THE DONNELLY ALBUM

THE COMPLETE & AUTHENTIC ACCOUNT OF CANADA'S FAMOUS FEUDING FAMILY
ILLUSTRATED WITH PHOTOGRAPHS

RAY FAZAKAS

FIREFLY BOOKS

A FIREFLY BOOK

A NOTE ON THE ILLUSTRATIONS

Copyright © Ray Fazakas 1995

No part of this publication may be produced or stored in a retrieval system, or transmitted in any form or by any means, electronic, mechanical, photocopying, recording or otherwise, without the written permission of the publisher, Firefly Books.

Canadian Cataloguing in Publication Data
Fazakas, Ray, 1932-
     The Donnelly album
Rev. ed.
Includes index.
ISBN 1-895565-61-8

1. Donnelly family. 2. murder - Ontario - Lucan.
3. Criminals - Ontario - Lucan. I. Title.

HV6810.L8F39 1995 364.1'523'0922 C95-930397-9

Published by:
Firefly Books Ltd.
250 Sparks Avenue
Willowdale, ON M2H 2S4

Firefly Books (U.S.) Inc.
P.O. Box 1338
Ellicott Station
Buffalo, New York 14205

Printed and bound in Canada

All illustrations are from material in the author's possession. The source for each, where known, is given in the accompanying caption. In identifying these sources the following abbreviations have been used:

Page	*Page's Historical Atlas of Middlesex*
PEI	Confederation Art Gallery and Museum, Charlottetown, Prince Edward Island
PAC	Public Archives of Canada
PAO	Public Archives of Ontario
Stanley	Spencer Armitage-Stanley
UWO	University of Western Ontario

CONTENTS

To Beverly, David, Sandra, and Derek

PREFACE

This book is not intended as a refutation of previously published works on the Donnelly story, but it perhaps fleshes out the legend as represented by Thomas P. Kelley's *The Black Donnellys* and the more factual account in Orlo Miller's *The Donnellys Must Die*. My personal feelings are that Kelley's Donnellys are rather too much larger than life while Miller's are rather too prosaic.

The material for this book came from the usual sources of government archives, newspaper and magazine files, and reference libraries and depositories throughout Canada as well as the United States and overseas. In addition, a wide-ranging correspondence carried on over a period of many years turned up a great deal of the anecdotal material and many photographs.

"It is too bad," friends have sometimes said, "that you could not have begun sooner while some of the older folks were still around to tell the story first-hand." While the point may be well taken, it is possible to overemphasize it. The story may have required about a hundred years of aging before many descendants of the families involved would talk about it openly, and some still do not. Probably the last person to have any vestige of association with it was Ida Porte, who died in 1968 at the age of ninety seven. She remembered the excitement in the years 1880-1 around the telegraph office of her father, William Porte, the Lucan postmaster.

While no one now alive was even remotely connected with the story, I did speak to or correspond with many of the older persons but one generation removed from the actual events. Of these I mention only a few, namely: Catherine Ryan, whose father, Zackariah McIlhargey, knew each of the Donnellys including old Jim and Johannah; Alice McFarlane, who wrote a fine paper for the London and Middlesex Historical Society on the subject in 1946; Elizabeth Quigley; Jennie Reycraft Lewis; Pat McGee; Fred McIlhargey; and Leonard Nangle, among many others. I mention also Spencer Armitage-Stanley, who took such a keen interest in local history and genealogical matters of Lucan and Biddulph, and who was kind enough to provide much valuable data and many photographs. I also met personally or contacted almost all the descendants of the Donnelly family, including the last one to bear the name. John Donnelly, the only son of William Donnelly, gave me a great deal of valuable material in the form of family background, photographs, and information about his grandparents and uncles.

To those mentioned and to all others who were so generous with their help I extend sincere thanks. While I have tried to make the account as accurate, authentic, and complete as possible, other information will doubtless turn up in the future which may, perhaps, be incorporated in revised editions.

1

HANDSPIKES

By pausing in her pioneer chores and cocking an ear at the doorway of her rude log shanty, Johannah Donnelly could just barely hear the distant din of the logging bee over at Maloney's farm. It was Thursday, June 25, 1857. Mrs. Donnelly could not help feeling anxious as she scanned the blackened treetops, for she knew that most of the neighbourhood men had gone there to work and to drink Maloney's whiskey. Among them was her husband, James Donnelly, and Patrick Farrell, a near neighbour and bitter enemy. The presence of both men at the bee could spell trouble.[1]

Maloney's farm was a short distance north of Donnelly's place along the road known as the Roman Line. Officially, the road was the allowance between concessions six and seven in the obscure backwoods township named Biddulph, in the County of Huron. The county formed part of the vast million acres of the Huron Tract, which had been granted by the British Crown to the Canada Company for exploitation of the land by its settlement.

The Roman Line, like most other pioneer roads of the day, straggled fitfully through the bush in varying degrees of obstruction. Most of the smaller trees had been cleared, but the path was strewn still with the burned and blackened stumps of bigger timber or the fallen branches of others. The latter had come from the great elms, killed merely by girdling. The dead giants stood stark and helpless, thrusting their brittle, spreading branches forlornly into the sky, to await gradual demolition by wind and storm.

The Roman Line was named after the men who lived there, all Irish Roman Catholics who had settled the road from end to end some ten or fifteen years before. From distant Tipperary they had come, to hack out, from the forbidding forests of the New World, a living more promising than that ordained for them in the restrictive confines of the Old.

At Maloney's, several gangs of men toiled with chains and oxen, enlarging the little clearing of five or six acres in which Maloney's shanty stood and in which a small patch of potatoes had already been planted. As was the custom at such pioneer bees, the Irish *usquebaugh* flowed freely. Water of life, the name signified, but Thomas McLaughlin, grog boss for the day, well knew that too liberal potions of the fiery liquid often resulted in the opposite effect. Among those partaking freely of the bog whiskey were James Donnelly and Patrick Farrell. The proprietor, William Maloney, was not at all happy to see Jim Donnelly at his logging bee. While Donnelly had always been friendly enough in the neighbourhood, the forbidding scowl on his face — for which he was well known — told Maloney that he had come more with the intent to make trouble than to work.

There were three teams of men, six men to a team. Jim Donnelly chose the job of driving the oxen of one team belonging to a man named Mackey. Mackey's brother, Martin, worked on another team consisting of Cornelius Lanagan, John Broderick, Michael (Mick) Carroll, and Patrick Farrell, and two other men. All of them lived close by: Broderick farmed the land immediately north of Donnelly's; Michael Carroll — usually referred to by the others as "the *respactable* Mr. Carroll", and related by marriage to Farrell — lived two or three lots north of Maloney; and Pat Farrell's farm was three lots south of Maloney's land.

The scowls of Jim Donnelly were directed at Pat Farrell. The two muttered angry words whenever their paths crossed. The words grew louder until by the mid-day break they were trading insults in full and heated argument. Farrell accused Donnelly of having tried to kill him with a gun; Donnelly accused Farrell of trying to steal his land.

About two o'clock in the afternoon, the teams had returned to work. When one of Farrell's crew shouted at Martin Mackey to lift the end of a heavy log, Mackey turned around to look for Farrell, who was supposed to be helping him.

"Look," exclaimed Mackey to the others, "Far-

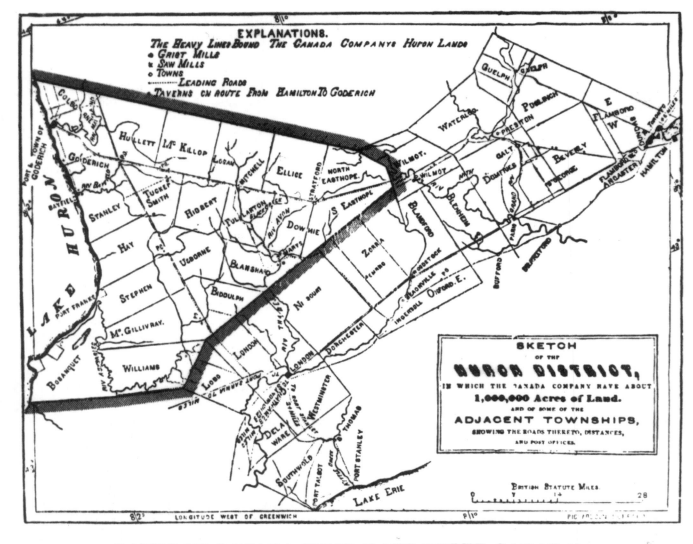

EXPLANATIONS.
THE HEAVY LINES BOUND THE CANADA COMPANY'S HURON LANDS
● GRIST MILLS
× SAW MILLS
○ TOWNS
——— LEADING ROADS
▲ TAVERNS ON ROUTE FROM HAMILTON TO GODERICH

SKETCH
OF THE
HURON DISTRICT,
IN WHICH THE CANADA COMPANY HAVE ABOUT
1,000,000 Acres of Land.
AND OF SOME OF THE
ADJACENT TOWNSHIPS,
SHOWING THE ROADS THERETO, DISTANCES,
AND POST OFFICES.

BRITISH STATUTE MILES.

LANDS IN CANADA WEST (LATE UPPER CANADA).

THE ATTENTION OF

EMIGRANTS, OLD SETTLERS AND OTHERS,

IS INVITED BY THE CANADA COMPANY TO THE

HURON DISTRICT,

CONTAINING ABOUT

ONE MILLION ACRES OF LAND,

IN ONE BLOCK,

Extending Westward from the Gore and Wellington Districts to the Shores of Lake Huron, which bounds it for sixty miles.

The Land in the Huron Tract is of the finest character, and of the description best adapted to the cultivation of Wheat. This Tract possesses advantages which render it peculiarly eligible to every class of Settler: scarcely a bad Farm is to be found in it: it is well watered by living Streams, and the climate is most healthy. The principal Port is Goderich, the District Town, which has a population of about 1200—good Stores or Shops, Mechanics, a large Grist Mill, a Fulling and Carding Mill, an Iron Foundry, places of Religious Worship, resident Clergymen, and good Schools, where the higher branches of the Classics are taught, &c. &c. &c.

rell's over there in the potato patch boxing with Donnelly."

Jim Donnelly was bare to the waist. Some of the onlookers began to joke about his attempting to emulate "the great Sir Dan", referring to the rollicking Irish pugilist Dan Donnelly, who, as every Irishman knew, had bested the Englishman George Cooper in a great bare-knuckle bout on the Curragh of Kildare just forty-two years before.[2]

"Donnelly's letting on to be a little high," was Maloney's opinion. A disapproving look at the grog boss must have conveyed the message, for Thomas McLaughlin, as if to absolve himself of further responsibility, quickly handed the whiskey bottle to Maloney.

There was little doubt about Patrick Farrell's condition. He was falling about drunkenly.

"Come on wid ye, bhoys," said Cornelius Lanagan walking over to the combatants and stepping between them. "Let's git back to work an' enough uv this."

Grog boss McLaughlin helped Lanagan separate the two men, and Farrell sat down on a log. When Lanagan and McLaughlin returned to their work, Donnelly walked over to Farrell and challenged him to continue the fight.

"I've had enough," Farrell mumbled. "I'll fight no more."

Donnelly cursed him then and called him a coward. "You're beat!" he taunted.

With a contemptuous swagger, James Donnelly turned away from his foe, nonchalantly picked up his shirt, and walked over to the *respactable* Mick Carroll to ask for a chew of tobacco. Carroll carefully scrutinized him, and he, too, thought that Donnelly was less drunk than he made out. "He's trying to keep the quarrel going," thought Carroll as he handed him the tobacco.

In the meantime, the taunt in Donnelly's last words gradually penetrated Patrick Farrell's benumbed brain. "I'm not beat," he muttered, struggling to his feet. Wobbling over to Martin Mackey, he wrested from him a wooden handspike used for levering the heavier logs. It was a short, thick piece

A pioneer logging bee in Muskoka (James Weston)

of hardwood about three feet long. As Mackey snatched it back, Farrell lurched forward and fell awkwardly to his hands and knees. The others, convinced that the two fighting men were too drunk to do each other much harm, again turned back to their work.

About fifteen or twenty minutes later, Cornelius Lanagan noticed Donnelly and Farrell fighting again, each with a handspike in hand. Again he went over to the two men, this time followed by Martin Mackey and John Broderick.

"Don't abuse yerselfs in sich a way," Lanagan chided.

But Farrell growled drunkenly at him, "Git to hell out uv my way. Don't touch me agin or I'll brain ye, too."

Farrell turned menacingly towards Lanagan. As the three men wrestled Farrell's handspike from his grasp, he again lost his balance and fell to the ground.

Meanwhile, as soon as the others had approached, James Donnelly pivoted away out of their reach, but when Farrell fell, he suddenly reversed his movement. With a quick, deadly, and yet graceful motion, he lifted his handspike over his head with both hands, brandished it in mid-air for a brief instant, and then brought it down upon the fallen Farrell.

Broderick caught a glimpse of the descending cudgel and threw his own handspike to ward it off, but it missed its mark. Farrell was half sitting and half lying, still struggling to right himself, when Donnelly's handspike caught him with full force on the left temple. Farrell fell back and never rose again. The blow left a gash of three or four inches running from the left ear to the top of the head. There was little blood, but the cudgel cracked Farrell's skull and on the opposite side it ruptured an artery, causing an immediate and massive flow of blood within the brain cavity. Patrick Farrell died within a few minutes.

James Donnelly, after striking the fatal blow, stood perfectly still. The others were also struck motionless with horror. Then someone yelled, "Murdher! Murdher!"

The rest of the crews came running. Pat Ryan and Mick Carroll heard the excited shouts and rushed from behind a pile of logs, the latter running up and kneeling on the ground beside the prostrate Farrell.

"Who did it?" he cried, lifting his head.

Farrell was beyond answering, but Carroll repeated the question: "Who struck the blow?"

Standing close by with a grim look on his face was John Toohey. "It was Donnelly struck him," he said quietly.

Someone then cried out, "Farrell, ye are dead!"

Other voices raised the hue: "Murdher! Murdher! Donnelly, ye have murdhered the man."

It was three o'clock in the afternoon and the Maloney logging bee had come to an abrupt end. Many of the men left for home immediately. They knew the law would be out on the Roman Line soon enough. Only a few of the men, for the most part those related to Farrell, stayed to pick up the limp body and carry it over to Maloney's shanty. Jim Donnelly watched them. Then he coolly removed his shirt, turned on his heel, and walked across the field towards his own shanty. He appeared perfectly sober now and did not at all stagger.

Although Patrick Farrell was killed in the British colony of Canada West, all of the men at Maloney's logging bee spoke the guttural brogue of North Tipperary, for the story of the Donnellys went back to another British colony, the Ireland of the time of the Penal Laws against Roman Catholics, roughly encompassing the seventeenth and eighteenth centuries. Cromwell's harsh campaign against the native Irish in 1649-50 merely continued a subjugation which had been going on for generations, and the famous Battle of the Boyne in 1690 was only a peak or a valley (depending on the point of view) in the defeat of the native and Catholic cause.

During the reign of Queen Anne, from 1702 to 1714, the Penal Laws became more rigorous. A statute of gavelkind or inheritance required that land owned by Catholics be divided up amongst the several heirs, unless the eldest should become a convert to the Established Church. In that case, all the property would pass to him. It is easy to imagine the family feuds which originated from such a law, rumbling from generation to generation, and easy to see also the origin among the Irish of Protestant counterparts to many of the old Irish

United Counties
of Huron & Bruce
To Wit

Informations taken of Witnesses severally and acknowledged on behalf of our Sovereign Lady the Queen, touching the death of Patrick Farrell, at the dwelling House of Robert McLean, known as the Exchange Hotel in the Township of Biddulph in the County of Huron on Sunday the 28th day of June, in the twentieth year of the reign of our Sovereign: Lady Queen Victoria, Before John Hyndman Esquire one of the Coroners of the said County, on an inquisition then and there taken on view of the body of Patrick Farrell then and there lying dead, asl follows to Wit: —

...

Cornelius Maloney of the said Township being sworn says as follows. I was at the logging bee on Thursday 25th June Am acquainted with Patrick Farrell deceased, saw him and James Donally fighting with their hands, I was distant from them about ten or twelve rods, I saw Cornelius Lanagan separating them, I saw the deceased Patrick Farrell struck by James Donally with a handspike deceased was lying down all the time that Donally struck him with the handspike only saw him strike him once to my knowledge. I consider I was three or four rods from them when the blow was struck, I did not see Farrell fall but saw him on the ground before he was struck.

By the Foreman
I heard some talk of an old grudge between them but saw no symptoms of it I did not see any one try to prevent Donally from striking him Donally was well able to walk about when he gave the blow after they were separated Donally wheeled away and then turned again I saw him raise the handspike with both hands and strike him (Farrell) across the head. I saw Donally leave the field after the deed, he did not stagger away.

his
Cornelis X Maloney
mark

...

William Maloney of the Township of Biddulph County of Huron, Sworn, saith there was a logging bee at my place on Thursday last 25 June when a quarrell took place between James Donally and Patrick Farrell, is aware that Patrick Farrell is dead did not see Donally strike Farrell but heard some one cry out Donally you have murdered the man, I was about five rod distant from the place, Farrell was drunk Donally let on to be a little high, saw both parties about nine or ten minutes before the blow was struck they were in the act of fighting and were put apart, heard Farrell say before he got the blow, that he had enough and would fight no more. All the crowd said that the man was murdered one voice said Donally the man is murdered

By the jury
Did not see Farrell take up a handspike at all, thinks it was Donally's intention to pick a quarrell with some one when he came to the bee more than to help to do anything

his
William X Maloney
mark

(PAC)

Catholic families. Consequently there were, in North Tipperary, Protestant Quigleys as well as Catholic Quigleys, and similar counterparts among the Carrolls, Thompsons, McLaughlins, and many other families, including the Donnellys.

The County of Tipperary in the Penal Law period was one of the most, if not the most, violent and lawless of all the unhappy counties of that unhappy kingdom. Echoes of its violence are heard in the story of the Donnellys: the faction fight, the family feud, the interminable lawsuits running from assize to assize and from generation to generation, the intermeddling of the parish priest in the bickerings of his parishioners, the petty animosities between neighbours. These were all part of an ancient Tipperary tradition which took root in the New World.

William Carleton made from first-hand knowledge the supreme record of the character, manner, customs, speech, superstitions, and daily life of the pre-Famine Catholic peasant in his *Traits and Stories of the Irish Peasantry* and related writings. He stated:

If Tipperary and some of the adjoining parts of Munster were blotted out of the moral map of the country, we would stand as a nation in a far higher position than that which we occupy... for it is surely unfair to charge the whole kingdom with crimes which disgrace only a single county of it....3

The agrarian outrage, the blunderbuss from behind the hedge, the death-dealing dagger from the roadside ditch, the forcing of the process-server to eat his papers were common enough incidents in a land where the rack-rent of the peasant was pitilessly raised, often after years of the tenant's labour to improve the land. He may have literally created soil out of bedrock by burning down heather, digging out stones, laying on lime, and hauling up manure and pushing it between the crags and boulders of his farm.

Little wonder that violence was often resorted to. "Something like a reign of terror prevails in Tipperary, Ireland," a newspaper account would read,[4] and Carleton noted that the massacre of entire families was almost a tradition in the country. "The murder of the Bolands, for instance, occurred in the year 1808," he wrote, "and the massacre of Carrickshock, as it has been called, in l832."[5] Between these two incidents the Tipperary outrage known as "the Burning of the Sheas" took place, in which an entire family was burned to death in its own home as an act of vengeance by a faction of its neighbours. A similar crime occurred in the County of Louth in 1820 when the home of the Lynch family, called Wildgoose Lodge, was burned down over their heads by a mob of neighbours. Carleton wrote of this incident:

> Both parties were Roman Catholics, and either twenty-five or twenty-eight of those who took an active part in the burning, were hanged and gibbeted in different parts of the county of Louth. Devann, the ringleader, hung for some months in chains, within about a hundred yards of his own house, and about half a mile from Wildgoose Lodge. His mother could neither go into or out of her cabin without seeing his body swinging from the gibbet. Her usual exclamation on looking at him was —"God, be good to the sowl of my poor marthyr!"[6]

Born in the County of Louth about the time of this massacre was Peter Crinnon, who grew up with the whispered tales of that terrible night etched indelibly in his mind and soul. Peter Crinnon became a Catholic priest. His very first mission happened to be in the wilds of Canada West, at St. Patrick's Parish, where a church was established on the Roman Line, in the Township of Biddulph.[7] During the few short years that Father Crinnon spent among the settlers from North Tipperary in the mission, he tried valiantly to get his unruly flock to mend their ways. But it was during this time that several murders took place there, including the murder of Patrick Farrell at the hands of James Donnelly.

BIDDULPH

The name Donnelly signifies "brown valour". Originally warriors seated at Drumleen, the Donnelly clan was in ancient times expelled and settled at a place which came to be called Ballydonnelly after them. Another branch were ancient chiefs of Muscraighe-Thire, which later became the barony of Lower Ormond in Tipperary.[1] According to one story, an ancestor of James Donnelly of Biddulph became involved in a dispute with a cruel and unjust landlord, who was shortly after found murdered. When suspicion focussed upon Donnelly, he fled his native district and settled in the Parish of Eglish, the modern name for which is Aglishcloghane, in Lower Ormond.[2] Here he began a new life but, in accordance with a common failing of the clan, fancied himself better than his neighbours and clandestinely courted a Protestant girl named Goodwin, daughter of a Justice of the Peace, and one of the local gentry. When the courtship resulted in marriage, the local Protestants resented the girl's attachment to "a Papist body", and Donnelly and his bride were forced to leave the district. They eventually settled in the townland of Tumbrikane, near Borrisokane, in Tipperary, where their descendants prospered.

James Donnelly was born on March 7, 1816, in the Parish of Borrisokane. In accordance with the general rule in nineteenth-century Ireland, he was much shorter than his Protestant neighbours. Although he was small and stocky, being only five feet five inches at manhood, his body was nicely proportioned and well muscled. With black curly hair, grey eyes, and a light skin with a very smooth texture about it, he was described, even by his enemies, as "remarkably good looking", and gave the initial impression of pleasant amiability. He was, however, never photographed in his lifetime.[3]

The character of James Donnelly is an enigma.

On the one hand he was known as sober, industrious, hard-working, kind and considerate, likable, a real gentleman, a warm friend to those he considered deserving, and a good man devoted to the church of his fathers. He was said to have received, as he deserved, the goodwill of his neighbours, to be open-hearted to a fault, and even to be a simple-minded, inoffensive little man who seemed quite mild and harmless. No doubt he was, at times, all of these. But by others, and under different circumstances, James Donnelly was known as a rollicking, drinking, quarrelsome Irishman, always ready to engage in dispute and to display his prowess as a pugilist whether by Broughton's bare-knuckle rules, or in rough-and-tumble, go-as-you-please bouts; shrewd, unscrupulous, wicked, vindictive, and revengeful in his thoughts, as well as belligerent, obscene, and offensive in his language, and extreme, intemperate, and vicious in his actions. But he was always cool under stress and was said to be capable of raising a ruckus "on his own behalf, if no one else would", carrying it to an extreme end just for the sake of sheer devilment; an unreasonable sort of person you could talk no sense to. There seems little doubt that Jim Donnelly was hardy to a degree, and that he prided himself as a match for any man in a fracas. He spoke with a strong Irish brogue and "was always very positive in maintaining any of his assertions".[4]

As a young man, James Donnelly worked as a coach-driver on the estate of a great Protestant landowner in Ireland. He soon "put his comether an" a girl from the next parish, Johannah McGee, who worked as a servant in one of the Big Houses. A long-boned, lanky woman, Johannah could sling stones with her stocking or apron with the best of the men in any faction fight. The courtship was frowned on by her father who asked her master to confine the girl to the second floor of their substantial Protestant home, but Donnelly managed to smuggle messages to her. Then one night he crept up to the house with a ladder and stole away his willing bride. Old McGee rode after them in a fury, but he was too late to prevent the legal ceremony. Undaunted, he dragged his errant daughter home, placed her under strict guard, and threatened to prosecute

James Donnelly, Sr., was never photographed in his lifetime. This sketch was made in 1880, after he had been murdered, by Robert Harris, later one of the most famous portrait artists in Canada. (PEI)

Donnelly for his alleged involvement in the "tithe throubles" then sweeping the country, along with the ever-increasing potato crop failures.[5]

His fortunes at a downturn, in 1842 James Donnelly decided to join his brother John and others of his countrymen, including two brothers named Ryder from neighbouring Nenagh, and ship out to Canada. They went to seek the millions of acres of cheap land in the New World crying out for ownership at a mere thirteen shillings an acre.

"What!!" says Paddy, "and with all the trees on it, too!!!"[6]

The Ryder brothers, Patrick and James, eventually acquired their fair share of Canadian soil and, in the course of so doing, managed to scrape through a great deal of trouble in which the fate of the Ryder and Donnelly families became inextricably mingled. And it was in the end the Ryders, along with the families of Maher, Carroll, Cain, and Toohey, who proved the nemesis of the Donnellys in Canada.[7]

During the time that James Donnelly was growing up in Tipperary, there was another group of dissatisfied people thinking of emigrating — a large community of free Negroes in Cincinnati, Ohio. Among them was J. C. Brown, born a slave in Virginia. His mistress being his own aunt, however, Brown was well treated and was educated to the mason's trade, eventually purchasing his freedom for eighteen dollars and settling in Cincinnati. In 1829, in Brown's own words,

the law of 1804, known as the Ohio black law, was revived in that State, and enforced. By this law, every colored man was to give bonds in $500 not to become a town charge, and to find bonds also for his heirs. No one could employ a colored man or colored woman to do any kind of labor, under penalty of $100.... 8

Brown thereupon formed a Colonization Society among the blacks to seek asylum in British possessions. Then he

went to Little York, where he entered into a contract with the Canada Company, for a township of land, agreeing to pay $6,000 a year, for ten years. It was the township of Biddulph.9

Two members of Brown's Colonization Society, Israel Lewis and W. Whitehead, were sent ahead to inspect the township. After wandering and living for days off bush berries, they found the land of Biddulph, on which a hermit named Doude had thrown up a temporary shanty. Doude hated to be crowded. The morning after the arrival of the two blacks, he picked up his few trappings and left. Lewis and Whitehead moved into his shanty and thus began the first real settlement of the Township of Biddulph.10

Named after one of the English capitalists who sat on the first board of directors of the Canada Company, Biddulph was a small, triangular township on the edge of the Huron Tract and about fifteen miles north of London. The contract for building a road through the township, a distance of six to seven miles, was completed in the summer of 1831 by the black settlers. The work was the equivalent of clearing fifty acres of bushland. The blacks also cleared their own little plots, planting Indian corn, and built small cabins with their peculiar clay chimney stacks on the outside, held in

place with thinly sawn horizontal boards. The latter were obtained from their own small sawmill. Early settlers of the black settlement included Caesar King, Leverton Pinkham, Peter Johnson, Mary Ann Thompson, George Washington, and William and Rosanna Bell, the latter known as Grandma Bell. Besides Brown, their leaders were Anstin Steward, who named the settlement Wilberforce after the great British emancipator; Peter Butler, who became treasurer of the settlement and died years later reputed to be worth a modest fortune; and Benjamin and Nathaniel Paul, Baptist ministers under whose influence "ardent spirits" were banned.

In 1832 Nathaniel Paul journeyed to England to raise money, gave evidence concerning the Wilberforce settlement before a Parliamentary Committee, and collected some six hundred dollars. But he gave too generously, he said, to the American abolitionist William Lloyd Garrison, who was also visiting England, and brought little of the money back. When he returned in 1835, however, he brought with him an English bride.

The settlement of Wilberforce began to decline when Mrs. Nathaniel Paul, horrified at the prospect of spending the rest of her life in what appeared to be a frightful forest, prevailed upon him to return to the United States. In the meantime, the Ohio Black Law had been relaxed, and the rest of the families who had planned to follow Brown wrote "that they could now walk without being pushed off the side-walks, were well used, and were living in clover", and therefore they decided not to come to Canada. The Colonization Society realized that an entire township was, in the circumstances, too ambitious a project and turned for help to the Society of Friends in Oberlin, Ohio. The Quakers sent Frederick Stover, but despite the building of a small, yellow frame church on the banks of the Sauble River and a log schoolhouse on the London-Goderich Road, the settlement faltered.

White settlers had in the meantime begun to encroach upon the district and hungrily eyed the lands of Biddulph, originally contracted for by the blacks. In 1831, the arrival of Big Jim Hodgins of Borrisokane, Tipperary, gave an impetus to their advance into the township.

James Hodgins and his wife, Mary. "Big Jim" Hodgins was the unofficial founder of Biddulph Township, and a land agent, whiskey distiller, and justice of the Peace. (Stanley)

Like Jim Donnelly, Hodgins was also in a sense fleeing the land of his birth. During a riot between the Catholics and the newly formed Protestant Peelers on Borrisokane Fair Day, March 26,1829, Constable James Hodgins had caught up with a fleeing Catholic rioter and, with one shot from his pistol, had blown the brains out of him, followed by the words, preserved in the evidence of his ensuing trial for murder, "Well, I have left one Papist low."[11] Six other constables were also tried for related murder charges at the same time, the prosecution witnesses bearing such names as Ryder, Heenan, Carroll, and Donnelly. But with Catholics excluded from the jury, all were acquitted. Nevertheless, Jim Hodgins thereafter considered himself a marked man in and around Borrisokane and emigrated with his family to Upper Canada.

Big Jim Hodgins arrived in Biddulph in 1832. As local agent for the Canada Company, he helped to locate many of his compatriots in the township when the Negroes could not complete their contract and the company decided to open Biddulph to the whites. Within a generation, there were at least forty-six different Hodgins households in the township, including those of Adam Hodgins, Benjamin Hodgins, George Hodgins, Edward Hodgins, Hiram Hodgins, Isaac Hodgins, Moses Hodgins, James Hodgins, John Hodgins, Richard Hodgins, Thomas Hodgins, and William Hodgins. Among the George Hodgins families alone, there were Bailiff George, Tavern George, Bunty George, Lame George, Dublin George, Hill George, Longworth George, Turkey George, and Aunt Ellen's George. Except for the Wilberforce Settlement, confined to the London-Goderich Road, the entire western third of Biddulph Township was settled by a solid phalanx of Protestant Irish from North Tipperary. The various road allowances were known after them as Big Jim's Line, the Armitage Line, the Coursey Line, and the Sadlier Line.

Big Jim Hodgins came to be called the founder of Biddulph.[12] He was the first appointed district councillor when local government was formed in 1842, the first clerk of the township in 1844, and the first elected reeve in 1850. He was a Justice of the Peace and an army officer, eventually Lieutenant-Colonel of the Sixth Battalion of the Huron Militia.

Hodgins was well established in Biddulph, the population of which was approaching one thousand, when Jim Donnelly arrived in 1842 with a party of Catholic settlers. Donnelly worked first in the city of London and in London Township. Perhaps when he drove stagecoach to Goderich he became familiar with the land of the Huron Tract. The middle portion of Biddulph was described by the original surveyor, the Highland Scotsman John McDonald, as "good, level land" covered with timber of "Maple, Beech, Elm, Hickory, Basswood and some Birch".[13] The Catholics, including the Hogans, Keefes, Ryans, Nangles, Mooneys, and Ryders, began to settle in this portion, and James Donnelly himself kept his eye on a plot on the road which came to be called the Roman Line, to distinguish it from the Protestant lines. And when Donnelly learned that Big Jim

Hodgins planned to make an excursion to bring more settlers from Tipperary, he asked him to get in touch with his wife.

Back in Ireland, Johannah Donnelly had apparently experienced married life long enough to give birth, in 1842, to a healthy young boy whom she named after his father. Young James was almost two years old when Big Jim Hodgins returned to Ireland. Old McGee had, with the birth of the boy, relented towards his daughter, for he did not wish him to grow up without the influence of a father, even a roguish one.

"Go and be damned wid ye," he told Johannah, and she and the young boy went back with Hodgins to the New World. When the youngster took sick during the voyage, two brothers named Francis and William Davis, also headed for Biddulph, came to the rescue. The latter, a herb doctor, rummaged among his bottles and came up with a potion which cured the illness, and the Donnellys never forgot the favour.[14]

In Canada West, as Johannah walked the Proof Line Road from London towards Biddulph, she heard often the familiar dialect of North Tipperary.

"God bless all here," she stated, after the manner of the Irish, as she entered a humble public house along the road. Then she halted in amazement, for there in front of her was her long-sought husband. James Donnelly was dumbfounded at the sudden appearance of his wife, a child of almost two years held firmly in her long, strong arms.

"Where the divil," he finally stammered, "did ye come from?"

She replied, "Where the divil did ye git to?"

Jim Donnelly was never a man of many words. "Well, come along wid ye," he said, and took charge of his newly found family.

The following year, Johannah Donnelly gave birth to a small, thin child with a deformed foot, whose bright eyes and alertness betokened for him a lively future. They called him William.

Jim Donnelly decided it would soon be time to claim a homestead. His friend, Michael Keefe, had already cleared five acres on the Roman Line of Biddulph, and four lots south of Keefe was an attractive piece of land. Patrick Fogarty had taken out the original lease from the Canada Company but made no claim to possession. The land, Lot 18 in the sixth concession, was timbered with maple, elm, beech, basswood, and a few wild cherry trees; birch swale, indicating less desirable low-lying land, was entirely absent. A small creek, which crossed the road allowance near by, drained the lot. James Donnelly laid claim to it in 1845. He did not occupy it until two years later when, with his wife and two small boys, he took possession of it in the spring of 1847.

Johannah Donnelly was, by then, pregnant again. She was completely enchanted with the abundance of spring greenery beginning to bud everywhere in the warm sunshine, and the wild cherry trees particularly delighted her.

"We'll call the place Greenland," she emphatically declared, and so it was named.

The land of the Donnelly homestead remained in the family name for almost a hundred years. It formed the base for its members during their ensuing decades of trouble and its soil became mixed with their remnant ashes.

FACTIONS

It did not take the Tipperary Irish in Canada long to put into practice their ancient heritage of the faction fight. Patrick Mooney, of the Swamp Line, the road immediately east of the Roman Line named after the huge cedar swamp which it skirted, was an early protagonist. At Thomas Cummins' house-raising bee in March 1847, as the company retired for dinner to the house of John Carty, John Kennedy and John Donnelly were following Mooney along the road when they saw him fall to quarrelling with a companion named Thomas Nangle.[1] Twice Mooney knocked Nangle down on the roadway before going into the house.

Nangle followed in a great rage a few minutes later, his face marked and his fist raised.

"Ye struck me wrongfully," cried Nangle, making a rush at Mooney, "and it's satisfaction I want."

Mooney was scornful. "I kin tie one uv me hands behind me back and bate ye still wid the other, Nangle," he said.

"Shush, bhoys," said Mrs. Cummins, who jumped between the two men, "come an wid ye."

Nangle would not be mollified. "Ye struck me wrongfully," he insisted. "I want ye to say ye struck me wrongfully."

Other voices joined that of Mrs. Cummins urging peace, and Mooney finally shuffled to his feet and muttered, "All right, for the sake uv pace in the house, I say I struck ye wrongfully an' I'm sorry for id."

Nangle went out, but in a few minutes he returned carrying a small stick and made a stroke at Mooney. Others intervened and persuaded him to drop the stick, and he took a seat near Mooney. In a moment he lashed out with his foot at his antagonist, who jumped up to defend himself. The company again intervened, but as they parted them Nangle muttered, "I'll git ye yit, when I git the chance."

The feud had begun two years before in April 1845, when Patrick Mooney lost a cow. His wife, Mary, went looking for it to the farm of John Kennedy, whose wife, Hanorah, was related to Nangle. When Mrs. Mooney called Mrs. Kennedy out of her shanty, angry accusations, denials, and insults were exchanged, but Mary Mooney's remarks carried more weight, for they were punctuated with a short stick applied forcibly to the other woman's back. The next day Thomas Nangle gave Patrick Mooney a severe beating on behalf of Mary Mooney. John Kennedy himself threatened to beat Mooney, as did Mrs. Kennedy, but the law intervened and the Kennedys were put on peace bonds for a year.

James Donnelly assisted in the various raising and logging bees of the Catholic Settlement of Biddulph, quickly erecting a log shanty in which a third son, John, was born on September 16,1847. He was named after Jim Donnelly's brother, who had also taken up land in the township.

The Donnellys, along with the rest of the Roman Liners of the Catholic Settlement of Biddulph, went to mass on Sundays at the corner of that road and the London-Goderich gravel road. Here St.Patrick's Church was built. Beside it Andy Keefe erected a large and pretentious two-storey frame tavern, and in Collison's grove near by, the annual Catholic picnics were held.[2]

The family of James Donnelly was augmented as the years passed. Patrick was born in 1849 and Michael in the late fall of 1851, followed by Robert in 1853 and then Thomas on August 30, 1854.

Most of the settlers first occupied their lands under Canada Company leases with the option to purchase. Leases and options were freely traded without too many formalities. Many pioneers simply squatted, defying anyone to dispossess them and intending in their own good time to make peace with the paper owner. James Donnelly laid claim to Lot 21 in the seventh concession on the Roman Line for a time, but dealt away his rights to a friend, John Grace, who, in turn, had in 1846 obtained paper title to Donnelly's original homestead lot. Grace had never registered his deed, probably with the expectation of trading it, or perhaps he and Donnelly had an understanding, for the latter never considered anyone imprudent enough to claim the land over his head.[3]

The Kennedy-Mooney feud resumed in 1849 when Kennedy, in company with John Donnelly, met Mooney on the road to Jerry McDonald's, near the church. He knocked Mooney down. McDonald ran out of his shanty when he saw Kennedy kicking his victim and shouted.

"Fer God's sake," he yelled, "he'll kill him. Help! Help!"

John and Sarah Kirkland also came running from their own nearby shanty, but Kennedy continued not only to apply his boots, but also to throw stones at Mooney on the ground. If he got up, he knocked him down.

When the Kirklands ran up, he demanded of them belligerently, "What do ye want?"

"Don't kill the man," replied Kirkland.

Kennedy then lashed out at the intruder with his fist, and Kirkland and his wife quickly turned and ran back to their shanty. Mooney survived the beating, went to law, and had Kennedy bound over once again to keep the peace for two years.

While the population of Biddulph was about this time sixteen hundred souls, settlers were only beginning to filter into nearby Stephen Township. Here another group of Tipperary Irish Catholics settled. Among them were the Carroll brothers, James, Bartholomew, and Roger, who arrived in the backwoods about the year 1850 and were enumerated by the census-taker early the following spring. He noted in the margin of his page:

Snow [k]nee deep no track no roads but blaze on a tree set[t]lers very far apart.[4]

That year Roger Carroll, his wife Catherine, and his small son James occupied a meagre shanty of Stephen Township. Across the road from them settled their relatives, James and Edward Maher, in 1854.

Many early squabbles between neighbours and at the various bees in the early days of both Stephen and Biddulph townships revolved around the ownership and possession of land. One mocking report read:

John Whalen has had the surveyors from London bekase the line fence between him and Mrs. Cain was not in the right place, and the result was the widow had to move the fence in on her farm three inches and 7/16ths.[5]

Patrick Gilgallin told of a typical skirmish at a bee in Stephen the year the Maher brothers arrived:

Was at a bee of Mr. Lawson's.... While some persons were taking their suppers some person or persons out of doors threw snow in at those at supper. Some person shut the door. I held a coat in a crack of the house to prevent snow from coming in. Edward Maher came in and accused me of holding the door. James Maher his brother struck at me with his fist. Edward took hold of me and threw me down.... I got a black eye, swollen on the cheek, also Thomas Gilgallin had a cut on his head and James Carroll had a black eye.[6]

Faction fighting was not confined to the Catholics. For years Big Barney Stanley, "the Tipperary Roarer", kept a hotel on the banks of the Sauble, beside the store of his brother Thomas.

SQUATTERS AND TRESPASSERS.

NOTICE

Is hereby given by

THE CANADA COMPANY

That their Commissioners are taking *active* *Legal measures* to protect their rights against those persons who are Unlawfully and Fraudulently *Squatting* or *Trespassing* on the COMPANY'S LANDS. And the Commissioners think it well to add, that, as during last year, there are now again many people going about the country in search of Improved Lands, occupied by Squatters with the intention of PURCHASING over their heads; and as the Canada Company can in no way interfere in such cases, but sell to the first applicant; the Squatters are advised forthwith to make arrangements for securing their Improvements, and the Lands they now illegally occupy, *to avoid the most serious consequences.*

Canada Company's Office. Toronto, 1st June, 1841.

(PAO)

The Stanley brothers coveted the nearby lands of the black settlers, and there arose such a squabbling between them that the Sauble Hill settlement came to be known as "Bunker Hill". In October 1848, Thomas Stanley claimed he saw one of the blacks, Mary Ann Thompson, take down Stanley's fence "so that the pigs got in and took out roots of clover". A few days later, the barns, strawstacks, and grain of three of the neighbouring Negro settlers, William Bell, Ephraim Taylor, and Daniel A. Turner, went up in flames. There was little doubt the fires were incendiary, and a government reward of fifty pounds was offered for the arrest and conviction of the arsonists.

The Wilberforce settlers suffered other misfortunes about this time. William Morgan's son was killed by a falling tree, and the Whitehead family was struck with a double disaster when a son-in-law, Duke, was killed while hunting raccoons, and old Mrs. Whitehead was found face down in the little stream which crossed the London-Goderich

Road before it came to the Sauble River. Said to have been a suicide, Mrs. Whitehead's death was a curious one.

It appears she was religiously mad, and to appease her strange god, tied her limbs together and lay down in the creek to drown.[7]

Young Joshua Turner also drowned in the Sauble River. Following this series of tragedies, many of the Negro settlers left the settlement. Whether the misfortunes had been accidental or deliberate, there is no doubt the hostility of the white settlers decided the fate of the colony. Although Wilberforce gradually dwindled, a few of the original settlers remained and their descendants live in the community to this day.

The Stanley brothers vied for Protestant supremacy in Biddulph with Big Jim Hodgins and his family. In 1848 Big Jim was hauling up the Stanleys for threats. "Whatever the consequences might be, you must fight us," they had challenged, and threatened to kick him into insensibility. Hodgins, for his part, seemed continually to be dogged by trouble.[8] Once he drove off John Ryan, who was scraping the road, and "struck with a sash whip several times" at Ryan's horses. Another time he went round to the house of Tom Coursey and broke the window panes. When Constables John O'Neil and Dan Siddall on one occasion approached Hodgins in his yard, he demanded: "Are you coming to serve summons or paper?"

When the constables nodded, Hodgins muttered, "I'll split your damn skulls!" and swung at them with an axe, embedding it into a corner of his log house. The constables quickly left.

As Captain of the First Company, Second Battalion, of the Huron Militia, Hodgins ordered his men to fall in on Parade Day in June 1848 at Flanagan's tavern. One of the men, John Jermyn, refused.

"I won't fall in," he said. "I'll be damned first."

Hodgins asked him why not, and Jermyn said that Hodgins owed him "that back tax". The captain grew furious at this and, reaching for the sword slung at his side, he bellowed, "Ye go to hell, ye blaggard pup. I owe ye no money, ye damn scoundrel. Dare ye talk to me so?"

He grabbed Jermyn by the cravat and pushed him not only out of the room but through the hallway and outside into the hands of Constable Alexander McFalls, instructing the latter to lock the upstart into the pig pen.

On another occasion, Henry Sutton charged Big Jim Hodgins with spitting in his face at Robert Hodgins' tavern, throwing a glass of whiskey at him, and calling him a "scamp, loafer, and long-legged yankee".

One of the most notorious of the families of the Catholic Settlement of Biddulph was that of Patrick Casey. His sons Thomas and William were often in trouble but gained their greatest notoriety in connection with the Brimmacombe murder.[9] Richard Brimmacombe was a Cornish Englishman who in 1856 moved to a lot beside the Caseys, on the extension into Usborne Township of the north end of the Roman Line. William Casey attended Brimmacombe's house-raising before the snow fell that year and, in a fight with some of the Englishmen, Casey was soundly beaten. He vowed to take revenge.

"You will be marked yet between this and the gravel road," he threatened Brimmacombe before leaving to get his head dressed. Returning the next day, he spotted one of his enemies on the roof of the new house. "And as for you, for one cent I'd come and twist your neck," he said. "Maybe you'll get a knock somewhere when you're not looking for it."

One of Brimmacombe's hired men was caught shortly after on the road and beaten. A friend of the Englishman was soon after accosted by old Patrick Ryder, father-in-law of William Casey. Ryder "swore a terrible oath" and said that he would murder Richard Brimmacombe the first time he saw him on the line.

A couple of weeks later, on Friday, February 6, 1857, Brimmacombe, returning in a sleigh with his hired man and a cow from his former home in St. Thomas, had just set out again after a warm beer at Andy Keefe's tavern when his sleigh upset in a snowbank just beyond St. Patrick's Church, about nine hundred feet from the tavern. Brimmacombe's knee was only slightly hurt in the upset but, not wishing it to stiffen up in the cold, he instructed his hired man to go on with the sleigh and wait for him in the Donnelly Schoolhouse while he caught up with the cow on foot. The hired man went ahead and waited as told but never saw his master alive again. Three hundred feet beyond a great elm tree which stood on the Roman Line not far from the house of old Pat Ryder, Richard Brimmacombe was waylaid and killed by a severe blow to the head. On the body, still warm when discovered, was found a $60 note given him by Andy Keefe in a horse deal, and some $12 to $14 in cash. Although many of the Roman Liners were out on the road that evening, none would admit to any knowledge of the murder. Patrick Whalen said he saw Pat Ryder near the scene "wid a small bit av a shtick in his hand", but later denied hearing Ryder say he had given Brimmacombe "a tap". Jim Donnelly was one of the first persons to know of the killing. He told Pat Heffernan as well as Thomas Casey, an uncle of the Casey brothers, who along with Pat Ryder were prime suspects in the case. But when the constables went to arrest old Ryder, he drove them away from his shanty with a "shot gun in one hand and pistol in the other". Ryder finally gave himself up on the advice of Pat Flanagan, the tavernkeeper, and the Caseys were also arrested. But the affair dragged on for five years, during which time Coroner John Hyndman complained bitterly about the careless manner in which the authorities prepared the case. During the long delay before trial, both Caseys fled the country after either jumping bail or escaping custody .

Another notorious family in Biddulph's early days were the Tooheys, for whom the Donnellys reserved a special antipathy. Living on the Roman Line about two and a half miles south of the Donnelly place, they were just far enough away to make good enemies.[10] The two families often tried their muscle against each other. The considerable brood of Toohey boys were, however, always squabbling amongst themselves, while this was a failing in which the others rarely indulged. The head of the family, old Dennis, born in the year of the great peasant uprising in Ireland in 1798, was one of the first to settle in the Catholic portion of Biddulph, in 1841. He raised a quarrelsome family of eight boys: John, Patrick, Timothy, young Dennis, Michael. Cornelius. James, and

Hugh. According to Will Donnelly, an admitted enemy of most of them, they were noted "for their treachery and rascality".

When the Railway Age came to Biddulph Township in the 1850s, the Grand Trunk Railway line cut diagonally across the farms of old Dennis Toohey and his son John. It was a windfall desired by all the farmers because of the cash received not only for the acreage, but also for the grading work. When the latter was advertised in 1856, the Tooheys defied any man to take the contract for the job through their farm. They wanted it for themselves at their own price. Andrew Keefe, the tavernkeeper, was prepared to take the risk and he bid on the job. Keefe was said to have been trained for the priesthood but became everything except that: soldier, distiller, grocer, contractor, tavern-

Dr. John Hyndman, the coroner who held the inquest on the body of Richard Brimmacombe, murdered on the Roman Line in 1857

keeper, and drawer of wood. Possessed of considerable capital for those days, he had the horses and equipment to do the job and got the contract. But on the night of July 25, 1857, Andy Keefe's barns went up in flames, devouring seven work horses, a valuable stallion, several tons of hay, and a peddler's wagon. The tavern, too, containing two kegs of blasting powder, was set on fire but was saved. Keefe could not complete the railway contract, and the Tooheys stepped in and finished the job. Charged with arson, they were arrested but were acquitted for lack of sufficient evidence at the Goderich Assizes.

The early troubles Biddulph gave it a bad name. D. G. Miller, a Woodstock lawyer who acted as Crown Counsel at one of the Goderich assizes, said: "There seems to be a clever crowd around Keefe's," and referring to the Brimmacombe murder, he went on:

The magistrates in the neighbourhood where the murder was committed seemed afraid or reluctant to act [and] the feeling of insecurity which existed among the inhabitants in that part of the Townships of Biddulph and Usborne where the deceased lived was so great that the value of property was depreciated and that respectable farmers and mechanics in

United Counties of
   Huron & Bruce
      To Wit

Deposition of Witnesses
Examined in the Township of Usborne and Biddulph before a Court of investigation by the Magistrates of Huron and Bruce, as directed by Daniel G. Miller Esquire — Counsel for the Crown Huron Spring Assizes March, 1857

John Longworth Esq. J.P. Chairman
Isaac Carling Esq. J.P.
Assisted by John Hyndman Esq. M.D.
Coroner, and Daniel Lizars Esq. Clerk
of the Peace   in the matter of
            The Queen
                vs
            William Casey
Suspected as accessory
to the murder of
Richard Brimmacombe
...

This deponent Mrs. Alice McGee wife of George McGee upon her oath saith as follows, That she knows the Prisoner William Casey, Deponent knows that Richard Brimacombe was murdered   heard of the murder on Saturday evening thereafter Deponent believes that Patrick Rider of Biddulph was in the neighbourhood on the Friday and was at the house of Prisoner and his father Patrick Casey on that day   Deponent has heard that suspicions were abroad against William Casey and Patrick Rider as the murderers this suspicion was raised by the neighbourhood as soon as the man was murdered, and after their apprehension. This opinion was founded in consequence of a fight at Brimacombes raising at which William Casey was beaten   Deponent has heard from Mr. Thomas Jaques or his son William that William Casey said on the night of the fight that the men or the Company at the raising would catch it although it should be in ten years time — Deponent is of opinion that from the malignancy of William Casey against Richard Brimacombe the latter came by his death, and Deponent considers William Casey to have been privy to it, Deponent is of opinion that Witnesses are afraid to give their evidence regarding this murder in consequence of threats —

Deponent has had a conversation regarding this murder with the mother of William Casey the Prisoner at Deponents house Mrs. Casey commenced by talking about Richard Brimacombe, that she was verry sorry that He had been murdered and she thanked God that her family was all clear of the murder, Deponent then said, well Mrs. Casey, you are well aware that the man was murdered through the spite that your William had against him   Mrs. Casey answered that she supposed so, And that her son was at home that night   She said it was a pity, or too bad that the man was murdered, that they might have given him a beating and then let him go   she said that her son William would have been up the line with Patrick Rider that night, Deponent did not believe all what Mrs. Casey stated — Deponent saw Old Mr. Casey's Cutter going up the line to Biddulph on the afternoon of the murder containing two men, Dept's impression is that the Cutter contained William and Thomas Casey   This impression was afterward confirmed by statements made to that effect by Catherine Casey and Ann Heffernan (married) and that a third person was in the Cutter when it came back, and Deponent was told that this third person was either Old Patrick Rider or his son Patrick Rider Junior, Catherine Casey told this to Deponent, Deponent had a conversation with Richard Brimacombe before the murder regarding the fight, when he stated that he was apprehensive of William Casey and had mind to sell off his place, but was dissuaded not to do so by his wife, Mrs. Brimacombe, Deponent believes that — that through the malignancy of the Casey's arising out of the fight that Brimacombe was murdered; and his hired man John Sutton had been grievously assaulted since the fight, Deponent considers the settlers have dread of the Caseys from the above cause.

                                                her
                                        Alice X McGee
                                                mark

Cross-examinde by Prisoner
The cutter with three persons in it was stated to deponent by her two sons Thomas and William McGee, to have returned upon the Friday about twenty minutes past five O'clock in the afternoon.

                                                her
                                        Alice X McGee
                                                mark

several instances had in consequence sold their property and removed from the neighbourhood, and others were desirous of following the same course if they could dispose of their land.[11]

It was an ironic but apt twist of fate that the unofficial Father of the notorious township, Big Jim Hodgins, had himself been tried for murder in Tipperary before coming to Canada to found Biddulph.

KINGSTON

The feud between James Donnelly and Patrick Farrell, who were possibly distant relatives, began in 1850 when Farrell moved to Lot 20 in the seventh concession on the Roman Line, just a couple of lots south of and across the road from Donnelly. Whether it was Farrell's abrasive character or the remnants of an ancient family feud, the two were soon at loggerheads. About 1855 John Grace, who held paper tide to the Donnelly homestead, sold the south half to Michael Maher of London Township. Donnelly defied Maher or anyone else to dispossess him, and the community heeded him, except for Farrell. The latter not only was related to Maher but was known as "a disturbing personage" who would go looking for trouble if it did not find him. Farrell took a lease of the land from Maher and went to claim it. In all likelihood he fought with Donnelly but could not budge him. Farrell went back to Maher, who brought legal action and in due course obtained a summons for ejectment of Donnelly in May 1855. A compromise was eventually made, through the intervention of friends, in which Donnelly yielded up the south fifty acres and obtained full legal title to the north fifty acres, but Donnelly took the loss

of half his original homestead in bad grace.

Not long after, Jim Donnelly bought a rifle in the newly incorporated city of London. As he was a crack shot, it was said he could easily have killed Farrell, had he wanted to, one day in December of 1855 when he took a shot at him. Farrell was not so sure the miss was intentional. "Donnelly tried to murder him," Mrs. Farrell later testified of the incident. Her husband swore out a charge of "felonious shooting" against Donnelly before Justices of the Peace James Barber and Daniel Shoff of Flanagan's Corners. Four days after Christmas that year, Donnelly was remanded to the Goderich Assizes. There he was bound over to keep the peace and be of good behaviour towards Patrick Farrell, promising "not to molest him again" for a period of one year.

Donnelly could hardly wait for the year to expire. On June 25, 1857, he met Farrell at Maloney's logging bee and killed him.

When Farrell's corpse had been removed from the potato patch to the shanty at the logging bee, Maloney's brother Cornelius went to notify the Farrell family. He stopped at the road and asked a little boy named Orange to fetch Mrs. Farrell. Sarah Farrell came quickly and, as soon as she saw Maloney's sombre face, she sensed that something was seriously wrong.

"Where's my man?" she asked anxiously. "Is he hurt, or killed?"

Maloney simply nodded. The woman groaned with grief, but in a moment she asked in a quiet voice, "Who done it?"

"Oh," replied Maloney simply, "who done it before. "

Patrick Farrell's corpse was taken home, carried past the Donnelly farm where, no doubt, some of Farrell's relatives muttered oaths of vengeance usual to such unhappy occasions. "Ye'll curse the day it happened," one might have said. "Bad 'cess to him and his childer," another might reply, and a third would enjoin, "May he niver die till he sees his own funeral."

Laid out to await the coroner, who did not arrive at the Farrell shanty for two days, the body of Patrick Farrell decomposed in the warm summer weather. When Dr. Charles Moore arrived for

> Michael Carroll of the Township of Biddulph and County aforesaid Sworn, Saith, I was at Wm. Maloney's logging bee on Thursday last 25th June, I am acquainted with the deceased Patk Farrell, in the afternoon he was drunk, himself and Donelly was quarrelling, began about an hour or two in the afternoon, I went to him when he was struck and raised up his head, and asked who struck him, I asked a second time, and John Townhy made answer that it was Donnelly that struck him, When Donelly struck him was about four or five rods from the place where they were, Donelly asked a chew of Tobacco from me about three or four minutes before the blow was struck;
>
> By the Foreman
>
> Did not see any blood where the body fell, I considered that Donnelly tried most to keep the quarrell going, had not see any one else but Donelly that had any dispute with Farrell on that day from what I hear it is my belief that Donnelly was the man that struck Farrell, the blow that killed him Donnelly was at my house on Sunday night was there also on Saturday morning between seven and eight o'clock and said he was sorry for what he had done, I have no doubt but it was Donnelly that did the deed, but did not see him do it I think Martin Mackey told me that he tried to ward of the blow from Farrell I heard that Martin Mackey and Lanigan had something to do in trying to take a handspike from the deceased when he got the blow that killed him.
>
> "Michael Carroll"

(PAC)

the *post mortem* examination, poor Pat Farrell was quite unrecognizable.

The coroner convened an inquest at Bob McLean's Exchange Hotel on the gravel road of Biddulph the following Sunday. After only two witnesses had been heard, the inquest was adjourned and the constables were dispatched to arrest James Donnelly. Appearing at his shanty, they were confronted by his defiant wife, who told them that her husband had "cleared out" The coroner would have to proceed without him.

Witnesses deposed that Donnelly had been seen standing in the doorway of his shanty the day after the murder. Cornelius Lanagan saw him there. Mick Carroll said that Donnelly had come to see him between seven and eight o'clock on the Saturday of that week, saying he was sorry for what he had done and begging forgiveness. He came again the next night. Carroll turned his face from Donnelly, and it was the last time anyone admitted seeing him again for many a day.

The jury brought in its verdict on July 1, 1857, at Patrick Flanagan's tavern, where the inquest had reconvened. It was that

James Donnelly...not having the fear of God before his eyes, but moved and seduced by the instigation of the devil...with a certain wooden handspike of the value of one penny...feloniously, wilfully, and of his malice aforethought...the said Patrick Farrell did kill and murder...and fled.... [1]

The rest of that summer and autumn, Jim Donnelly hid in the thick woods which covered the back of every farm in Biddulph. His wife and the older boys, James who was 15, Will who was 12, and John who was 10, took turns stealing provisions out to him. Occasionally he was seen by neighbours, cultivating one of the stump-studded fields in the garb of his wife. But whenever the constables visited the farm, he was nowhere to be found. "Such is the state of society in his neighbourhood," one official complained of Donnelly's successful evasion of the law, "that as soon as the officers of Justice approach he is apprised thereof and hitherto has escaped. "[2]

But Donnelly's offence, described in a government report of the day as "a most brutal murder ...committed in open day", was well advertised in notices offering rewards for his apprehension as well as for information leading to the conviction of persons suspected of harbouring him. When the central government was applied to for further rewards, Attorney General John A. Macdonald replied in a communication dated January 20, 1858:

In this case a reward of four hundred dollars having been offered by the municipality, it does not in my opinion appear necessary to offer an additional reward.[3]

Hiding in the winter was more difficult. Sometimes Donnelly spent days in a strawstack or stable, and there are numerous stories in the township of his living in the caves on the banks of the Sauble River, on the farm, for example, of the Neils. Or he hid or was hidden on the farms of other Protestant families, such as the Kents and the Hasketts, where he would help out with the chores. On one occasion Mitchell and Mary Haskett hid Donnelly in bed among their children while the constables searched the house and the barn. He may even on occasion have sneaked back to the tavern of his old friend, Andy Keefe, at the Catholic Church Cor-

REWARDS !!

$400   **AND**   **$100**

THE Municipal County Council of the United Counties of Huron and Bruce, offer a reward of $400 for the apprehension and delivery in the County Gaol, Goderich, of JAMES DONNELLY of the Township of Biddulph in the County of Huron, accused of murdering Patrick Farrel of the same place, on Thursday the 25th day of June, 1857. A further reward of $100 is also offered to any person giving such information as will lead to the conviction of the person or persons harbouring the said James Donnelly.

D. H. RITCHIE, County Clerk,
HURON & BRUCE.

County Clerk's Office,
Goderich, Oct. 6, 1857.

n36-4t.

(PAC)

Charlotte Haskett. When she was a child James Donnelly, Sr., was supposed to have once been hidden in a bed among the Hasken children to avoid being captured by the police. (Stanley)

ners for the odd "sup uv the crathur".

Certainly "the bhoys" missed him at the tavern. On Christmas Eve that year, Thomas Casey sat in the bar-room getting drunk with only the bartender, Michael Ryan, to keep him company. It had been the day of the election poll in Biddulph, and a great party of sleighs bearing the Orangemen, who had gathered at McLean's Hotel along the road, soon drove by shouting, "Hurrah for the Tipperaries! Hurrah for Holmes! To hell with the Papishes!" The Orangemen supported Holmes, the Reform candidate, while the Catholics of that day stood up for Cayley, a right-wing member of the Conservative party. The Protestants drove by Andy Keefe's "Papish house" just to stir up trouble, and they succeeded when Casey, half drunk, ran out to challenge the Orangemen. They piled out of their sleighs and attacked the tavern, leaving it a shambles. Despite the odds, it was one of the Orangemen, Edward Coughlin, who was almost fatally injured in the melee. A principal ringleader of the Orange mob was Big Barney Stanley.[4]

During the remainder of Jim Donnelly's hiding, a general feeling of sympathy gradually grew up in favour of the fugitive. Farrell, it was now generally agreed among the community except for a small knot of his relatives, had been a troublemaker and had provoked the quarrel from the beginning. And while Donnelly may have acted rashly at the logging bee, the consensus of the community was that by "the verdict of the general public, he was hardly guilty of wilful murder".

Thereupon, on May 7, 1858, James Donnelly, in company with his supposed captor, Mitchell Haskett of Biddulph, after having been a fugitive from justice for a little less than a year, walked into the office of the man who had been the original surveyor of Biddulph Township but was now the Sheriff of Huron County. The day that Donnelly gave himself up to Sheriff John McDonald was just four days before the opening of the Goderich Spring Assizes. When Haskett applied for the reward, however, the municipal county council balked. A suspicion persisted that the prisoner had arranged for Haskett to "capture" him, the reward to be split between captor and captive, with the latter thereby financing his defence. Despite the affidavit filed by Johannah Donnelly disclaiming any connivance, and Haskett's submission of an account for his travel expenses, the reward money was refused.

Jim Donnelly needed a good lawyer. Who better to retain than Honest John Wilson of London, a man very well experienced in murder cases? Years before, Wilson, still a law-student, had successfully defended himself for murder, the case arising out of the last fatal duel ever fought in Canada West, in 1833. Moreover, he was a lawyer popular with the common people, having

> passed his early days upon the farm and endured a full share of those hardships which the early immigrants to Canada were obliged to face.... It was here that he acquired the knowledge of farm life [and] that sympathy with a farmer's lot and its trials.[5]

Surely Honest John Wilson would know about the feeling of a pioneer for his land, and about logging bees, and how best to defend James Donnelly.

Sir John Beverley Robinson, Chief Justice of the Court of Queen's Bench for Canada West, was the presiding judge at the trial of James Donnelly, which came before him on Friday, May 14. Robinson was a highly esteemed jurist, whose law was so sound that he had never once been overturned by an appeal court, and who, twenty-four years before, had presided over the trial of Honest John Wilson himself. Crown Counsel was another London lawyer, Frank Cornish, a well-known character of the day.[6] Among the jury were Thomas Case and Simon Young, sometime constables of the district, the latter from Biddulph itself. Another juror was James Stanley, prominent among the Orangemen of Biddulph.[7] Cornish called ten witnesses for the prosecution, most of them being men who had attended Maloney's logging bee, as well as the medical doctor and Farrell's widow. Then it was time for the defence.

Honest John Wilson was supposed to be an advocate "most powerful before a jury". His eloquence was characterized as unadorned, but it "bristled with common sense, and was strong in those great Saxon words which express so much." In the case of James Donnelly, Wilson followed his usual course before a jury, which was

> to simplify a case, bring it within their comprehension; seize hold of the strong points and press them

home. With the subtleties of the law he did not care to trouble them.[8]

The theory of the defence was that the fatal blow was "an unlucky stroke given in drink". Only two defence witnesses were called, Michael Feeheley and Dennis Darcey, Sr., both near neighbours of Donnelly. The lawyers then put their arguments and the judge charged the jury. It soon returned with a verdict: Guilty. The judge thereupon donned the black cap and pronounced the dreaded sentence:

> That you, James Donnelly, be sentenced to be taken to the Gaol from whence you came, thence on the 17th day of September next to the place of execution, there to be hanged by the neck until dead.

The curses of Patrick Farrell's friends and relatives seemed certain to be proved true, for Jim Donnelly was about to be favoured with the prospect of being invited to his own funeral.

Donnelly's only hope now lay in petitions for clemency. His wife spent every waking moment for the next few weeks circulating them for signature.[9] Donnelly was remembered as a goodlooking, likable kind of fellow who circulated widely in the Queen's Bush between London and Goderich, perhaps while driving stagecoach. Farrell, on the other hand, was often referred to as "a desperate character". Many residents of Huron, to which the Township of Biddulph was in those days attached, signed the petitions. They included those "from the wife of the Convict, from several Inhabitants of the Township of Biddulph, and from the Reeves of the several municipalities in the United Counties of Huron and Bruce...." There were petitions from the Mayor and others of the town of Goderich and from the parish priest of St. Patrick's Roman Catholic Church in Biddulph.

When Governor General Sir Edmund Walker Head arrived in Goderich on a tour of the country, it was said that Johannah obtained a personal audience to present the petitions. Whether this is merely part of the legend, it is a fact that the Executive Council of Canada considered the matter of clemency for James Donnelly at a cabinet meeting on July 26, 1858. Based on the petitions and the opinion of the trial judge, a recommendation for mercy was made by the Attorney General

"Honest John" Wilson, defence counsel for James Donnelly, was once himself on trial for murder.

Sir John Beverley Robinson, the trial judge who sentenced James Donnelly to be hanged by the neck until dead

for Canada West, John A. Macdonald. The sentence of death was accordingly commuted to seven years' imprisonment in Kingston Penitentiary.

Ten days later, James Donnelly left the sombre grey walls of Goderich Gaol in company with Sheriff McDonald. On August 6, 1858, he entered Kingston Penitentiary.

In October that year Johannah Donnelly gave birth to her last child, a daughter. She was christened Jane but throughout most of her life was called Jenny by almost everyone. The following year came hard times in their seemingly inevitable cycle. In the midst of the economic depression, the Donnelly shanty saw the old Irish fare of "potatoes and point" served regularly.[10] The farm itself was burdened with a loan secured by a mortgage bearing interest at twenty-four per cent! The mortgage went into default and foreclosure proceedings commenced. When Patrick "Grouchy" Ryder came in the spring of 1861 to enumerate the census, he found sickness and desperation in the little

shanty. Young Tom was on the point of death. When all the traditional Old Country remedies had failed, Mrs. Donnelly turned, as a last resort, to summoning a young physician who had not long before hung out his shingle on Glendenning's Hotel at Flanagan's Corners. Dr. James Sutton came, cured the illness, and remained a fast friend of the family ever after.

Misfortune continued to beset the family when John Donnelly joined his older brother in Kingston. In company with Keefe's bartender, Michael Ryan, and another companion named Thomas Knight, John had taken a job as labourer on the gravel road between Brucefield and Goderich. The trio were among the first to collect their pay in Marsden's Hotel at Brucefield, and had no sooner got outside than they realized that the tight-fisted paymaster had deducted $1.25 per man for a shovel. Furious, the three men stormed back to the paymaster's table.

"I'll hev the price uv the shovel or I'll spill yer

blood," cried Donnelly, and when the paymaster made no move to comply, he grabbed for the tumbler of money sitting on the table. "Well, thin, I'll pay meself!" he exclaimed.

But the assistant snatched the tumbler away and scuttled out of the room with his employer before Donnelly and his companions could catch him.

"There won't be another man paid heer today, I tell yeez," Donnelly shouted after them, "an' ye won't be gittin' out uv heer wid yer life."

Ryan pounded the door behind which the paymaster and his assistant cowered, and swore, "I will leave the mark of me shovel on yer face before I leave Brucefield."

Donnelly, Ryan, and Knight laid siege to the hotel but were arrested shortly after when the paymaster escaped in a carriage, running over one of them. The three men were arrested, convicted at the Goderich Fall Assizes for "rioting", and each sentenced to three years in Kingston Penitentiary.

Upon his release, if he returned to Biddulph at all, John Donnelly did not remain there long. He left the district, went to the United States, and was reported to have met his death years later by drowning in a canal in Toledo, Ohio.[11]

During the years that James Donnelly spent in Kingston, his wife remained the backbone of the family. "In the darkest days of our need," recalled her daughter Jenny, "her loving arm... never failed to throw its protection around and provide for all of us." Johannah, whose name was sometimes shortened to Julia, Judith, or even Judy, had a will of iron and a physique to match. She stood a few inches higher than her husband, with long, strong bones and powerful limbs. Her body was large and her head also, with a skull perhaps deeper than average from front to back, a characteristic she passed on to one or two of her children. After the Irish manner, she smoked a clay pipe.

By dint of her great efforts, the circumstances of the household were gradually turned around. The foreclosure proceedings were somehow compromised and the land saved. When better times returned generally, the Broderick family, on the north side of the Donnelly farm, built a large house of hewed logs standing one hundred and fifty feet back from the road. It looked like a mansion compared to the humble Donnelly shanty,

but Judith Donnelly dismissed it to her children as pretentious and too draughty and pretended to prefer the shanty, which stayed warm and cozy during the coldest winter. The Donnelly boys grew into strong, healthy, hardworking lads, and a local historian noted that "under their mother's management they carried on the farm and actually improved the family's financial position."[12]

Meanwhile their efforts to free the head of the household did not cease. Father Peter Crinnon, of St. Patrick's was prevailed upon to dispatch further petitions in May and June of 1859, and again in 1862. All petitions to shorten the term of imprisonment were denied. Father Crinnon was later transferred to Stratford and eventually succeeded Bishop Farrell in the Hamilton diocese, where he died in 1882. But it was during his pastorship, on Christmas Day in 1859, that another notorious murder took place in the Catholic Settlement of Biddulph. James, the son of Michael "Butt" Cain, beat to death with a wooden wagon seat a neighbour named William Cahalan during an altercation on the road.[13] Still another murder was committed not far from the Donnelly farm when John Drought concluded a disagreement with a neighbour over a small gore of land by beating him to death with a stick.

Thus, the murder of Patrick Farrell was not a single, peculiar occurrence in a generally law-abiding district. Violence to life and property was not unusual in and about Biddulph, and strangers entered this society at their peril. "In 1860 a strange man named Mitchell came on the Roman Line with a threshing machine," related William Donnelly about those days, "but this not suiting some of the inhabitants, they went in the night and cut his machine to pieces." Thomas Hodgins, a friend of the Donnellys, also brought his threshing machine into the Catholic Settlement some years later, intending to compete with a couple of the Catholic farmers' for custom threshing. But the ears and tails of Hodgins' horses were cropped in the night to scare him off.[14]

William Donnelly also told of an Englishman who built a shanty on a Canada Company lot adjoining Biddulph. The land was coveted by a Biddulpher who, with a gang of accomplices in the dead of night, toppled trees on the little shack and

Francis E. Cornish, Crown counsel in the prosecution of James Donnelly, Sr., for the murder of Patrick Farrell

26th July 1858. 39

Several Municipalities in the United Counties of Huron & Bruce, praying for a Commutation of the said Sentence.

The Circumstances of this case having been fully Considered by his Excellency in Council, in Connection with the Opinion of the learned Chief Justice who tried the Case, and the recommendation of the Hon. Attorney General (U.C.) in favor of a Commutation of the said Sentence, His Excellency was pleased to Order, And it is hereby Ordered, that the Sentence so passed on the above Named James Donnelly be Commuted into imprisonment in the Provincial Penitentiary for the term of Seven years.

The record of the Cabinet decision that saved James Donnelly, Sr., from the gallows (PAC)

frightened the Englishman away. The "bushwhacker" moved in and squatted there for years, until the Canada Company put him out on the road with all his possessions. They amounted, Donnelly recalled, "to a table and an ox-yoke".

Then there was the case of Patrick Donegan. Donegan arrived in Biddulph via the East Indies and settled amidst the Harrigans, Cains, and Tooheys, on a lot opposite the Cedar Swamp Schoolhouse. He had the temerity to accuse one of his neighbours of stealing a valuable oak tree from his lot. At a raising bee held shortly after, Donegan's neighbours mobbed him, stripped the clothes from his back, applied red-hot irons to his flesh, and put him behind the back log of the fireplace until he screamed for mercy. They then threw him outside into a mud-hole.

"What about the oak tree now, Donegan?" one of them mocked as he struck him on the head with a rail-splitting mall.

The crowd threatened to cut the wretch's ears off until the mistress of the proprietor finally persuaded them to leave poor Donegan alone.

Father Peter Crinnon's personal motto, "In all things, charity", was sorely tried during his years at St. Patrick's in Biddulph. He visited Donegan the following day and

when the priest turned him in bed the flesh actually fell off his bones. The good priest, horrified at the sight, looked to heaven and said he was afraid the hand of God would fall on Biddulph.[15]

Jim Donnelly had completed half his allotted term when the Brimmacombe murder trial was finally held in Goderich. Thomas and William Casey, along with the latter's father-in-law, Old Patrick Ryder, faced the judge on November 13, 1862. The Roman Liners, according to William Donnelly, "chewed the key of Heaven to pieces" in attempting to avoid implicating the defendants in the crime. Crown Counsel Harrison could only elicit the following harmless testimony from witness Pat Heffernan:

Coming home about eight or nine o'clock at night I saw the body. My wife was with me, an sez she, "Och, Paddy, is this a log or a man in the shnow?" An, sez she, "I think he's a Englishman name of Cornish." Indade, if I was goin' to die I didn't hear

Peter Crinnon the parish priest at st Patrick's in Biddulph in 1857-9, later Bishop of Hamilton

SCHOLARS

anyone say it was Brummgum, an Danelly that's now in Pinitinshery was the first man that towld me....[16]

The Crown prosecutor eventually threw up his hands in disgust when the witnesses proved too evasive, and he in effect abandoned the case for the Crown. All three accused men were directed to be acquitted of the murder.

"The crime has not been brought home to you," admonished Chief Justice Robinson in releasing them. He advised them to return home and lead exemplary lives in the future.

While serving his time in Kingston Pen, Jim Donnelly in 1861 scrawled his X on a deed to a small plot of land off the northeast corner of his farm. On this plot a well-built hewed-log schoolhouse was put up. The third school built in Biddulph, after Coursey's and Atkinson's, it occupied almost all of its tiny forty-by-fifty-foot plot, without a fence, and with room only for an "office" at the rear, for use when nature called. The scholars of the day were thoroughly familiar with the rugged features of Johannah, and with the Donnelly horses, whose noses "almost touched the windows as they turned the furrow-heads that ended at the schoolhouse".

Young Will Donnelly often stayed home and scraped on a borrowed fiddle, even though the schoolhouse was close by. "I am sorry if my lack of education shows itself," he once said with a trace of bitterness, "but my mother often had no clothes to send us to school in." While never becoming really expert, Will could certainly fiddle well enough to saw out in tolerable fashion the jigs and marches of the boisterous soirees in the Catholic Settlement. He made up for the lack of a formal education with a native intelligence which made him, in the end, the most literate of the family. Of the brothers, James and Robert were the least inclined to book-learning. While both could scrawl their signature if pushed, they usually resorted to making a mark after the manner of their father. Michael, Thomas, and Jane were reasonably well educated and capable of good expression, while John and Patrick fell somewhere in between.

Attending the Donnelly School, as the schoolhouse for Biddulph School Section Number Three was known, were the Feeheleys, Sullivans, Ryders, McLaughlins, McGees, Quigleys, Careys,

Hogans, Regans, Farrells, Carrolls, Kelleys, Keefes, Cains, and Caseys, among others. The schoolyard alliances and factions no doubt shifted back and forth, and the *argumentum fisticuffum* was often engaged in extracurricularly. As far as such activities went, "The only way in which the family suffered during the father's absence," it was said, "was pride, for the Donnelly boys at school and on the road were often the butt of rude remarks regarding their father's absence from home [and] naturally they avenged these insults with their fists...." Jim Feeheley, usually a close friend of the Donnelly brothers, once admitted, "One of the Donnellys nearly beat me dead once."

Pedagogic punishment was meted out by rawhide. But as some of the early teachers could attest, it was not always the scholars who were on the receiving end. One day in August 1857, James Burns of the Roman Line took exception to the classroom conduct of the schoolteacher, Patrick Leonard, and, striking the teacher several blows with his fist, he tore his clothes and sent him scampering down the line. And the story is told of the new teacher, perhaps James Ryan, who was determined to treat his charges like ladies and gentlemen in hopes they would reciprocate.

"How do you do and what is your name?" he asked as he went around and shook the hand of each in turn.

A large, broad-shouldered youth with a mop of straight white hair grasped the teacher's hand and pumped it vigorously up and down as a huge smirk spread over his face.

"How do you do," he said, "I'm Tom Donnelly, sir."

The pedagogue shook no more hands that day. All four of his fingers were broken.

Donate Crowe, an Italian who taught at the Cedar Swamp School in the 1850s, came up to the standards required for survival in Biddulph. One cold winter's day he pushed young Maggie Harrigan out of doors without a coat and said, "She put her tongue out at me and made a noise with her mouth like the whores of Limerick. She is a whore, a bitch and a flirt. She is a sheep-stealer and the family they are an ill-bred lot."

Mr. Crowe challenged the young roughs of his school to try their muscle with him any time. "There is not a man in Buddulph able to fight me,"

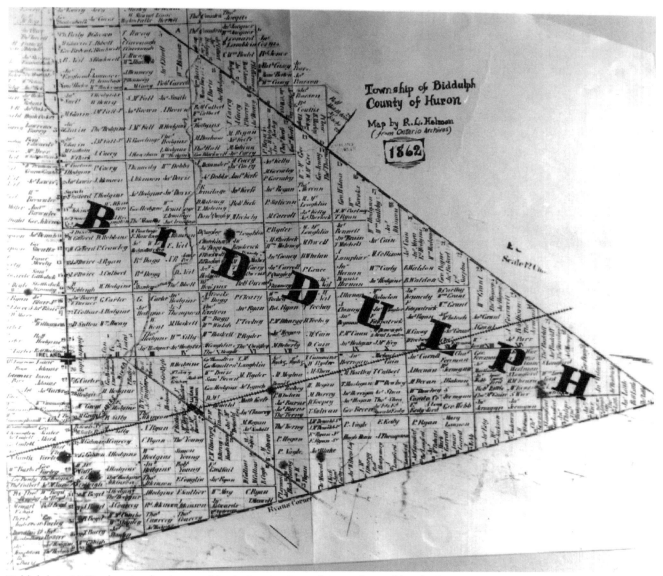

Biddulph in 1862, showing landownership during the time of the early troubles (PAO)

he once raged in front of his pupils, sending the stone ink stands flying when he brought down his heavy wooden rule with a bang. "I will not leave Biddulph until I have made Tom Nangle and Ned Ryan and others of their like sup sorrow." Nangle heard of the challenge, went to school to accept, and was soundly thrashed.

Although few of the teachers boarded in Mrs. Donnelly's crowded shanty, she always maintained a special solicitude towards the lady teachers. One wet morning she saw the schoolmistress hurry by the farm.

"Good morning, miss," she called out, "come in and dhry yerself before goin' to school."

The young woman thanked her but said she had not time.

"Shure but yer feet is all wet," Johannah insisted. "Do come in till I git ye a pair of dhry shtockings."

But the teacher hurried on, smiling. Judith Donnelly fetched a pair of stockings from the house and handed them to a scholar with the words, "Tell the teacher to change her feet."

Female scholars of the day had the additional

risk to endure of assault with ardour. In November 1861, Julia Madigan was set upon by young Michael Shea, who had followed her on the road. The young man, in the words of the female complainant,

> laid down a plough point which he carried in his hand and laid violent hands upon me, catching me by the breast and forcing me up against the fence, at the same time using his best endeavours to lift up my dress.... I seen he was determined to abuse me. I then called on Paddy Grace with all my might. He clapped his hand on my mouth.... I bit him.... He stooped down and put his hand under my clothes as high as my knees and says, "I must have it! I must have it!" I got away from him [but he] got me right down; he kneeled on to me. I gathered all my clothes under my legs. I gave him one kick of my two feet into the stomach and throwed him off, I suppose two or three yards. I shouted triumphs of joy and thanked the Lord.[1]

Hannah Coughlin was similarly accosted by young Joe McIlhargey, who rode up to her on his horse on a lonely stretch of Biddulph road. "I intend to have you mine," said the youth, "and I will put you in a way that you will be mine." He jumped off his horse, threw the frightened girl to the ground, and began to unbutton his pantaloons. She screamed.

"Stop!" he hissed, "I'll murder you if you don't shut up."

But the girl's shouts fetched young Tommy Whalen. "Shame!" he cried at McIlhargey.

"Take care of yourself, Whalen," the other warned him.

"Don't you dare go, Tom Whalen," the besieged girl cried out. Young Whalen stayed and Hannah Coughlin's virtue was preserved.

Among the early school superintendents were William Elliot and John Dearness. Elliot later became a lawyer and then Judge of the County Court of Middlesex, and he thereby became well acquainted with each of the Donnelly boys as they grew up from rowdy schoolboys into rowdy men. John Dearness inspected the Donnelly School regularly and always quartered his horse in the family's stables. He found them to be "always kind and considerate".

John Dearness. As a young man Dearness was a schoolteacher in pioneer Biddulph. Then and later, when he became a school inspector, he often stopped off at the Donnellys'.

The schoolhouses of the day were social centres where dances, weddings, and political meetings were held. In the case of the Donnelly and Cedar Swamp schools of the Catholic Settlement, they served also as small chapels, which the parish priest would periodically visit. There he would say mass for the older people who found it difficult to journey to the church. When the Donnelly School burned down in the early morning of February 20, 1878, it was rebuilt of frame that summer and equipped with a large, bureau-like altar for this purpose.[2]

Jenny Donnelly did not see her father until she was almost seven years old and going to school. She was a comely girl with a sturdy, prepossessing look about her.[3] When fully grown, she was five feet five and one-half inches, and thus slightly taller than most women of the Catholic Settlement, and weighed one hundred and forty-five pounds at maturity. Even in her later years she had a not unattractive appearance, although at first

The Donnelly schoolhouse was situated on the northeast corner of the Donnelly farm. This is the building erected in 1878 following a fire that destroyed the original schoolhouse.

blush one might think her stern and hard-faced by modern standards. But in the flower of her youth, there is no doubt she was a bright, handsome girl and "the idol of a family who were noted for their love and kindness to each other through all their troubles".

Although Detective Hugh McKinnon of Hamilton had no great liking for Jenny's brothers, he described them as "fine looking, muscular men, with an air of cool desperation that awes at first sight". James Donnelly, Jr., was a handsome youth with fine and regular features, of medium height and build, but muscular and rugged.[4] He sometimes exhibited a low and cunning mentality with a vicious streak. Being only fifteen years of age when his father went into hiding, he had quickly to assume the burden of the male head of the household.

But during those dark days it was Johannah who continually shored up the morale of her sons. "The boys were goaded on by their mother to

Johannah Donnelly in later life (*The Globe*)

resent the insults," it was reported. Urged on by her, they would "scarcely stop at anything to resent a real or fancied injury [and] in this one failing lay their weak point." It was said that the mother, "a woman of masculine will [but with] her share of the natural ability which characterized the whole family",

> prayed on her knees that the souls of her sons might for ever and ever frizzle in hell if they ever forgave an enemy, or failed to take revenge.[5]

This may have been an exaggeration, as were the tales of her vowing she would never be satisfied until each of her boys had killed his man,

but there is no doubt, as her neighbours said, that "she was a hard talker."

While Jenny's involvement with the family troubles was small, the boys' brushes with the law began soon after their father had fled to the bush. Annie Robinson's saucy tongue may have been the provocation, but young Jim and John Donnelly, along with a chum named Jimmy Atkinson, were soon hauled up before Magistrates James Kelley and Jim Hodgins for assaulting the young girl, knocking her to the ground, ripping a cap off her head, and tearing her clothing. They were assessed minor penalties.

Aside from the questionable gallantry of this

(UWO)

youthful scrape, it was the general opinion that the Donnellys "had energy and ability much above average". The opinion was especially apt in the case of the second-born, William Michael.[6] "The clubfoot cripple", as his enemies called him, became the acknowledged brains of the family early on. "In general intelligence and cunning he is the leader in the township," it was reported, and his quick and ready intelligence astonished men of much greater learning. He was "acknowledged to be one of the most naturally astute men in the county", said Goodspeed's *History of Middlesex*, and a Toronto newspaper reporter once stated, "He is as sharp as a steel trap and possessed of an iron will, being cool, determined and far-seeing. He thinks twice before he speaks and always acts on his determination." Once in the witness-box for six solid hours, without a note, he never once made a blunder, nor was he tripped up on cross-examination by experienced legal counsel.

Sharp-visaged, with a high forehead, and long, dark hair hanging "down his neck in clustering ringlets", Will Donnelly sported a light-coloured and wispy moustache and, in later years, an imperial. Like his brothers, he wore the finest clothes he could afford when he grew up and affected a more polished and cosmopolitan air than the ruder playmates of his school days. His familiarity with the outlandish legalese of official documents, perhaps dating back to his experiences in rounding up signatures for petitions, and his later familiarity with the inside of a courtroom, earned him the sobriquet of "the Lawyer". He "wrote a good letter" and acquired a facility of expression which the better educated might have envied. "I have no big words to give you but will use my own name and defy contradiction," he once said when relating some of his family's history. On another occasion he offhandedly penned the following lines in the autograph book of one of the daughters of the Lucan postmaster:

When Father Time with his big sword
Shall slay old William Porte,
I trust his daughter Emma will
For lifetime hold the fort
But should one less agreeable
The business attend to,

I seldom will look through the hole
I often see you through.[7]

Will Donnelly's honesty evoked the sharpest difference of opinion. According to Big Barney Stanley, the leading merchant of the community, Donnelly was guilty of the worst possible sin: he could not be trusted to pay his debts. "I tell yeez," he once puffed, "that Donnelly is so bad, I have known him to take a piece of property and hold it till I had to git the Sheriff to put him off it." Others called him "a spoiled priest", "the plotter of the family", and stated he could not be believed on oath. "He'll swear to anything," said one. And Pat "Grouchy"' Ryder, who had been a close friend for thirty years until they quarrelled, swore an affidavit that Donnelly was "vindictive and unscrupulous". On the other hand, there were those in the community, including Grouchy's own brother, who took their oath that Will Donnelly was completely honest.

The third brother, John, was quiet, cheerful, and likable, with a genial disposition unless aroused to anger, and for the sake of peace would even take a blow without retaliation. The enemies of the family would not concede so, however, and insisted he was as vicious as the others but only less demonstrative. Described as "a fine built fellow, his physical development being complete", John Donnelly grew up to be a muscular and broad-shouldered man with a barrel chest, his lungs being authoritatively reported as "perfect models". He most closely resembled his mother in countenance, with his hooked nose, large jaw, and shoulder-length hair. Notwithstanding, he was considered a handsome fellow. John was the favourite of his parents. He was generally to be seen with a smile playing on his lips, while even the enemies of the family would often exempt him from their hatred. John Dearness, the Biddulph School Superintendent, once boarded in the same house with him and recalled, many years after in 1946, "I found him a decent and respectable working man and never knew anything against him."[8]

Next came Patrick, the middle brother of the seven. At the age of eighteen he went to London to learn the blacksmith's trade in John Campbell's works, where he was known as a quiet, industrious person, popular with his fellow workers as well as his employer. While their enemies said it was Pat's "absence from the paternal roof at an early age [which] saved him from the evil of the others", it was generally agreed that he was an uncomplicated and straightforward fellow whom one could trust instinctively. He minded his own business and kept to himself, but was nevertheless a tough little man. One recorded conversation about him went:

That's him.
Who? The little fellow?
Yes, the small man.
My eye! I thought those Donnellys were giants.[9]

Pat was "a right smart chap", who dressed well and was ambitious, going on from Campbell's in London to work at such places as W. T. Holmes & Son in Clinton, and eventually establishing himself as carnage-maker on his own.

The younger brothers, Mike, Bob, and Tom, were sure to be in evidence when rascality of any sort was called for, whether it was Professor Linder, "the great mind reader" visiting the area to give a demonstration of his amazing occult power, or mesmerizers, bell-ringers, ventriloquists, cartoonists, or musicians who needed to be harassed. Michael Donnelly was the leader of the younger set. He was a good-natured and likable fellow, who made friends easily and was quickly recognized by his wide, burly shoulders tapering to a trim waist, and by his peculiarly shaped head sitting atop a strong, sinewy neck. Like his mother, he seemed to have a long skull from front to back, high forehead, and features rather small and delicate. Described by some as an easy-going and good-hearted fellow who was not at all quarrelsome, friend and foe alike agreed that he would "not allow himself to be run on", and he did, on occasion, tend to be short of temper and loud of voice. He began driving stagecoach when about twenty years of age.

Robert Donnelly, born in 1853, was the second-youngest of the boys, perhaps the handsomest, and certainly the fanciest dresser. Although only five feet eight inches, he was well proportioned and weighed about one hundred and sixty-five pounds in his prime. Unlike his brothers Jim and

Tom, Bob never drank to excess, having taken the pledge early in life and kept it. John also gave up drink, after a few early bouts, while Will once boasted that he had never been the worse of liquor in his life. The others apparently followed their father's habit of remaining temperate for long periods, but when they "fell off the wagon", they fell hard.

The youngest boy was Tom, reputed to have been a sickly child, but who grew up into a great, strapping fellow, with a beefy, hulking presence and a crude sense of humour which could be at once reckless and brutal. Five feet and eleven inches in height, he was a handsome fellow with regular, clean features, almost white hair, and a skin which was light, smooth, and fine-textured like his father's. He used every possible occasion to push his muscle around. Will would sometimes admonish him, "Tom, must you fight every day of the week?"

Tom Donnelly never forgave a slight and was often "the central figure in all the scrapes". "He possessed a retaliatory nature and through his general bravery ran into many a disturbance and brought trouble upon his head." With some justification, it was alleged that "the constables in Lucan and Biddulph [were] afraid of Tom Donnelly," and it was their failure to act which encouraged the boys in their sometimes outrageous conduct in bullying the peaceable citizenry. Hugh McKinnon, writing of one incident, stated:

Isaac White kept the Hotel. He is inclined to favour the Donnellys. He at one time went, I think, Tom Donnelly's bail for some of his pranks. [10]

Some of the other hotel proprietors were not as kindly disposed towards Tom. George Swartz, who kept hotel at Birr, related:

One day Thomas Donnelly sat in the bar, somewhat under the influence of liquor, when he carelessly pulled a revolver from his pocket, pointed the muzzle over his shoulder and fired, regardless of the consequences. The bullet passed uncomfortably close to Mr. Swartz's head, burying itself in the wall. Donnelly then fired another shot, with as much nonchalance, which lodged in the ceiling....[11]

The Donnelly brothers, when they grew up, were said to be real gentlemen, at least until you crossed them. They then "made the quarrel of one of their number a family matter, and wreaked vengeance upon their opponents in the most approved Ku-Klux fashion." Labelled as "the Terrors of the Township for many years" by the newspapers, the journalists delighted in quoting their enemies. "They burned and cut," they said, "and were cut and burned."

LUCAN

The village of Lucan had the misfortune of growing up with the Donnellys.[1] Whether its bad reputation in the nineteenth century was attributable to the family or whether it was the other way around

can long be argued, but it is with the name Lucan, rather than, more properly, Biddulph, that the Donnellys are always associated. The site of the village was first populated by about 150 blacks of the Wilberforce Settlement. Then, between Castleconnel Henry Hodgins' hewed-log tavern built in 1842 and Patrick McIlhargey's large brick tavern built around 1850, the white settlers formed a hamlet where the Grand Trunk Railway crossed the London-Goderich Road on its run from Montreal to Sarnia. Big Barney Stanley forsook his old stand on the Sauble River and built a huge two-storey "Cash Store" in 1859, the same year the tracks themselves were laid. Surveyor John McDonald, who had been paid in land for his work in Biddulph, subdivided his holdings here into small village lots and named the subdivision Marystown. The name was soon after changed to Lucan.

The Protestants insist to this day that Dublin Tom Hodgins timidly suggested the new name, in honour of his former wealthy employer in Ireland,

McIlhargey's Tavern, built about 1850 and still standing on the southern outskirts of Lucan, where several of the early inquests were held

Barney Stanley's Cash Store, which stood for a hundred years on Main Street in Lucan (Stanley)

at a public meeting at George Hodgins' tavern. The Catholics, on the other hand, maintain that Father Peter Crinnon chose the name to commemorate the birthplace of the great Irish Catholic patriot Patrick Sarsfield. At any rate, within ten years the cluster of small buildings, including the old Wilberforce log schoolhouse, to which William Porte returned with his young wife to teach school after the Negroes abandoned it, was soon transformed into a bustling market village of several hundred residents. Grocery stores, livery stables, boot shops, many houses, and several taverns sprang up, including Bob McLean's Central and John O'Donohue's Queen's.

While the great Civil War raged in the United States the prosperity of Canada West flourished. In 1864 it was said of the fast-growing village of Lucan that "the petty feuds and jealousies common to most villages are rare."[2] It was a curious statement which would not again be applied to the place until years after.

From the beginning a faint aura of disrepute clung to the village, for it was here that several of the blacks had suffered misfortune, including death, apparently by accident. Then, from about the time that James Donnelly was imprisoned, rumours began to circulate in the district that members of a certain family in the vicinity were enthusiastic believers in the maxim "God helps those who help themselves." It was reported:

About that time the petty thieving that subsequently was the cause of much trouble in the township began, and the name Donnelly was mentioned in connection therewith, but no open charge was ever preferred against them.[3]

However, in fairness, it is said in the district to this day by those who would defend the family that "If a farmer's wife left her fresh baked pie on the doorstep to cool, and the dog ate it, why she would blame the Donnellys."

While it may have been true, on the other hand,

that "no open charge was ever preferred against them," they were often enough accused, both formally and informally. In 1864 Will Donnelly was charged, along with a neighbour's boy named Michael Sullivan, with larceny of wood, and Mrs. Donnelly herself was charged with receiving the stolen goods. But the result, which so often repeated itself in following years in connection with theft charges, proved an exoneration of sorts. In this instance the Grand Jury threw them out.

Much of the early lawlessness of Lucan was associated with its frequent fires. Many of the first taverns burned to the ground: William Morgan's hewed-log inn in 1864, Madill's hotel in 1865, Leonard Hodgins' tavern in 1866. It was, of course, in the taverns where the Donnelly boys were usually to be found. Will Donnelly was once charged with stealing a bottle of whiskey and arrested, perhaps at the instance of Barney Stanley, who said: "He was before me for stealing when a small boy." And one of the Tooheys once accused Will of stealing sheepskins. While nothing came of either case, it was said of the many thefts:

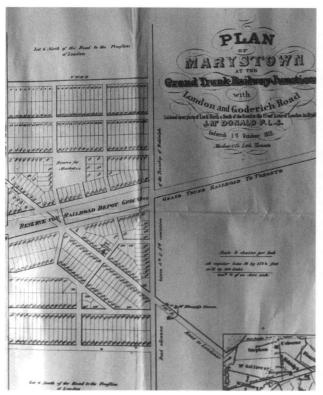

Plan of Lucan (Marystown) as laid out in 1853 (Stanley)

There was no moral doubt among the people as to the parties who committed these things. A great number of them were traced directly to the Donnellys. But there they stopped. Nothing further could be done for want of evidence. The Donnellys knew this, which encouraged them in their lawlessness and ...they even threw out hints in their reckless way of what they had done, or what they intended to do, so as to intimidate the people still further. They wanted to show that they were masters of the situation and they did it pretty well.[4]

Soon it was reputed that "farmers were afraid to bring their grain into market, as they were in danger of being robbed of the proceeds before they reached home." Again, a neighbour of the family once said, "A great deal of pork and cattle stealing have taken place in our neighbourhood [and] the Donnellys are suspected of having committed many of these crimes." Specific thefts were even enumerated: Dearness's grain, Jones's wheat, and the cattle of Foster, Nangle, Morley, and Dan McDonald.

Nevertheless, the thriving village continued to attract the neighbouring farmers, especially during holidays such as the Queen's Birthday and the Glorious Twelfth of July. The first May 24th celebrated in the village was in 1863 when a flag-pole was erected near the post office, now run by William Porte, the former schoolmaster. The horsemen of the Kalathumpians held a grand procession arrayed in outlandish costumes, and a splendid cannon was cast at Diamond & Jackson's local foundry to usher in the holiday. But

on the third discharge it burst into pieces, injuring several bystanders and the man who was firing it severely. A large piece came down through the roof of the foundryman's house into the kitchen, and sent the stove into fragments just as the owner was starting a fire to make breakfast

But the crowd of 2,500 who had poured into the village were determined not to allow the festivities to be so easily dampened.

At 9:30 the athletic exercises commenced on the grounds near the drill shed and were kept up with great spirit until 5 p.m.... At 6 p.m. the horse races came off.... In the evening there was a fine display of fireworks which were let off from the Band Stand and a torchlight procession....[5]

Dublin Tom Hodgins and his wife. Dublin Tom was said to have suggested the name Lucan for the village. (J. Bilyea)

Sure to be among the celebrants would be the Donnelly brothers and their chums. Not only did the progeny of James Donnelly inherit his knack of making friends wherever they went, but they seemed to inspire amongst their companions a fierce loyalty. "The Donnellys are a bad crowd to meddle with," wrote someone who knew them well, "not only them but the crowd that will almost die for them."

It is true that the boys' home on the Roman Line was open to many visitors from both far and near. Inside Johannah's massive body beat a heart to match, and it went out especially to the orphans and derelicts her boys would often bring home. One of these was John Purtell, a large and muscular fellow, albeit a trifle dim-witted at times. His widowed father, roaring drunk, one day tried with his bare hands to stop one of the trains which came rushing through Lucan, with predictable result. Young Tommy Ryan was another orphan. He found himself, at the tender age of sixteen years, facing an assize court for shooting at Mick Carroll's son.

The Kennedy boys, Joe, Big Jack and one-armed Rhody, were intimates of the Donnelly brothers. Young Joe Kennedy took an enforced sojourn in Kingston when, in June of 1865, a couple of Protestant lads named Surplice evinced an interest in the youthful Kennedy girls, Sarah and Margaret, then sixteen and fifteen respectively. Their brothers invited the Surplices to a frolic, but on the way the guests "were waylaid by the very parties who invited them, assisted by several others" and given a savage beating. Young Kennedy was sentenced to five years for this escapade.

Other youngsters who were frequent visitors at the Donnelly house were the young Darceys, Sullivans, Farrells, Hogans, Feeheleys, and Keefes. Young Dan Keefe was a bosom companion. In the fall of 1871 he was convicted of stabbing Martin O'Meara and served six months in prison. Having no sooner got out of jail, however, he was back in trouble again, and the following was typical of one of his frequent forays into Lucan:

Before Squire O'Neil, last week, Daniel Keefe was fined $20 and costs for breaking into Widow Craig's house, making use of abusive language and otherwise ill-treating the poor woman. The wretch pleaded "liquor" as usual in such cases....[6]

With their numerous comrades, bold manner, and great numbers, the Donnelly brothers had the run of the boisterous little village. Many tavern-keepers and shopkeepers were afraid of them. Those who were not part of their chosen circle steered clear of their company. The McLaughlins, Whalens, and McGees all lived close by the Donnellys and got along with them as long as they stayed out of their way. Even at that, as Mrs. Whalen would say, "the boys would sometimes have a tiff."

Patrick McGee was a quiet and inoffensive young fellow who one winter's day sat modestly in his sleigh on the main street of the village wrapped in a buffalo robe. One of the Donnellys came along. He struck McGee in the face, pulled him out of the sleigh, and flung him into the street. Why? "Oh, for no reason at all," McGee's grandson related, "but they were the town bullies and simply wanted to let Grandfather know who was running the place."[7]

It is not surprising that the Donnellys, while popular with their friends, made bad enemies. "In all justice it must be stated," said one man who was friendly towards them, "they would scarcely stop at anything to resent a real or fancied injury." It is therefore not surprising that the reputation of the little village of Lucan sank low, and it was reported about that time that

so disorderly and lawless a state has the place become that it is often impossible to get magistrates to issue, or for constables to execute, processes when required.[8]

But because the brothers were "good looking, healthy, well set up lads", they were at first forgiven some of their petty transgressions by their neighbours. However, in the moral code of the farmer, city and town were essentially corrupt, and because the brothers frequented the village and travelled so much more often to London than most farm boys, they gradually acquired, in the eyes of some Biddulphers, the corrupting ways of town life. "There used to be people coming around," said Mrs. Pat Whalen who lived across

Richmond Street, London, Ontario, in 1865

Dundas Street, London, Ontario, in 1860

the road from them, "strangers and people they used to be acquainted with. A man from Toronto who had been out of prison had once been there."

On the other hand, some of their companions such as Big Jack Kennedy, for example, would visit London only three or four times a year. Martin McLaughlin only went once a year. Tom Ryder, although he had been born and raised in Biddulph, was in London not more than once a year after his marriage. The Donnellys, in the meantime, acquired such questionable city friends as William Denby, who was often in difficulties with the city police. And they got to know many urbanites, including almost all the entire London legal fraternity.

About Lucan, at this time, it was reported:

Lucan boasts four magistrates, but no lawyer; peace and order reign in the village. Whether this is owing

to the presence of the former or the absence of the latter is hard to say.[9]

But the peace and order was relative only, for the passage of a week or so without a commotion in the street was considered worthy of comment:

There has not been a *taste* of a fight for ten days — not as much as a blow struck or an ear bit for over a week.[10]

The first *bona fide* resident lawyer of Lucan was William McDiarmid, who came in March 1874. Several had sojourned for short periods before that, including one William Grant. His practice, it was said, was "principally confined to the hotel bar", and he was later charged with killing a man in a brawl near Lucan.

It is true that the entire blame for the bad reputation of Lucan could not be laid at the door of the Donnellys in the 1870s. For example, when two youngsters fell to quarrelling in a village orchard one day, one of them named Brown ended the argument by blowing off the head of the other, a son of Mitchell Haskett, with a shotgun. The boys were ten years old. It was incidents like this which gave Lucan the name of "the wildest town in Canada".

RETURN

In the year 1865 the newspapers carried headlines such as that on February 8 which read: "The Confederation Scheme". The story below it described the proposed union of the British colonies in North America. A few weeks later, on April 10, the newspaper headlines proclaimed: "Lee's Army Surrenders", followed within a few days with the news: "President Lincoln is Assassinated". The London Advertiser put out an extra edition for the last story. In Lucan, the village flag in front of the post office was lowered to half mast out of respect for the dead American president, but this was too much for one Confederate rebel who was living in the village for the duration of the war. The Southerner, Dr. Theodore Alfonso White, took a shot at the half-raised Union Jack in protest.

It was during the events of this exciting year that James Donnelly came home from Kingston. He was still only forty-nine years of age, while his eldest son and namesake was already twenty-three. The elder Donnelly was a hardy and compact man who had endured in reasonably good spirits the seven long years in the penitentiary. And his heart leapt with excitement when he stepped off the train and clapped eyes on his family: a sturdy wife and seven fine and healthy sons, not to mention the stout, bright-eyed little girl with the brazen face. The older man marvelled at the size of his boys as he grinned from one to the other, seeing, no doubt, in their twinkling eyes the mischief which he well knew must be there, if they were really Donnellys.

"It's sivin divils I've raised for ye, Jim," Mrs. Donnelly proudly said to her husband as she presented them in turn. "An' this here's young Jinny," she proclaimed as she pushed the little girl toward her father.

On the happy trip back to the old homestead, Johannah Donnelly told Jim of the many hardships they had endured, although she had never mentioned these in her letters. She talked of the deadly epidemics which had struck the neighbours but had always spared the Donnelly household, and how well the farm was doing. The returned convict marvelled at the changes in Biddulph since his departure. The population of the township was now about 3,000, including the villages. A fine new yellow brick church stood at the Roman Line corner, while along the road itself the fields stretched farther back from the roadway and there were fewer stumps left studding the fields.

James Donnelly quickly settled back into the humdrum of farm life on the Roman Line, but he never forgot the long, wasted years in Kingston Pen or the friends he had made there. Upon their release, some of the latter would visit him in Biddulph. This was not at all unusual, for it was characteristic of James Donnelly that he made friends easily, and his wide circle of acquaintances included a broad range of the society of the day.

While the farm of Greenland continued to prosper, one night in the fall of 1867 the family were roused at three o'clock in the morning by the sound of the fierce roar of flames devouring their barn, including the year's grain harvest. The fire had been deliberately set, an act of vengeance and a show of defiance by their enemies. The nucleus of the families who continued to bear ill-will against the Donnellys remained the Mahers. James Maher had left his old farm in Stephen opposite the Carroll homestead and, having married a Biddulph girl, had moved to the Roman Line a mile or two north of the Donnelly place. Maher's wife was Ellen Cain, a woman of large proportions who could handle herself in any brawl. Known as "a masculine minded woman [of] determined will and stiff in opinion", she kept her own revolver. It was her definite opinion that the Donnellys were her enemies.

Her brother, John Cain, went to live on the farm which had originally formed the south half of the Donnelly homestead, after the departure of Michael Maher, who had taken eviction proceedings against Jim Donnelly. The latter and his wife continued to resent the loss of half their original land. On one occasion John Cain had wanted to sell the farm to Patrick Casey, from whom he had taken a deposit of one hundred and fifty dollars. Mrs. Donnelly met Casey on the road a few days later as he was making his way to Cain's to seal the bargain. She warned him that any purchaser would take the land at his own risk, implying that her boys would "cut the guts out" of anyone who defied them. Mrs. Donnelly's "jawing" was enough to convince Casey that the bargain was a bad one. He backed out of the deal. Incidents like this helped to persuade Cain that his relatives, the Mahers, were correct in their assessment of his neighbours and helped to align the Cains and the Caseys behind the Mahers and Carrolls in opposition to the Donnellys.

About the same time that John Cain moved next door on the south, there was also a change of occupants on the north side of the Donnelly place. In 1867 the Brodericks sold their land with its new log house to old William Thompson, a well-to do farmer of McGillivray Township, and his son, William Thompson, Jr., a bachelor, went to live on the Biddulph property.

Besides the village of Lucan, Granton was the only other sizeable village community entirely within the bounds of Biddulph. In the eastern part of the township, the little village was not far from the Kennedy farm. In 1867 Queen Victoria's birthday was celebrated in Granton in grand style. The little place attracted many of the farmers from the surrounding country, and the Kalathumpians paraded in the morning while in the afternoon "the athletes of the neighbourhood measured their capabilities in many well contested games, affording every satisfaction to the spectators, and reflecting credit upon the contestants." The young Donnelly boys — young Jim, 25; Will, 22; John, 20; Pat, 18; Mike, 17; Bob, 14, and Tom, 13 — probably participated in the field sports and cleaned up on the prizes that day. A fireworks display at night — young Bob was always especially intrigued by fireworks and flames — brought "the national holiday" to a close. As for Confederation, in Lucan the first Dominion Day was celebrated with a bonfire. Thereafter, the real national holiday celebrations varied in intensity from year to year but never amounted to much in comparison with Queen Victoria's Birthday or the Twelfth of July. In 1870, to mark the entry into Confederation of Manitoba, "a Riel tom-tom procession" was held. But Bob Donnelly liked the bonfires the best.

Except for the burning of their barn, which may have been connected with the scaring off of Patrick Casey from the purchase of John Cain's farm, good fortune for the Donnellys generally continued and was so constant that the family finally decided to replace the original log shanty with a large new log house. Robert Thompson, the carpenter hired in 1870 to construct the new dwelling, was not related to the Donnellys' new neighbour, but he did copy the latter's house in size and design. From trees cut at the rear of the farm and hauled to the site by the strapping young men of the family, Thompson built a fine, hewed-log building. The Donnellys were shanty Irish no longer!

Compared to the old home, the new log house was a mansion.[1] Resting at each of the four corners on a large field stone, the hewed logs, carefully fitted at the angles by the expert framer and standing nine high, formed a building twenty-six feet long by eighteen feet wide. Besides the workman-

ship in its finely dove-tailed corners and well-finished joints, the frames of the end-windows and the doors were, at Johannah's insistence, painted. As a result, for its time and place, it was considered rather more pretentious than the other houses of the neighbourhood. A front door faced east, and a back door west. Windows looked out to the north and south.

Inside the house two bedrooms, separated by a one-inch board partition, were positioned along the south wall.[2] In the northwest corner, a small staircase led up two or three steps to a landing, then turned and continued up to an attic on the second floor which was boarded but unpartitioned. A single window upstairs faced south. A little cupboard was built under the stairs. There was no stone cellar, as in some of the later houses, but a simple dirt hole about three or four feet in depth was scooped out of the earth and was reached by a trap door from the front room. The latter formed the main part of the building. The following year, Robert Thompson came back and built a large frame kitchen twelve feet by sixteen feet on the back of the house. Another small bedroom near the stove was partitioned off the kitchen.

Over the years the house came to be comfortably furnished. One day Mrs. Donnelly's fancy was taken by a great bed which was up for sale at the London second-hand market, and she bought it for her and Jim's bedroom. It was made of dark wood with huge bedposts that reached almost to the eight-foot ceiling. For privacy, curtains ran around the bedposts. Everyone who saw the bed remarked on its size and kingly appearance and Johannah took great pride in it. The only other stick of furniture in the tiny bedroom was a small wash-stand. Usually a gun or two stood in the corner behind the door, including the gun with which Donnelly had shot at Pat Farrell years before. The other bedroom contained a normal-sized bed, a wash-stand, and a trunk or two. In the front room, which was called the sitting room, stood a big bureau along the west wall, on which sat a large clock. Religious pictures depicting Jesus and the Blessed Virgin hung on the north wall near the doorway of the enclosed stairs. At this wall, too,

Covent Garden Market, London, Ontario, in 1870, where Johannah Donnelly purchased the high four-poster bed with curtains

stood a table near a stove, and one or two other firearms rested in a corner of this room also. All in all, it was a secure and comfortable farm home.

A young man always welcome at the Donnelly house was William Farrell, son of the man whom James Donnelly had put in his grave. The family's kindness to young Farrell was apparently Johannah's act of contrition on behalf of her erring spouse. "No matter how much his father may have desarved whot he resaved," she might say, "shure it's not the bhoy should suffer for't."

Down the road from the Donnellys, poor Pat Farrell's widow struggled to keep her fatherless children together. Besides young William there was little Joseph, Daniel, Mary, and Margaret, the last barely one year old when her father was killed. Not long after that event, Sarah Farrell married Pat Flannery, who then farmed his wife's land on the Roman Line. More children arrived. Eventually the Farrell–Flannery family broke up, one or two of the girls marrying Biddulph farmers but the others drifting out of the township, with the younger children being parcelled out to relatives and neighbours. William Farrell remained in Biddulph, making his home with his relatives the Cains, but spending a lot of time at the Donnelly place.

The charity of the Donnellys to the offspring of their old enemy only pointed up the contrast between their prosperity and the relative poverty of their rivals. Some of their neighbours were envious and resentful of that prosperity. Whether fired by old grievances or new misfortunes, the resentment increased when ill fortune somehow always spared

Lucan businessmen, c. 1870, by Alfred Smart, the photographer, who is prominently featured in the centre of the picture (number 27)

Those who figure in this book are:

1   John O'Donohue, founder of the Queen's Hotel

4   Robert H. O'Neil, the first reeve of the village, who once boasted of being one of the few Lucanites who had never been burned out

5   James H. McRoberts, butcher and drover

10   George Porte, son of the postmaster and comrade of the Donnelly brothers

13   John Farrell, druggist

14   Robert McLean, founder and long-time proprietor of the Central Hotel

16   James Curry, complainant in a case against Tom Donnelly of robbery and assault

19   George Atkinson

22   James McCosh

26   Daniel McCosh

28   Michael Crunnican, a Catholic shopkeeper and Justice of the Peace who was accused of shirking his magisterial duties

32   William Matheson, jeweller

33   Thomas Dight, reeve

34   William Ellwood, the first tailor of the village

35   Sylvanus Gibson

40   John Robinson Armitage

42   Bernard (Barney) Stanley, proprietor of the Cash Store, leading citizen and principal promoter of the Liberal-Conservative Party

44   Henry Collins, tinsmith

46   William Stanley, J P., who sat on many of the Donnelly cases

47   Dr. James Sutton, the long-time family physician and friend of the Donnelly family

55   William Porte, the Lucan postmaster and telegraph operator

61   David Atkinson

63   William Henry Atkinson

74   Dr. Thomas Hossack, coroner

75   Patrick McIlhargey, J.P.

76   Ted Crowley, partner of the Flanagan brothers in the stagecoach business

(Stanley)

the Donnellys. At the home of the *respactable* Mr. Carroll, young Mickey Carroll, the pride of his father at fourteen years of age, died tragically in the year 1867. Across the road from Carroll, the eldest of the Feeheley boys and a sister, eighteen and sixteen respectively, were also struck down. Young Jimmy Corcoran died in his twentieth year.

James Donnelly, Sr., did not forget his people in Ireland during these years, but he sent no letters nor received any. The homeland across the wide Atlantic was far away, and Jim Donnelly was too busy for letters in the bush of the New World.

CASWELL

The village of Lucan was formally incorporated on January 1, 1872, with a population of about 1,000. Its first reeve was Robert Hill O'Neil, so popular that in later years he was able to boast that he was one of the few villagers who had never been burned out. Anticipated benefits of incorporation included wooden sidewalks and the riddance of "those pools of stagnant water which for years had been an eyesore to the village". But many of the expectations were not always realized, for the newspaper continued to note that "swine roamed throughout the streets uninterruptedly," and stated:

> The attention of the village fathers has been called to the carcass of a dead pig lying on Main Street, between the railway and the English Church, for several days.[1]

And to the editorialist the new wooden sidewalks became a source of irritation:

> Will nothing prevent those unemployed clerks and nominal wheat-buyers from sitting in front of stores on shutters and empty boxes, making coarse remarks and rudely staring at ladies as they pass?[2]

The young Donnelly boys were doubtless among this company, not only on the sidewalks of the village but in its several taverns. There were, by the 1870s, at least eight hotels in the village, with their freshly painted signposts, well-stocked bar-rooms, and commodious sample rooms where commercial travellers displayed their wares. In addition to the Central, Queen's, and John Carroll's Royal on the main street, William Deacon ran the Dominion, which he leased from Charley McRoberts, and George Hodgins operated the Dublin House, while William Walker's stand was the Western Hotel. The last three were all on William Street. Then there was Hugh McPhee's Revere House at the corner of Main and Alice, while further along on the latter thoroughfare stood William McLaughlin's Australia House, although McLaughlin soon sold out to Joseph Fitzhenry. As well as at the taverns, grog could be purchased by the bottle in the several shops or saloons operated by, among others, Hugh Murphy, Henry Quarry, Edward Mara, Michael Crunnican, Thomas

Hodgins, and James Gleeson. Altogether there were about fifteen places where liquor could be bought.

The village also provided four "lemon ice cream saloons and one Arctic soda fountain", as well as "a pop factory …two coloured barbers and an African white-washer". A local wag asked, "Is it a fact that hair grows faster here than in other localities?" and hoped not, "for some physiologists say that much hair denotes little brain." The barber-shop was the traditional gambling parlour and outlet for illicit liquor, especially on a Sunday when the bar-rooms were closed, and it was reported:

Boys have been amusing themselves lately by throwing stones at the door and shutters of a certain barber shop situated in the front street. This is a gentle reminder to the inmates that there is more going on inside than the mere shaving of beards and other tonsorial trimmings.[3]

The Main Street of Lucan in winter, about 1890 (Stanley)

The respectable parents of the boys were intimating that the barber, William Berry, was too "spiritually inclined [for] gathering around him congenial spirits, also that he and his friends were too aristocratic in their taste and spend their evenings with kings and queens, and of course, where there are kings and queens there must be knaves."

The Donnelly brothers were frequent visitors to the barbershops for legitimate reasons also, as well as to the tailor shops and the boot and shoe stores, for they always took pride in their appearance. The older boys continued to farm or hired themselves out as farm hands. The average wages of an experienced labouring man in Biddulph in those days were good, particularly when prices picked up following the American Civil War, a trend that continued for several years afterwards.

Even as farmers or hired hands, the Donnelly boys were full of the fun and high spirits which made them ever popular with their companions. Caulcannon, the traditional Gaelic meal of white vegetables, was eaten on All Hallows Eve, and the Lanphier family has never forgotten the Hallowe'en when young John Donnelly was working at their farm on the Swamp Line. As the family sat down at the table a strange, shaggy beast suddenly came shuffling through the door. The women screamed and the children cowered behind their skirts at the grunting, growling animal which looked like nothing known, until it finally ambled out the back door of the kitchen. Young "Tone" Lanphier seized the family shotgun and crept out after the beast. He was about to pull the trigger when a familiar voice called out, "Don't shoot, Tone, it's me." John Donnelly then pulled off the head and skin of a freshly killed sheep and fell down, convulsed with laughter at the terrible fright he had given the family.[4]

A couple of years after James Donnelly returned from Kingston, young Jim Donnelly decided to strike out on his own. On the eleventh concession of Biddulph, just up from the Kennedy farm, was a parcel of fifty acres, half of it cleared, then in the possession of Michael Devine. Devine sold his improvements to young Jim for four hundred dollars with a small down payment, the balance to be paid in instalments and with the new owner taking over the Canada Company lease. One of Jim's new neighbours was a Presbyterian farmer named Joseph Caswell, of little means, who had married early in life. On the other side was Edward Maher, tenant of Anthony Heenan and related to Michael Maher, who had ejected Jim Donnelly from the south half of his farm, and to James Maher, whose brother-in-law occupied the farm next to the Donnelly homestead. They all agreed that none of the Donnellys was too scrupulous about appropriating items of private property belonging to their neighbours. Will Donnelly always resented these accusations. "The only time I ever committed a theft," he was able to boast once from the witness box to the county Crown attorney, "was when I stole your servant girl!"

Still, there was the time in 1871 that Will was accused of assisting in the theft from Robert Burns Orme in Lucan.

> Early on Saturday morning last the bedroom of Mr. Oram [sic], of Lucan, was entered by thieves and a cash box containing $400 stolen therefrom. Mr. Oram awoke in time to give the burglars a pretty hot chase, but they eluded further pursuit by taking to the woods. The cash box was, however, found next day secreted in a granary, and its contents untouched.[5]

Tom Gray, the "affable and careful" bartender at his brother-in-law Robert McLean's Central Hotel, was apparently not careful enough in choosing his companions, for he was arrested along with Will Donnelly on suspicion of committing the crime. However, on September 15, 1871, the Grand Jury refused to bring in a true bill and, in effect, threw out the charges.

But even before this escapade the Granton Job took place. In the little railway village of Granton, not far from young Jim Donnelly's farm, was the cobbler shop of James Jamieson, a Scottish Presbyterian with a large family, who augmented his income by operating the local post office. One night in 1869 someone broke into Jamieson's shop and rifled the post office of its contents. Suspicion at once focussed on two of the Donnelly boys, young Jim and Will, along with two young Kennedys, Jack and one-armed Rhody. They were arrested, but on July 22 John McLaughlin, J.P., found the evidence insufficient to send them to trial, and they were released.

Shortly after, when fresh evidence in the case

was discovered, young Jim Donnelly disappeared from Biddulph and, although a warrant was issued against him, it was never served. Donnelly was reputed to have left home in a hurry. Biddulph boys on the lam usually headed for the lumber camps of the "thumb" district of Michigan. Here Jim Donnelly bided his time for several years, learning to cope with the rough, violent, and sometimes brutal life of the bush camps, making an occasional foray into Detroit for diversion.

His brothers continued casually to work young Jim's farm, and even James Donnelly, Sr., would visit it on occasion. But the Canada Company lease fell into arrears, the buildings began to sag, and a stranger to the district would have taken the place to be abandoned. Bob Donnelly, not yet twenty years of age, visited the place a few times in the spring of 1873.

In the meantime Joe Caswell, who had a dozen mouths to feed, considered the Donnelly acres, thirty of them cleared, an irresistible attraction and better than his own mere lease-hold of rank bog and forest.[6] He had heard not only that Donnelly was in arrears to both the Canada Company and Michael Devine, but that the latter had commenced legal action. The lawsuit was eventually compromised when the Donnelly family agreed to pay two hundred dollars in final settlement of Devine's claim, but the Canada Company put out a broadside listing the farm for sale.

Joseph Caswell insisted that when he journeyed to the Canada Company offices in Toronto in the latter part of 1873, he had no intention of buying the Donnelly farm. There was no harm, however, in asking about it. Oh no, the Donnellys had no claim whatever against the property, he was told, for they had been legally evicted. As the land was a good bargain, Caswell thought the matter over for about two seconds and decided to buy it, assured by the company officials that he was not buying the property over the heads of the Donnellys.

But shortly before taking possession of the farm, he met Bob Donnelly in Lucan and decided that prudence was the wiser course. "Oh, Bob," he opened the conversation with Donnelly, "I've gone ahead and made a deal with the Canada Company to buy that old farm your brother Jim used to keep, next to mine."

Robert Donnelly only scowled at him, and Caswell went on, "Now I've not got it yet, mind you, but I hope to take possession soon. That is, if it's all right with your family."

Donnelly stared coldly at him but did not answer, and Caswell continued uncomfortably, "About the improvements, Bob. I was wondering how much you wanted for them?"

"You look here, Caswell," Bob Donnelly said. "That property does not belong to the Canada Company and your bargain isn't worth the paper it's written on. The hell with the improvements! We won't settle for anything less than the value of the place."

Bob left Caswell to mull things over. Perhaps the good bargain was more than he had bargained for. But on the other hand, why should he have to pay for the land twice over? He decided to take possession.

Soon after moving on to the farm, Joe Caswell began to suffer misfortune. First, his neighbour, Thomas Fulton, charged him with stealing wood, having followed tracks in the snow all the way to Caswell's from his own farm. Squire Pat McIlhargey of Lucan convicted Caswell, and he was forced to appeal and have the conviction overturned by the Queen's Bench before his name was cleared. Caswell claimed that the Donnellys had deliberately placed the stolen wood on his land, but could not prove it. His troubles in Biddulph were only beginning.

"FEMAILS"

By the end of the 1860s the Donnelly boys were all grown to manhood and, being "well-built, muscular men, with curly hair and well-cut features", it was almost unanimously agreed that "a finer looking family did not live in Biddulph." The boys were, besides, "always the life of any party or dance" and were very popular with the female sex.

Traditions are alive in the area to this day that the girls of many households would have dearly loved to go with the Donnelly boys but for fear of parental wrath. Some, like young and wilful Kate Quigley, defied their families. Her niece related:

> Aunt Kate was asked to go to a dance by young Jim Donnelly. Her brother Will forbade her but Donnelly had a beautiful rig and they always had the best-looking horses and, being a foolish girl, she went. When Uncle Will walked into the dance hall that evening, the first couple he clapped his eyes on were his sister Kate and Young Donnelly. He was furious. But Kate later told her brother that she went only to save their barns from being burned. It was a lie, of course.[1]

Especially in their younger days, the brothers were accused by their neighbours of "deluding our femails [sic] and robbing them of their charactor [sic]", although they were not totally suspicious of the marriage vow. John Donnelly ventured a brief experience in matrimony at about the age of twenty-four when in 1871 he wedded Fanny Durham, setting up house in Lucan. He left her after a short time when, it was said, her family refused to give him money.[2] In April 1874, while driving stagecoach to Exeter, John Donnelly met pretty young Susan Pebber, of Stephen Township, and whatever their relationship in the beginning, it ended up badly, for she charged him with indecent assault. Donnelly intimated at the time of his arrest that he was not afraid of the charge. When the court case came up in Exeter, the female complainant was nowhere to be found, and the charge against John was dismissed. The long period of time between the incident and the laying of the charge, four months, suggests there was more to the matter than appears from the court record. "It is supposed," a newspaper speculated, "that the woman was enticed away."

Bob Donnelly was perhaps the handsomest of the seven brothers. He was said to have become engaged to a girl of the Biddulph Catholic Settlement, but shortly before the wedding date her brother handed him a fairly large sum of money — a common custom, it appears, to preserve the family honour — which Bob promptly spent and then failed to keep the engagement.

Tom Donnelly was also reportedly engaged at one time to a local damsel but, having received two hundred dollars from her family in anticipation of the blessed matrimonial event, he pocketed the funds and paid little more attention to her. Tom and young Jim Donnelly never did marry.[3]

The brothers were popular, however, not only because of their good looks and their prominence in fisticuff engagements, which were often worked up to impress the fair sex, but because "they spent their money freely" and had about them an assured and confident air. "The boys were perhaps as fair and good looking a lot of young men as could be found in any one family in the Province," it was reported, and "they were at the same time extremely affable and obliging in their demeanour, and would go any length to accomplish anything they undertook for a friend." And again: "Whatever may be said of the Donnellys their worst enemies never accused them of lacking in courage or shrewdness or intelligence." [4]

The Thompson family discovered that attractive girls were unsafe near the Donnelly boys. In 1867 when young William Thompson, aged twenty-five and a bachelor, left his father's house in McGillivray and moved into the old Broderick farm beside the Donnellys, his younger sisters were dispatched to Biddulph to keep house for him. First came Sarah, who eventually caught the fancy of one of the eligible bachelors of the Roman Line and left the Thompson house to become Mrs. James Toohey. To replace her came Maggie, two years her junior.

Margaret Thompson quickly attracted the attention of Will Donnelly, then engaged in farming the Donnelly homestead. He was in prosperous circumstances and was soon to invest in the stagecoach business, where a couple of his brothers were already working as drivers. But Maggie Thompson, then only seventeen, was not about to have much to do with the Donnellys, for she had been forewarned about them. Of course, she found it very convenient, nevertheless, to travel with the brothers on their many trips with the stagecoach to and from the farm into Lucan, and to her home in McGillivray. On Will's orders, the trips were always free of charge.

William Donnelly's engaging manner soon began to have its effect and word got back to the old folk on the home farm that one of the Donnellys was sparking their daughter. Worse still, the girl appeared not to be discouraging the affair.

"Have no fear," she assured her parents when questioned about it, "I would rather suffer death than marry William Donnelly."

The family was reassured, but they underestimated the persuasive powers of Clubfoot Bill. He wore fine clothes, called himself "gentleman", played the fiddle at dances, and, with his quick mind and ready wit, kept the girls laughing. He, too, began driving stagecoach for Hugh McPhee of Lucan and had money to burn. His blandishments soon turned poor Maggie's head completely, and she fell madly in love with him.

During the summer of 1872 and into 1873 their romance flourished. By this time Will Donnelly had begun his own stagecoach line and had taken up residence in the village, but he continued seeing Margaret Thompson frequently, and when they were not visiting they exchanged letters. One read:

Biddulph, April 22, 1873

Dear William, —

I address you with these few lines, hoping they will find you in good health, as they leave me enjoying the same blessing at present. Dear William, I was a long time about getting this picture for you. You can keep it now, in hopes you think as much of me as I do of you. At the beginning of another term of our future summer, which we can look back upon with pleasure, I desire to bear testimony to the faithfulness with which you have labored for my benefit, and the kindness which you have ever shown towards me.

Yours truly,
MAGGIE THOMPSON.[5]

The kindness shown by William Donnelly to his lady love continued, and it was not long after that he proposed marriage. She replied:

April 30th, 1873

William Donnelly: —

Dear Friend, — I take the pleasure of writing you these few lines, hoping they will find you in good health, as they leave me enjoying the same blessing at present. I now wish to inform you that I have made up my mind to accept your kind offer, as there is no person in this world I sincerely love but you. This is my last and only secret, so I hope you will let no person know about it. But I cannot mention any

certain time yet. You can acquaint my parents about it any time you wish after the 1st of November next. Any time it is convenient to you will please me if it is in five years after the time I mentioned. If it does not suit you to wait so long you can let me know about it, and I will make it all right. Do not think I would say you are soft for writing so often, for there is nothing would give me greater pleasure than to hear from you, but no matter now. I think soft turns is very scarce about you. If you have ever heard anything of the kind after me I hope you will not attribute it to a desire on my part to give you pain, but regard it as thoughtless behavior of youth; and that the blessing of God may ever attend it the sincere wish of your affectionate friend.

MARGRET THOMPSON

In August of that year "a genuine 'Black Crook' company from New York" played three nights running at Spettigue Hall in London. At about the same time, old Mr. Thompson again heard rumours that the Black Crook in Biddulph — Will Donnelly was said to look like him when he walked — had poisoned the heart of his daughter Maggie.

Later that fall when Margaret Thompson returned to her parents' home and hinted that it was time to make preparations for a wedding, old man Thompson could not conceal his outrage. "I would rather see ye goin' to yer grave than iver ye should have me consint to marry William Donnelly," he declared emphatically. "So ye've been looking after him, have ye? Well, he is a son uv a bitch, I say, and I have sons kin back me up in sayin' so. Ye are to come home right away and I forbid ye iver to see that man again, or any one uv that blackleg crowd. I'll be the manes of sendin' thim all to Kingston yit where they all belong, jist like that devil uv an owld man that spawned thim."

Although Mr. Thompson pawed through his daughter's effects searching for letters, Maggie managed to conceal and burn them before they were found. The enraged parent forbade her to leave the parental roof. About November 1 her clothes were brought home from Biddulph, and for weeks she was kept virtually a prisoner. Finally, on the day before Christmas, she was allowed to accompany the family on a brief shopping trip to the nearby hamlet of Offa, known also by the more euphonious name of Limerick. Here Maggie managed to steal away for a few moments to the post office where she scribbled the following hurried lines:

December 24th, 1873

William Donnelly, —

Dear friend, — I adress you with these few lines to let you know I am well, and hopes you are enjoying the same blessing. I wish to let you know a little about the performance I had to go through since I came up here. My friends herd all about me writing Letters to you, which caused an awfull storm, so that I could not attempt to ask to go any where, and on that account you will please excuse me for not writing to you. Dear William, I would rather be in the grave than home, at preasant, for the way my people abused me on your account hinders me of ever forgiving them. I will never have anything like a chance of fullfilling my promise of marriage with you except you come and take me away by force, and if you think as much of me now as you did always I trust you will relieve me before long, and if not you will please send me my Letters to Offa P.O., and I will try to put up with all. I burnt your Letters when they commenced to abuse me about you, for they would shurly get them if I did not do something with them. Excuse my bad writing, for I am in an awfull hury, as it is in the office I am writing it. No more at preasant from your loving friend.

MARGRET THOMPSON

The letter was an open invitation to abduction from a willing victim. Will Donnelly decided to act on it. On the night of Friday, January 9, 1874, eight men — Will, Mike, and Tom Donnelly, Daniel Keefe, James Keefe, William Atkinson, Robert Corcoran, and Patrick Quigley — all heavily bundled and muffled to the ears, drove up in a sleigh to the farmhouse of Mr. William Thompson, Sr., on the fourth concession of McGillivray Township. While Will stayed outside in the sleigh, the other seven trooped up to the door and knocked.

"Open up in the name of the Queen!" one of them called.

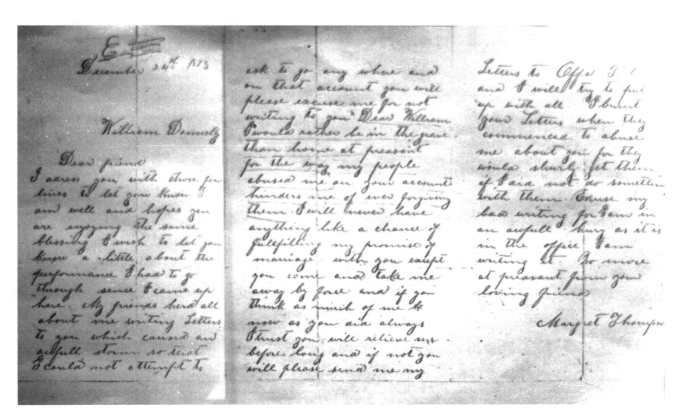

One of Maggie Thompson's letters to Will Donnelly (UWO)

"What is it?" came a voice from inside. Michael Thompson, a younger brother of Maggie, came to the door and partly opened it.

"What do you want?" he asked.

"We've got a warrant for a horse thief," they answered. "Let us in."

Pushing past young Michael, they crowded inside.

"Get some chairs, boy," old Thompson, who was waiting for them, barked at his son. When they were seated he said, "All right, show me the warrant."

"Have you anything to eat?" one of the intruders replied, ignoring Thompson's request. "We want supper."

"There's no women around to git it," Thompson answered a little testily, but he could not suppress a little note of triumph in his voice, for his daughter had been secreted elsewhere in the event of just such an invasion of the household. Then he added, "The tavern's but a half-mile away. Ye kin git yer food there."

The crowd was stumped. After a little silence one of them said, "Have you an overcoat?"

"Why," the old man replied, "I scarcely have enough to cover meself widout me givin' ye clothing."

"Well, then, I reckon we'll stay the night," rejoined the other and glanced significantly at his comrades.

Mr. Thompson was beginning to lose his patience.

"All right, boys," he said, "what is it ye want?"

"We have a warrant for a horse thief and we're out to get him," Tom Donnelly said. "We have to search the house."

"Well, thin, read the warrant. Show me the warrant, would ye," old Thompson demanded.

None of them made a motion to produce anything, and the old man's voice rose, "It's not a horse thief ye're afther at all, but my daughter. Ye're lookin' fer my daughter!"

One of the men replied, "You're right, Thompson, we've come to get your daughter. Where is she?"

A smile of grim satisfaction creaked across the old man's face as he answered, "She's not heer, bhoys, I warrant ye that. Ye'll not git her heer."

The men quickly went through the rest of the house. Finding nothing, they trooped out and drove off.

Old Thompson could hardly contain his glee at having outwitted the gang. He had to tell someone about it. Donning his coat he started for the house of widow Ellen Fogarty, a relative who lived a short distance to the south, but just as he got to the sideroad he saw the sleigh carrying the eight men heading eastward. They saw him at the same time. Quickly turning the sleigh around they caught up to the old man just as he reached the widow's fence. Two of the men jumped out of the sleigh and grabbed hold of him, one putting his hand across Thompson's mouth to stifle his shouts. But Thompson managed to break away.

"Mrs. Fogarty! An axe! Get me an axe!" he shouted.

The others had now all jumped out of the sleigh. One of them fired a couple of shots from a gun and the bullets whistled past the old man as he ran up to the house and pushed in the door. He was partly inside when the men caught up and, crowding him ahead, barged into the house.

"Search the house," they shouted, "she must be here."

"What do you want?" cried Ellen Fogarty, completely taken aback at the sudden intrusion into her house.

Mike Donnelly addressed Thompson. "We want your daughter, Thompson. Where is she? We'll have her wherever she is."

Thompson replied, "That, Donnelly, ye will niver git."

Tom Donnelly came up to Thompson and struck him on the ear with his fist, bowling the old man over like a tenpin. As Thompson pulled himself up from the floor he muttered, "Ye'll pay fer this."

When the men failed again to find their quarry, they left.

Ellen Fogarty did not forget the visit of the Donnelly gang. Her daughter, Rebecca, married James McGrath of Biddulph, and the McGraths were related to the Blakes, besides the fact that it was a Fogarty who had held the original Canada Company lease to the Donnelly homestead. The Thompsons, Fogartys, McGraths, and Blakes be came bitter enemies of the Donnellys.

After driving north from Widow Fogarty's, the search party turned back to Biddulph, where, even though it was four o'clock in the morning, they called upon the house of William Thompson, Jr., beside the Donnelly farm. The younger Thompson got up out of bed to answer their knock, let them in to satisfy themselves his sister was not there, and then bade them good morning.

Will Donnelly returned to Lucan empty-handed and unwed. He and his friends spent the rest of the day drowning their disappointment in strong drink. That evening, young William Thompson went to Lucan in company with a number of the Tooheys, including his brother-in-law, James Toohey. It was at the home of the latter — known as Long Jim — that Maggie Thompson had been placed in hiding the evening before the raid on the Thompson homestead. The Tooheys drank and bragged about their complicity in thwarting the designs of Clubfoot Bill.

When Will Donnelly, in company with Dan Keefe, saw Thompson and the Tooheys on the streets of Lucan that evening, he called out, "Thompson, I want to speak to you."

Donnelly approached them, and said, "I was at your father's place last night and at your place, too. And I'll go there again."

He challenged the Thompsons and the Tooheys to try their muscle and it is likely that they obliged, for the *Exeter Times* reported:

A riot between some of our villagers and a number of people from Biddulph who had spent the day in laying in a stock of whiskey took place on the Main street last Saturday evening. The result was a few cracked heads.[6]

Three weeks later, on Saturday, January 31, 1874, the younger William Thompson took himself a wife. She was Mary Carroll, daughter of "the respactable" Mr. Michael Carroll of the Roman Line, who had been one of the principal witnesses against James Donnelly in his murder trial many years before. Will Donnelly used the occasion to vent his frustrations by getting his brothers and some of his friends together again and giving the newlyweds "a musical and literary entertainment", better known as a "shivaree".

Most of the Donnelly brothers took part in the charivari — only young Jim and John being absent — and it is even said that old Jim Donnelly himself assisted in the proceedings. They smashed the windows of the house with clubs. They fired pistol shots through the broken windows. They whooped obscenities at the couple inside, and fired bullets through the roof of the barn and then at the chimney of the house until part of the latter came tumbling down. Finally, they piled up some of the fence rails in front of the house and lit them into a great bonfire.

A day or two later the Thompsons, father and son, repaired to the London law office of Hugh Macmahon to complain of the outrages against their households. They showed him a letter written by Will Donnelly to the elder Thompson. Macmahon sent them to the police, charges were laid, and Detective Harry Phair arrested the Donnellys. Thompson, Jr., eventually agreed to withdraw charges upon payment of fifty dollars' compensation, but ever after he harboured a bitter grudge against the family next door.

A few days later, on February 10, Dan Keefe encountered Long Jim Toohey in a Biddulph hotel known as the Huron House. Urged on by Will Donnelly and his brothers, Keefe commenced cursing the entire Toohey family. Long Jim Toohey naturally responded with his fists, and Keefe seemed to be getting the worst of it when he pulled out a knife and carved Toohey up quite severely.

Charges were laid all around, each side choosing its magistrate with care. Henry Ferguson, J.P., of Birr, fined Toohey $1 for assault and battery and assessed costs against him of $11.55! Toohey laid his own charge of "abuse and assault" before Squire Robert O'Neil of Lucan, who fined Keefe $2! Not satisfied, Long Jim Toohey went to the authorities in London and in the result a Grand Jury brought in a true bill on the more serious charge of "assault, stabbing and wounding", on which Dan Keefe was convicted.

Thus ended, for the time being, the Maggie Thompson affair and its immediate repercussions. Little wonder was it said: "The Donnelly boys seemed to have some queer adventures in the matrimonial line."

Even the marriage of Jenny Donnelly was a

curious affair.[7] Jenny was a headstrong young girl of only seventeen years when the focus of her will and desire fell hard upon a stalwart young man from Glencoe named James E. Currie. Mrs. Donnelly was impressed immediately with the young fellow's bearing and courtesy upon his delivering her daughter to the homestead one day. Currie helped Jenny out of the coach like a real gentleman before going round to shake hands with her parents and brothers. But the young man was a Protestant, and when he left Mrs. Donnelly warned her daughter that he was of the wrong religious persuasion to be considered seriously as the object of her affections.

"I don't care if he is, mother," Jenny replied, "he's a good man and I will have him if I want."

Johannah paid little attention to her daughter's rash words — the girl was, like herself, outspoken — until a day shortly after when she found her unexpectedly gone from the house along with most of her clothes. Gathering together two or three of her boys, Mrs. Donnelly immediately lit out after her.

The trail led to the home of the Currie family near Glencoe in the southwest part of Middlesex County. James Currie's father had been raised a Catholic in Londonderry, Ireland, but had brought his own children up in his wife's Protestant faith. When the invaders from Biddulph burst into his home, he presented a rifle with a bayonet at them.

'We ain't goin' to hurt no one in the house," Mrs. Donnelly said, "we just want our girl back. Where is she?"

Finally, one of the Curries said, "She's gone to Melbourne." The place was a little village east of Glencoe, and the Donnellys piled into their sleigh — it was in February, 1874 — and headed east.

But James Currie and Jenny Donnelly had in the meantime left Glencoe shortly before the arrival of the latter's mother and brothers and had gone west to the village of Bothwell. There they were married in a Protestant ceremony in the Anglican Church.

Jenny's family reconciled themselves to the marriage not long after. "A man cannot help what he's born," they said then and years later, "and his religion should not count against him." But they prevailed upon their daughter at least to remarry

within the rites of the Roman Catholic Church and this event was accomplished in St. Thomas. The Donnelly family always had hopes that Currie would change his religion, but he never did. Nevertheless, the marriage proved a happy and bountiful one, and Mrs. Donnelly even joked about the elopement later.

"She got hold uv 'im and wouldn't let 'im go," she said, "fer she always could drive any damn horse — or man! He is a good one, even though Protistint, an' my Jinny was not goin' to let any Protistint girl git 'im.

The Donnelly household on the Roman Line changed perceptibly when Jenny left. Only Mrs. Donnelly's rough femininity remained to smooth the predominant masculine influence of the home, and the curtains around the big four-poster bed in the parents' bedroom — deemed by Victorian respectability to be no longer necessary — were removed.

10

HAWKSHAW

In 1972 the name Donnelly, of Biddulph and Lucan renown, was on the verge of dying out. John William Donnelly, the sole survivor bearing the marked surname[1] and the only son of Will, spoke of his family: "I'll tell you why they killed them, it was because they were jealous of them. My father and uncles had fine clothes, nice horses and stagecoaches, and they were good business men. Their enemies were jealous of all these things and tried to beat them up but when they found they couldn't, they killed them."

The voice of the old man rose excitedly. Despite his eighty-nine years it was a strong voice, booming from deep in his chest. Its harsh and cutting edge softened considerably as he recalled the youthful memories of his father.

"I remember my father telling me that after the trials he was broke," he related, "having spent all his money trying to get justice. When he came to Appin he had hardly a penny in his pocket, but he went and borrowed $1,000 from a doctor friend and with it bought a stallion called St. Nicholas. He bred it and inside a short time was making $2,000 a year, which was quite a lot in those days."

Whatever else their enemies accused them of, they never once said the Donnellys were lazy. And the business enterprise for which the family will ever be known was the stagecoach line between Lucan and London.[2]

In 1826 a canny Scot named Peter McGregor founded the city of London by erecting a log tavern in the wilderness of Upper Canada, at the Forks of the Thames. Within thirty years the Great Western Railway had joined by rail the lusty little frontier settlement to the more sedate and civilized cities to the east, but its only connection with the Canada Company town of Goderich, on the shores of Lake Huron, remained by road. Situated on this road of sixty miles was the little village of Lucan, through which the stagecoaches passed.

James Donnelly may have driven the early stages which left London from Darby's Huron Hotel on Richmond Street, opposite the Catholic Church. In 1856 a James Donnelly, stage driver, was convicted of furious driving and failing to leave half the road free in the Township of Goderich. One Thomas Rutledge testified that Donnelly had left his own side of the road and crossed towards the other vehicle, whose driver tried to avoid him but failed when the wheels of the two vehicles locked and Rutledge was forced off the road. It sounds very much like James Donnelly of Biddulph. Stage-driving seemed only natural for a family which always possessed a certain affinity for fine horseflesh.

"I'm strictly a horse man," declared the son of Will Donnelly a hundred years after his own father had begun to drive stagecoach, and Jack Donnelly (as his wife of over fifty years called him) went on to make an almost incredible statement about horses and automobiles, considering he lived most of his adult life in Detroit and Pittsburgh, both spawned by the era of the automobile. "I never owned or drove a car in my life," he said. "I'm strictly a horse man."

Richmond Street, London, Ontario, in 1864

In the 1860s the stagecoach mail contract between London and Clinton was worth a thousand dollars per annum, a tidy sum for those days and more than enough to pay the expenses of drivers, horses, and equipment. It made the receipts from cash-paying passengers at $1.50 a head for the full trip a matter of pure gravy.

The Donnelly family ran stage on only a small part of the route, the south leg, from London to the villages of Centralia, Crediton, and Exeter. If Clinton was included, it was for a brief period only. And they operated the line for only a few years, probably no more than ten as drivers and only five (between 1873 and 1878) as proprietors. But in those few short years, the Donnellys earned a reputation as the scourge of all rivals and made their name notorious throughout southwestern Ontario.

By 1869, stage travel had increased to such an extent that at least two rival lines were competing on the route between London and Goderich. One left Hayden's Hotel in the morning, while the other left at three p.m. from the City Hotel at Dundas and Talbot streets. The crowded stagecoaches, which stopped at the platforms of the various hotels and taverns along the route, brought a great rush of business to Lucan:

The Lucan hotelkeepers have been obliged to increase their accommodation. Large three-storey brick additions have been built to the Central and Queens hotels.[3]

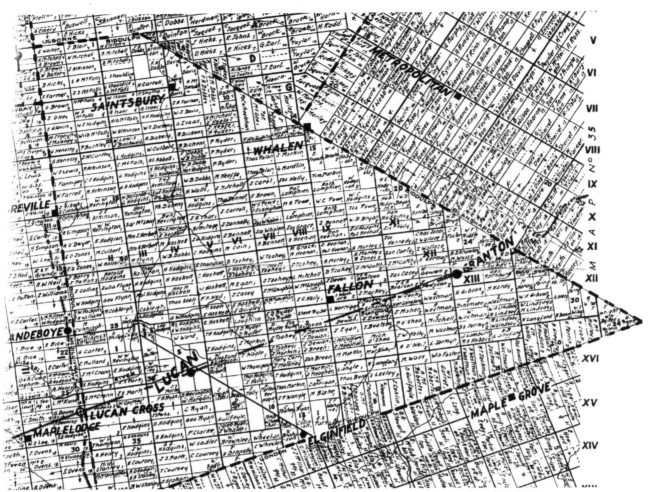

This map for Biddulph Township is from a much later date but shows many of the places where stagestops were made during the years of rivalry. (PAC)

In April 1871, three years after William Diamond of Biddulph contracted to transport the mail from London six times a week for $957.50 per annum, the unfinished balance of his contract was taken over by Alexander Jamieson of Exeter. It was then that Michael Donnelly began to drive stagecoach between Lucan and London. John and a couple of his brothers quickly followed him, and at one time or another all of the brothers, with the exception of Patrick, engaged in stage-driving on the Proof Line Road.

The Donnelly boys grew very familiar with the sights along that stretch of the London-Goderich Road. South of Lucan, just beyond the toll-gates and the old McIlhargey tavern, the huge elm tree at Dinney Dorsey's blacksmith shop towered over the road, while further along stood the new brick house of Michael Fox, built in 1872 to replace the old log dwelling. The big new brick house of the Catholic priest stood beside St. Patrick's Church, whose grand spire, also completed in 1872, towered majestically 120 feet over the Biddulph landscape. A short distance along was the large brick hotel built by William H. Ryan, at the intersection no longer called Ryan's Corners but Elginfield. Thomas Nangle's Grand Trunk Store and Stephen McCormick's grocery stood here, while further along in London Township the taverns Bluejay, White Pigeon, and Nighthawk beckoned at the twelfth concession, along with the Talbot House at the eighth, the Montgomery House still further south, and the Mason and McMartin houses at Masonville Corners, where the Sarnia Road crossed.

By 1872 the Hawkshaw family was well established in one of the stagecoach lines. William Hawkshaw operated the Mansion Hotel in Exeter, out of which his brother John ran the stagecoach. The latter was known, at least around Exeter, as "the Stage King". By leasing the Biddulph Township toll-gates for $1,269 in 1870, Hawkshaw obtained an edge in competition over the rival line. John Hawkshaw was then in his mid-thirties, but one of his drivers was a nephew of the same name and a couple of years younger. In 1930 the nephew recalled his stagecoach-driving days. "I never once forgot a single errand or parcel entrusted to me," he stated, "although I never committed anything to writing." Other drivers who worked for Hawkshaw included Robert and James McLeod, Alexander McFalls, William McIntyre, and the well-liked William Brooks, born and raised on the Biddulph boundary near the Catholic Settlement.

One or two of the Donnelly boys may have broken into stagecoaching with Hawkshaw, or, more likely, Hawkshaw acquired them as drivers when on April 1, 1872, he bought out the opposition line and amalgamated it with his own. With Hawkshaw holding a monopoly on the road, fares went up slightly, and the southern terminus of the line became the Western Hotel in London.

John Hawkshaw had a kicking horse. One day while harnessing the animal, the driver, named McFalls, was kicked square in the face and knocked insensible. He lay in a corner of the stall until a passerby heard his moans and found him half unconscious and bleeding. Now Mike Donnelly, a young man with a very quick temper who "would not allow himself to be run on" whether by man or beast, may also have had an encounter with Hawkshaw's kicking horse. One day shortly after the amalgamation of the two stage lines, the London *Advertiser* carried the following small item:

LUCAN...A dastardly and cruel punishment has been inflicted on Mr. John Hawkshaw's kicking horse. The party in charge, losing his temper, attacked the animal with a pitch-fork, and stabbed it so unmercifully that fears are entertained for the animal's recovery.[4]

If it were indeed one of the Donnelly boys who taught the kicking horse a lesson, it may well have signalled the end of their association with the Hawkshaw Stagecoach Line.

In any event, it appears that shortly after Hawkshaw became the owner of both lines, the Donnelly brothers made an attempt to establish their own stage business. They continued to patronize the City Hotel, one of the traditional junctions in London, and Will Donnelly became a financial backer of his brother Mike in the enterprise while continuing to farm his father's homestead. But the effort was sadly lacking in capital, and the equipment threadbare – an old wagon, one or two overworked nags, and a highly unpredictable schedule. Although the opposition to the Hawkshaw line was feeble, mishaps such as the following began to be reported:

An accident occurred to the stage running between London and Lucan. One of the wheels came off when the vehicle was near the city, in consequence of which an upset occurred. Fortunately there were but a few slight cuts and bruises inflicted upon the passengers.[5]

Soon plans for a full-fledged opposition line were rumoured. A few weeks later this was confirmed when orders were placed for brand-new coaches and the purchase was made of horses for the enterprise. The new proprietors were Hugh McPhee and Andy Keefe, with Will Donnelly acting as a go-between. McPhee, a Scotsman who had for some time past operated the Revere House at the corner of Main and Alice streets in the village of Lucan, knew Will Donnelly well and liked him. "I have trusted him with a great deal," he once said, "and never found anything wrong with him. He always behaved himself first rate."

The other associate, Andy Keefe, flitted from one business to another during his lifetime and went through fortunes that others only dream of. Of the old Irish Catholic petty aristocracy, his father was reputed to have been colonel of the militia at Clockfergus in Tipperary. Here Andrew Keefe was born;[6] he was destined to be a priest but instead fell in love with a daughter of Lord Windymore and forsook Maynooth College. But spurned by his lady love, he took up the more familiar art of soldiering and emigrated to Upper

Canada, where he claimed to have commanded a regiment in the Rebellion of 1837 and to have received a decoration for his achievements from Queen Victoria herself. After selling a flourishing brewery in Delaware for the then astonishing price of $47,000, he built in Biddulph Township the imposing two-storey frame tavern beside St. Patrick's Church. But he soon retired from tavernkeeping, describing it as "the last of all business" when in one year alone several murders occurred in the Catholic Settlement, including those of Farrell and Brimmacombe. "The society in that section not being congenial to him", Keefe took up the life of a gentleman farmer in Biddulph, until the American Civil War prompted him to rally to his many friends in the Deep South. Among them were perhaps the wealthy Carrolls of Carrolton, South Carolina, where Keefe was appointed colonel of a regiment of four hundred men. He fought with the Confederates as "one of the most trusted friends of the late General Stonewall Jackson, also a near and dear friend of General Robert E. Lee..." until the capitulation of the Army of the South at Appomattox. Andy Keefe then returned to Biddulph. Finding his farm had in the meantime been lost in foreclosure proceedings, Keefe flung himself into the efforts to salvage and even recoup his former fortune. He wrangled with James Maher, who had in his absence established himself on the Roman Line, over the possession of certain land and they "lawed each other" in the courts. He quarrelled also with William H. Ryan over the boundaries of certain woodlots which he purchased in the Cedar Swamp near Elginfield. He worked as a gravel-road contractor in Biddulph in 1866. Then along came William Donnelly proposing he join forces with McPhee and open a new stage line.

The new partnership, with headquarters at McPhee's Revere House in Lucan, was inaugurated on August 1, 1872. Shortly after the new line got started, one of the horses died mysteriously in its stall, and while cause of death was attributed to "the heaves", foul play was not altogether ruled out. But the travelling public cared little about such trifles. It rejoiced at the "opposition stages between Lucan and London" and exulted that "the result will be cheap riding." Cheap riding or

not, there was soon much more excitement on the road between Lucan and London, and items such as the following began to appear in the news:

INTERRUPTING THE STAGE. – Andrew Keefe was fined $1 and $10 costs today on charge of crossing and delaying the stage, preferred by Mr. Hawkshaw, the driver.[7]

Characteristically, however, Andy Keefe soon lost interest in the new business. He and McPhee dissolved their partnership. Keefe went into custom threshing; McPhee also gave up the stage line and restricted himself to tavernkeeping.

But the failure of the new line was a glorious opportunity for the Donnellys. Not only were horses and equipment available for purchase but, as luck would have it, a new post office was about to be established at Centralia, on the bend in the Exeter Road where it skirted the Big Marsh on the town line between McGillivray and Biddulph Tradition has it that the Donnelly Stagecoach Line was inaugurated on Queen Victoria's Birthday – May 24 – in 1873. The Crediton – Centralia mail contract for stage delivery ran for one year from July 1.[8] At the urging of his old friend William Porte, and perhaps with a good word from Thomas Scatcherd, the federal Member of Parliament who had always been on good terms with the Lucan postmaster as well as with the Donnellys, Will Donnelly bid on the contract and obtained it. Although not a major undertaking, it was enough to pay expenses and enable Donnelly to pay for the horses and stage equipment bought from Keefe and McPhee.

Hawkshaw countered the new competition by putting on the road a handsome vehicle "just turned out from the factory of John McKellar" and said to be "a credit to maker and proprietor". Notwithstanding Hawkshaw's new coach, the Donnelly Line proved popular and the business lucrative. Will Donnelly and his brothers were at all times pleasant and affable, and their engaging manner attracted a great deal of new custom.

"More obliging people never lived," recalled George Essery. "My mother would take berries to sell to the Devon store and she always took the Donnelly carriage. The boys could be counted on to help her carry the berries into the store."

Another of their passengers said: "Their horses were well fed and well groomed and the stagecoach kept neat and in repair. The drivers were always courteous, obliging, and punctual."

Elizabeth Sinclair recalled her experiences on the London-Goderich stagecoach run. "I remember going on another stage on a wet day, and the water poured through the roof. The Donnelly stage was never like that."

The merchants of Crediton and other places recalled their transactions with the Donnellys as always very satisfactory. One man related the story of his first trip to Lucan, as a small boy, carrying a large bag which contained all his earthly possessions.

"Is there anything valuable in here, boy?" Donnelly had asked as the young lad approached the fearsome Donnelly stage, about which he had been warned but which was the only one available at the time.

"It's all I own, sir," said the boy as he handed over his bag, convinced he would never see it again .

At the end of the trip the driver not only returned the luggage safely but, after putting up the horses, took the small boy to his exact destination in the village to make sure he got to the house safely.

"That's what the Donnellys were like," he recalled in later life, and no once could ever convince him otherwise.[9]

By way of contrast, the following news item relating to the opposition stage was reported about this time:

THE LUGAN STAGE. – Before Squire Peters this afternoon William McIntyre, driver of the Hawkshaw stage, was charged by E. T. Keays with robbing him of $17 in money and some gold studs... [10]

11

BARNUM

For a year and a half the Hawkshaws and the Donnellys struggled for supremacy on the road between London and Exeter.[1] Autumn was a lucrative period for the carrying trade. It was then that farmers and their families made their most frequent trips to market and the many fall fairs. In August 1873, P. T. Barnum's "Great Travelling Museum, Menagerie and World's Fair" made a one-day stand in London, broadsheets proclaiming it as "Ten Times Larger Than Any Other Exhibition in the World" and titillating the fancies with the anticipation of "over 1,000 men and horses...100,000 cardinal curiosities" including the "only living Giraffes in captivity". And the canny showman wrote to the local paper:

To the Editor of the Advertiser.
In consequence of the immense throngs that have crowded my exhibitions daily since leaving New York, thousands being invariably turned away for want of room, I am admonished that my manager has made a mistake in arranging for one day only in your city.... In view of this I would respectfully urge ladies, children and all who can do so to attend the 10 a.m. exhibitions, as those are rarely crowded....
The public's obedient servant,
P. T. BARNUM.[2]

On the great day, the infectious carnival spirit took hold as the people for miles around poured into London. And in Lucan

on account of Barnum's show at London, the 8th instant was declared a public holiday by the people of Lucan. Mr. W. Matheson informs us that the stream of waggons, buggies and horses that filed by all night Sunday night and Monday forenoon baffles description.[3]

John Hawkshaw put an extra coach on the line for the occasion. Both his vehicles loaded their passengers at Christy's Hotel in Exeter, but when the first stage started up, it went only a short distance before one of the front wheels spun away and the coach crashed to the roadway. The startled horses thrashed about excitedly, shaking the passengers inside, until driver William Brooks managed to calm them. The dishevelled passengers crawled out of the coach, wishing they had taken the second vehicle which remained standing at the hotel platform. There were no serious injuries, but examination of both vehicles revealed that "some evil disposed person had on Sunday night removed the nuts from the front axles of both stages..."[4] Hawkshaw was sure that it was the Donnellys but he never obtained proof, despite offering a large reward.

Later that month the annual Western Fair in London took place. Once again Hawkshaw put an extra coach on the line and once again trouble erupted. The *Advertiser* reported:

QUARRELING STAGES. – Squire Peters this morning settled a dispute between two Proof Line stage drivers by fining the defendant in the case, with costs, $7.25. The complainant had been assaulted by the other.[5]

As the measures in restraint of trade practised by the opposition line took effect, many of Hawkshaw's customers decided to patronize the other line. Criticism was also reported about the quality of the mail service which Hawkshaw provided:

For some time past the hour of the receipt and delivery of the mail at our office has been very unsatisfactory...the mail for Exeter per G.T.R...does not arrive here in time to be distributed till about eight p.m....[6]

There were no complaints, on the other hand, about the mail handled by William Donnelly. Nevertheless, the diary of William Porte, the Lucan postmaster, recorded under date of April 15:

Wrote Mr. Griffin – that Donnelly would not keep the Centralia and Crediton contract for another year and that he must advertise it.[7]

Will Donnelly had bigger plans in mind centring on one Alexander Calder of London. Calder not only had political pull, but he was also the proprietor of the London Omnibus Line. With a brand new set of imported coaches far more luxurious and comfortable than local vehicles, he offered to carry passengers to any part of the city for the modest charge of ten cents. Scenting opportunity, Will Donnelly in the spring of 1874 made Alex Calder a proposition he could not refuse. With each omnibus costing as much as nine hundred dollars, it would take a lot of fares at ten cents each to recoup such a huge investment, Donnelly argued. But if the two outfits were to join forces, Donnelly supplying the horses and drivers and Calder his fine carriages, together they could dominate the Proof Line carrying trade. With their well-made, powerful, imported springs, Calder's large vehicles could comfortably seat eighteen or twenty passengers without difficulty. The fare to Lucan could be reduced to fifty cents and the opposition confounded.

Calder agreed, and the new line – called Calder & Company's Stage – started up in the middle of March in 1874. Calder successfully applied for the contract to carry the London-to-Centralia-and-Crediton mail for four years commencing July 1. Headquarters for the new line was the City Hotel, corner of Dundas and Talbot streets (which billed itself as "the Only Real Farmer's Hotel in the City" which did not "keep Circus horses to crowd out the Farming Community"). Coaches left London at 7:45 a.m. and Lucan at 2:15 p.m. As planned, the fare to Lucan was fifty cents. The new proprietors, doing everything to oblige, advertised that "intending passengers who leave their address by 7 p.m. at Tytler & Rose's Grocery store the night previous will be called for in any part of the City."

That same spring John Hawkshaw lost his own London-to-Exeter mail contract to another newcomer to the trade, S. S. Armitage. It is possible that the Armitage and Hawkshaw lines found it convenient to work in close concert in opposition to Calder and Donnelly's line. Both the former quartered at the Western Hotel, at the corner of Fullerton and Richmond streets. Their stages left at 7:30 and 8 o'clock in the morning and again at 2 o'clock in the afternoon.

Travel on the road continued strong, but there was hardly custom enough for three lines on the

Will Donnelly. This photograph, taken about 1874, was provided by
Will's only son, John, shortly before he died in 1973.

Proof Line Road and the fierce competition for passengers soon began to take its toll. When the Hawkshaw Stage dropped out briefly, Calder and his partners immediately added a new coach to Exeter. The *Times* of that village noted:

> A very lively trade will be carried on between this place and London in the carrying line…. Messrs. Calder & Co. have now put a line of stages on this route. Stages are comfortable and drivers obliging.[8]

In the meantime Armitage was trumpeting the virtues of his own coaches. "Ho for London!" proclaimed his advertisements, which stated that "his stages afford every accommodation". Hawkshaw soon reappeared on the scene, billing his stage as "the Old Line". He put a handsome side-seated coach on the road, touting it as far superior to the front-seated coaches of the other lines.

The competition resulted in a great juggling of schedules, each line trying to find the optimum departure and return times. The Armitage coaches left the Western Hotel at 7:30 a.m. and returned from Lucan in the afternoon, then shifted to 8 o'clock and 3 o'clock respectively. In Lucan, the Calder & Company's Stage made its headquarters at the Queen's Hotel. The old hostelry founded by John O'Donohue had been acquired by William Bowey, who had fitted it up with spanking new furniture. The Hawkshaw Stage left Exeter at the disagreeable hour of 4 a.m. and left London to return at 2 p.m. Perhaps because of the popularity of Hawkshaw's principal driver, William Brooks, or because of the early start, the rival Exeter run began to falter and by the middle of June the town's newspaper reported: "The opposition morning stage from London has been taken off." Hawkshaw then began to run to Crediton in an attempt to take patrons from the Calder and Donnelly stage, which had the run from London to Crediton and Exeter as well as to Lucan. In July the *Exeter Times* reported:

> Opposition. Hawkshaw is now running a daily stage to Crediton connecting morning and night with the main line at Devon. Both lines have put comfortable rigs on the route and will have a lively tussle for the carrying trade.[9]

Calder and Donnelly countered the Hawkshaw

threat by putting on a new run from Exeter, also leaving at four in the morning and scheduled to arrive in London at nine, leaving for the return trip at two.

The travelling public became quite aware of the commercial warfare, as the newspapers chortled:

> Opposition between the rival stages is very keen, and language the reverse of parliamentary is sometimes freely indulged in by the respective drivers when canvassing for passengers. Sometimes it is said that passengers are carried free rather than that they should patronize the other line. This may not pay the proprietors, but the travelling public appear to be satisfied.[10]

To some, the conclusion was questionable. On one occasion, a patron stood at the corner of the eleventh concession of London Township and the Proof Line. His slight bemusement at the appearance of not one but two stagecoaches heaving into view and racing towards him turned into consternation when Donnelly's stage was the first to charge up. The driver jumped off, seized the man bodily, and threw him into the coach scarcely before it had stopped.

Another incident involved two men intending to travel from London to Lucan, word of which reached the Donnelly brothers. The latter made a polite call upon them, intimating that for their own safety the two would be better off to take the Calder & Company line. When they wondered why, the answer came back loud and clear: "You might get shot if you take the other stage!"[11]

During this early period the citizens of Lucan tended to favour the Donnelly stage anyway. "Everybody sided with the Donnellys," it was claimed, not unnaturally, for the family was more familiar to the Lucanites than were the Hawkshaws from Exeter. Lucan nevertheless remained a battleground where "one party or another was getting a beating almost every other day," including one reported to have been administered by Bob Donnelly to young Hawkshaw.[12]

There is no doubt that the village was a lively place. A vignette from that year reads:

> One of the frame taverns for which Lucan is celebrated was "discoorsed" in a manner detrimental to gilt

labelled decanters and cut glass goblets. The landlord retired with a shanty over his eye.

"It's a shame!" cried the landlady, but the rioters continued to riot until "the performances terminated with a free fight among themselves, in which a pistol was fired." Then the landlord reappeared

with a loaded pistol, backed up by his wife with a poker, and the hostler with an axe helve. The array was truly formidable, and finding themselves threatened on flank and rear the rioters broke and fled.[13]

The respectable citizenry bemoaned that "the want of a lock-up is severely felt in this village", and complained that much of the trouble was caused by rowdies from the neighbouring countryside. A "patrol policeman" was needed, for cases of violence on the streets quickly followed one after the other.

The first was a rough and tumble fight witnessed by at least one magistrate....
The next was a tirade of the most horrible blasphemy, yelled out by a man who fancied he had been insulted, each volley of vile language being prefaced by a scream which had the effect of gathering a crowd of boys and girls....
Again on Saturday last a sort of faction fight took place on the Main street, stones were freely used by the combatants of whom there were five engaged....[14]

Front windows of the Lucan stores were now and then smashed, and innocent bystanders suffered. "In the past week two of our villagers have been struck in the face with stones," it was reported.

As the Donnelly brothers frequented London more and more, their name became increasingly familiar to the court officials there. When old man Thompson laid a charge of "shooting with intent", arising out of the attempted abduction of his daughter Maggie, Magistrate Lawrence Lawrason committed for trial William, Mike, and Tom Donnelly, along with Dan Keefe and Billy Atkinson. Two other defendants, Pat Quigley and Jim Keefe, were released on account of insufficient evidence. The case came off in the summer of 1874. Defence counsel Warren Rock of London prevailed upon Will Donnelly to yield up Maggie's

love letters as part of the defence and, much to the chagrin of Donnelly – to say nothing of that of his lady love – they were published in the city's daily press. The tactic proved a success, however, for the jury returned a verdict of Not Guilty.

Southwestern Ontario began to take note of the boisterous society in Lucan. More than one traveller discovered that "classic but pugilistic spot" as a good place for strangers to avoid. For example:

A few days since, Mr. M. Calovan, of Parkhill, left Exeter with the intention of going to Minnesota. Before starting he obtained $400 for a note of hand, and went on his way to Lucan to take the cars from that point. Reaching Lucan about dusk he fell in with some roughs, who, finding him walking the streets in a no very sober manner, thought to make easy prey of him. He says he was clinched from behind, a slung shot put at his head, his overcoat jerked away from him, and he was robbed of all he had.[15]

A Biddulph farmer by the name of Isaac Langford made the mistake of visiting Lucan in February 1874 and lost just about everything but his shirt. A fellow named Ryan walked off with his two coats, his pants, and a pocketbook containing $40, and it was only by good fortune that Constable Robinson was able to put the clamps on the thief just as he was about to depart by train.

Meanwhile, the usual Lucan night-time activities continued. On New Year's Eve, the boot and shoe shop of Cavanaugh was broken into, while that same night the shutters of another bootmaker, William Cathcart, resisted the burglar's attempts. Shortly after, someone raided Galloway's poultry house, ransacked Thompson's hen roost, and broke into John Frank's store and stole $150 worth of goods. Then Alex McDougall's butcher shop was entered and a quarter of beef taken. Many other minor thefts were reported in Lucan that year: Knowlton lost $15, Savage the druggist $18, and Isaac Hodgins, teller at Molson's bank in the village, wanted badly to "lay hould of the dirty spalpeen who went through him for six dollars". Many of these petty crimes were blamed upon the Donnelly boys.

When a villager out for a sidewalk stroll near Walker's Hotel stumbled over the body of ironmoulder James Simpson, the latter's death was

James Currie, who married Jenny Donnelly

Jenny Donnelly

attributed by some to the intemperate use of alcohol or, as reported, to "a ruptured blood vessel". But whispers made the rounds for years that the rupture had come about by foul means, and that Simpson had in actuality been waylaid and robbed and his skull crushed in.

In August of 1874, the Donnelly brothers and Alex Calder had a falling-out. Their partnership was dissolved and Calder put both the Omnibus Line and the stagecoach line up for sale by auction. "Satisfactory reasons given for selling out" proclaimed the notice of sale. Hawkshaw, the rival proprietor, attended the sale and pulled off a coup by buying up the four omnibuses, ten horses, and the harness of the omnibus line, in addition to the stage vehicles and eight horses. He had "now the whole road between London and Exeter to himself".

That year John Hawkshaw ran two stages to the Western Fair and, at a round-trip fare of $1.50 a head, cleaned up. It was, however, the last gasp for the Stage King. Shortly after the Western Fair tents were packed away for another season, he sold out, determined to retire from stagecoaching "to the scene of a more peaceful life". He had learned that the Donnellys were furious at being ousted from the road. They had anticipated that no one would have the audacity to bid for Calder's equipment and they would then buy at their own price, especially since Calder owed them the price of certain horses.

Hawkshaw's departure was accomplished by the sale of his business to Patrick Flanagan and Ted Crowley. They persuaded the popular William Brooks to stay on as driver. The new proprietors immediately announced the stage would continue leaving Exeter at half past four in the morning.

William Donnelly, in the meantime, took legal action against Calder, retaining the assistance of William McDiarmid, a lawyer who had just settled in Lucan. Judgment against Calder was secured for $242, the price of a number of horses sold and delivered for the now defunct stage line. The stake was enough to recommence the line, and before the year had expired the Donnelly brothers had new coaches built and horses purchased, and were back in business. The Exeter newspaper noted:

OPPOSITION STAGE. – Messrs. Donnelly have put on an opposition stage to run from Crediton to London, calling at Lucan, so the public will have increased accommodation and fares will probably be lowered. [16]

But the entry of young Pat Flanagan, backed by his older brother John, who ran the family store and tavern at Flanagan's Corners, signalled a new and intense period in the stage rivalry which was not long forgotten. "Residents there still remember," Alice McFarlane stated in 1946, "the fights, the rifle shots, the yells that accompanied the arrival of the stage on so many occasions."

FLANAGAN

Patrick Flanagan, of County Mayo in Ireland, emigrated to Canada early in the nineteenth century. He worked as a contractor on the Rideau Canal at Bytown and as a shipper in Little York, then built the first hotel and distillery in Waterdown, fought to rout Mackenzie and his rebels in 1837, and later helped to construct the Wabash and Erie canals. In 1844, Flanagan settled in the Huron Tract. Here he built a log tavern at the crossroads of the Biddulph and McGillivray Town Line and the London-Goderich Road. With the addition of a general store and post office operated by the enterprising founder, the hamlet flourished and soon became known as Flanagan's Corners.[1]

Although Patrick Flanagan married a "Prospyterion" girl born in Scotland, he remained a staunch Roman Catholic. But he feared his fellow countrymen in the Catholic Settlement part of Biddulph. "They are a bad set down there," he said, "and I would not like to be out at night in that neighbourhood." Flanagan told Constable Joseph Case, investigating the Brimmacombe murder in 1857: "It's not your business to be interfering so much about this matter." When the constable suggested this was not a proper attitude for a Justice of the Peace, Flanagan replied, "How would you like to have your bones broken by them?"

Pat Flanagan died in 1865 and his funeral attested to his popularity. The cortege of 185 sleighs to the little cemetery beside St. Peter's, the other Catholic church in Biddulph, was the largest ever seen in those parts. Flanagan's business enterprises were inherited by his four sons, John, Patrick the younger, James, and William, who added to them when, in 1874, John Hawkshaw bought the Britannia House in Exeter from his brother and re-tired from stagecoaching. Hawkshaw sold the stagecoach line to the Flanagans in October that year.

On the banks of the Sauble River, not far from Flanagan's Corners, stood the large frame building of St. James' Anglican Church. With its glebe house beside it, the church had been built in pioneer days on a parcel of twelve acres donated by the Canada Company through the efforts of Big Jim Hodgins. Although a well-built, commodious structure, by the 1870s "people's tastes [had] become more cultivated", and the edifice was considered no longer appropriate for a building which "had the style and finish of a barn". A new brick church was therefore built and, notwithstanding "lack of care in laying the foundation and a mistake in the plans", it stands to this day. Upon completion of the new building in 1873[2] the old frame church was desanctified and unceremoniously auctioned off. The Flanagans purchased it to house the horses and stagecoach equipment of their new business. In partnership with Ted Crowley,

Flanagan's Corners. Later known as Clandeboye, in its early days the village was the fiefdom of Patrick Flanagan, Sr.

they began their stage-line operations on November 1, 1874.

The winter that followed was so severe that travel by road was drastically restricted. In February 1875, a great snowstorm blew in which clogged the roads for weeks, and Lucan became so quiet that the correspondent to the *Exeter Times* grew puzzled. "One week past and no case of lawlessness to chronicle. Truly Lucan is improving," he marvelled. For the rest of that year the reporter was hard pressed to repeat the observation, for with the arrival of spring and the drying up of the roads, the stagecoach business improved. Upon the entry of Crowley and Flanagan on the road, the Donnellys set out to establish themselves as "monarchs of the line" and advertised their schedules in the London newspaper:

Crediton and London stage. – Leaves Crediton every

morning at 4 and Lucan at 6, arriving at London at 9 o'clock. Returning, leaves the City Hotel at 2 p.m., and Lucan at 5 p.m., arriving at Crediton at 7 p.m.[4]

For the rest of 1875,

Competition became so acute that the whole countryside came to be divided into two camps, those who travelled "by Flanagan", and those who travelled "by Donnelly".[5]

A wholesale dealer in London once made the mistake of dispatching a parcel of confectionery to John Flanagan's store by way of the Donnelly stagecoach. When Donnelly walked into the store with the parcel, Flanagan flung it to the floor and trampled it under foot. He ordered Donnelly out.

"But I want you to pay me," Donnelly insisted, "or sign the receipt."

Flanagan refused and Donnelly grabbed him by

the shirt, "You may not want to take it, Flanagan, but it's yours and you're going to pay for it even if I have to go to law over it."

Donnelly sued for the confectionery and Flanagan laid a charge of assault. Although a compromise was eventually reached, the ill will between the two families persisted. Each swore to drive the other off the road.

Shortly after, two lady passengers wanted to go from London to Crediton. While Flanagan & Crowley's Stage ran straight to Exeter and did not come within two or three miles of Crediton, the Donnelly stage ran there direct. Pat Flanagan had volunteered to drive a rig especially to Crediton in order to keep the two fares from going by the rival stage, and the Donnellys were furious when they heard of it. William, John, and Michael Donnelly drove over from the City Hotel just as Flanagan's rig was about to leave. John Donnelly ran to Flanagan's team, seized the horses' reins, and quickly unhitched the harness. His brother Mike jumped up on the driver's seat and grabbed Flanagan, an epileptic. Before Flanagan had a chance to protest, muscular Mike had pulled him off the coach and flung him down into the roadway. William Donnelly in the meantime opened the stagecoach door in his best gentlemanly manner. "Come along, ladies," he said with a gracious bow. "I understand it's to Crediton you're wishing to go. The Donnelly Stage is at your service."

Patrick Flanagan lost little time in complaining to the London authorities about his rough treatment. In a day or two the Donnelly trio were speedily arrested, tried, and found guilty of assault by J.P. James Owrey. Michael Donnelly was fined $10 and costs, and his brothers $5 each, and all three were bound over to keep the peace against Flanagan.

Following the long, hard winter of 1874-75, part of the reason for the quickening of the pulse of life on the Lucan-to-London road was the return of young James Donnelly. Jim, aged thirty-two years going on thirty-three, had been away for almost five years. The lumber camps of Michigan had weakened his constitution – he sometimes had a sickly pallor now, and he coughed often – but had hardened his character.

James Donnelly, Jr., a sketch made from a photograph

Young Jim had invested some of his earnings in the purchase of eighty acres near Bad Axe, in the Township of Lake, County of Huron, Michigan, but the rest of his capital he brought back with him. He immediately put most of it into his brothers' stagecoach business and assumed the titles of "Gentleman" and "stage proprietor", but despite these claims to seeming respectability, a dissolute and unhealthy air clung to the eldest of the Donnelly brothers.

Joseph Caswell, who had taken over young Jim's farm, had been forewarned of the return of James Donnelly, Jr., to Biddulph. Caswell had heard nothing more from the Donnellys after his encounter with Bob Donnelly in Lucan, until one day John Donnelly called at the Caswell farm.

"My brother Jim is coming back from the States," he said, "and he'd like to have his old farm back."

"Well, now, John," Caswell replied slowly, "I have spent money on this place, you know."

"Yes, I know," John Donnelly went on amiably,

coolly running his eyes over the log buildings which Caswell had propped up. "But suppose Jim pays you for what you've laid out. He's done all right in the States, you know."

"Well, in that case," said Caswell, feigning relief, "I welcome him back with a thousand welcomes. Of course he can have the place back. All I want is the cost of my improvements," he lied. He did not really wish to give up the farm, but he feared the Donnellys would do him personal injury if he did not agree with them. He would simply have to negotiate, he thought, a high enough price for his improvements.

About a month after this conversation James Donnelly, Jr., returned to Biddulph. Before long he went to have a look at his old farm. He and Caswell talked about setting a price for the improvements and, surprisingly, Donnelly's reaction did not seem overly hostile. But he scoffed at the sum mentioned by Caswell.

"At that price," Donnelly said as he prepared to leave, "I don't want the old farm in any way, shape, or form. Why, I can buy better and cheaper land elsewhere for that money."

On Christmas Eve, 1875, Joe Caswell's sheds and barns – the improvements which he and Donnelly had been dickering about – burned to the ground. At dawn, Caswell followed tracks leading away from his still-smouldering buildings, down the side road past the Swamp Line, and down the Roman Line several miles distant. They came to an end at the Donnelly homestead. Caswell continued on to the village of Lucan and presented his findings to one of the Justices of the Peace. While the magistrate was sympathetic, he pointed out that the tracks alone were insufficient to identify the culprits. No, he had better get more evidence or forget it.

Joe Caswell returned to his farm not yet a ruined man. But in July his haystacks were burned to the ground, and not long afterwards he woke to find his two horses lying in the field with their throats cut and their bellies slit open. He subsequently learned that on the following day young Jim Donnelly was seen in Exeter with blood on his coat. Caswell was convinced it was the blood of his horses.

With no horses and most of his crop of 150 acres standing in the field, Caswell grew desperate when his neighbours would not lend him horses or assist him. One of them, George Westman, finally helped in the late fall to bring in the little bit of crop that had not rotted and Caswell managed to struggle on, but the following year's planting was set on fire and consumed where it stood in the field. One thousand dollars' worth of produce, Caswell claimed, went up in smoke that day.

In the meantime, whenever any of the Donnelly brothers met him in Lucan or Granton, said Caswell, they threatened him, and tried their best to pick a quarrel. When Caswell again went to a J.P. in Lucan to complain, he was told: "Take my advice and forget it. Why, if the Donnellys attacked you all of Lucan could not save you."

The attitude of the J.P. was prevalent throughout the community. Timothy Toohey, one of the oldest pioneers of the Catholic Settlement, had been elected to the township council year after year as the representative from the Catholic ward of Biddulph. Respected and popular as he was, Toohey admitted: "I myself dared not speak for fear of the consequences. I was not fool enough, after working hard all my life, to run the risk of having my own barns and stables burned." Most of the Tooheys were never fond of the Donnelly family.

In desperation, Caswell notified the officials of the Canada Company in Toronto of his harassment. The company authorized its local agent to advertise a reward, and broadsheets were posted throughout the district. Whenever a group of farmers met in front of such a poster, they would wink and exchange knowing looks. Sometimes one of them would even murmur, "It's the Donnelly gang." But before doing so, he would always glance over his shoulder.

One night in the spring of 1878, when Joseph Caswell had left the eleventh-concession farm in the possession of his son James, someone crept into the field where Caswell's reaping machine stood and broke all its iron work to pieces. Joe Caswell and his family finally decided they had had enough. They packed their belongings and left Biddulph, but resentfully. For years afterwards they talked of their farm "up home", as they always called Biddulph, and how the Donnellys had driven them from it.

Other residents of the township also resented the presence of the Donnelly family. Old Mick Carroll, who lived but three farms from them, claimed that one Saturday night about the time of the return of young Jim Donnelly, the boys had removed an iron gate from the wall of the Carroll milk house, which stood near the house, and, breaking through a thick plank nailed inside the grate, had removed two barrels of pork. It was first-class meat, Carroll complained, and although he had no legal proof, he was sure it was the Donnellys and William Farrell who had done the deed. William Farrell was the son of the man James Donnelly had murdered.

The manner in which Old Mick Carroll complained about this outrage against his property gives a clue to the bitter feelings of hatred and jealousy that had grown up against the Donnelly family among some of their closest neighbours. In the early days of Biddulph, Old Mick Carroll had been a relatively prosperous farmer, looked up to by the rest of the settlers, but the general economic depression of the mid-1870s hit him hard. He complained of those who "roll in unbounded wealth", meaning the Donnellys with their stagecoaches and thriving business, during "the very hard times with which some are now so intimate". The year before, for example, the Donnellys had augmented their fifty-acre farm by purchasing an outlying parcel of twenty-five acres from Cornelius Maloney, just across the road. The slip of land was part of the very farm where James Donnelly had laid Pat Farrell low. In 1874 Old Donnelly was paid eleven dollars by the township for installing a culvert on the Roman Line, while, aside from the stage business of the sons, on his farm he kept four head of cattle, ten head of sheep, one hog, and two horses.

Some neighbours suspected that the prosperity of the Donnellys was ill-gotten. In the summer of 1874, two new butcher shops were opened in Lucan, making a total of three in the village. Within a few months both shops, belonging to Alex McDougall and Willard Hutchins, were broken into and robbed of meat. At this time the Donnellys kept their stage equipment and horses in the stables behind Hugh McPhee's old Revere House, now operated by Alexander Levett. It is likely the Donnelly brothers took turns sleeping in the stables with the horses, and during cold nights kept a stove burning. Stoves require stovewood, and that winter the respectable citizens of Lucan complained that, among other things, a great deal of cordwood seemed to disappear. "Don't leave any wood outside!" the word went around. "Them Donnellys manage to keep their stove going but never seem to buy any wood."

And about this time the newspaper reported:

A man named Williams was robbed of a sum of money near Lucan. It appears that whilst under the influence of liquor the person alluded to kept constantly pulling his money out of his pocket and shoving it under people's noses. Some party or parties, as yet unknown, wishing to obtain a closer inspection of the "flimsies", not being satisfied with a mere smell of the article, contrived to relieve the foolish man of his superfluous coin.[7]

The party in question became known not long after. The victim, Samuel Williams, a young man of twenty-two, descended from one of the Wilberforce settlers, identified the robber as Daniel Keefe, an intimate friend of the Donnelly brothers and their constant companion. Keefe was arrested and convicted. When about to be sentenced, he asked the Justice to wait until a petition might be got up as to his previous good character.

"I do not put much faith in petitions," the judge replied, "for nowadays a lengthy one can be procured in a very few minutes. Do you have anything to say before the sentence of this court is pronounced upon you?"

"I am not guilty," said Keefe.

"Now that is strange," the judge answered, "that not one of the prisoners convicted at the present sittings of the court believed themselves guilty. Yes, strange indeed. However, the various juries have thought otherwise from the evidence brought before them."

Keefe was sentenced to five years in Kingston. He thereby missed the ensuing excitement in the next few months of the continuing stagecoach rivalry between the Flanagans and the Donnellys.

13

DAN CLARK

Dan Clark was William Maloney's hired man. He eventually purchased one-half of Maloney's fifty acres, but never proved a very successful farmer, and finally agreed to sell his slip of land to Patrick "Grouchy" Ryder, who owned the adjacent farm. On St. Patrick's Day in 1875, Dan Clark walked to Lucan to meet Grouchy and conclude the bargain. It was a big day for Dan Clark but he did not survive it. He died in mysterious and, in the minds of some of the inhabitants of Lucan, suspicious circumstances. It was later alleged by the enemies of the Donnelly family that three of the boys – young Jim, Bob, and Tom – were somehow implicated in Clark's death.[1] The allegations were founded on rumour and suspicion only. A private detective from Hamilton tried to work up the case against the suspects the following year but claimed that one of the prime witnesses, an iron-moulder named William Easdale then living in Lucan, who was supposed to have witnessed the murder, refused to give evidence for fear of reprisal.

At 8 o'clock in the morning of March 17, Clark appeared in the bar-room of the Revere House in Lucan and asked Richard Tapp, bartender, for a drink. Tapp considered it too early for Clark to start drinking and refused him.

"Come on, Dan," said William Berry, a barber who was known on occasion to dispense illicit liquor from his shop next door, "let me give you a shave."

Clark went, but in the process of getting his shave also got quite intoxicated. Later that morning he teetered back into the Revere House bar-room in company with young Jim Donnelly,

and here he stayed the rest of the morning treating all who entered. Tapp and the proprietor, Alexander Levett, later swore they gave Clark no more liquor, but their testimony was unconvincing. Clark was still there at 3 o'clock in the afternoon, boasting that he had got money from the bank and was going to get more. His listeners were young Jim Donnelly, now joined by his brothers Bob and Tom, Mike Sutton and William Easdale, and an old pensioner. Levett finally got tired of their carousing and put Clark, Sutton, and the old pensioner out. The others were allowed to stay. They either boarded at the hotel or, like the Donnellys, kept horses in its stables.

It was a raw spring day and Dan Clark wandered from shop to shop, trying to stay near a stove but otherwise without seemingly rational purpose. Michael O'Connor saw him in Crunnican's store shortly after 3 o'clock. A half-hour later he staggered into the shop of James D. McCosh and sat himself down near the stove. McCosh was unhappy about drunks frequenting his store.

"What do you want?" he asked Clark testily.

"I want to buy a hat," Clark blubbered.

"Have you got any money?"

"No, I don't," Clark stammered, "but I expect to get some. I'm meeting someone to give me some. He owes it to me."

McCosh put him out and Clark said he would go over to Stanley's. Jim Churchill, a veterinarian friend of the Donnellys, saw him from inside the Revere House retracing his steps along Alice Street. It was 4 o'clock in the afternoon. Clark staggered into John Walker's harness shop, speaking so incoherently that the harnessmaker could not understand him. He stayed about ten or fifteen minutes and left, mumbling words which Walker took to be, "I'm going over to Stanley's to buy a hat."

Fifteen-year-old Susie Dight, daughter of the reeve of Lucan, saw Dan Clark about twenty minutes before six as he was entering Bruin's store. She was the last person to admit seeing Clark alive.

About six o'clock Joseph Berry, of the barber's family, heard moans emanating from Levett's stable while carrying in stovewood but did not bother to investigate. Mary Patterson had been in the stable shortly before this to milk a cow but had seen nothing untoward, and Richard Tapp had been there at half past five and had seen no one.

Tapp returned to the stables at 8:30, and noticing the back door of the building ajar, went to close it when he caught sight of a man lying in the back stall. It was Dan Clark and he was dead. The body lay on its right side, the coat turned up a little, the pants unbuttoned, and the shirt hanging out. Two bruises were visible on his forehead and one on his left hand.

"Boys, boys, there's a man dead in the stable," Tapp yelled, running out, his cries soon fetching Churchill and Levett. William McCombs, Robert McLean of the Central Hotel, John Walker the harnessmaker, and others soon joined them. Churchill turned the body over just as William Deadman, another Lucan veterinarian, arrived.

"It's Dan Clark," he said. "Look, there's a mark on his forehead. It looks like foul play."

The news spread quickly, a murdered man in Levett's stable! Reeve Thomas Dight, living just a door or two away, consulted with Barney Stanley and early next morning they penned the following:

Lucan, March 18th, 1875
To Thos. Hossack, Esq., M.D., Coroner in and for the County of Middlesex.
Sir,
We the undersigned beg to request you to hold an inquest on the man by the name of Daniel Clark who was found dead in Alexander Levett's stable last night – as it is said or surmised that some foul play was the cause of his death.
Thomas Dight, Reeve
Bernard Stanley, J.P.

Dr. James Sutton of Flanagan's Corners was sent for. He examined the body and at the inquest gave what appeared to be the conclusive evidence in the case:

After viewing the body of the deceased carefully I could easily understand how the external injuries were caused. They were of such a trifling nature as to be of no use as to accounting the cause of death. The slight bruise on the forehead could easily be caused by the fall. I am satisfied the deceased came to his death from natural causes.

The jury rendered a verdict accordingly: death from natural causes.[2]

Despite the verdict, rumours persisted that Dan Clark had been done in and that other evidence had been suppressed by either fear or favouritism. Dr. Sutton's testimony was called into question. It was pointed out that his own nephew had been in company with the Donnelly boys that afternoon and may have been implicated, and they had been plying Clark with drinks all day.[3] Clark had bragged about meeting Grouchy Ryder to get more money. He had no close relatives. His whereabouts from shortly before six to half past eight were unaccounted for. It was said that William Easdale knew where he was, and that he might even have witnessed the foul play, but Easdale was saying nothing. He boarded at Levett's hotel and was on good terms with the Donnelly brothers.

Shortly after Dan Clark's death, an itinerant fruit peddler named Thomas Gibbs pulled his wagon into the yard of Levett's hotel in Lucan to find lodgings for the night.[4] Gibbs and his young son, Johnny, helped the hostler put up the horses before retiring. Between six and seven o'clock the next morning, young Jim Donnelly sauntered into the stables and, as it was Sunday and the stage was not running, he thought he might even ride over to St. Patrick's Church for mass. On entering the stable, he was surprised to find the wagonload of oranges and lemons. "God helps those who help themselves," he thought as he began stuffing the fruit into his pockets.

In the meantime, young Johnny Gibbs was sent out to get the horses ready for the day's trip. Catching sight at the stable door of Donnelly stuffing oranges into his pocket, he ran back to get his father. The older man hurried out. Quietly coming up behind him, he clapped his hand on young Jim Donnelly's shoulder and sternly commanded: "Leave them alone!"

Donnelly swung around, startled. Gibbs's face told him the fruit peddler meant business. Donnelly quickly put his right hand into his coat pocket and brought it out again, his fist encased in a set of steel knuckles.

"I'll knock your brains out, by God," he

Deposition of James Donnelly, Jr., in the inquest into the death of Dan Clark (UWO)

exclaimed and went to work on the fruit peddler, smashing the man in the face and breaking his jaw.

Young Johnny Gibbs fled in tears and ran into Richard Tapp, the bartender, standing at the barroom door.

"Help! help!" the little fellow cried. "There's a man in there beating my father!"

All Tapp could do was help the bleeding and shaken Gibbs get medical attention. But the fruit peddler laid charges of theft and assault before two of the Lucan magistrates, Robert O'Neil and William Stanley, who sent Donnelly to London in custody for trial.[5]

William Donnelly was immediately called in.

Assault was one thing, but a charge of theft was considered a blot on the family name, to be avoided at all cost. After intense negotiations a compromise was reached, and when the trial came off, Donnelly was held Not Guilty on the charge of larceny but Guilty of common assault. Avoiding the conviction for theft proved costly: the fine for assault was $1 and costs of $25 as well as payment of $27.50 to Thomas Gibbs "in full of all claims for damages for assault". The enemies of the family pointed out that the only reason there was a conviction at all in the case was that Gibbs, being a stranger to Lucan and vicinity, did not have to live with the fact of his successful prosecution of them.

Depositions in the case against young Jim Donnelly, charged with assault and stealing oranges and lemons, April 1875 (UWO)

Towards the end of April 1875, iron-moulder William Easdale, who boarded at Levett's hotel, received some bank notes, one for $100 from the Bank of Commerce in Lucan.[6] Exchanging the notes with his landlord for cash, he went on a binge in the city of London, returning in about a week between six and seven o'clock in the evening via the Donnelly stagecoach. The driver, Tom Donnelly, rejoined Easdale in the bar-room after putting up the horses. During the ensuing revelry, Easdale pulled out his pocketbooks to lay bets on some triviality. Tapp, the bartender, thought they were betting about a horn and saw Tom Donnelly keeping a close eye on Easdale and on his pocket-books. There were two of them, one containing his keys and the other his currency. When Easdale headed for the stables at the rear to relieve himself, Tom Donnelly asked Tapp for some liquor to take out.

"What for?" asked Tapp.

"To treat him," Donnelly replied, nodding after Easdale. "Get him drunk."

At half past eight, Easdale staggered back into the hotel and up the stairs to his bedroom on the second floor. Dropping his pants over a chair near the head of the bed, he fell atop the bed and was sound asleep in a few minutes. William Dew, another of Levee's boarders, came up shortly after and had to cross Easdale's room to get to his own bedroom, which he shared with Tapp, the bartender. As Dew passed through with a light in his hand, he noticed Easdale sound asleep. He left the door between the two bedrooms partly open as he knew that Tapp would soon be up.

In a minute or so William Dew saw someone enter the outer bedroom. It was Tom Donnelly, in his stocking feet. Donnelly picked up the pants from the bedstead, searched through the pockets, and dropped them back. Noticing Dew's presence, he went over to the second doorway and showed him Easdale's pocketbook that contained the keys.

"Look here," he said to Dew, "the old bugger has no money in his pocketbook now."

Donnelly went out but bumped into Richard Tapp on his way up the stairs. He held out the pocketbook to Tapp.

"He hasn't got a damn cent in it," Donnelly said, and turning around he returned to Easdale's room and replaced it.

But Tapp had hurried downstairs to inform Alex Levett and his wife that Tom Donnelly was upstairs snooping around, and this brought the landlord upstairs immediately, just as Donnelly was coming out of Easdale's room.

"I cannot keep you, Tom," said Levett. "You'll have to go."

Donnelly left and Richard Tapp returned upstairs and tried to rouse Easdale but could not.

Early next morning William Easdale immediately noticed that his pocketbook containing the money was missing. He rushed downstairs and met Mrs. Levett, Richard Tapp, and Michael Donnelly near the bar-room, and told them his money was gone.

"Tom Donnelly's got your money," Tapp said.

"Where is he?" Easdale asked, and when the landlady motioned towards the stables, he ran out in that direction.

Michael Donnelly immediately got up and confronted Tapp. "I'll kill you," he said, "if you ever say again that Thomas has got his money."

Easdale met Tom in the stables. When he accused him of taking his money, Donnelly took hold of him in his huge fists and snarled, "If you ever accuse me of robbing you again, Easdale, I'll cut your black heart out."

WILLIAM DEW – sworn   I am a Bricklayer – I lived in Lucan last spring – I remember Wm Esdale being robbed about the last of April or first of May – I was then boarding at Lavett's Hotel – I remember the night of the Robbery – I slept in adjoining room and had to go through Esdales room to get to my bedroom – Tapp & I slept in same bed same Room – I took the light & went up to room at about 9 or 10 o'clock. Esdale was lying on the bed when I passed. I don't remember whether he had his clothes on or not – He went upstairs before that and was the worse of liquor – I was in my bedroom waiting for Tapp & the door partly open – I saw the prisoner come in and go up to the bed where Esdale was lying, and I saw him apparently taking something from the person or pocket of Esdale – who appeared to be asleep – Then he came into my room and shewed me a pocket Book – he showed me the pocket Book which had some keys in it – and said to me "Look here the old bugger has no money in his pocket book now" – then he went away taking the pocket book away with him – I went away shortly after and saw Donnelly then in sitting room –
Cross Examined

"William Dew"

Sworn before me London 17 March 1876
"L. Lawrason" P.M.

Shortly after, Easdale gave up his job at the local foundry and left Lucan. No charges were laid until many months later, when Easdale was finally persuaded to go to London and give evidence against Donnelly after the latter had been taken into custody on other charges.

With their victims afraid to prosecute, the Donnelly brothers seemed to have the run of the village and township. An account of another incident of this period reads:

By the spring of 1875 a farmer had cleaned up a load of oats for seed, and had them on the barn floor ready for sowing the next day. Early in the morning he heard a wagon driving away from his barn, and going out found his oats had been stolen. He followed the wagon a short distance up the road, when one of the Donnellys got out of it and coming back to him ordered him back to the house if he wanted to escape with his life. The man turned back and said no more of it.[7]

The Lucan postmaster, although a friend of the family, feared that the influence of Will Donnelly over his brothers was too great. Porte often wrote to Pat Donnelly, who was then living in Thorold and whom he considered a level-headed fellow, imploring him "to come up and take away or get rid of your brother William, who was becoming a terror in the community".

There was some suggestion, too, that there were firebugs on the loose in the district. In the spring of 1875, disastrous fires visited each of the three village communities of Biddulph Township. First there was the Easter Monday fire in Lucan when Henry Collins' tin shop and dwelling, Bosworth's "Red Mortar" drug store, and William Thompson's harness shop and dwelling house burned to the ground, and Mellon's large wagon shop had to be pulled down with grappling hooks to prevent the flames from spreading. The Collins family escaped in their nightclothes, Collins losing everything, including his pants which contained $150 in cash. The fire left a great gap on Main Street between the Central Hotel and the shop of Henry Quarry. Five days later, on April 2, a fire broke out near the hotel at Flanagan's Corners and destroyed five buildings, including William Howard's cabinet shop. Not long after, a large fire in Granton levelled Edmund Brooks' Ontario House tavern and stables, and Grant Brothers' store next door. Suspicions were aroused that the fires may have been incendiary, particularly when it was pointed out, for example, that there had been no fire in Howard's cabinet shop stove, where the blaze seemed to originate, for at least three or four days prior.

After the disastrous Easter fire, the Lucan Hook and Ladder Fire Company prevailed upon the village fathers to erect huge water tanks, 12 feet in diameter by 8 feet in depth, at each point in the triangle which formed the nucleus of the village: Porte's Corner, Frank's Corner, and the Dublin House corner. And the works of the ancient fire engine, purchased shortly after the town's incorporation in 1872 and dubbed Old Rescue, were overhauled.[8]

One of the members of the Lucan fire company was Michael Donnelly, who took up permanent residence in the village about this time. He had been driving stagecoach for about four or five years and on his many trips to London had passed the home, near St. John's, of a London township horticulturist named Francis Hines.[9] The beauty of Francis Hines' flowers was surpassed only by that of his three daughters, Catherine, Ellen, and

Mary. Michael Donnelly wooed and won the middle daughter, more familiarly called Nellie,[10] and the couple set up their household in a house on Alice Street rented from Benjamin Blackwell. It stood near the Revere House where the stage horses were stabled. The groom's several brothers and the bride's brothers and sisters were frequent visitors to the little household, among them being Nellie's brothers, Harry and Tom. William Donnelly would often stay with his brother in the village.

The Donnellys were thus securely ensconced in the village in the year of 1875, and few would challenge the brothers' running of at least the street and tavern life of the place. They seemed masters of the village. "There was a reign of terror in Lucan in those days," wrote Charles Hutchinson, the County Crown Attorney for the County of Middlesex, to the Attorney General's office the following year, and the attitude of the townspeople was that "no one dare go against the Donnellys."

Mary Hines in later life. Her sister, Nellie Donnelly, resembled her a great deal. (C. Andrewes)

14

BERRYHILL

On July 2, 1875, William Brooks started out to drive the Crowley & Flanagan stage from Exeter to London at the usual early hour in the morning. He made the customary few brief stops at Moores-ville and Irishtown. At Lucan, the half-way point, the stagecoach was changed and, although it was later alleged that the back-up manoeuvres in that process had loosened the wheel-nuts of the vehicle, there were other more sinister explanations for what followed. Although it had left Lucan after the Donnelly stage, it passed the latter on the way because of Donnelly's more frequent stops to pick up fares. The Crowley & Flanagan stage carried only eight passengers. Donnelly's stagecoach was nevertheless close behind, going at about five or six miles per hour, as both coaches reached the brow of Mount Hope hill. Just as they started downhill, Donnelly drew up and tried to pass on the narrow roadway. Brooks kept his vehicle determinedly in the centre of the road.

Suddenly, the left front wheel of the Crowley & Flanagan stage came off the axle and rolled away. The vehicle lurched and thundered to the ground. Brooks and one of the passengers who had been riding with him on the box tumbled off the coach. Thrown in front of Donnelly's horses, the passenger miraculously rolled clear of hoofs and wheels, but William Brooks was not so fortunate. He struck the whiffletree on the way down and, tangled up in the harness and reins, was dragged by the frightened horses a distance of twelve hundred feet, his head thumping the road all the way along.

The horses finally stopped at Oxford Street in London. Some of the passengers had managed to jump clear or were thrown out of the vehicle.

Two, an Exeter magistrate named David Johns and Robert Dempsey, ran after the runaway stage, but it was a McGillivray farmer named Cobbledick who stopped his wagon on the road and was the first to reach Brooks.

"He's killed! He's killed!" Cobbledick shouted as he lifted Brooks' limp body from the harness.

Cobbledick was wrong. Brooks still lived, and as the other stagecoach drew up, Donnelly jumped off and with the help of Robert Dempsey lifted his mangled body to the bed of Cobbledick's wagon, on which he was taken to the Western Hotel. Doctors could do little and William Brooks died that afternoon at 3:15.

Later that evening a coroner's jury was quickly convened and an inquest held. The jury finding read:

> We the undersigned jurymen upon the inquest held upon the body of William Brooks do hereby agree that deceased came to his death from injuries received by being thrown from the Exeter Stage which was caused by the fore wheel of said stage coming off and that the deceased came to his death accidentally.[1]

One of the jurymen refused to sign this verdict, the dissident being none other than Patrick Flanagan.

The death of William Brooks resulted in only a brief pause in the stagecoach war. A few weeks later the *Exeter Times* reported a curious incident:

> A few evenings since, as Crowley and Flanagan's stage was waiting at Centralia for the Crediton mail, two young men were testing the running powers of the respective beasts which they bestrode. On coming near the stage, one of the equines, probably fancying he would be better employed if in place of one of the stage horses, made a bee line for the position, but barely missed his mark, going past the stage, but in the bolting process succeeded in unseating his rider and sending him head first through one of the stage windows....[2]

The account did not identify the actors.

A more serious encounter took place on Tuesday afternoon, August 31, 1875, when once again the Donnelly stage left London at the usual hour of 2 o'clock. Again because of its heavier load, it was passed by the Crowley & Flanagan stage containing only eight passengers, at St. John's. The driver of the latter vehicle was Robert McLeod, an experienced Scotsman who had driven for Hawkshaw. Donnelly's vehicle contained ten passengers, but in addition it was heavily loaded with luggage and parcels, including a great vat of vinegar. Three passengers sat up on the box with driver Tom Donnelly, including Isaac White, proprietor of the Dublin House in Lucan.

When two of Donnelly's passengers, Martha and Louisa Lindsay, passed word up to the driver that they would like to stop at Birr for a drink of water, Tom Donnelly was happy to oblige. Perhaps with an air of bravado in order to impress the ladies, he spurred on his horses, for it was a point of pride with Tom never to be second at the hitching post. Glancing over his shoulder as they approached Birr, McLeod urged his team into a quick trot but kept close to the centre of the roadway, for Donnelly was close behind. At the

driveway to Swartz's Hotel, Tom Donnelly cut his horses to the right, intending to make a beeline for the first position at the platform and confound his rival at the last moment, as he had so many times before. All he had to do was squeeze between the other vehicle and a pump beside the driveway. Around the pump was a huge pile of stones, no doubt as fortification against stray carriage wheels.

"Tom, be careful!" yelled Isaac White, who realized what Tom Donnelly was up to. "He won't let you through."

To block Donnelly, McLeod also pulled his horses to the right. In swerving to avoid the coach in front, the wheels of the Donnelly carriage ran up on the stone pile, and the vehicle tilted dangerously. The passengers inside screamed, the hind wheel of the Crowley & Flanagan stage caught the

Main Street, Birr. The collision between the Donnelly and Flanagan stages occurred in front of the Birr Hotel, the building at the far left of this photograph.

front wheel of the Donnelly coach and then tangled itself in the traces of the Donnelly horses and struck the animal's legs. The horses bolted just as the front wheel of the Donnelly carriage fell apart. The coach lurched and fell against the other, knocking it off balance. Both vehicles tumbled on their sides, spilling passengers and luggage.

McLeod landed on his feet and immediately ran over to Donnelly.

"What did you do that for?" Tom Donnelly yelled at him.

"If I have the chance, Donnelly," McLeod replied vehemently, "I'll do it again."

Luggage and passengers were strewn everywhere on the roadway, soaked by vinegar from the broken vat. Damage to the Donnelly stage amounted to thirty dollars. Worse still, personal injuries were claimed to have been suffered by several passengers, including Martha and Louisa Lindsay in the Donnelly coach and, in

the other, George Sanders, with a cut in the face, and Mrs. Edworthy, with an elbow in the eye. Lawsuits were threatened all around.

A few days later an indignant correspondent wrote to the London *Advertiser*:

It is too bad that the lives of the public are to be so endangered when they think proper to visit London and take the stage route, which for Lucanites is by far the shortest and most desirable route. The drivers are continually at war, get running races, and care little or nothing for either horse flesh, stages or those that are inside the stage....[3]

The Donnellys blamed McLeod for the collision and were angry at the wrecking of their stagecoach but were reminded of that ancient Irish adage, "Don't get mad, get even." A couple of weeks later, on September 17, the Crowley & Flanagan mail stage left Exeter loaded with twenty passengers. At Mooresville, while the carriage was crossing a small wooden bridge, one of the axles of

THOMAS DONNELLY, sworn.   I am a driver for my Brother Michael Donnelly. live in the Tn Biddulph. I remember 31st August. I was driving my brother's stage coming from London to Lucan when another stage on the road Mr. McLeod is driving it. I left London at 2 o'clock. I left before Flanagan's stage. Flanagan's stage passed me at the 11 con of London Township. I kept close behind him. he was before me approaching Birr. When between Mr. Young's store and the pump I turned in and he didd not turn in. he McLeod turned and opposite the – I was going for the nearest post. When I got opposite the heap of stones there was about seven – eight feet between us   we were then side by side   he then turned into me   he made a quick turn as quick a turn as ever I seen. he made a short turn to the right crowding me right into the stoens. he pulled me right up on top the stones he brock one of my wheels   he wheel caught in my harness and pulled up the horse and caught my horse hind leg and broke the tong and upset the stage to the left. I got to me feet and faced towards Lucan. I had ten passengers three in the drivers seat besides myself seven inside. there was a qanty of luggage on my stage. there was about 7 dollars worth of vinegar destroyed and about thirty dollars of repairs to the stage. The wheels of my stage ran up in the stones at the pump. he McLeod crowded me up on them. McLeod came back to me. I asked him what he done that for. he would do it again if he got the chance. Thomas Kenney Mr. White and another person were in the front of the stage   there was plenty of room between him and the pump for me to pass if he had kept on the way he was going. The pump is about eight or ten feet from the first tiepost at the Hotel.

By the Magistrate.   I believe the he McLeod done it maliciously.

X Examined.   He McLeod turned off the road about half way between the store and the pump. I turned in front of the store. We were side by side when he McLeod turned of the road in front of the stable   it is about 30 feet from stable to the pump. in coming in a direct line from where McLeod turned he would be about 14 feet from the pump. McLeod's horses were within three feet from the pump when he turned in on me. He turned about 6 feet on me. I also turned a foot or so. McLeod's hind wheel caught in my front wheel. Before we got up the the stones the stages did not strike. It was right opposite the stones when the stages struck   it was about the centre of the stones around pump that we struck together. I swear that Mr. White did not tell me not to drive in there. I am quite shure no body said anything to me from the time we saw Birr till the time the accident happened. I said what meade hime do it. He McLeod would do it again if he had the chance.

Re-examined.   I turned off the road first. he McLeod was keeping the centre of the road straight for Lucan. Then after he turned in at the time McLeod turned in there was about 6 feet between the sides of the stages. When McLeod turned in suddenly there was about 14 feet from the pump on west side. The reason I could not hold up was because of my heavy loads.

Re X Examined.   I intended to tie at the hitching post nearest the pump. Sometimes I tie and sometimes I don't. The ladies wanted a drink of water at Swarts Hotel.

"Thomas Donnelly"

Witness presents
"Henry Ferguson" J.P.

(UWO)

the vehicle broke and the box crashed down on the planks, hurling driver, passengers, and baggage into the stream bed below. No one was hurt although the vehicle was considerably damaged and one of the horses injured. Whether this accident was caused by the intentional weakening of the axle or by pure accident is not known. But it seems that the Donnelly boys were in a distinctly jubilant and defiant mood in Lucan that evening.

Joe Berryhill thought he could control them. As big as three men and with the strength of an ox, Berryhill was the local strongman. On one occasion, still remembered in the district, he simply got under a farmer's broken wagon overloaded with grain and lifted it by sheer brute strength to allow the wheel to be replaced. On the evening of the latest stagecoach upset, Berryhill had finished selling a load of apples at the Lucan market and had dropped in at Levett's tavern, where he had lately boarded, for a little diversion. With him were Robert Taylor and Daniel Perley.

Pat Donnelly, at home on a visit, happened to be having a drink with a boyhood chum, Jimmy Keefe, when Berryhill and his companions came in.[4]

"So the runty blacksmith of the family is trying to be a proper gentleman," Berryhill remarked to the others, noting Donnelly's fancy city clothes.

Pat Donnelly was not amused. As part owner of a prosperous carriage-making business, he considered Berryhill an ill-mannered oaf for so attacking him without provocation.

"There's no cause for the likes of you poking fun at me, Joe Berryhill," he said. "Watch what you say or you'll regret it."

Berryhill roared with laughter. "You come back and say that when you've grown up," he taunted. But the two men with him did not laugh as heartily.

James Keefe, who was closer to Berryhill's size, came to Pat's defence. "You may be a big man, Berryhill," he said, "but you need not act the bully around here. Watch yourself."

"Are you threatening me?" Berryhill demanded truculently. He looked hard at Keefe, then back at his two companions, and added, "I'll have to lick someone yet before I go home."

Pat Donnelly replied, "You better watch you

Patrick Donnelly, from a sketch made in 1880 by Robert Harris (PEI)

don't get licked yourself, Berryhill"; then he said to Keefe, "Never mind him, Jimmy, that bastard is too smart and will get what's coming to him yet."

But Keefe continued the exchange. "Yes, and I'm the man to do it. And I'll do it before this day is over. "

"Well, then," Berryhill answered, "where do you want to fight?"

"It's really no matter," said Keefe. "I will meet you to fight, don't worry."

Berryhill and his friends finished their drinks and left, but not without a parting shot from Berryhill. "I'm going over to Walker's," he said; "I can lick you any time you want."

Word quickly spread through the village that Jim Keefe was to square off with Joe Berryhill. Joe had sauntered over to Walker's Hotel near the railway station on William Street, where there soon congregated many of the young roustabouts, including barber Peter Anderson, butcher George Henry, Cornelius Gleeson, and Mike Heenan, along with Taylor and Perley.

At Levett's Jim Keefe had a few more pulls of courage on the bottle and in about half an hour, egged on by three or four more of the Donnelly brothers who arrived on the scene, the delegation trooped out and headed over to Walker's. Led by Jim Keefe, it consisted of Pat, Will, young Jim, Mike, and Tom Donnelly. Along the way each man stooped to pick up from the road-bed two large stones weighing from one to two and a half pounds each.

When they reached Walker's Hotel, Keefe barged through the bar-room door followed close behind by young Jim, Pat, and Tom Donnelly. The other two remained outside. Joe Berryhill, standing with his back to the door and talking to the proprietor Walker who was behind the bar, turned. Before anyone in the room knew what was happening, Keefe seized Berryhill by the waistcoat and struck him on the head with the stone clutched in his hand. It was about twice the size of his fist. The force of the blow stunned the big man, for it was strong enough to cut not only the victim's hat but the hatband as well. Seizing the other's bushy beard, Keefe jerked it so hard he pulled out a clump of the hair by its roots.

Young Jim Donnelly, standing just inside the doorway, yelled, "Give it to him, the son of a bitch."

But Berryhill, although stunned by the fierceness of the sudden attack, was a long way from being beaten. He clutched at Keefe. As they grappled, all five of the Donnellys flung their stones at Berryhill, striking him on the head, shoulders, and back. One of the stones knocked out two of his teeth and loosened a third. Beside the stove was a heavy wooden bar chair which young Jim Donnelly seized and, reaching over the stove, brought down hard on Berryhill's head and right shoulder. Berryhill fell but dragged Keefe with him. As they struggled on the floor, the others pummelled the big man with their boots, all the while yelling, "Give it to him! Give it to him!"

But Berryhill nevertheless seemed to be getting the upper hand. When he put Keefe under him and tried to struggle to his feet, James Donnelly again hammered him with the bar chair.

The sudden and ferocious barrage of stones had sent the other inmates of the bar-room skeltering for cover. The proprietor scurried out from behind the bar and fled up the stairs. Perley and Taylor

The Western Hotel, Lucan site of the Berryhill fight In later years the hotel was owned by Robert Donnelly and stood on William Street until it was torn down in 1967.

took refuge in the kitchen. When Taylor peeked out and saw young Jim Donnelly strike Berryhill with the chair the second time, he ran out to help, but Tom Donnelly seized him and they both fell to the floor. Taylor happened to land on top, but young Jim quickly picked up one of the largest stones lying on the floor and, with a deft blow to the back of his head, put Taylor out of commision.

The second blow of the bar chair had caused Berryhill to loosen his grip on Keefe. The latter scrambled to his feet and was about to strike his opponent, still struggling to get up, when Mike Donnelly ran into the room and threw himself between them.

"All right, boys, that's enough," he cried, and the fight was over.

In a few minutes the dust had settled. Taylor regained consciousness. He and Joe Berryhill staggered into the kitchen to wash up and attend to their wounds, one of them a deep gash over the big man's eye.[5] A large patch of his beard was missing and several large lumps graced his noggin.

It was about eight o'clock in the evening. Friends and well-wishers of Keefe and the Donnellys crowded into Walker's, among them John McConnell, Billy Atkinson, and James Churchill. For about twenty minutes they treated each other to drinks, and then someone suggested, "Let's go over to White's."

Province of Ontario
City of London
County of Middlesex
The examination of JOSEPH BEREHILL taken on oath this 10th day of March in the year of our Lord 1876 at London, in the said City & County in the presence and hearing of James Donnelly who is charged this day before me for that, the said James Donnelly at the Village of Lucan in the County of Middlesex on the 17th day of September 1875 did assault beat and wound him the said Jos. Berehill.

This Deponent Joseph Berehill upon his oath, saith as follows: I lived in London Township on 17 September last. I was in Walker's Hotel in Lucan on 17 September 1875 – between the hours of 7 & 9 o'clock P.M. – I had been in Walker's Hotel about half an hour before I saw the prisoner. I was talking to Walker who was inside the Bar – and I was standing by the Bar talking to him when James Keefe came in the door followed by the Defendant & Thomas Donnelly – who came close behind him – James Keefe followed by defendant came immediately up to me, & struck me with a stone on the head, cutting my hat band and hat through and raised a mark on my head – at same time he seized me by the Beard – the Blow stunned me & I might have fallen from it but from the hold he had of me – I struggled with Keefe and would have got rid of him but for the Defendant who struck me with a stone and also with a chair, as well as his brother – The Prisoner was assisting Keefe, who I thought was trying to take my life – I had three wounds in my head from stones, my head was severely cut the scars of which I now shew, Two of my teeth were knocked right out with a stone, and another injured so that it came out afterwards – From a blow of stone on my shoulder my shoulder was severely injured and my right arm disabled – & it remains disabled so that I have not the proper use of it now – he pulled out part of my beard – I heard the Donellys call out, "Give it to him" several times during the attack. Prisoner James Donelly was one of the foremost amongst those assisting Keefe – The wounds in my head were dressed by Dr. Hossack afterwards.

"Joseph Berehill"
Sworn before me London 10 March 1876
"L Lawrason" P.M.

(UWO)

The whole gang trooped out and swaggered along the wooden sidewalk toward the Dublin House at the corner of William and Frank streets then operated by Isaac White. Along the way they came upon James Curry, a boarder at Walker's. Curry was no relation to the man who had married Jenny Donnelly but a Lucan Volunteer who had been out for parade muster with the Fourth Battalion Rifle Brigade. He had been given money that day: $6.20 by Captain McMillan and $10 by one of the Blackwells-Freeman or Richard, Curry could not remember which. After paying his landlord $2.30 for board and lodging and 25 cents for his supper, he had bought several drinks and was feeling no pain when he met Keefe and his companions. One of them knocked him into the ditch while the others laughed. Curry struck his face on the edge of the sidewalk and began to bleed. Tom Donnelly, one of the last of the troupe, stepped off the sidewalk and with his huge fist struck Curry a blow in the chest, knocking him flat. Then, according to Curry, Donnelly lifted up Curry's coat and pulled the man's pocketbook out of his pants.

"Take all I have but for God's sake don't touch me again," Curry groaned. "I am bleeding to death now."

Donnelly removed all the currency from the pocketbook – a five-dollar bill, Curry thought, and $2.75 in silver – and carefully replaced the pocketbook. Then he kicked the half-prostrate Curry flat on his face before hurrying along to catch up with the others.

The group also passed Rhody Kennedy standing on the sidewalk near White's tavern. Rhody was a brother of young Joe and Big Jack Kennedy, who were all intimate friends of the Donnelly family at this time. He was well known around Lucan as the man with one arm. He had spent the day threshing at Benn's. Young Jim Donnelly, partially intoxicated, lurched up to his old pal and flinging one arm around Kennedy told him about the Berryhill fight. According to Kennedy, Donnelly concluded by saying, "Rhody, I want to know if you'll do one thing for me."

Kennedy asked him what it was and Donnelly continued in a confidential tone of voice, "I want you to burn out Flanagan's stables." Kennedy said he would not do it, but Donnelly persisted. Pulling out a five-dollar bill, he held it out.

"Here, take it," he said. "This is what it's worth to you."

Kennedy pushed the money away. "No, Jim, I won't do it," he said. "I never did the like and I won't now."

"But Rhody," Donnelly insisted, "you might as well do it and earn five dollars." Then he added, "Because if you won't do it, I will!"

"Jim," Kennedy replied, "don't you have nothing to do with it. You'll be sorry if you do."

Rhody Kennedy could see that young Jim was well on his way to being drunk, and he wanted to get away from him. But Donnelly, forgetting all caution, called out after him as he left: "Remember, Rhody, wherever you are, a week or two weeks from Sunday night you will hear of its being burned to ashes. I'll leave that bastard not worth one shilling, or I will have his life."

Young Jim Donnelly joined the others in White's bar-room. Within a few minutes, Jim Curry came in staggering and bleeding from the ear. "I've been robbed!" he blurted out.

Nobody paid any attention to him. Curry left and went back to Walker's to get his wounds dressed by Dr. Thomas Hossack, who was attending Berryhill.

The crowd at White's Dublin House spent the next hour or two in drinking and carousing. About half past ten Churchill noticed Tom Donnelly and Billy Atkinson get up and leave. Young Jim Donnelly had by this time become obnoxiously drunk, and Churchill, wanting to get away from him, bid his leave and went out. It was a clear moonlit night. Churchill took the shortest route to his lodgings at the Queen's Hotel—up Frank Street to Main Street and around Albert Goodacre's cabinet shop to the alley leading to the rear door of the hotel. As he crossed Main Street, he noticed Billy Atkinson standing on the sidewalk in front of Mason's foundry.

"What are you doing, Billy?" he asked.

"Oh, I'm just waiting for Tom," Atkinson replied. "He's gone in round the back."

Churchill continued. As he approached the stables belonging to the Queen's Hotel, where Patrick Flanagan's stagecoach equipment and horses were housed, he noticed a dark form mounting a board propped up against the northwest corner of the building. The person had clambered up on the board about four feet off the ground and was holding a lighted match over his head. As he stretched to reach a clump of hay sticking out of the little door of the loft, the board broke and the man fell to the ground, landing on his feet, but the match went out.

"Is that you, Pat?" called Churchill in a low voice.

Startled at the sound of the voice, the man froze. It was Tom Donnelly.

"Churchill," Donnelly growled when he recognized him, "if you say anything about this, I

swear, by God, I'll have your life." Then, after a pause, he added, "I'm giving it up tonight, but I'll carry it through some other time for I'll have my revenge yet."

James Churchill had set up practice as a veterinary surgeon in Lucan in May 1874, and in the year and a half that he spent in the village he remained on good terms with the Donnelly boys most of the time. But shortly after encountering Donnelly in the alley, he began to find the atmosphere of the village uncongenial to him and he left Lucan to set up practice in Sarnia. While their enemies said he was afraid of the Donnellys, the latter ascribed other reasons for his departure, namely, the size of the debts he had accumulated over the months with the Lucan merchants. "Lately he has been in the habit," it was said, "of leaving his pocket book at home on top of the piano, and 'Put it in the book' has in consequence become with him a household word." Many of the Lucan merchants grieved when they heard of his departure.

With the death of Brooks and other serious personal injuries inflicted, both accidentally and wilfully, the stagecoach warfare on the London-to-Exeter road had accelerated to dangerous proportions. It seemed apparent, too, if Rhody Kennedy and James Churchill were to be believed, that the many fires in Lucan and vicinity were not all accidental.

15

FALLING OUT

The old Anglican church in Biddulph, fitted up as a barn for the Flanagan stage, served its new purpose for less than a year. On the night of Thursday, September 30, 1875, at half past 8 o'clock, it perished in a blaze of fire. Flanagan's horses and equipment had been put up at the Queen's Hotel stables in Lucan and survived, but he did lose 1,500 bushels of grain and other valuables totalling $4,000. Flanagan soon thought he knew who had set the fire. His only doubt was: Which of the Donnellys did it? Suspicion eventually settled upon Mike, and he was charged with the arson, but not until several weeks later.[1]

In the meantime, on the evening of October 4, Patrick Flanagan locked up the stables at the rear of the Queen's Hotel in Lucan and went up to his room. Flanagan was uneasy, for Churchill had warned him that the stable, containing the stagecoach and eight horses, was marked for burning. Moreover, Flanagan had earlier seen some of the Donnellys lounging in front of Farrell's drug store across the street. Young Jim and his brothers John, Bob, and Tom were there in company with Billy Atkinson, Billy Farrell, Peter Anderson the barber, and young George Porte. Flanagan would have been even more uneasy had he known what the Donnellys and their pals were joking about as they passed a bottle of whiskey from one to the other.

"Hey, George," one of them called out to young Porte, "have you got some matches?"

Porte obliged by handing over a box.

"Thanks," the other replied, "we don't know how often we're going to use these tonight."

Later, about midnight, a Lucan butcher, George Henry, was putting his horse away behind his home on Frank Street not far from the Queen's when he noticed two men step off the sidewalk and walk away into the shadows. They turned their backs so he could not identify them. He thought it strange to see two men out walking that late and, having earlier seen the gang in front of Farrell's, he was suspicious.

Upstairs in the hotel, Malcolm McIsaac, who shared Flanagan's bedroom, was fast asleep. Flanagan himself remained restless and awake although he had been in bed for an hour. At about one o'clock he suddenly became aware of a flickering red light reflected on the window and jumped up to look out. The north corner of the hotel stables below was entirely ablaze. He quickly roused McIsaac, and the two frantically pulled on their pants and rushed outside, all the while shouting to waken the other inmates.

James Churchill was already on the scene trying to get the horses out. Frank Hyland, one of Flanagan's drivers, was the next to appear and the four plunged into the smoke-filled stables and managed to retrieve all eight of the stage horses before the flames engulfed the rest of the contents, including the stagecoach. The Lucan Fire Company with Old Rescue in tow arrived too late to save the building, and its efforts were concentrated on preventing a spread of the flames. A great crowd gathered. Hyland noticed that young Jim and Tom Donnelly arrived together. Flanagan saw them, too, and thought they were enjoying themselves immensely while only pretending to help. Young Jim helped George Henry, the late-retiring butcher, to hook up the fire engine pump. Others noticed Mike Donnelly among the crowd. By three o'clock in the morning the Queen's Hotel stables were nothing but a pile of smouldering ashes.

Two or three days after the fire Rhody Kennedy, still working on the threshing team which had moved to the farm of John Carroll, was putting up the horses for the night in the Carroll stables when Tom Donnelly walked in. Donnelly had a wide grin on his face.

"There was a big excitement in Lucan on the night of the fire," he said.

"I suppose there was," replied Kennedy, continuing with his work. Although he had only one arm, he prided himself on being able to do a full day's work and sometimes serve as constable besides.

They talked of the fire and then Tom Donnelly said, "You remember the night of the Berryhill fight, Rhody? Well, I went to do it then but got caught at it, and couldn't."

"Who caught you?" the other asked.

"It was that horse farrier that lives in Lucan," Donnelly answered. "If that bastard ever squeals on me I'll take his life."

A few days after, Rhody Kennedy went into Lucan to view the huge parade the Catholic Temperance Society of the district had organized. Over two hundred marchers paraded through the streets of the village with "flags flying, banners waving, brass bands in full blast". Some of them were mounted on horses magnificently arrayed while others were decked out in resplendent uniforms with "costly white feathers in their hats [and] bright and beautiful sashes". It was a grand sight, and as they passed the Central Hotel the brass band of the Father Mathew Society of London blared out "The Harp That Once Thro' Tara's Halls". Everyone agreed it was a great day in Lucan in the battle to put down Demon Rum and that "great credit [was] due the R.C. clergy of Lucan and Biddulph for their untiring efforts in the great cause of temperance." After the parade, the entire company sat down at the Fitzhenry House on Alice Street, recently acquired by Joe Fitzhenry who began to attract the custom of the Catholic Settlement as the only Catholic hotel in the village, and in the evening listened to a lecture on temperance.

But those who had merely been spectators at the parade broke up and dispersed to the various other taverns of the village for a few snorts of the hard stuff before going back to work. As Rhody Kennedy sauntered over to the Revere House at 4 o'clock he met his old friend James Donnelly, Jr., in front of Walker's harness shop. For a confirmed souse like young Jim it was quite late in the drinking day, and he was already well under the influence.

"Did you hear about Flanagan's fire?" Donnelly leered and grinned at his old pal.

Kennedy allowed he had and Donnelly continued, "Didn't I tell you that stable had to burn, eh, didn't l?" And Jim Donnelly cackled before he added, "Well, Rhody, I'm the very man that did it."

It was the last time that any of the Donnellys ever confided in any of the Kennedy brothers, for just a few weeks after this incident, a sudden shift of alliances took place between the younger sets of the two families.

The cause of the falling-out was a matter of love and courtship. As soon as many of the girls of the Catholic Settlement reached the age of about sixteen years, eager to escape the drudgery of farm life in Biddulph they sought positions as domestics in London. A younger sister of the Kennedy boys,

RODAY KENNEDY – Sworn   I reside in Biddulph – I know James Donelly, Thomas Donelly & John Donelly, the Prisoners – & all the Donellys, I recollect having a conversation with Thomas Donelly about the burning of this stable – after the fire took place – I met the Prisoner James Donelly in the street – in Lucan on the night of the Berehill fight after the fight – He wanted to know if I would do one thing for him – asked him what it was – He said he wanted me to burn out Patrick Flanagan's Stage Stables in Lucan – I said I would not do it – Then he puts his hand in his pocket and pulled out a five dollar Bill and offered me th five dollars to go & burn the Stables – I told him I would not & never did the like & would not do it – He said I might as well do it and earn five dollars, for if I did not, he would do it – I said to him you had better have nothing to do with it, Jim, & if he did he'd be sorry – I started to go away, and he said "Remember where ever you are, a week or two weeks from Saturday night you will hear of its being burned to ashes. This conversation took place I think about ten o'clock at night – I met him again about a week after the fire near the Donelly stables – at about 4 o'clock in the afternoon. He asked me did I hear of that fire. I said Yes – He then said "Did not I tell you that I was going to burn that stable" I said yes and he then said I am the very man that did it." About three days after the fire I had a conversation with Prisoner Thomas Donelly. He said there was a big excitement the night of the fire in Lucan – I said I suppose there was – Then he told me that the night of the Berehill fight he went to do that but got caught at it – I asked who caught him – He said a Horse Farrier that lived in Lucan – He said "if he ever squeals on me I'll take his life" I was at this time friendly with the Donellys. One of them is married to my sister.

Cross examined   Before the 17th September I was not a particular companion of the Donellys – I would not have gone to them for any kind act sooner than I went to others. I thought I had a great deal better friends than they were – I had many more intimate than the Donellys – Afterwards I had a difficulty with them – They brought me before a Justice of the Peace for assault & battery – & I was committed for 40 days – I was in 25 days – I then went to Magistrate [Owrey?] to get a warrant against them for an assault but did not get it – it was for what took place on the occasion of the assault – I have been arrested by Wm. Donelly on a charge of perjury & have given Bail to appear at the Assizes – that is an unjust charge, The first conversation I had with James Donelly was on the sidewalk between Levett's Tavern and Walker's Harness Shop – no other person present – I met him on the sidewalk. I was going from the direction of Lavitt's Tavern when I met him. I had taken liquor but was not drunk – The conversation I had with Thomas Donelly was a little after dark at John Carroll's place in Biddulph – He came into the stable where I was unharnessing my Horses – I think it was Wednesday but I am not positive. I am sure it was in the month of September – no other person present.

His
Roday X Kennedy
mark

Sworn before me London 11 March 1876
"L Lawrason" J.P.

(UWO)

Norah, thus obtained employment as a housemaid in the home of Charles Hutchinson, who happened to be the Crown Attorney for the County of Middlesex. Norah Kennedy was reputed to be "very far from being unpleasing", despite features described as "somewhat peculiar" in that she had prominent cheekbones and "a somewhat pointed nose and chin", with "a fine forehead and mouth". William Donnelly was seven years her senior.[2] He had managed to live down the embarrassment of the publication in the London daily press of Maggie Thompson's love letters and, while the whole affair added stature to the reputation of the brothers as Lotharios, it made the fickle female population of the district wary of serious romantic entanglements with the likes of William Donnelly. But Donnelly and Norah Kennedy had known each other since childhood, and on the stagecoach trips between London and her home in Biddulph they had plenty of opportunity to renew their youthful acquaintance. A strong bond of matured friendship grew up between them, and in the fall of 1875 he proposed marriage, she accepted, and they were wed. All six of Will's brothers stood up with him at the wedding altar, and the officiating parish priest said he had never seen such a fine group of young men.

The marriage pleased Norah's parents, although by the peculiar twists of the older Biddulph society the elder Kennedys were not on speaking terms with the elder Donnellys. Mr. and Mrs. Kennedy nevertheless welcomed Will Donnelly wholeheartedly into the family. They seemed genuinely fond of him, even aside from the fact that Norah was the favourite of their five daughters and in their eyes could do no wrong.

Big Jack Kennedy's opinion of the marriage, on the other hand, was in direct contrast to that of his parents. "I consider," he said, referring to the event, "that Donnelly insulted me."

The Kennedy and Donnelly boys had grown up and raised hell together as youngsters. As youths they had chased girls together and as young men had bragged to each other about their sexual prowess and amorous conquests, no doubt embellishing their licentiousness with a vigorous imagination. As so often happens, it was, in such circumstances, a shock to Kennedy when Donnelly

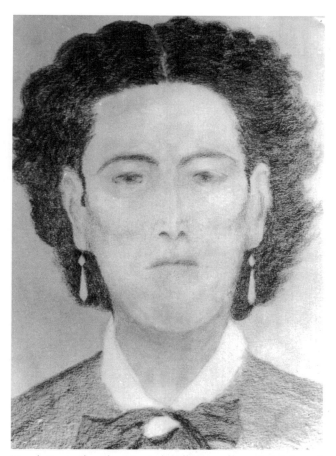

Norah Kennedy, who married Will Donnelly, a sketch based on a photograph

dared to ask for the hand of his sister, and worse still when she accepted. It was one thing to go wenching with a fellow but quite another to have him turn around and marry your sister!

"They are a gang of thieves and robbers," John Kennedy told his one-armed brother Rhody, "and no respectable person in Biddulph will have anything to do with them."

But Big Jack Kennedy had another motive for fearing his new brother-in-law. He suspected Donnelly of the same propensity displayed by his younger brothers for using matrimony, or the promise of it, to extract material reward from the families of their girls, and the plain truth was that, because Norah had always been "their pet", Kennedy was afraid his parents would leave their property to her. Old John Kennedy himself once said that this was what his son feared more than anything.

John Kennedy (*The Globe*)

About the last week of November 1875, not long after the marriage, Will, Bob, and Tom Donnelly met Big Jack and Rhody Kennedy at the Fitzhenry House in Lucan, where, it appears, they "discoorsed" on the subject of the recent nuptials.

"Kennedy began at me," William Donnelly said in describing the origin of the affair.

One thing led to another and the former bosom friends were soon trading invective as only formerly intimate friends can.

"Well, brother-in-law," Kennedy sneered, "whose house are you going to burn down next?"

Donnelly replied in the same vein, and Kennedy added, "If I ever hear of a house being burned I'll swear it on you at all hazards 'cause you'd be the one that did the job."

"You just see that you don't get burned out!" Donnelly retorted.

Donnelly won the repartee easily, not only be-

cause of his keener wit and sharper tongue, but because he knew that Kennedy stood in mortal fear of him. Despite his powerful appearance, said William Donnelly, Big Jack Kennedy was a "natural born coward".

"Nor did he ever look for a chance to attack me," Donnelly said. "He knew better than that. He'd never try it the second time if he did it in the daytime. It's altogether probable I would have fixed him."

Kennedy's method of revenge was to devise various schemes to get Donnelly into trouble. Once he offered to steal a steer from his father, make a gift of it to a Westminster Township man, and blame the theft on Donnelly. The rift between son and parents worsened when Kennedy himself married a woman to whom the elder Kennedys took a dislike. They quarrelled, and things came to such a pass that the parties hauled each other up in court on charges of obscene and threatening language.[3] The rift lasted until the deaths of the old people not too many years after.[4]

It goes without saying that the William Donnellys and the Big Jack Kennedys never visited. "He knew better than to come to my place," Donnelly said. "I have often avoided him for peace's sake and kept away from his father on that account."

After their argument at the Fitzhenry Hotel, Will Donnelly and Jack Kennedy never spoke to each other again. But Kennedy would often stand in a crowd cursing and sneering at his "brother-in-law", spitting out the latter phrase with venom, but he always took care he had plenty of friends around him when he did it.

Following the marriage of their sister, the two Kennedy boys suddenly became fast friends of the Flanagans.[5] Despite the double burning inflicted upon them in the fall of 1875, the Flanagans were determined to retain the mail contract. New stagecoaches were quickly obtained and were back on the road within a couple of weeks. Convinced that their property had been fired by the Donnellys – James, William, Robert, and Thomas – along with William Farrell, they were determined to get revenge. But shortly after getting back on the road, Pat Flanagan was making his way early one morning to the rebuilt stables at the rear of the Queen's Hotel when he was waylaid, given two stiff knocks on the head, and left cut and bleeding. Flanagan claimed he would have been murdered in cold blood but for the fact that the weapon, a cudgel with a heavy knob on one end loaded "with lead ...of sufficient weight to fell an ox", broke in two at the second blow.

As 1875 came to a close, the fortunes of the Donnelly brothers took a bad turn when the results of many of their past misdeeds caught up with them. First, Martha and Louisa Lindsay made good their threat of legal action and commenced a lawsuit for damages against the proprietors of the stagecoach, William and Michael Donnelly. The sisters charged them with having conducted them "negligently and unskilfully [in their] stage or covered wagon [and] negligently and maliciously ran races with other stagecoaches", resulting in personal injuries to the plaintiffs. Next, Tom Donnelly was arrested by Detective Phair and bailed to appear in London Magistrates' Court for assaulting Joe Berryhill. The principal assailant, James Keefe, had cleared out of the district. Tom was also charged with assaulting and robbing James Curry. Then Robert McLeod, the driver of the Flanagan and Crowley stage who had been convicted at the instance of Michael Donnelly for "malicious driving" as a result of the upset at Swartz's Hotel in Birr, launched an appeal of his conviction to the County Court. And Rhody Kennedy laid a charge against young Jim Donnelly of attempting to bribe him to commit arson.

But the worst blow of all struck not only the Donnellys but also their rivals. It was the commencement of operations of the London, Huron and Bruce Railroad from London to points north. The opening of the railroad signalled the end of the lucrative period of stagecoaching on the Proof Line Road. As noted in the newspapers, "North and south, the passenger coach is completely filled, and but little more crowding will demand another coach to be placed on the line."[6] Every passenger who went by train was one less passenger for the rival stagecoach lines to squabble over. The *Exeter Times* observed:

> Since the opening of the railroad, the travel by stage has fallen off so that the morning stages to London are taken off entirely, while the Clinton mail is carried in a single buggy....[7]

As the number of stage passengers dwindled, the competition for them intensified and the constant juggling of schedules and routes by the rival lines continued at an even more hectic pace. One of the Donnelly coaches remained on the run to Crediton, while the other concentrated on the London-to-Exeter route. The London *Free Press* carried the following advertisement at the beginning of 1876:

> DONNELLY'S EXETER AND LONDON STAGE. Leaves Exeter every morning at 4 and Lucan at 6, arriving in London at 9 o'clock. Leaves City Hotel at 2 p.m. & Lucan at 5 p.m., arriving at Exeter at 7 p.m. First class accommodation. Charges moderate.[8]

And the Flanagans, in addition to enlisting the Kennedys to their cause, called in other paid help.

16

MCKINNON

Highland games were very popular in the days of the Donnellys. The home-town track-and-field athlete was a favourite who upheld the local cause not only in the large competitions but in matches between neighbouring villages and towns. Alexander C. Reid, better known as "Sandy", was such an athlete who sometimes made his home in Lucan while making the rounds of the North American Highland games competitions in the 1870s.[1] Another was big Hugh McKinnon of Hamilton. Standing six foot three in his stocking feet and weighing 215 pounds "when in training", Big Hugh reached his prime about the year 1875. He was then thirty years of age[2] and well known.

> From 1874 to 1879 McKinnon, one of the most noted all-round athletes Ontario has ever had, held the heavyweight championship [in throwing] in both the United States and Canada, retiring in 1879 undefeated. In these years he won a thousand medals and

Hugh McKinnon, wearing the many medals he amassed in Highland Games competitions

cups with championships in European contests and also in Philadelphia.[3]

McKinnon had joined the Hamilton Police Force but was expelled when a local magistrate found him guilty of aggravated assault because of a too exuberant enforcement of the law. The verdict was reversed on appeal but the case left McKinnon's police career under a cloud. He became, instead, a private detective, a career which left him greater latitude to travel about the country cleaning up on both medals and criminals.[4]

McKinnon was said to be a paragon of honesty. Besides reputedly possessing an abundance of humility,

modesty amounting to shyness was his, and though a

public character known to many thousands of citizens everywhere in Canada, his intimate circle of friends was always a limited one.[5]

One who entered that innmate circle was Sandy Reid of Lucan. The two would meet often at the various games, and when they got to talking about their respective home towns, the subject of the Donnellys would inevitably arise. The newspapers had taken frequent note of the general spirit of lawlessness in Lucan, and the London *Free Press* in particular often referred to the Donnelly brothers as "The Lucan Ku-Klux". The *Free Press* about this time noted:

For months past, the village of Lucan has been brought into unenviable notoriety, mainly through the lawless conduct of a few of its inhabitants, the most prominent in the work being members of the Donnelly family – 5 or 6 young men. Two of them have owned a couple of stages for years past, and we doubt not have amassed considerable money in running them between this city and the villages and towns to the north of us.[6]

It was only natural, therefore, that the Flanagans, who considered the early-morning assault on poor Pat to be the final turn of the screw, were determined to find the necessary evidence to put the Lucan Ku-Klux behind bars and turned, on Sandy Reid's advice, to the big detective from Hamilton.[7]

Hugh McKinnon had one short interview with Pat Flanagan and then went to work. He believed that he had entered Lucan anonymously under the guise of a mild-mannered and innocent stranger, "a sporting man who had not only a superabundance of muscle but plenty of money". The Donnellys, however, told a different story. Thomas Johnston, a constable in London East and a good friend of the brothers, said of McKinnon's coming: "He arrived in Lucan one evening and Mike Donnelly told me in London next morning that there was a detective up there to watch them." Again, McKinnon claimed that he quickly and skilfully ingratiated himself into the brothers' confidence. "I never sought the society of the Donnellys, but conducted myself in such a manner that I knew they would be sure to come to me." But once more the Donnellys told a different story, claiming they "used" McKinnon almost immediately. The burly sleuth did later admit that "for some time, however, I made slow progress [for] I had shrewd, desperate men to deal with, who did not take strangers into their confidence.... "

In McKinnon's own words, this is the way he went about his plan:

One day shortly after arriving in Lucan I was sitting in a bar-room and heard a man railing at the Donnellys in a most violent manner. The opportunity was too good a one to be lost, so I immediately turned to the irate talker and rebuked him for scandalizing people who were not present to defend themselves and to whom he dared not speak in such terms to their faces. One word brought on another, and finally I was obliged to end the discussion by giving the man an open-handed slap in the face. As soon as this incident reached the ears of the Donnelly boys, it convinced them that I must indeed be their friend, and I thereby gained their confidence.[8]

It is more likely, however, that the brain of Will Donnelly raced far ahead of Hugh McKinnon's plodding police mentality and that the incident was a ruse to smoke him out. Big Hugh, of course, would never admit such a thing. A *Globe* reporter who interviewed him later effused: "...Mr. McKinnon evidently had no desire to make himself prominent in the story he had to tell. So strong was his inclination in this direction, indeed, that I was more than once during the conversation led to the belief that if he had been less modest he might have furnished me with a more interesting story."

McKinnon managed to suppress his modesty sufficiently to narrate the following story of his activities after befriending the brothers:

I spent an evening in the house of Mike Donnelly and some of the other brothers were there. They were scuffling and wrestling among themselves in a friendly way but I could see that their real object was to draw me into a contest in order to gauge my abilities in "rough and tumble". I was ready for them, however, and when one of the best of them – I forget which of the brothers it was (it might have been John) – closed with me I put forth the most vigorous effort. I am a trained athlete, you understand, and therefore I threw my opponent with such quickness that it thoroughly astonished the whole gang of them.[9]

Concluded McKinnon modestly: "They knew I

was strong, but this display of science and agility took them completely by surprise."

It is possible the brothers were setting up their new-found friend to their own advantage. A little charade was worked out with him beforehand and then put into operation. As part of this plan, they spread the word among the villagers that there was a stranger in the village who could lick Tom Donnelly. The rumours titillated the sporting instincts of the good citizens of Lucan, who knew a good bet when they saw one, and they laid heavy money on the contest. The locals knew Tom Donnelly and they bet on him. But the brothers, through the likes of accomplices such as Billy Atkinson and Billy Farrell, clandestinely covered all bets. The outcome of the episode was unwittingly reported in the *Free Press* a few days later as a bona fide encounter:

A species of the "rowdy" class of beings was exceedingly well punished at Lucan the other day. It appears that in the village named, as well as in most places, there are a number of representatives of this class. And on the occasion named, one of them – a man named Donnelly – was as neatly "set down" upon as one could wish. He went into an hotel, and got liquor, treating all and sundry. He had the "assurance", too, without paying for it, to ask for his change. The bar-tender, of course, remonstrated, whereupon the pugilistic individual braced himself up, and not only threatened to annihilate the poor bar-tender, but all and sundry in the room who denied he had not given the money. The noise brought "mine hostess" to the bar, a ponderous piece of cordwood in hand, bent, no doubt, on administering chastisement on the disturber of her usually quiet domain. When she was told that it was "Donnelly", the club dropped; she knew his pugilistic fame, and deemed non-aggression the most prudent policy. The "rowdy" was determined on having the disturbance completed, and he challenged to combat a peaceful individual who sat by, in an insolent manner demanding he should fight. The young gentleman referred to got up, and gave him such a blow as sent him sprawling out of the door where he lay for some time as if dead. He received every attention from those in the hotel, however, and soon regained consciousness. It is generally understood he has resolved within himself to be more careful whom he insults in the future. For a time, let us hope, he has retired from the "ring".[10]

All bets were quickly scooped up from the confounded gamblers of Lucan, and McKinnon later said: "Mike and his brothers pocketed a few dollars by the operation, but I took care two or three of my friends whom I had in the neighbourhood were in on the secret and should throw cold water on the affair to such an extent as would prevent outsiders from being seriously victimized."

Outsiders may have been protected, but several Lucanites were not, and when word soon leaked out that the match had been a set-up, some of the losers were furious. Among them were Thomas Culbert, who kept a livery stable in the village, and Rhody Kennedy. Despite Rhody's reversal of loyalty, he had considered himself shrewd enough not to bet against Tom Donnelly and thought to pick up a few easy dollars. Upon discovering the trick, Kennedy and Culbert marched over to Fitzhenry's Hotel where they confronted Bob and Tom Donnelly and demanded the return of their bets on grounds of fraud. The two brothers laughed and told them to go to hell. A "terrific fight" ensued between Tom Donnelly and Culbert, followed by a "general scrimmage" in which Rhody Kennedy, with only one arm to defend himself, was badly abused not only by Bob Donnelly but also by Tom, after the latter had dispensed with Culbert.

On the whole, Hugh McKinnon's mission to Lucan on this occasion was not particularly fruitful. "The Donnellys by some means or other," the detective perplexedly explained, "get a great deal of information concerning the doings in London of anything concerning themselves, such as when an officer was going out to arrest them, and who." The brothers themselves boasted of this to McKinnon.

In the meantime, the stagecoach war continued unabated, as appears from the following newspaper item that month:

Exeter and Vicinity. SET ON FIRE. – Crowley and Flanagan's London stage on Tuesday evening last was set on fire by placing some straw in the bottom of the sleigh as it stood in front of the Mansion House stables. It is supposed to have been done by some maliciously inclined persons.[11]

The Flanagans took some consolation in the Lindsay sisters' obtaining judgment against the Donnellys at the end of the year, Martha for $15 and Louisa for $20, and in the conviction of Tom Donnelly for assaulting Joe Berryhill. He was given a hefty penalty of $20 fine and $12.25 costs. But while Crowley and the Flanagan brothers had been in the stagecoach business for only slightly over a year, in that short period their drivers had suffered physical beatings, one of them had been killed while racing with the rival stage, their carriages had suffered upsets, and two large stables with coach and equipment had been burned to the ground. While they continued to advertise for patronage, privately they decided to quit the road.

The Flanagans found a buyer for the stagecoach business in Richard Bryant. Bryant, forty-two years old and originally a farmer in McGillivray but lately moved into the Piper Survey of the village, was a member of the Church of England. He agreed to take over at the beginning of the New Year, to be assisted in the enterprise by a brother-in-law, James McMahon. They planned to run the line out of the Central Hotel in Exeter but to keep some of the equipment and stable horses at McMahon's farm, conveniently located at the Elginfield intersection just south of Lucan. McMahon held a small grudge against the Donnellys: he had been a passenger on the Crowley & Flanagan stage when it was upset in front of Swartz's Hotel in Birr the previous fall. As for Bryant, he had no illusions about the dangers of carrying on business against the Donnellys. He expected trouble and it came soon enough.

In the second week of January 1876, while Richard Bryant was driving his new stagecoach to London, an axle of the vehicle suddenly broke as it neared the city. Bryant was thrown off the box and a wheel ran over his leg, breaking it. Bryant quickly enough found himself out of commission as a driver of his own stage. On the following Saturday night, the carriage itself was also retired from business when some unknown person or persons, under cover of darkness, crept to its resting place for the night and, drawing it away by hand a quarter of a mile up the road, proceeded to saw it into pieces "as small as stovewood". The next morning many of the Lucan villagers took a quiet Sunday stroll out to inspect the pile of firewood,

The Central Hotel, Exeter. Note the typical stagecoach of the period in front of the hotel.

formerly a stagecoach, and to shake their heads. One reporter stated that "to say that people were surprised when they saw one of the stages last Sunday cut up in small pieces would be incorrect for rowdyism and flagrant outrages of law are such common occurrence in Lucan that the discovery of the crime appears no longer to create any astonishment. "

Richard Bryant had no intention of giving up without a fight and quickly procured new vehicles and hired new drivers. Among them were a man named Carling from around Exeter, a Scotch farmer named Peter McKellar from London Township, and none other than Rhody Kennedy, the one-armed sometime constable. Carling did not last long. Within a matter of days, on January 20, Bob Donnelly met him in Lucan and administered a severe and, as Carling claimed, unprovoked beating. Carling quickly retired from stage driving. The others were a little hardier and better prepared.

"I heard times were rough in Lucan," Peter McKellar declared when asked about the gun he carried, "and I was advised to borrow the revolver to protect myself."

McKellar long remembered Monday, January 24, 1876. On that day he was accosted and threatened in turn by at least five of the seven Donnelly brothers. The first instance was early in the morning between six and seven o'clock when McKellar drove the Bryant stage up to the platform of the Queen's Hotel in Lucan. Sitting up on the box with him was the intrepid Rhody Kennedy, acting as guard.

"Anybody going to London?" McKellar called out, and then, "Let me have the robe and cushion."

As the articles were handed up, the two men spied young Jim, John, and Bob Donnelly, who stepped out from across the street and approached the stagecoach.

"Come on, boys, let's have a drink," one of them said in a seemingly friendly tone and motioning to the bar-room door of the Queen's.

"No," replied Kennedy, tucking the buffalo robe around his feet and knowing full well the Donnellys were anxious to get them down off the carriage.

"Come on," insisted both John and Bob Donnelly as they came closer. "If you won't drink at Bowey's, then we'll go over to McLean's."

Bowey's was the Queen's and Bob McLean's Central was across the road just a few dozen yards away, neither of them much frequented by the Donnellys.

"I won't do it," McKellar replied with determination.

He slapped the reins to start off. He was not now concerned with passengers, nor even intending, in the circumstances, to stop at the platform of the Central as he normally would have done. John and Bob Donnelly ran alongside the coach. Opposite the Central Hotel, when they realized that McKellar was not stopping, Bob Donnelly spurted in front of the team and, catching hold of the harness, stopped the horses. His brother jumped up on the wheel and seized the buffalo robe around McKellar's legs. When McKellar drew his legs back, Donnelly struck at him.

"You son of a bitch," he said, "I'd like to have you alone. Listen, McKellar, I'll have your life if you don't quit driving this stage before a week – you or any other man that will drive it."

McKellar drew off his mitt and reached for his gun. "Let go the horses!" he shouted.

Donnelly jumped off the wheel hub and called to his brother, "Come on, Robert, let's go," and the two of them ran off in a trot.

Shortly after five that evening, McKellar and Kennedy returned from London. They expected trouble. After putting up the horses at the Queen's, they went inside and met Henry Bryan, whose revolver McKellar had borrowed; from there they went to Alex Levett's Revere House for a drink, coming out just as the Donnelly stage pulled into the village. It was dark, but they could see the driver, Michael Donnelly, get off the coach. He saw them also and came over immediately. Henry Bryan braced himself. He had once been a county constable, and Mike Donnelly, he claimed, held a grudge against him.

But instead, Donnelly walked up to McKellar and, glaring at him, said, "You keep driving that stage, McKellar, and I'll have your life."

Without flinching, McKellar replied with a silent but determined look which seemed to enrage Donnelly. The latter pulled out a roll of steel balls from his pocket and, clenching them in his fist, took a fighting stance. "All right," he challenged, "let's fight it out right now."

Bryan interrupted in a conciliatory tone, "You leave him alone, Mike."

Michael Donnelly may have been more quick-tempered than usual, for his wife Nellie was expecting the first grandchild in the Donnelly family.[12] The waiting was getting hard on Mike's nerves. At Bryan's interruption, he exploded. "You son of a bitch!" he yelled, and commenced cursing and swearing at the top of his voice, continuing in this vein until the trio retreated.

Bryan decided to retire, asked McKellar for his revolver back, and departed into the darkness. It was half past five now, and McKellar and Kennedy, joined by Tom Robinson and a man named Ryan, stood around talking over the events of the day and then headed over to the Central Hotel. As they clambered up on the platform they met Mike Donnelly, who was still sufficiently truculent to exchange insults with Kennedy as they went into McLean's bar-room. Coming out about five or ten minutes later, they found that Mike had been joined on the platform by his brother Will. What happened next is uncertain.

According to Will Donnelly, he was standing quietly when McKellar pointed a gun at his breast and said, "You son of a bitch, Donnelly, leave my way or I'll put a ball through you."

Needless to say, Peter McKellar's version of

what happened on the platform of the Central Hotel was different. He said he had no gun to point at Donnelly at all, having given it back to Bryan, and that it was Donnelly who had threatened him.

When McKellar then took his leave to retire to his lodgings at Walker's Hotel that night, Henry Collins told him, "Look out for yourself, Pete."

"Don't worry," replied McKellar, "I've got a good pair of legs."

The day ended without harm to either faction, but the air of Lucan was heavy with the threat of violence. The brothers Donnelly were unaccustomed to being challenged on the streets of the village with impunity.

Other minor fracases which occurred about this time involved Tom Donnelly and his new brother-in-law, Jim Currie. They got into a scrap with Joe Hauley. Needless to say, Hauley lost. And Michael Donnelly made threats to shoot, for the second time, a Lucan blacksmith named Alfred Brown, who also acted as county constable. It was apparent the Lucan pot was simmering, and its lid blew off at Tom Ryder's wedding celebration in February. But before that happened, Rhody Kennedy was dealt with.

17

RHODY

Most members of the Donnelly family were relatively experienced with the law courts. During the 1870s every single member of the family save the father and Jenny[1] appeared in front of the bench as a defendant. Several of the brothers knew the inside of a courtroom better than some lawyers. Although they were personally acquainted with the leading defence counsel of London, including Warren Rock, John Bartram, Edmund Meredith,

William R. Meredith, John Taylor, and Hugh Macmahon, among others, the family's favourite lawyer was always David Glass.[2] That is not to say, however, that they were not adept at legal manoeuvring on their own.

For example, on the afternoon of November 23, 1875, Detective Hugh Murphy arrested Tom Donnelly in London on charges by Berryhill and Curry, and he was bailed to appear for his trial in a week. Then came the legal stratagems. First there was the tactic of delay. On November 30 the case was postponed for two weeks by J.P. Lawrence Lawrason when witnesses were said to be unavailable. Curry had apparently been cajoled into having a few drinks on the way to court and landed up instead in the London drunk tank. Other witnesses would be given related treatment. One of the brothers, feigning friendliness, would invite the prospective witness "for a throw" at a nearby tavern. During the ensuing conviviality allusions would be made to the impending court case and to "poor Tom", the harassment of the authorities, or the callousness of "black-hearted villains who would swear away a man's freedom", and, if the witness happened to be a Catholic, talk would sometimes turn to the belief that "the Law Bible" usually found in court would not bind a man's conscience, for only "the Church Book" could do that. Veiled or unveiled threats might be made, their degree of disguise varying with the weakness of the person at whom they were directed. In the case of Tom Donnelly, all treated in this manner were the witnesses John McConnell, a merchant tailor of Lucan, Nelson W. Warburton, the railway station agent in the village, and George Henry, the Lucan butcher. When the case finally came up at noon on December 13 and after Curry and one or two of the other witnesses had given their evidence, the magistrate adjourned until 4 o'clock. When court resumed at the time appointed, however, Curry had disappeared. The defence thereupon made a motion for dismissal, and the magistrate wavered but finally set the matter over to the next day.

Meanwhile, in the Berryhill assault case, notwithstanding that a Lucan witness named George Alloway failed to give evidence when he was found intoxicated by Detective Murphy on the stairs leading up to the police courtroom, Tom Donnelly was found guilty and given a hefty fine with the option of working it off by two months in jail. He paid the fine. The defence tactics fared better in the Curry cases the next day when the court stated that the evidence of McConnell, Warburton, and Henry was equivocal and dismissed the charge of assault. The robbery case was not proceeded with, as the magistrate felt there was insufficient evidence to corroborate the complainant.

Thus Curry was fairly easily dealt with, but the man who learned at first hand of the Donnellys' skill at legal machinations was Rhody Kennedy. Following his falling-out with the Donnellys, Kennedy took up with Flanagan, who persuaded him to lay a charge of arson against young Jim Donnelly. In retaliation, the brothers laid a countercharge against Kennedy of assault upon Bob and Tom Donnelly at Fitzhenry's,[3] and one-armed Rhody was speedily arrested by Constable Charles Ferguson, and just as speedily convicted on December 4 by the constable's father, Henry Ferguson. He was sentenced to the severe penalty of forty days in jail!

It appears that Ferguson was unaware that Robert H. O'Neil of Lucan had in the meantime remanded young Jim Donnelly to appear for his trial before the Birr magistrate. Both Justices of the Peace were notoriously friendly towards the Donnellys.[4] Ferguson, upon discovering what had happened, wrote to Crown Attorney Hutchinson:

> Please let me know how I am to get Rhody Kennedy who is now confined in jail when his time expires to come and prosecute Donnelly for the burning of Flanagan's stable....[5]

But after serving twenty-five of his forty days, Kennedy was released. He immediately asked London Police Magistrate Lawrence Lawrason whether his conviction prevented him from laying a charge against the same two Donnellys whom he had been convicted of assaulting. Lawrason referred him to the Crown Attorney. Hutchinson replied that "from Kennedy's story it would appear he was badly used" and advised Lawrason to accept the charge. "I don't think Mr. Ferguson's conviction conclusive as to the merits of the case," he added. Bob and Tom Donnelly were thereupon

charged, arrested, and given bail before Squire O'Neil in Lucan. Billy Atkinson and Tom Hodgins acted as bondsmen. Their trial was set before a London J.P., James Owrey, on January 13, 1876. On December 30 Rhody Kennedy testified before Ferguson in Birr that young Jim Donnelly had tried to bribe him with five dollars to burn Flanagan's stable. William Donnelly then stood up and said he wished to lay a charge of perjury against Kennedy. The tactic took the magistrate completely by surprise. Ferguson adjourned the case to seek the Crown Attorney's advice and the latter replied:

> I think you will be right in dismissing the case against Donnelly for the alleged burning of Flanagan's barn. Donnelly might lodge an information against Kennedy for perjury before you – You would then issue a warrant for Kennedy's arrest.[6]

Thereupon Kennedy was again arrested and remanded to appear on January 13, the same day that he was to prosecute Bob and Tom Donnelly in Squire Owrey's court in London!

When the Donnelly brothers' case came up before Owrey and the defendants had not bothered to show up, the J.P. was about to issue a bench warrant for their arrest when he noticed the bail bond was defective. He thereupon drew one up in proper form and dispatched it to Squire Robert O'Neil in Lucan for his signature. But O'Neil merely scratched his name through the original bond and returned it to Owrey in a few days' time. The papers were now in a mess. James Owrey complained to the Crown Attorney, who was beginning to lose patience with the Justices of the Peace for constantly pestering him about the Donnelly cases, but he nevertheless wrote to O'Neil about the alteration of the bail bond:

> Will you please explain the reason of it? ...I can not suppose you do not desire to aid in the preservation of order nor that you wish in any way to assist parties accused of crime to evade the investigation into the matters charged against them ...?[7]

Bob and Tom Donnelly did appear before Squire Ferguson at Birr on the 13th day to prosecute the charge of perjury against Rhody Kennedy.

Tom Donnelly took the witness box and stated on oath:

I swear positively that James Donnelly never offered Rhody Kennedy $5 to burn Flanagan's stable, on that night. This was on Friday night about the middle of September. I swear that I slept with James Donnelly on that night and he could not have offered Rhody Kennedy $5 to burn Flanagan's stable without my knowledge....[8]

Young Jim and Will also gave testimony. Will stated: "I positively swear that Rhody Kennedy did commit wilful and corrupt perjury against James Donnelly by swearing that James Donnelly offered him five dollars to burn Flanagan's stable and also by swearing that Flanagan's stable was burned. I swear Flanagan's stable was not burned at all!"

The ultra-legal reasoning of William Donnelly was that Flanagan's stable in Lucan could not have burned because Flanagan owned no stable in Lucan – he merely rented it! On this evidence Squire Ferguson committed Kennedy for trial at the next assizes in London.

In the early morning of January 24, Peter McKellar was accosted several times in turn by some of the Donnelly brothers in Lucan. Rhody Kennedy slept with McKellar that night in Walker's Hotel and doubtless advised the Scotchman to lay criminal charges. The Donnellys, however, took the initiative when Will charged Peter McKellar before Squire Ferguson with pointing a gun, and Charlie Ferguson arrested McKellar. The case was heard on January 28. The Birr magistrate again consulted the Crown Attorney:

I regret very much to have to trouble you so often, but I have got into those unfortunate cases in and about Lucan.... My brother magistrates do not wish to have anything to do between those violent parties so the weight falls upon me.[9]

Ferguson went on to complain that he had two or three cases "nearly of the same nature" involving the same parties and that "they are so excited that I am of the opinion that if something is not done there will be lives lost."

Hutchinson advised Ferguson to dismiss the charge. The other cases referred to by the Birr J.P.

were charges of abusive and threatening language against Rhody Kennedy and countercharges against William and Michael Donnelly of assault and threats, all arising out of the events of January 24.

Fresh incidents were soon added. On the day that the case was heard in Birr, Peter McKellar went to London and laid charges of threats made by John and Robert Donnelly on January 24. Rhody Kennedy was appointed a special constable to effect the arrests. Armed with the warrants, Kennedy rode back to Lucan on McKellar's stagecoach. As they pulled into the village, he immediately spotted Robert Donnelly on the platform of the Central Hotel. Kennedy quickly jumped off the stage, ran up to Donnelly, and took hold of him with his one arm.

"I've got a warrant for you," he cried out, "and I arrest you as my prisoner in the Queen's name."

Bob was startled, but quickly reached into his coat pocket and pulled out a revolver. "Let me go, you son of a bitch," he said, striking Kennedy in the face with it. But the one-armed constable clung resolutely to his quarry as Donnelly continued striking him again and again.

"Help, help, in the name of the Queen!" Kennedy yelled, bleeding profusely.

RODAY KENNEDY – sworn   I came from London with McKellar on 24th arrived at Lucan between 5 & 6 o'clock – we got off the stage at the Queens – I went with him from the Queens Hotel – went first to Lavetts and then to McLeans – I was with him when he met Michael Donnelly – The only place I saw the Defendant was on Platform – I heard no words exchanged between McKellar & Defendant there. I was with McKellar the whole time – I know nothing about the revolver McKellar could not have called the defendant a "son of a Bitch" or told him to: "leave his way or he would put a ball through him" without my hearing it – I continued with & went home with McKellar to Walker's Hotel, and slept same room with him –

Cross Examined – I am: not on good terms with Defendant who is my brother in law – Defendant abused me – McKellar was with me – I think McKellar might have heard it—McKellar & I went into McLeans – Robinson was there about same time – I think Robinson came out or just after as I saw him there on the Platform.

his
Roday X Kennedy
mark

Sworn before me London 12 February 1876
    "L. Lawrason" P.M.

(UWO)

Peter McKellar jumped off the stagecoach and ran toward the struggling men but was confronted by John Donnelly waving a pistol in his face.

"Stand back," John warned him, "stand back or I'll shoot you."

Young Jim Donnelly suddenly appeared on the scene and, slipping off his coat, went to his brother's assistance.

"Let him go, you bastard," he said to Kennedy, catching him by the arm. Rearing back, he kicked Kennedy several times. Rhody Kennedy fell to his knees, dragging the other down with him. When they fell, Bob Donnelly began to pummel, bite, and scratch Kennedy like a cornered wildcat, sinking his teeth into his face. Young Jim also continued to pound poor Kennedy whenever he could get a blow in.

Finally, attracted by the crowd of some forty or fifty bystanders who had gathered, Constable John Bawden rescued Kennedy. As he pulled young Jim away, John Donnelly ran up and jerked his brother Bob out of Kennedy's grasp. Bob Donnelly, his revolver still in his hand, slipped through the milling crowd and escaped. Bawden lifted Kennedy to his feet. His face was covered with blood, there were great bleeding gashes around his eyes, and a piece of his lip was missing. The fight had only lasted two or three minutes but Rhody Kennedy was a badly beaten constable.

In the meantime, Peter McKellar had turned around and laid a charge of perjury against William Donnelly arising out of the evidence that Donnelly had given in the McKellar assault and threatening case. McKellar could not have threatened Donnelly with a gun, went the reasoning, for he had given it back to Bryan a short time before. Donnelly was arrested in London on this charge on February 4.

Then the charge of assault and threatening by Will Donnelly against Rhody Kennedy was heard. Once again the Crown Attorney replied to Ferguson's appeal for advice:

It is difficult to decide between parties who are both considerably in the wrong and when the evidence is contradictory. In this case, it is evident there had been considerable wrangling before the alleged assault and threatening occurred, and it is impossible to say who was the original aggressor. Donnelly's evidence is open to considerable doubt. Did he not accuse McKellar of having threatened him with a revolver on the same occasion?[10]

Hutchinson advised Ferguson that "it would be safer and better to dismiss the complaint."

Before this advice reached Ferguson, however, Lawrence Lawrason in London heard the witnesses Peter McKellar, Henry Collins; Henry Bryan, Thomas Robinson, and Rhody Kennedy in the case against William Donnelly for perjury. The latter considered the case of sufficient importance to retain the services of London lawyer John Taylor. Notwithstanding his argument that there was insufficient evidence, the police magistrate committed Donnelly for trial at the assizes.

In a day or so the parties were back in court before Henry Ferguson, but the Birr J.P., contrary to the advice of the Crown Attorney, bound Kennedy over to the assizes. He furthermore set bail at the enormous sum of seven hundred dollars! There seemed no doubt in Ferguson's mind at least that Kennedy was the trouble-maker.

But William Donnelly was not through with Kennedy yet, laying a fresh charge against him in Lucan before Squire Patrick McIlhargey of using abusive language. McIlhargey was a Catholic, a long-time friend of the Donnelly family, and a freshly appointed Justice of the Peace. On St. Valentine's Day, Rhody Kennedy was arrested, tried, convicted, and sentenced to a fine or twenty days in common jail. Being unable to pay the fine, he was quickly transported, doubtless via the Donnelly stagecoach, to the old fortress at Dundas and Ridout streets behind the Court House in London, accompanied by the ditty:

Rat, drink and be merry, Rhody,
For the next twenty days
At Lamb's hostelry.

The charges continued. In London the next day, Peter McKellar charged John Donnelly with threatening to kill him on January 24, and Detective Murphy shortly after asked Donnelly to accompany him to the police station. Donnelly at first refused, but Murphy was an old hand and knew how to handle the boys. Hard threats had to be coated with soft words. He gave him time to round up two bondsmen, William Penny and

Alfred Panton, and they soon all trooped down to the station, where Donnelly was bailed for his appearance two days later.

When the case of Rhody Kennedy versus Michael Donnelly, assault and threats, was called in Magistrate's Court in London, the defendant had not bothered to appear, for he knew that Kennedy was in London Jail. A bench warrant was nevertheless issued for Donnelly's arrest. In the next case of Peter McKellar versus John Donnelly, threats, the defendant again failed to show, and he was ordered arrested and his bail bond forfeited.

In the meantime Private Detective Hugh McKinnon had returned to Lucan. Upon his inquiring after Rhody Kennedy, all that anyone could tell him was that he had been arrested at the instance of one of the Donnellys and had not been heard from since. McKinnon thereupon dispatched a message to the office of the Crown Attorney in London: "What has been done with Kennedy upon the last arrest of the Donnellys?"

Charles Hutchinson wrote back informing McKinnon of Kennedy's imprisonment for using abusive language against William Donnelly. McKinnon was furious and quickly scribbled a reply. "How refined and delicate the feelings of the Donnellys are," he fumed, "when poor Kennedy can hurt them so easily."

Kennedy had in the meantime complained to the Crown Attorney of the excessive costs charged against him by Constable Charles Ferguson. Hutchinson agreed the complaint was valid and ordered the constable to return the excess costs. Hugh McKinnon then presented himself at Hutchinson's office, demanding that Kennedy be released to enable him to prosecute the old charge of assault against Tom Donnelly. McKinnon pointed out that in his zeal to incarcerate Kennedy, Squire McIlhargey had committed Kennedy to twenty days in jail without the option of paying his fine. Even though McKinnon was prepared to pay the fine, it seems the warrant had still to be amended before Kennedy could be released. Hutchinson immediately ordered McIlhargey to amend the warrant to forestall any suit for false imprisonment, and also arranged for Kennedy's attendance in court to give evidence against Tom Donnelly.

The case came up on February 22, and Donnelly was fined $10 and $7.80 costs. Two days later County Court Judge William Elliot heard the appeal by Robert McLeod from his conviction by Henry Ferguson at the instance of Michael Donnelly for "malicious collision". The injuries and fine had amounted to the fair sum of $35. Judge Elliot quashed the conviction and awarded costs against Donnelly. Despite all the legal manoeuvring, it was a bad week for the Donnelly boys, and Hugh McKinnon saw to it that the pressure was maintained. The corrected warrant of committal was finally returned by Squire McIlhargey, the fine paid, and Kennedy released. But he was hardly out of jail before he was back in court again, this time as complainant in a charge of assault against Michael Donnelly alleged to have been committed on January 24. Donnelly was convicted of this charge and fined $5. William Donnelly was also convicted of using abusive language towards Kennedy and fined $5 and costs.

Following Bob Donnelly's escape from Kennedy's grasp, warrants were issued against him for assault, beating, and wounding. His brother Jim was charged with the same offences, as well as aiding Bob in resisting arrest and escaping. Bob Donnelly disappeared from the district after this and stayed away for a year and a half, until the excitement of 1876 had died down.

Later that year, on May 24, 1876, Rhody Kennedy saw a fight between Jimmy Howe of Lucan and William Kent of London. When Kent knocked the Lucanite down with a shovel, Kennedy ran up, wrested the shovel from Kent, knocked him down, and began to kick him. Jimmy Howe died from his wounds, Kent went on trial for murder, and Rhody Kennedy decided he had had enough of Canadian courts for the time being. He fled to Michigan. Thus ended the tribulations of Rhody Kennedy, as far as the Donnellys were concerned.

18

FITZHENRY'S

"Unchecked rowdyism," said the *Exeter Times* of Lucan at the beginning of 1876, "is hurting the village more than the opening of the London, Huron and Bruce Railway."[1] A prime example was the events of Thursday, February 24, that year. It all began innocently enough when Tom Ryder married Hanora Mackey at St. Patrick's Church.[2] The bridal couple were then driven to Joseph Fitzhenry's hotel in Lucan, for now that the youngest of the numerous Ryder brothers had married, the family planned a celebration befitting their prosperous standing within the Catholic community. Large numbers of the Roman and Swamp Liners crowded into the little hotel for the sumptuous feast. About three o'clock in the afternoon, eight or ten of the guests wandered over to the Revere House near by for a short respite from the noisy crowd and a few quiet drinks. Among them were William Donnelly and his brother James, Jr.

Suddenly Constable John Coursey entered the bar-room of the Revere House and walked straight up to young Jim. "All right, Jim," he said, "you're under arrest. I've got a warrant against you for beating Rhody Kennedy."

Coursey patted the paper in his waist pocket. It was Lawrence Lawrason's warrant for assault and other charges arising out of the attempted arrest of Bob Donnelly by Rhody Kennedy almost a month before. Young Jim meekly went out, with Coursey accompanying him, toward Stanley's store where J.P.s Barney and William Stanley would bind Donnelly over for his court appearance. They had gone about thirty feet along the wooden sidewalk when Will Donnelly stepped out of the hotel after them.

"Jim, come back here," he called out to his brother, "don't go letting yourself get dragged along the street with that fellow. Come back here."

The touch of scorn in Will's voice was enough to prick his brother's pride. He glanced at Coursey and then turned and followed his brother back into the Revere House Coursey also went back, but on his entering Will Donnelly stepped between his brother and the constable, holding in his hand a pistol.

"I'll blow the breast out of you, Coursey, or any other man who tries to take him," Donnelly said grimly, and added, "or, for that matter, who tries to take any of our family."

Young Jim started removing his coat. "Don't worry, Will," he said, "there is no constable in Lucan that can take me."

He threw his coat down and faced the constable. Coursey looked around at the smirking faces of the crowd, all anticipating a little blood-letting and secure in the knowledge that the odds were favourable enough to ensure that it would be Coursey's .

"Have it your way," the constable muttered and left. Coursey went to see his friend and fellow constable John Bawden, a large-sized Englishman from Devonshire and a stonemason and bricklayer who had built many of the first brick buildings of the village. He knew the Donnellys well. "One night to save his own life," his niece related years after, "he jumped a freight train and was never heard from for over a year, going out West to avoid the brothers whose enmity he had incurred."

"I'll take him," Bawden replied when Coursey opined that young Donnelly's arrest should stand over until after the wedding celebration. "Just give me the warrant and some help, and we can get Reid and Ryan, too, and maybe some others."

Hugh McKinnon, before leaving the village three or four days earlier, had organized a kind of vigilance committee, with John Reid, a brother of the athletic Sandy Reid, and William Ryan, a young farm boy of McGillivray, having been appointed deputy constables. By four o'clock in the afternoon the four constables headed over to the Revere House. They found that the stray wedding guests had returned to Fitzhenry's. As the constables approached the Catholic tavern, they spied

Hugh McKinnon

Tom Ryder, at whose wedding celebration at Fitzhenry's Hotel in Lucan the Donnelly brothers fought with the Lucan constables. Sketch made in 1880 by Robert Harris. (PEI)

Stratford
Feby 22, 1876

C. Hutchinson Esq
Barrister
London
Dear Sir –

I have been for some time back engaged in ferreting out the perpetrators of certain crimes which have been committed in Lucan & its vicinity. I have sufficient evidence in my possession to convict certain parties who have committed those crimes – I don't know if Pat Flanigan ever laid an information before a magistrate either for the burning of his stable or the attempted murder of himself – If he has not done so before the Police Magistrate in London would you please write him to come in to do so at once – His address is McGillivray P.O. He resides in "Irish town". I would also want Caswell who had his barn burned stock killed & crops destroyed to do the same but we will attend to his case again – In the meantime we want to attend re Flanagan's barns. I presume you are already familiar with a great many circumstances connected with those crimes & offences which from time to time have been committed in Lucan by the so-called "Ku-Klux" – When do your Assizes take place and who is to be the Judge – I am at present in Stratford where I will remain until I hear from you – Please let me hear from you by return mail – Do not mention my name to any person but Flanagan at present – For the past 3 weeks I was in Lucan & so managed matters that only to those who should know was my real character known & so make use – & so I desire thus to remain for a few days yet.

Yours truly
Hugh McKinnon

P.S. What has been done with Kennedy upon the last arrest by the Donnellys?

H. McKinnon.

(UWO)

young Jim Donnelly and his brother entering the bar-room.

With John Reid in the lead, the constables burst in after them. The small room contained a huge crowd. Reid had to push through the wedding guests toward the rear kitchen, leaving Bawden and the others simply scanning the many faces. John Donnelly suddenly appeared out of the crowd, in his shirt sleeves.

"Bawden, what's this about?" he demanded, catching hold of the constable's coat.

By way of reply John Bawden seized hold of Donnelly's shirt and declared, "You're under arrest."

"What?" said Donnelly. "Can't you leave us alone this day and mind your own business? Remember, Bawden, when you arrested me before, I went with you like a man, didn't I?"

"Yes, when you had to," Bawden answered.

"Then let go of me," said Donnelly heatedly. "Let me go or I'll kill you, you son of a bitch."

At this moment Reid came back from the kitchen and ran up to John Donnelly. "You are under arrest in the name of the Queen," he cried out, also taking hold of him. "I have a warrant for you."

The Main Street of Lucan, taken in the early morning of july 19, 1888

"Go away, you son of a bitch," Donnelly said turning to Reid. "Let me go or else I'll kill you." Then, struggling to get away, he turned to the crowd and yelled, "Help! Help!"

Standing around were a trio of young Keefes, Jimmy, Pat, and young Bob, as well as William Farrell, William Denby, and one or two of the young Hodgins boys. "Let him go! Let him go!" they cried out and closed in around the constables.

Bawden shouted, "In the name of the Queen, I call upon every man present to help arrest this man. He is our prisoner."

Bedlam broke loose. Ryan and Coursey, who had remained near the door, pushed through the throng, and all four constables took hold of John Donnelly and tried to shove him towards the door. The crowd pushed them back. Bawden's feet were knocked out from under him, but as he fell he dragged Donnelly down with him.

As Reid bent over to help Bawden, Will Donnelly suddenly appeared brandishing a four-barrelled pistol in one hand and a heavy cudgel in the other. "Let him go," Will yelled at Reid, "or I'll shoot you."

John Bawden, the Lucan constable, in his Fenian Raid uniform, 1866 (A. O. Williams)

William Ryan and his wife. In 1876 Ryan was a Lucan deputy constable who participated in the affair at Fitzhenry's Hotel (Mrs. E. Rankin)

Donnelly fired a shot into the ceiling. Reid reacted by reaching into his pocket and pulling out his own gun, a six-barrelled revolver, but before he could make use of it William Denby made a grab for it. Young Farrell, standing beside Will Donnelly, then seized the cudgel from Donnelly's hand and with a deft stroke brought it down on the nose of the constable. Reid fell in a daze, gushing blood on everyone and raising the excitement to a fever pitch. Will again fired into the ceiling. With his free hand he pulled out a second revolver and brandished both pistols wildly.

In a matter of seconds Reid staggered to his feet. Bleeding profusely and still in a daze, he managed to spot Farrell about eight feet away. Pointing his revolver, he shot. One account has it that the shot missed its mark, but another version – the Donnelly one – states that there were two shots from Reid's gun and both hit William Farrell, though neither of them hurt him seriously. Wounded or not, Farrell seized the four-barrel pistol from Will Donnelly, gave back the cudgel that had just broken Reid's nose, and ran out into the hallway with the constable after him. Reid caught Farrell by the collar in the hallway and began to beat him "about the head in a fearful manner" with his gun. He dragged him to the outside door, Farrell doubled over trying to ward off the blows but still hanging on to his gun. At the doorway the two men stumbled over the tongue of a sleigh which had been carelessly left at the entrance. As they fell, Farrell's pistol, pointed at Reid's stomach just below the ribs, went off. The first shot may have been accidental, but there was no doubt of the second. Young Farrell scrambled to his feet and taking point-blank aim at the constable, wounded and struggling to get up, shot him again in the stomach. Reid fell back. Farrell ran off with Coursey and Ryan after him.

Inside the bar-room John Donnelly and Bawden were still on the floor, the former on top and pummelling the constable. Donnelly suddenly jumped to his feet and made his way to the bar. Bawden also scrambled up, and followed and seized hold of him again.

"You son of a bitch," Donnelly cried, "if you don't let me go I'll kill you."

Will Donnelly stepped up to Bawden still brandishing his cudgel in one hand and with the other he raised the revolver to Bawden's face. "You son of a bitch," he said, "if you don't let him go I'll shoot you."

When Bawden refused to release his grip, Donnelly fired over the constable's head. Still Bawden did not flinch. Instead, he shoved John Donnelly towards the door. John seized the constable's coat as he lurched forward. The two men hurtled over the bar-room stove and went down once more to the floor. Will fired again, aiming just to miss the constable, and then clouted him several times over the head with the shillelagh. With the help of the crowd, John Donnelly scrambled to his feet and ran out the door, but this time when Bawden tried to follow, one of the Hodgins boys tripped him just as he reached the door. The fall knocked the wind out of him. Donnelly had escaped. The crowd in the little room quickly dispersed until, besides the constable, only young Hodgins and one other person were left.

Bawden slowly got up, retrieved his hat and watch dropped in the melee, and went out to find Reid Lying beside the tongue of the sleigh. His hat was on the ground beside him and he was bleeding. Coursey and Ryan appeared at just about the same time, empty-handed. They picked Reid up and carried him over to Barney Stanley's store. Dr. James Sutton, on his arrival, found that both bullets had entered the abdominal cavity, and Reid's life was feared for.

JOHN REID – sworn   I was a county constable on 24 Feby last – I had a warrant which I now put in marked A for the arrest of John Donelly, one of the defendants for an Assault – I went with that warrant with John Bawden & John Courcy two other constables – I was aware that Bawden had a warrant to arrest the prisoner James Donelly & I went with him to assist him in executing that warrant. I went into the Bar room and from that into the kitchen in search of James Donelly – did not find him – I then returned to the Bar room – I there saw Prisoner John Donelly, in hold with Constable Bawden – John Donelly made use of the words "Let go of me Bawden or I'll kill you you son of a Bitch" – I then arrested John Donelly in the name of the Queen telling him I had a warrant for him – I took hold of him & took him towards the door, and he resisted & threatened me – He hallo'd for me to let him go, and for help from the crowd – When I told him I had this warrant he said "Go away you son of a bitch" – I got him towards the Door and several of the crowd pulled him back – Three of the Keefes and one Denby were assisting him – Bawden & John Donelly fell on the floor & Donelly was beating Bawden with his fist on the floor – William Donelly stood by and swore that if I did not let him go he'd shoot me – I drew my revolver out of my pocket and Denby grabbed it and tried to wrench it out of my hand – I got John Donelly & Bawden on their feet again & got them towards the door – Then I saw Wm Donelly with a Revolver in his hand & heard the report of a pistol – immediately after that William Farrell got a heavy walking stick from Wm Donelly and struck me a heavy blow with it across the nose which broke my nose in and cut my face in two places which left scars and broke the bridge of my nose – Then I shot at Farrel – he was about eight feet from me at the time. Farrel ran and I followed him and caught him in the Hall & dragged him out of the door – I fell over a sleigh tongue dragged him with me & then he fired one shot at me which took effect in my side – I then let go of him & I was helped away by Bawden & another man – On examining the wound at Stanley's store about 8 or 10 minutes after I found I had received two pistol shots I don't know when I received the other shot – Doctor Sutton attended me I was laid up 17 days – and was confined to my bed for six days from the wounds – I did not see James Donelly – John Donelly did not strike or kick me – but was kicking & striking Bawden when I had him under arrest.

Cross Examined – I was appointed a County Constable 3 or 4 days before this took place – I live at Lucan – I got the warrant form Bawden, two days before – Bawden did not tell me that he read the warrant over to the Donnellys and that he did not intend to enforce it – I only fired one shot at Farrel – don't know whether it struck him or not – I don't think that Farrel had a pistol in the Bar room – or in the Hall – I first saw the pistol in Farrel's hand when he got up after falling over the sleigh tongue. I think it was a four Barrel pistol – mine was a six Barrel revolver. I went in first to make the arrest – I don't know where this warrant was previous to its coming into my hands – I saw a pistol in Wm Donelly's hands a Revolver. I heard the report of one pistol in the Bar room & I think two in the Hall. I did not draw my revolver until after William Donelly had his drawn in his hand, and had threatened to shoot me, when I drew it in self defence.

"John Reid"

Sworn before me London 10 March 1876
        "L Lawrason" J.P.

(UWO)

Word quickly spread that the Donnellys had "over-awed" the constables at the Catholic tavern, and had shot Constable John Reid. The news aroused the Orange blood of the predominantly Protestant villagers, especially since all of the constables involved were Protestant, and the fracas had occurred at the Catholic wedding celebration. Potentate Barney Stanley deemed it necessary to call out the militia. Soon the stalwart butchers, stonemasons, carpenters, shoemakers, grocers, and assorted yeomen of Number Five Company of the Fourth Rifle Brigade of the Sixth Battalion (better known as the Lucan Volunteers) were issued their Enfield rifles at the drill shed on the edge of the village square. Before the ranks could be drawn up, a message arrived that the foe had decamped. The Donnellys, the Keefes, and the rest of their supporters had all piled into a sleigh driven by blond, bewhiskered Robert Keefe and had headed for the Roman Line. Undeterred, and about thirty strong, the Lucan Volunteers requisitioned a wagon and a team of horses and followed.

Sometimes demanding admittance in the name of the Queen or, depending on the house, without any warning, the militiamen of Lucan stormed into house after house on the Roman Line. Their foray must have evoked the exciting tales told by their fathers and grandfathers of the old days in Ireland when the local Orange Lodge enforced the laws against contraband Catholic arms, while to the Catholics whose houses were searched it brought back less pleasant memories. Those days were recalled by William Carleton, the Irish writer:

...One night in midwinter there was a battering at the door of his father's house, much bellowing of uncomplimentary remarks about traitors and rebels. The yeomen crowded in over the threshold, armed and uniformed, bayonets screwed on their guns and pointed menacingly at his father.... They wanted the old man's gun, the papist gun, the rascally rebel gun. They called his father a liar. They called his mother a liar. They jabbed his sister in the side with the bayonet because the bed in which she lay might conceal a gun.... He remembered that incident against yeomen. He remembered it against Orangeism, against bigotry, against the glorious, pious and immortal

memory of me Dutch king who crossed the Boyne on a white horse....[3]

The militiamen eventually came to the farm of Matthew Keefe, who had long since departed to meet his Maker, but who had been succeeded on the farm by his son Dan. On this occasion, however, Dan Keefe was unable to greet his unexpected company, for he was serving five years for highway robbery. The Volunteers entered. In a minute or two they found James Donnelly, Jr., in one of the bedrooms, hiding sheepishly between two feather ticks. They dispatched him to Lucan, handcuffed and with an armed guard, while the rest of the men pushed on up the Roman Line.

On the way they met William Casey, himself a fugitive from justice almost twenty years before on the charge of murdering the Englishman Brimmacombe. He and the Donnellys were not good friends. What assistance Casey may have given the militiamen is not known, but as they approached the Donnelly farm they were wary. A figure of a man suddenly ran out the back door of the house.

"Halt!" they shouted. "You're under arrest."

The man kept running through the open field towards the woods at the rear of the farm. Three shots were fired at the fleeing form. As the bullets whistled uncomfortably close to him, the running man stopped in his tracks and, taking off his cap, waved it high in the air.

"Mercy, boys, mercy," cried John Donnelly. "I'm coming. I'm coming." And he gave himself up.

Flushed with success at capturing two of the Donnelly desperadoes, the Volunteers made a meticulous search of the house and farm buildings and then returned to Lucan with the second prisoner.

Back in the village "the greatest excitement prevailed amongst the villagers ...and threats of lynching were freely indulged in by the exasperated populace." Rumours straggled back that Will Donnelly and young Farrell had fled the district, while other rumours had it that they had been tracked to a large swamp in McGillivray Township, that a large party had gone out and surrounded the swamp, and that it was just a matter of time until they were caught. Still other rumours circulated that Will and Farrell had not left the Catholic Settlement at all but had spent the night continuing the wedding celebration at the old Ryder homestead on the Roman Line.

Hugh McKinnon was quickly summoned back, and the Lucan Vigilance Committee sent telegrams to all of the towns and villages of the surrounding countryside to be on the lookout for the fugitives. William Porte, the postmaster who also served as telegraph operator, harboured little sympathy for McKinnon and the constables, but what finally provoked him to an outburst was the constables' request for a telegram to the Chief of Police in St. Catharines asking for the apprehension of Porte's particularly good friend, Patrick Donnelly. In the bar-room of one of the Lucan hotels, Porte, after a few drinks, was heard to bellow, "I'm a Donnelly man, by Christ!" The St. Catharines police refused to comply with the request anyway.

Driving the stagecoach to London the next day, Michael Donnelly, short-tempered and short-handed, showed no restraint in expressing his opinion of the uproar. He, too, was arrested, it was reported, "for using some distasteful language with reference to the affair" and bailed to appear the next day.

Upon receipt in London of a report that "the Donnelly boys were murdering everybody in Lucan, and assistance was wanted from the London police," Detectives Harry Phair, Hugh Murphy, and Thomas Johnston were dispatched to the village. Although there was a great excitement in the streets, they found nothing particularly amiss. When the three policemen paid Michael Donnelly's house a call, he met them at the door, informed them none of his brothers was there, and invited them to look through the house. The three men returned to London questioning the emotional equilibrium of the Lucanites who had called for help .

But the villagers insisted they knew only too well how the Donnelly Gang, as they called them, could go on a rampage and have little proved against them. About this time it was reported that in nearby McGillivray

a man named Barry and his wife were sleeping at home one night, when the house was broken into by the Donnellys and Farrell and some other of the gang, and robbed of a keg of butter, a chest of tea, and some tobacco, knives and forks and about a dollar in money.[4]

Another report stated that "the gang broke down the door and took one dollar and some pork – failing to get $300 which Barry had recently got in trade but had wisely left with the parish priest." A third report said the men battered down the door and held a gun to old Barry's head while demanding the whereabouts of his money. Warrants were sworn out for the arrest of Tom Donnelly and his alleged companions in the episode.

William Denby, of London, in the meantime remained at Michael Donnelly's house following the brawl to help operate the stagecoach. But on the following Monday, Denby, not generally known in the village, made a foray into the enemy's camp, representing himself as "deputied by the Press of London" to inquire into the recent excitement in the village. He explained his presence at Donnelly's as an attempt to get the other side of the story. In this guise Denby made the rounds of the local taverns until

in his perambulations he came across Detective McKinnon...and that gentleman having heard of his business, offered him every opportunity of becoming acquainted with the facts, ending by soliciting him to visit the magistrate's office. This, however, the bogus Press man would not do, having, as McKinnon alleges, "smelt a large mice".[5]

The next morning McKinnon and his Vigilance Committee called at Mike's house. They summoned Denby out, escorted him to the village limits, and told him to clear out. It was only after banishing him that McKinnon and his crew realized that Denby had in fact been a party to the fracas at Fitzhenry's. A warrant was issued for his arrest, but he had by then decamped for London.

Up to this time Detective Hugh McKinnon had suffered under the delusion that the Donnelly brothers were unaware that he was operating as an undercover agent. It was time, he felt, to reveal himself. On Wednesday, March 1, he drove out to the Donnelly homestead with the warrant for the arrest of Tom Donnelly in his pocket. The warrant related to the robbery of the man Barry. McKinnon knocked on the door and Mrs. Donnelly answered.

"Is Thomas here?" asked the detective.

Just as he spoke, Tom Donnelly, "the most dangerous of the gang" and a man to be reckoned with on any occasion, appeared from another room.[6] McKinnon produced his private detective's badge and said, "I want you to come with me. You are my prisoner."

As McKinnon later told the story: "For a moment the man was thunderstruck, but realizing the trick that had been played, with a terrible oath he sprang for a weapon of defence." Then McKinnon modestly conceded, "But I was too quick for him, and in order to secure him as my prisoner I had to punish him severely."

Both James Donnelly, Sr., and his wife were present on this occasion and, aside from the Hamilton detective's version, it is difficult to know exactly what took place, but it is entirely likely there was no violence at all and that both parents admonished their son not to resist arrest. As Tom was being taken away, however, old James Donnelly addressed McKinnon.

"There be only one thing I ask of ye, sar," said the curly-haired old man, "and that is to leave me, when all is done, wid me son John."

Tom was taken to Fox's store in Lucan, where three Lucan Justices of the Peace, the two elder Stanleys and William H. Ryan, committed him for trial in London, along with young Alex Levett.

Later that day when Michael Donnelly returned to the village after the day's stagecoach run, the Lucan Vigilance Committee picked him up, too. According to Donnelly, it was Big John Bawden who jumped him, and after a hard struggle the constable and his cohorts managed to get a pair of handcuffs on him and led him, thus manacled, through the streets and alleys of Lucan to the Central Hotel. He was lodged in an upstairs bedroom and held prisoner for four days. No warrant was out for his arrest.[7]

For a short while longer the Lucan Vigilance Committee remained active. At three o'clock in the morning of March 2, it visited the home of Billy Atkinson. In the heavily muffled crowd, besides McKinnon and Bawden, were Sandy Reid,

Arthur Gray, Henry Collins, Albert McLean, Jim Hodgins, and Jacob Palmer, as well as Billy Atkinson's three brothers, David, Jim, and Thomas.[8] Billy's wife Rebecca answered the door. McKinnon told her to get her husband, that he was to get dressed and accompany them. Atkinson was blindfolded, loaded into a sleigh, and driven off toward the Sauble River.

"Tell us about Donnellys' burning of Flanagan's stable," they demanded, but Atkinson made no reply.

"Who stole Mick Carroll's meat?" another asked.

Atkinson answered, "I heard it was Farrell."

"Who else?"

"I don't know," he responded, and after further prodding, "I heard it was the Donnellys, but I don't know anything about it."

"Where is young Farrell?"

"I don't know."

"What about Henry Collins' sheepskins, what do you know about them?"

"Nothing."

"Where is Farrell?"

"I heard he's gone to Seaforth."

"What else do you know?"

"Nothing else."

"We don't believe you. Come on, tell us everything or you'll be sorry."

Finally the sleigh came to a stop beside the river flats and everyone got out. A rope was produced, Billy's hands were tied firmly behind him, and then the rope was slung around his neck. Two men climbed into a tree and stood on a strong limb holding the other end.

"Now, I want you to tell all you know about these Donnellys," ordered McKinnon, for Atkinson recognized his voice. When Billy insisted he knew nothing, the detective said, "All right, boys, pull him up."

Billy was hoisted into the air by the two men above – he recognized them as his own brother James, and Arthur Gray, when the bandage slipped away from his eyes – his heels dangling above the ground. Then they let him down and repeated the question. Five or six times they elevated him, but he refused to talk.

Finally they untied Atkinson and took him back to the village. As soon as he was freed, however, John Bawden came up, the scarf now removed from his face, and said, "You're under arrest."

For a day and a night Billy Atkinson was kept locked in a room of the Queen's Hotel before being released.

Billy returned home, nursing a sore neck. Slinking around the village with shoulders hunched and coat turned up at the collar, he showed the raw rope burn on his neck to two or three Lucanites, including shopkeeper Michael Crunnican. The whole village seemed strangely quiet. Atkinson went over to Mike Donnelly's house. No, Nellie did not know where her husband was and had not seen any of his brothers for days, although she had heard that Tom had been taken in custody to London along with Alex Levett. She didn't know about the others. Billy Atkinson decided to take an extended vacation with friends in Kalamazoo, Michigan, and quietly slipped out of the village. He stayed away for several weeks.

ASSIZES

The list of criminal charges which the Donnelly brothers had to face during the first three months of 1876 alone is awesome:[1]

1. James Donnelly, Jr., arson of Flanagan's stable in Lucan;
2. James Donnelly, Jr., assault on Joe Berryhill;
3. James Donnelly, Jr., resisting arrest by Constable Coursey;
4. James Donnelly, Jr., arson of John Flanagan's barn;
5. James Donnelly, Jr., assault and wounding Rhody Kennedy;
6. William Donnelly, perjury charged by Peter McKellar;
7. William Donnelly, arson of Flanagan's stable in Lucan;
8. William Donnelly, obstructing a lawful arrest;
9. William Donnelly, abusive language against Rhody Kennedy;
10. William Donnelly, shooting with intent;
11. John Donnelly, assault and threatening Peter McKellar;
12. John Donnelly, arson of Flanagan's stable in Lucan;
13. John Donnelly, assault and wounding Constables Bawden, Reid and Coursey;
14. Joho Donnelly, arson of John Flanagan's barn;
15. Patrick Donnelly, assault on Joe Berryhill;
16. Michael Donnelly, threatening Peter McKellar;
17. Michael Donnelly, threatening Henry Bryan;
18. Michael Donnelly, assault on Rhody Kennedy;
19. Michael Donnelly, threatening to shoot Brown;
20. Michael Donnelly, abusive language;
21. Michael Donnelly, arson of Flanagan's stable in Lucan;
22. Robert Donnelly, assault on Rhody Kennedy;
23. Robert Donnelly, assault on Carling;
24. Robert Donnelly, assault and wounding Rhody Kennedy;
25. Robert Donnelly, arson of Flanagan's stable at Lucan;
26. Thomas Donnelly, assault on Rhody Kennedy;
27. Thomas Donnelly, assault on Joseph Hauley;
28. Thomas Donnelly, robbery of Barry;
29. Thomas Donnelly, attempted arson of Flanagan's stable in Lucan;
30. Thomas Donnelly, arson of Flanagan's stable;
31. Thomas Donnelly, arson of John Flanagan's barn;
32. Thomas Donnelly, theft from Easdale;
33. Thomas Donnelly, assault and robbery of James Curry.

But, as Michael Donnelly would say, "there are always two sides to a story", and the cataloguing of the charges in this fashion produces an exaggerated effect. Some of the items consist of one charge against several defendants, and several of the incidents out of which the charges arose relate to a period of time before the three months' period referred to. At least two of the charges – against Tom Donnelly for the robbery of Barry and Michael Donnelly for the arson of John Flanagan's barn – seem not to have been pursued formally beyond the arrest or, if pursued, were thrown out by the Grand Jury, while several of the charges, such as the one against Patrick Donnelly, went so far as the finding of a True Bill by the Grand Jury and were then dropped.[2] Again, many of the offences were minor and were disposed of by Justices of the Peace.

Nevertheless, the fact remains that at the Spring Assizes for the County of Middlesex, which commenced in London on March 10, 1876, with Mr. Justice Joseph Curran Morrison presiding, there were at least a dozen criminal charges facing the brothers, and it is little wonder that the sittings were referred to as the Donnelly Assizes. The Grand Jury found True Bills in the following cases against them:

1. The Queen vs. Thomas Donnelly, attempt at arson;
2. The Queen vs. William Donnelly, John Donnelly, William Earrell, James Keefe, and William Denby, assault on a constable;
3. The Queen vs. Thomas Donnelly, arson;
4. The Queen vs. William Donnelly and John Donnelly, assault on a constable;
5. The Queen vs. William Donnelly, shooting with intent;
6. The Queen vs. James Donnelly, Jr., assault on Rhody Kennedy;
7. The Queen vs. John Donnelly, assault on Peter McKellar;
8. The Queen vs. Thomas Donnelly, and James Donnelly, Jr., arson;
9. The Queen vs. Thomas Donnelly, larceny from Easdale;
10. The Queen vs. James Donnelly, Jr., and William Donnelly, assault on Constable Coursey;
11. The Queen vs. James Donnelly, Jr., Patrick Donnelly, and James Keefe, assault on Joe Berryhill;
12. The Queen vs. Thomas Donnelly, highway robbery of James Curry.

Their fortunes at a low ebb, the brothers in custody retained David Glass as defence counsel. He applied for bail on behalf of Jim and John Donnelly, but the magistrate refused on grounds that the charges were much too serious; besides, he

Justice Joseph Curran Morrison, who presided at the Middlesex Spring Assizes at London in 1876

stated that John Donnelly had been bailed before him shortly before and had not appeared as required.

Meanwhile Michael Donnelly, after four days of incarceration in an upstairs bedroom of the Central Hotel in Lucan, finally found himself unguarded and broke out through a window. He stole into London and went to see David Glass. Glass advised him to stay out of sight for a few days yet.

The Donnelly Stagecoach had in the meantime ground to a halt. "The stages have ceased to run between Exeter and Lucan," the press reported, and "the mail stage between the same village has come down to an old white horse driven by Mr. Hobbs...." Johannah Donnelly, said to be "on

David Glass, defence counsel for the Donnelly brothers at the Spring Assizes, 1876 (Manitoba Archives)

Zackariah McIlhargey. An altar boy at St. Patrick's in his youth, he was related by blood or by marriage to a great many of the families of the Catholic Settlement in Biddulph. (J. McIlhargey)

the warpath" and vowing to wreak vengeance on Hugh McKinnon at first sight, persuaded her husband, then sixty-one years of age but still spry, to resume for the time being his old occupation of stagecoach driving.[3] He was assisted by Michael (Mick) O'Connor, married to Mary Hastings who as a girl had lived on Dan Keefe's farm. The O'Connors were notorious for operating an illicit groggery in Lucan, which the licence inspector had closed shortly before.[4]

Before the beginning of the Assizes, the Donnelly brothers were brought up from the cells again and again, whether for trial of the minor charges or for preliminary hearings in preparation for the higher court. A witness, Edwin Grange, showed up one morning so drunk and loud that he was thrown into the cells to sober up. On Friday, March 10, James Donnelly, Sr., came to court and was sitting in the body of the courtroom when three of his sons – James, Jr., John, and Thomas – were brought up in chains for preliminary hearing in the Berryhill assault. As Joe Berryhill related from the witness box how Keefe and several of the brothers had mobbed him, the grizzled old man rose up in his seat and, pushing his way out through the spectators, muttered half aloud, "Ye'll sup sorrow yit, Joe Berryhill."

Meanwhile, Will Donnelly remained at large. The daughter of Zackariah McIlhargey has told of his coming to her father's home and, quite relaxed, picking a fiddle off the kitchen wall and knocking out jigs and reels by the score without seeming the least apprehensive about his fugitive status. He told the family to take word back to the authorities in London that he had not left the country as reported by some sources, but was within a couple of miles of Lucan and would give himself up if the search parties ceased. He objected to being taken by a mob. The manner of his final surrender was related by his only son: "When things had quieted down a bit, he took the gray mare and rode it into London to give himself up."

The day was Wednesday, March 15. Donnelly went first to consult A. J. B. Macdonald, and this legal worthy advised him to consider very seriously the consequences of surrendering. When Donnelly insisted he was innocent of all charges and would assume the responsibility, the lawyer accompanied him to the Court House. There he was taken in charge by an old acquaintance, Deputy Sheriff Sam Glass, a brother of the brothers' defence counsel.

Young William Farrell was never brought to account for his part in the Fitzhenry Hotel fracas. For a time he remained in hiding, nursing his wounds. The Donnellys claimed he had been given a fearful beating about the head in the melee, "leaving several gashes which will take some time to heal". Farrell then disappeared from the district and apparently never returned.

A couple of days after Will's surrender, John Donnelly, charged with assaulting Peter McKellar, came up before the police magistrate. "The defendant says he is not prepared for his defence and prefers to have the case sent for trial at the Assizes," it was reported, and the court obliged. On the same day Will Donnelly was convicted of using abusive language towards Rhody Kennedy and fined $5 and costs or twenty days. Already confined on more serious charges, he took the twenty days.

In the meantime, the intrepid Hugh McKinnon was zealously rounding up witnesses against the brothers. He learned of the whereabouts of James Churchill and immediately took the Grand Trunk Railway to Sarnia.

He called upon him, and told him that he had a sick horse in Ailsa Craig which he wished him to visit. He gave him money to purchase his ticket, and got on the train with him. As they neared Ailsa Craig he told the farrier that he had neglected to mention that the sick horse was in Lucan, and that his name was Donnelly. Churchill understood at once what was wanted...but was exceedingly loath to give evidence, and it was only after a great deal of persuasion that he was induced to do so.[5]

The first case involving the brothers to be tried at the Spring Assizes for the County of Middlesex in 1876 was that of William Donnelly, charged with shooting with intent. It was an exciting trial, held March 29 in a crowded courtroom. The various constables all gave their testimony, describing the wild melee at Fitzhenry's, how the wedding guests had set upon them, and how the defendant had wantonly fired his pistols at them. Then it was the turn of the defence. John Donnelly testified on behalf of his brother that the pistol William Donnelly had brandished was broken and could not be fired. "It would not go off," he swore, "though prisoner had wished to discharge it." He could not explain on cross-examination, however, why the gun had in that case been loaded with shot. It was after six o'clock in the evening when the jury brought in its verdict on the three counts of common assault, aggravated assault, and shooting with intent to maim. The verdict was Guilty on the third count.

Post-trial machinations immediately followed. Mr. Glass asked that the jury be polled, but this did not alter the result. Then the foreman of the jury, George Randall, handed in a note to Justice Morrison stating that the jury had made a mistake, and the Judge said he would take the matter under consideration in meting out sentence. A report of the incident in the newspaper prompted the following letter shortly after:

To The Editor of the *Free Press*.
Sir,
In your report of the Queen vs. William Donnelly it is stated Mr. Randall, foreman of the empanelled jury in the above case, sent a communication to the Judge that the jury intended in finding the prisoner guilty of the third count in the indictment was finding him guilty of the offence of common assault. It was distinctly understood that the prisoner was guilty of

shooting with intent to maim, which was the third count in the indictment, and such finding was thoroughly understood by each juror in the jury room; and we were not consulted in said communication in any way by the said Geo. Randall.

Signed,
ONE OF THE JURY.[6]

Meanwhile, the sentencing of William Donnelly was postponed until the judge had time to reflect upon the appropriate penalty.

At the conclusion of the case, another curious little scene occurred. Defence counsel Glass rose from his seat and addressed the court: "My Lord, I wish to refer to the action taken by the detectives who worked up the Donnelly case just concluded. Several of the brothers are now in custody, and in lawful custody, but one of them, Michael Donnelly, has been kept by the detectives for several days locked up without a warrant. He is now free of custody, and he has instructed me to state that if there is any charge to be made against him, I am able to undertake to have him appear in court tomorrow."

Mr. Justice Morrison shook his head. "I know nothing of what you say, Mr. Glass," he told the lawyer, "and I can give you no answer in regard to this matter. The detectives, of course, would be best able to deal with the matter, if they see fit."

The next day James Donnelly, Jr., was tried for the assault on Joe Berryhill, the jury bringing in a verdict of Guilty on the count of aggravated assault. Again the Judge reserved sentencing. As John Donnelly was being brought up from the cells for the next case, Glass got together with the Crown Counsel acting at the assizes, Frederick Davis, Q.C., of Sarnia, for some plea bargaining. A deal was struck and as John Donnelly entered the dock, Glass addressed the court. "My Lord," he said, "in the next case of The Queen versus John Donnelly, on behalf of the prisoner I am consenting to a plea of Guilty being entered if the prisoner is arraigned on the charge of common assault."

The charge was accordingly read and the clerk of the court intoned, "How do you plead to the charge, guilty or nor guilty?"

"Not guilty," Donnelly replied in a firm, strong voice.

Glass quickly jumped up and went over to his client, hurriedly trying to explain the bargain that had been made with the Crown whereby the more serious charges would be dropped if he pleaded guilty to the least serious of them.

"How do you plead to the charge?" the clerk asked again.

"Not guilty," John Donnelly replied once more. "I had nothing to do with the row at all. Let the trial go on."

"My Lord," puffed Glass, "may I beg the court's indulgence for a word with my client." Glass then took great pains to point out to Donnelly that the evidence against him was strong enough to have just convicted his brother William and that it was sufficient to convict him, too, on the more serious charge if he persisted in his folly. Donnelly was finally persuaded to enter a plea of Guilty.

Justice Morrison then meted out the punishment to the three who had been convicted. He sentenced each to the Central Prison in Toronto: John for three months and James and William for nine months each. Court was adjourned for the day and the sittings concluded with no other Donnelly cases disposed of.

While most of the public seemed generally satisfied with the result of the Donnelly trials, there were great cluckings among some about their cost. In one day alone, it was reported, the Judge had signed an order for $178 to cover expenses of witnesses and "in that quarter the amount paid the county, including the amount payable by the Government, for the one item of witnesses in these cases against the Donnellys was $593.95 [which] is exclusive of all costs incurred for constables' attendance, preliminary magistrates' suits, etc." The report concluded: "The expense of the administration of justice on account of that lawless faction in Biddulph, in the last 4 or 5 years, has been extraordinary."

Upon conclusion of the assizes, the Bailiff of the Central Prison arrived in London by train on the evening of April 10 with four prisoners in tow and left the next morning for Toronto with seven more prisoners added to his chain, including young Jim and John Donnelly.[7] Will Donnelly did not form part of this chain gang.

Will was said to have scoffed at his sentence. "A

paltry nine months!" he is reported to have said. "Why, that much I can do on my head." He decided instead to do it on his back. His enemies claimed that he tricked the authorities by "playing sick" and persuaded them to place him in the Debtors' Ward of the London Jail. Here he was reported to be lying ill "of a low fever", and so serious was the illness, it was said, that his wife Norah was allowed to minister to him in jail. The authorities had been persuaded that he was suffering from a disease of the spine which in all probability would prove fatal. "Spinelessness!" his enemies muttered. "Afraid to take his punishment like a man."

Nevertheless, his doctor was reported to have said, "Nothing but the Lucan atmosphere will restore tone and vigour to the drooping William," and after allowing him to languish for a month in the jail, they released him to return home to die. On April 30, exactly one month after being convicted and sentenced to nine months' imprisonment, William Donnelly rode home to Lucan in a hack, a free man.

20

DAMAGES

Michael and Nellie Donnelly's first child arrived at the Donnelly homestead on February 8 in that turbulent year of 1876.[1] The stagecoach troubles were then rampant, the air was thick with charges and counter-charges, and Hugh McKinnon had come back to Lucan as the month began after his first short visit in the fall.

Shortly after the fracas at Fitzhenry's and before he himself was locked up, Michael Donnelly wrote a letter of protest to the editor of the London *Advertiser*. It read:[2]

It has been represented that the Donnelly family are a terror to the neighbourhood in which they live, and no one dare oppose them as stage drivers on the road between Lucan and London. This assertion I beg

leave to contradict, and have no doubt it is made for the sole purpose of injuring my character and confidence in me as a driver....

He stated that the fight at Fitzhenry's was the fault the constables who provoked his brothers into it.

Reid and Bawden, although they had a warrant for the arrest of them for some time previous in their possession, failed to execute it for weeks although daily opportunity offered for their doing so. But on the 24th February there was a wedding party being held at Mr. Fitzhenry's tavern...and then and there, in a most provoking and unjustifiable manner, Constables Reid, Bawden and Coursey proceeded....

Moreover, he stated the constables exaggerated their injuries.

Reid was reported fatally wounded, and Bawden cut badly about the head. But Bawden's wounds were not of so serious a nature as reported in the newspapers, for he was around the same evening as hale and hearty as though nothing was the matter with him. And he came to London the next morning with the prisoners.

And as for the Flanagans, Michael Donnelly said, revealing perhaps more than he intended:

I and my brothers have met with every kind of opposition at the hands of a certain party residing in the vicinity of Lucan for some time back, and every attempt made by us to frustrate them has failed. They have done our business much harm without any just cause. All this is done in order to run us off the road....

Donnelly concluded his letter by stating he hoped his "true statements of the case" might prevent the minds of the public from being altogether poisoned against "the Donnelly Tribe, as one of your local papers chose to term us".

The letter was dated March 1, 1876. The next day John Bawden and the Lucan Vigilance Committee pounced on him and locked him up in the Central Hotel.

Michael Donnelly escaped the Spring Assizes, but his brother William remained in London Jail for another month while John and James, Jr., were in Toronto's Central Prison. Tom Donnelly also remained in London Jail to await his trials, the

John Bawden (E. Quigley)

Crown Attorney worrying that the witnesses against him could not be found. He referred, among others, to Rhody Kennedy "I heard he was in hiding," wrote Hutchinson. He notified the Attorney General's office in Toronto that Detective Hugh McKinnon was anxious that Tom Donnelly be refused bail, and the Hamilton detective himself wrote to the Attorney General in the same vein.[3] Bail was accordingly refused.

In mid-April came another disappointment for Michael Donnelly and the stagecoach line when the six-month mail contract from London to Exeter and Clinton was awarded to Richard Bryant. Bryant himself was still convalescing from complications from his fractured leg. He nevertheless assumed the contract and hired a new driver, one Joe Watson, of Lucan. Watson was reputed to be a tough egg.

Pressed for funds and doubtless guided by his brother Will, Michael Donnelly went to the office of the County Crown Attorney.

"Mr. Hutchinson, sir," Donnelly said, "in a case where a party is required by a magistrate to put up a peace bond, should the complainant or the party putting up the bond pay the costs, I would like to know?"

"Well, certainly, in my opinion," Hutchinson replied, "it is the complainant, except perhaps the cost of the recognizance. But why do you ask?"

"You made Mr. Ferguson, at Birr, return such costs which were charged against Rhody Kennedy, if you recall the case."

"Yes, certainly."

"Well, then, I want you to do the same in my case. I was arrested in this city at the instance of Peter McKellar and taken before Mr. Lawrason, and gave bail to him. I had to put up a recognizance to keep the peace and Mr. Lawrason made me pay all the costs, between three and four dollars. I want you to get Mr. Lawrason to repay me the money as you did in Kennedy's case."

"But, my dear fellow," protested Hutchinson, "I would rather not interfere. Mr. Lawrason is, after all, in charge of his court."

But Mike persisted. "You did it for Kennedy," he said, "and I want you to do the same in my case."

Hutchinson had to agree with Donnelly's logic. "Oh, very well," he said finally. "I will write to Mr. Lawrason and see what I can do."

A few days after Will's release from jail, Michael Donnelly called for a trunk at the Western Hotel in London at two o'clock in the afternoon. The landlord, no doubt a trifle peeved at having the now notorious Donnelly carriage stopping at his respectable premises, said: "It's already loaded, now get off with you." Mike took offence at the insolent tone and told the proprietor, without subtlety, what he thought of him, until "an immense crowd of persons gathered" to hear what the shouting was all about. "Neither of the parties was badly slaughtered," noted one observer, "but the talk could have been heard blocks off."

Michael Donnelly ran into more trouble in London the next day when he encountered the opposition stage from Lucan driven by the new man, Joe

Watson. Donnelly, claiming that Watson drove his vehicle furiously at his stage in an attempt to scare the horses, went to the authorities and charged Watson with furious driving. "As our readers are aware," the *Advertiser* stated, "there is a good deal of ill-feeling between the parties, and this prosecution is doubtless more the result of that than any overwhelming desire to prohibit fast driving." But James Owrey, J.P., was a little more sympathetic to the complainant. He convicted Watson and fined him five dollars and costs.

During this period William Denby assisted Mike Donnelly in keeping the stagecoach on the road, but in May he, too, was arrested for his part in the brawl at the Fitzhenry Hotel. He resisted arrest but the constables, Johnston and Allan of London, overpowered him.

The Donnelly brothers began to counter-attack. Mike Donnelly instructed David Glass to commence a lawsuit for damages against Constable John Bawden as a result of his apparently unlawful confinement in the Central Hotel for four days back in early March Next came Tom's case. Efforts were made to bring back Billy Atkinson from Kalamazoo, Michigan. Tom Donnelly made an affidavit that Atkinson was an essential witness for his defence in the Flanagan arson charge and that money had been dispatched on May 29 to pay his return fare.

In attempting to have the trial of Tom Donnelly postponed when Atkinson did not return, however, Glass incurred the displeasure of the Crown Attorney. At the beginning of June, Hutchinson asked Glass if he would be ready in the case. "Unless I hear soon," he wrote, "I shall hardly be able to get ready." Glass immediately acknowledged Hutchinson's request but in a follow-up note stated he was not sure whether the defence would be prepared. Hutchinson, perhaps misinterpreting the message, wrote to Hugh McKinnon in Lucan to round up Rhody Kennedy and James Curry, two of the more elusive of the witnesses. All other Crown witnesses were subpoenaed for the June Sessions of the Peace. But when Glass later intimated that the defence would be requesting an adjournment, Hutchinson was furious. In a bristling exchange of notes each accused the other of bad faith.

Meanwhile, Hugh McKinnon left the village of Lucan at the end of June, and Mike Donnelly went to the German Settlement near Crediton for recruits to help run the stagecoach, pending the release of his brothers. Before long the following report emanated from the village: "A Dutchman at large with a revolver is the latest that disturbs the tranquility of peaceful pedestrians."[4] The Dutchman had been hired by Donnelly to guard the family stagecoach.

Despite an affidavit filed by "Thomas Donnelly, a prisoner confined in the Common Gaol [that] if any trial is put off until the next assizes I will be able to procure the attendance of the said Atkinson", Glass's motion to postpone failed, and Donnelly was arraigned on Tuesday, June 27, on the charge of setting fire to Patrick Flanagan's stables in Lucan the previous October. The evidence of James Churchill, the veterinarian, was not as solid as the Crown had hoped, and Glass was able to rattle his story considerably on cross-examination. He had, after all, as the Crown Attorney himself conceded to the jury, once been a close companion of the brothers, and that in itself made his evidence suspicious. Rhody Kennedy, who had been flushed from hiding, was the other witness. He was a man easy to dislike. On the other hand, the jury seemed to take a liking to Tom Donnelly, a broth of a boy, and they were out for only an hour before returning a verdict of Not Guilty. The prisoner was next arraigned on the charge of theft of money from William Easdale. Witnesses listed on the indictment included William Dew, Alexander Levett, and Hugh McKinnon, but the Crown decided to call only Easdale, the alleged victim, and Richard Tapp, the barman of the Revere House. Once again the jury returned a verdict of Not Guilty. The only charge left pending against Tom Donnelly was for the robbery of James Curry. The Crown was not ready to proceed in this case, as Curry could not be found, and Donnelly therefore gave bail to appear at his trial when called upon and walked out of court.

At the June Sessions, Michael Donnelly was bound over to keep the peace in the amount of $400, apparently as a result of threats made. His sureties were his father and William McBride, a Lucan carpenter, in the sum of $200 each.

Hugh McKinnon

By the end of that month John Donnelly had been released from prison and had returned home, bringing back word from his brother James that as far as he was concerned, whatever the brothers decided to do about the stagecoach business was all right with him. It was apparent that the lucrative days of the carrying trade were over. Will Donnelly therefore decided to retire from the business, advising his brothers to do the same, and soon concluded a deal for some of the equipment and horses with W. Dewart of Fenelon Falls. Michael Donnelly began to look for another occupation. Along with William McBride, his recent bondsman, he applied to the authorities for appointment as a county constable under the patronage of an old friend of the family, Patrick McIlhargey, a Lucan J.P. But the Crown Attorney, understandably, wrote that "it was not considered advisable...to make the appointment...."

Rejected for the constabulary, Mike turned to the railroad. In those days railroading was a dangerous occupation. Every few weeks a brakeman was reported to have been fearfully crushed or mangled by the cars. But the pay was good and surely it could be no more hazardous than driving stage along the Proof Line Road. As for Will Donnelly, having miraculously recovered from his spine illness, he thought he could obtain employment as fireman of the heating plant at the London Insane Asylum and asked David Glass to put in a good word for him with the superintendent. On receiving Glass's letter, however, Superintendent Bucke turned it over to the Crown Attorney, perhaps scandalized that Donnelly, with his reputation, would dare even to ask for the position. John Donnelly also retired from the stagecoach and arranged with his father to farm the additional twenty-five acres the family had acquired across the road two years earlier. In November 1876, the advertisement of the Donnelly stagecoach in the London *Free Press* was dropped.

That summer, Richard Bryant also sold his stagecoach line to a newcomer to the carrying trade but an old hand in hotelkeeping, William Walker, proprietor of the Western Hotel on William Street in Lucan. Walker took possession of the business on July 10, with Joe Watson re-maining on as driver. Richard Bryant had never recovered his health following the breaking of his leg in the stage accident, and within a month of disposing of the business to Walker he was dead.

Billy Atkinson witnessed the large Masonic funeral of Bryant, for he had finally returned from Michigan. It had been a quiet summer in Lucan without Atkinson and several of the Donnelly boys, the most exciting event of the season having been the muster for parade drill of the Lucan Volunteers, forty strong, on the village square under the command of Captain McMillan on August 24. The old Revere House, at the corner of Main and Alice streets, closed its doors for good as a public house when Alex Levett sold out to Buckley Thomas Hodgins, who converted the building into a grocery store.

The lawsuit by Michael Donnelly for damages against John Bawden for malicious arrest and false imprisonment came on for trial at the Fall Assizes in London before Mr. Justice Burton with a jury. David Glass appeared for Donnelly and a promising new lawyer, Edmund Meredith, acted for the defence. After listening to the testimony, the judge ruled against Donnelly on a technicality. Donnelly instructed his counsel to appeal.

Two days later Tom Donnelly was back in the prisoner's box to stand trial on the old Curry robbery charge. As the complainant was still missing, the Crown offered no evidence and an acquittal on all three counts in the indictment was, of necessity, recorded. At the same assizes, Will Donnelly was also called to stand trial on the old charge of obstructing Constable John Coursey in the lawful execution of his duty, but the case was put over to the next assizes.

The following week Billy Atkinson instituted proceedings against Hugh McKinnon and the so-called Vigilance Committee of Lucan before James Owrey, J.P., of London. Constables Thomas Johnston and McLaughlin went to Lucan and arrested six of the men: Arthur Gray, barkeep of the Central Hotel; Jacob Palmer, a carpenter of the village; David Atkinson, a semi-successful grain merchant of Lucan; John Bawden, the bricklayer and county constable; and James H. Hodgins, a butcher better known by his nickname of Greasy

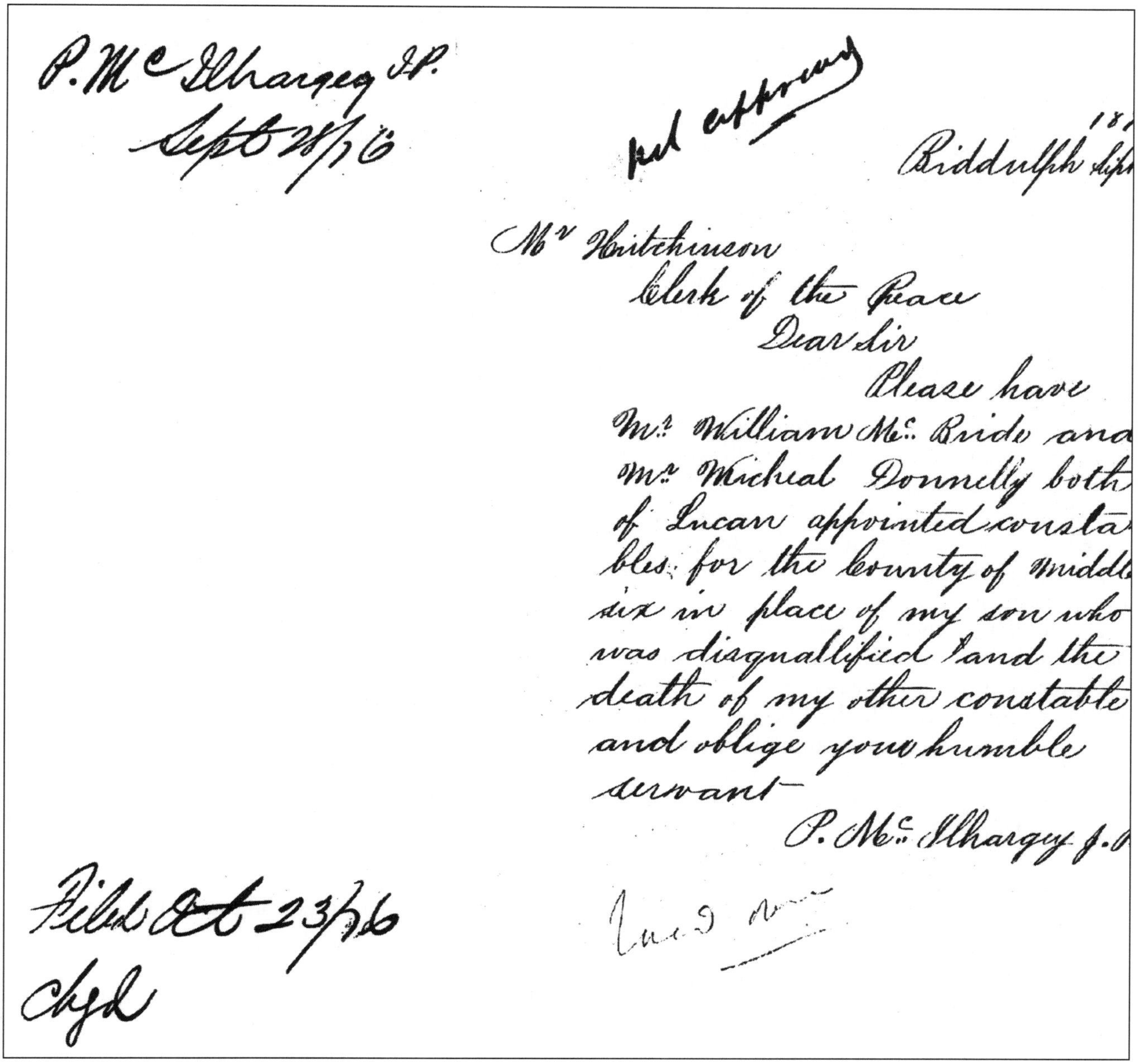

P. McIlhargey J.P.
Sept 28/76

pd attorney

Biddulph Sep... 18..

Mr Hutchinson
Clerk of the Peace
Dear Sir
Please have
Mr. William McBride and
Mr. Micheal Donnelly both
of Lucan appointed consta-
bles for the County of Middle-
sex in place of my son who
was disquallified and the
death of my other constable
and oblige your humble
servant
P. McIlhargy J.G

Filed Oct 23/76
chgd

Jim. Later, McKinnon himself was also arrested along with five more of the defendants: Henry Collins, tinsmith; James Atkinson, a former chum of the Donnelly boys and brother of the complainant; another brother, Thomas Atkinson, an incipient cattle dealer; Albert McLean, son of the owner of the Central Hotel; and Sandy Reid, the athlete.

Hugh McKinnon was chagrined at this turn of events. Then at the height of his athletic fame, he had as usual taken first prize in September that year in the heavyweight hammer throw at the Guelph Caledonian Games, with a winning throw of 79 feet and 10 inches. In a letter to his hometown paper, the Hamilton *Spectator*, he expressed his indignation at Atkinson's charge:

Without entering into the details of the charge which is made against me, conjointly with a number of the most respectable men of Lucan...I will content myself for the present by denouncing the affair as a fraud from the beginning, which I feel confident will be shown to the satisfaction of everybody when the case is further examined into.[5]

The other defendants were not as sure as McKinnon. When Will Donnelly, who was managing the prosecution for Atkinson, offered to settle the case upon payment of one thousand dollars, some of the defendants favoured negotiating, on the grounds that it would be difficult to establish alibis after so long a lapse of time. But McKinnon advised them to fight it out. He, for one, was prepared to go to court with witnesses to prove that on the night in question he was in Glencoe in company with Detective Murphy. McKinnon's advice prevailed. The defendants decided to fight it out in court and retained Edmund Meredith as defence counsel.

On the day of the trial Billy Atkinson gave evidence in the morning, but when court resumed in the afternoon he was nowhere to be found. While the Donnellys claimed he had been spirited away, Crown counsel stated his opinion that the remainder of the prosecution evidence would not corroborate Atkinson's testimony and he did not feel warranted in taking the case further. The judge accordingly directed the jury to bring in a verdict of Not Guilty and the prisoners were discharged.

Toward the end of November that year, young James Donnelly returned home from Toronto by train. But at Ingersoll he was pinched by Constable Henderson for failing to pay his fare. Although at first he denied it, giving his name as Alex McDonald, he finally admitted the charge, paid the fare plus costs, and continued home to Biddulph. The atmosphere of the Central Prison had not improved young Jim's health. Shortly after his return, he was arrested on two old assault charges laid many months before by Rhody Kennedy and John Coursey. But at least in the London Jail young Jim found friends, one of them being William Feeheley of the Roman Line, who had been picked up in the city on charges of drunkenness and vagrancy on December 8. Then there was William Denby who, in December, was found guilty of an assault on Constable John Reid the previous February and was sentenced to one month in jail.

At the same court sessions the case of John Donnelly for assaulting Peter McKellar came up. The Crown Attorney wrote Donnelly:

You had better come in tomorrow for the purpose of having the indictment against you disposed of. You will be liable to have your recognizance forfeited unless you appear, notwithstanding the absence of the prosecutor and his witness.[6]

The witness referred to was, of course, Rhody Kennedy, who was reported to he "still away, somewhere in Michigan, and cannot be found". As for McKellar, he had taken a trip across the ocean. John Donnelly was accordingly happy to appear in court the next day in company with his defence counsel, John Bartram, when the jury brought in a directed verdict of Not Guilty.

The only outstanding charges now remaining against the brothers were finally disposed of at the Spring Assizes, 1877. The Crown could offer no evidence on the charge against James Donnelly, Jr., of assaulting Rhody Kennedy. In the case of The Queen versus the same defendant along with his brother William, accused of assaulting Constable Coursey in the execution of his duty, the Crown likewise offered no evidence and the brothers were acquitted. Out of the dozen formal accusations against them at the Spring Assizes of the previous year, therefore, the only convictions were the three against John, James, and William, who received their sentences on March 30 and were all free again by the end of that year.

Thus, towards the end of 1876, peace broke out in Lucan. A quiet period of regrouping followed the surfeit of court cases, and it was reported:

This village may now boast of being one of the quietest and most law-abiding in the Dominion. The finger of scorn continues no longer to be pointed at her inhabitants, nor is the demon of intemperance and discord rampant as of yore. Order prevails in her streets, and peace and harmony in her outhouses. As proof of this our attention was called to the fact that Bill Donnelly's horses are at the present moment in the same stable with Collins' cow.[7]

The last statement was true, for the end of the year

Hugh McKinnon in later years when he was Chief of Police in Hamilton

found one or two of the family back in the stagecoach business. In a deal negotiated by Will, Tom Donnelly went into partnership with Joe Watson and William Walker, the rival driver and proprietor respectively. The coaches had always worked in pairs, and it was agreed that the Walker & Watson vehicle would work in concert with the Donnelly coach, owned by Thomas Donnelly and assisted on occasion by his brothers Michael and young Jim. With Levett's hotel converted into a grocery, Tom Donnelly rented Collins' stable to house the stage horses, at least one of which belonged to his brother Will. "The hatchet was buried at last," reported the newspaper of the deal, continuing:

The ceremony took place last week. Donnellys, Walkers, Watsons, and the individual known as

"Wicked Will" rushed into each other's arms; wept on each other's neck; bought stages from each other; exchanged whips, jack-knives, tobacco pipes, and other tokens of affection; pledged each other in flowing bowls, swore eternal friendship, and are prepared to go to their necks in water for each other on occasion of the first thaw.[8]

At the same time, old enemies retired from the field. The Hawkshaw family retained a small connection with the carrying trade when Thomas Hawkshaw set up a short route known as the Omnibus Line between Lucan and the new station of the London, Huron and Bruce Railway at Clandeboye, the new name for Flanagan's Corners. And Hugh McKinnon, also casting about for a more settled position in life, asked the Middlesex County Crown Attorney to write a letter of recommendation on his behalf "From what I have observed of your conduct in the discharge of your duties as a detective," wrote Hutchinson,

I have formed a high idea of your zeal, intelligence and activity as a peace officer, and shall be glad to hear of your appointment to the office of Chief of Police at Belleville, for which position I would consider you well qualified.[9]

McKinnon won favour with the Belleville council on grounds that he possessed "the necessary ability and plenty of muscle" and gained the appointment in January of 1877. The Donnellys were glad to be rid of him and their paths never crossed again.

David Glass took to the Court of Appeal of Ontario the case of Michael Donnelly against John Bawden, but in dismissing the appeal the court quoted with approval from the trial judge's notes:

. . . The peculiar circumstances of the village at that time, when a general terrorism prevailed, and the military had to be called out, and other offences were daily occurring, is sufficiently shown in the plaintiff's own evidence to warrant me holding that there was reasonable and probable cause [for the arrest]. [10]

21

TERROR

Although the village fathers did not so plan it, 1877 turned out to be a rebuilding bonanza in Lucan. The first of a great rash of fires, in what came to be melodramatically called "the Reign of Terror", occurred one Saturday night in January, burning Sylvanus Gibson's planing mill and sash factory. Many of those who had taken part in the hanging of Billy Atkinson either were employed at the mill or depended upon it for a livelihood. Two of Billy's brothers worked there. One of them, Jimmy, lost his $200 carpenter's kit in the fire, while the proprietor lost new machinery recently installed in the building, as well as the finished woodwork for several new houses in the village, for total damages of $2,000. Gibson only had $1,500 worth of insurance. A high wind blew sparks from the fire clear across the village which could easily have ignited many other buildings but for the heavy coating of snow on the roofs.

Other members of the mob at the attack on Billy Atkinson suffered misfortune. Butcher Greasy Jim Hodgins had his shop broken into and his animal hides scattered over the ice of the Sauble River one week, followed by the smashing of his shop windows the next, and by the kicking to smithereens of the panels to the front door the next.

But at the same time, when the "usual plundering and stealing [became] more than usually ascendant" in Lucan, mutterings were heard among the villagers of reviving the Lucan Vigilance Committee. A particularly galling example was the theft of Grundy's pig,

a choice Berkshire...got up expressly for family use. The utmost care had been evinced in the nurture and sustenance of this quadruped. The superfluous moisture from the culinary department together with modicums of vegetables and an occasional handful of grain tended to develop the bone and elevate the muscle, if not to some slight extent the adipose deposit of the pig in question.

And then

the killing day arrived but with it came a villain who watched the operations through a crack in the fence. Mr. Grundy had occasion to "see a man" and during his absence the dressed hog disappeared....[1]

Meanwhile, the stagecoach partnership between Tom Donnelly and William Walker did not last long. Upon their falling out, both expressed an intention of taking over the entire route for themselves, Joe Watson siding with Donnelly for the time being. As neither would sell his equipment to the other, new stagecoaches were ordered from the local blacksmith and wagon shops. Tom Donnelly had one built at Maloney's wagon shop. Walker placed an order elsewhere. At this point, coach and wagon shops and stables harbouring stage horses began going up in flames at an alarming rate. First, on February 17, the flames devoured the blacksmith and wagon shop of James Hodgins in Clandeboye, along with Hodgins' house and that of a neighbour. In March a flax-mill building on the outskirts of Lucan, containing $3,000 worth of dressed flax seed and a span of horses, burned down. The Lucan flax merchants, Messrs. Pieper and Hogg, some of whose employees had also helped to hang Billy Atkinson, had no insurance against the loss.

Perhaps to deal with the increasing lawlessness, three new Justices of the Peace for Lucan were appointed: Samuel C. Hersey, James D. McCosh, and Michael Crunnican. "With the assistance of a few new policemen and a lock-up," it was said, "Lucan might be considered safe for pedestrians at nightfall." The movement for a lock-up was given impetus by a "friendly ruction" which was reported by the London *Advertiser* under the headline "OLD-FASHIONED FACTION FIGHT IN LUCAN":

One night last week the villagers were aroused from their slumbers by the firing of revolvers, accompanied by heavy tramping and shouting. This sort of thing was kept up at intervals through the night much

Dignan's blacksmith shop, Lucan. Although of a later date, this is typical of the blacksmith shops of the nineteenth century. (J. Bilyea)

Buildings on Main Street, Lucan, about 1890. R. H. O'Neil was the first reeve of Lucan. (Stanley)

to the annoyance of the peacably-disposed Lucanites who next morning held committees of inquiry in front of their respective places of business.[2]

Known as Corkonians and Tipperaries, the two factions had met at an old-fashioned Irish wake in a shanty on the outskirts of the village. The incident was enough for the Village Council to decide at their next meeting that they "should make an addition to the police and petition the County Council for a lock-up."

Shortly afterwards, the wagon shop of James Maloney on the Robins Corner in the village burned down between midnight and one o'clock in the morning. Tom Donnelly's new stagecoach survived the conflagration, but Maloney's loss was thought to be $400, with only $150 worth of insurance, carried by the Ontario Mutual of London. On the following Saturday, St. Patrick's Day, the stage equipment and horses of Joe Watson and Tom Donnelly had been as usual housed in the stable of tinsmith Henry Collins, but at 11:30 that evening the building was seen to be on fire. The alarm was sounded and the Lucan Fire Brigade, "thundering upon the scene amid the wildest enthusiasm, immediately unlimbered for action." But a bystander nonchalantly pointed out to the firemen that they had forgotten to bring the hose. "In about half an hour" that essential item was brought to the scene and, undaunted, the fire brigade thrust the hose into a neighbouring well and began to pump. But, alas, "the 'hydrants' were frozen and the machine refused to squirt." Some of the villagers assisted those of the Donnelly brothers who had rushed to the fire by the less sophisticated but more effective means of water buckets and huge snowballs. They could not save the building. Meanwhile, after much effort and fiddling with Old Rescue, the firemen got the contraption into working order, but

as by this time the fire had completely died out, the aforesaid officers directed their energies to playing a stream through the strainer of the suction pipe (which, in the darkness, they mistook for the nozzle), upon a prominent and unoffending citizen.[3]

With the firefighting fiasco ended, Tom Donnelly and Joe Watson counted their loss at four sets of harness and other equipment, and a quantity of grain and hay belonging to the stage business. Saved from the flames were Donnelly's stagecoach and Henry Collins' cow, as well as one of Donnelly's horses, although the latter was "in a singed condition". A horse belonging to Watson died in the flames. The partners had no insurance and the total loss was four hundred dollars. As Watson was wiped out by the fire, he and Tom Donnelly terminated their association. The parting was not amicable.

Since Tom's new coach had survived the fire, he continued to run. But Watson, too, remained on the road, for he hired himself out as driver with the rival line of William Walker. Walker had ordered a new stagecoach built at the wagon works and blacksmith shop of Judge and Cook, located near his hotel on William Street. But on April 10 the Judge and Cook works, along with five dwellings adjacent to it, burned down in a fire which had been deliberately set between twelve midnight and one o'clock. Total loss was between $5,000 and $6,000.

The following night Tom Donnelly's business, too, came to a sudden end. While his new stage was resting in the drive shed of the Montgomery House on the Proof Line Road, two men drove out from Lucan with a can of coal oil. Under cover of darkness they spilled it over Donnelly's stage, which in a few seconds was burning brightly. The London *Free Press*, in reporting the incident next day, attributed ownership of the vehicle to Watson, which provoked Tom Donnelly to write:

To the Editor of the *Free Press*.
Sir, – I notice in today's issue of your paper a news item headed "Incendiary Fire" wherein you state that "one of Mr. Watson's London and Lucan stages was burned while standing in the driving shed of the Montgomery House," etc.

I beg you will have the kindness to correct an error which has crept into the above paragraph, whether accidentally or not on the part of your informant I am unable to say. The stage in question did not belong to Mr. Watson, nor has he any interest whatever in it. It belonged solely to your correspondent, neither Mr. Watson nor any other person having the slightest claim thereto except myself. Owing to this fact, I am of opinion that Mr. Watson will not turn many stones in order to find out the perpetrators of the dastardly act.

I am, Sir, &c.,

THOMAS DONNELLY.

London, Apr. 13, '77.[4]

Tom Donnelly ordered a new stagecoach built. Two weeks later the Lucan and London stage route claimed another victim when the nut on the fly wheel of the Walker stage loosened and the wheel fell off on the Proof Line between the fourteenth and fifteenth concessions of London Township, just after leaving Birr. In the tumult an elderly passenger of seventy years, Joseph McGuffin, suffered a severe cut on his forehead and was paralysed by a fracture of his spine. He died a few days later.

James McMahon continued his connection with the stagecoach line even after his late brother-in-law, Richard Bryant, had sold the business to William Walker. When Lucan was considered unsafe for stage property, McMahon quartered the horses on his farm, which lay near Elginfield. On the night of April 25, 1877, McMahon's barns and stables burned to the ground. Five horses died in the fire, at a total loss of $2,000 with insurance of only $400.

In the village, the Lucan Fire Brigade was coming under increased criticism. Bad enough that the "antiquated fire engine", of 1851 vintage, had been discarded by the city of London many years before. Worse was "the ambition of each Lucanite to act either as a chief engineer or 'branch man', when handling the old veteran", leaving but few hands "to run the machine". There was also some skulduggery in the works. At the Judge and Cook fire, Old Rescue was on the ground in time, but despite strenuous pumping, only a pitiful stream of water four to six feet in height could be coaxed out of the machine – "of little avail when brought to bear against the burning sides of a large frame building." Next day came "the astounding discovery that some cordwood had been mysteriously introduced into the pump valve". When practice was held a few days later, the firemen were out and running in magnificent style and "ere the expiration of three and a half minutes (some say three) the gallant old Rescue was throwing a stream of

water upon two imaginary fires." It seems it was only with real fires the fire brigade had trouble.

One night in April "Mr. Joseph Watson, of Lucan stage notoriety, got a whack of a club across the ear on Saturday night, from an unseen hand, which knocked him senseless."[5] Watson was on his way to his boarding house from the stables where he had just checked the stage horses. He was not seriously injured.

On the early morning of Friday, May 11, six more stage horses burned to death in Lucan, and another died later from the effects. This fire was set, well after midnight, in the stables of Robert McLean's Central Hotel. Four of the horses belonged to McLean and were valued at $1,000, while the other three had been brought in by a stranger for Walker and Watson's stage. Conveyances and harness, hay, and oats were also destroyed. The flames spread to John Drought's cabinet factory and dwelling and the stables of William Porte and George Shoebottom. Shoebottom was a carnage and wagon maker who worked with Alfred Brown, one-time constable, who on at least one occasion had a run-in with Michael Donnelly. Most of Lucan blamed this fire on the Donnellys.

In the wake of the McLean fire, the villagers were tense and expectant. Robert McLean had been a respectable and inoffensive tavernkeeper in the place for decades, and if his premises were not safe, no person's were. Every serviceable gun in the village was loaded for use. Then, late on the night of that same day or early Saturday morning, the rear of the hardware storehouse of Barney Stanley was set on fire. Although some of its contents were saved, the building burned to the ground, with the loss of several hogsheads of sugar. Damages were said to be $4,000, while Stanley had only $600 worth of insurance. When the flames had died down, the astute merchant, knowing the predilection of certain Lucanites to help themselves to booty, took the precaution of hiring two armed guards to watch over the exposed merchandise, which sat piled in the alleyway behind the store. The guards were an English house-painter named George Gear and another man named Delmage. Their orders were to shoot on sight anything that came close to the merchandise.

The Central Hotel, Lucan, as it appeared in the nineteenth century. It operates as a hotel in Lucan to the present day. (Stanely)

Very early the next morning a number of young men of the village, who had armed themselves and were supposedly on the watch for fire-bugs, began to engage in target practice. Most of them had been at the Stanley Hardware fire and some were drunk. Soon Gear was struck from behind by "a stray bullet [which] in a most unaccountable manner...found a lodging place in the soft part" of the watchman's leg. It was said to have been a pure accident. During the same night, however, or early Sunday morning, May 13, William Berry's barbershop near the Stanley warehouse was broken into. All the contents were smashed to pieces and the interior of the shop was left in a shambles. The shot which struck Gear may have come from the barbershop.

On the night of the next day, Monday, May 14, the Lucan firewatchers fired at two figures lurking behind the Queen's Hotel and they fled. But at least one of the shots seemed to have found its mark. The newspaper account of the incident reads:

Almost the only thing spoken about in Lucan on Tuesday was the exciting encounter of two of the night watchmen appointed in consequence of the recent outrages, which took place on the previous (Sunday) night.[6]

It should be noted here that "the recent outrages" could only have referred to the wrecking of Berry's barbershop and the Stanley Hardware fire. The account continues:

The Queen's Hotel, Lucan

It appears that whilst in the vicinity of the Queen's Hotel, the watchmen saw two suspicious looking characters stealthily walking round by the back of the premises. The watchmen called upon the party to halt, but the latter heeded not and ran away. A second demand to stop was made and not responded to, whereupon the watchmen fired the revolvers upon the fugitives. The rascals, who evidently had no good object in view, got clear away. Tuesday morning, traces of human blood were discovered near where the party were when the watchmen fired, leading to the supposition that one of them, at least, had been wounded. Who the men were remains a mystery; but rumour points to the absence of a "suspicious one" from his accustomed place in the village Monday, as a solution, it being supposed that he was the person wounded....

The day following the shooting, May 15, 1877, young James Donnelly died in his bed at the old Donnelly homestead. He was thirty-five years old. His remains were buried in a family plot at the northwest corner of the burying ground beside St. Patrick's Church, on the Roman Line of Biddulph.

The first death in the Donnelly family caused great excitement in Biddulph and Lucan. Cause of death was reported in the newspaper to be "inflammation of the bowels", but the enemies of the family were convinced that it was young Jim who had been shot behind the Queen's Hotel the night before he died. The Donnellys denied it and pointed to Dr. Sutton, who attended young Jim at his death and who certified the cause of death as pulmonary consumption.[7] The enemies of the family circulated stories, however, that the physician had signed the death certificate "death from lead poisoning"! At the very least, they said, the final illness of young Jim Donnelly was accelerated by a gunshot wound which the family concealed.[8] Little else is known of the death of the eldest of the brothers. William Donnelly said that "James, when dying, refused to drink liquor, even on the doctor's order." It was a curious statement, for it was well known that, at least since his return from Michigan, young Jim Donnelly had never hesitated at all in "takin' a dhrap av the crathur".

Whether the death was natural or not remains a moot point, but the following few days saw a terrible spite wreaked upon the enemies of the Donnelly family. First, there were the horses of William Walker and Joe Watson. The rival stagecoachmen had pastured the horses in the field of baggage-master Timothy Carey near the railway station on the outskirts of the village.[9] The following morning Walker's three horses were found lying "in a dead state" in the field, their throats cut and their bodies slashed and mutilated. Watson's horse was alive but almost disembowelled, waiting for death to relieve its misery. The tongues of the horses had been cut out of their mouths.

Two nights later, with a strong northwest wind blowing, an attempt was made to fire the Oddfellows' Hall in the village, and it was reported:

...A gloom of a most appalling nature is gradually settling down on the inhabitants of unhappy Lucan. The torch of the incendiary looms on the midnight air and dark forms, knife in hand, prowl near the dwellings of the sleeping villagers. Women move from house to house with hesitating steps....[10]

"The utmost excitement and terror reigns in Lucan," the neighbouring inhabitants of Ailsa Craig learned. "Watchmen patrol the streets all night. Many of the inhabitants contemplate leaving." In view of the location of the Oddfellows' Hall and the wind blowing that night, it was felt that if the attempt to burn it down had succeeded, the whole village might have gone up in flames. "Almost every morning brings tidings of

some new outrage," the report went. "A store burnt, dwellings destroyed, stables, filled with valuable horses, consumed, horses with their throats cut." Some Lucanites, before retiring, took to laying out a large blanket into which, in the event of fire, their valuables could be thrown and dragged out in the night. Up to forty-six armed men at one time kept watch in the streets and alleyways of the village throughout the night, and numerous man-traps were set to catch fire-bugs.

On Queen Victoria's Birthday that year several Lucanites spent the holiday fishing for trout near the neighbouring village of Brecon. The hot and sultry river banks were soon forsaken for the cool shade of a tavern. When the visitors from Lucan expressed a wish to settle in Brecon, the citizens of the latter were disturbed. "This place can accommodate quite a few," they said, "but we don't want a certain class from Lucan or we will want to sell out also."

On Saturday, May 26, Constable John Reid's horse was stolen in Lucan and found the next morning with its throat cut. Reported to be the nineteenth horse killed or burned to death in Lucan, it prompted a newspaper to state: "The reign of terror is once again fairly established in Lucan." Another asked, "Why don't the vigilance committee get to work?"

Early in the morning of June 11 the Queen's Hotel was discovered ablaze, apparently set on fire by someone who had crept through the cellar and was seen fleeing from the rear of the building. Shots were fired but he escaped. The fire brigade, however, made a timely appearance and confined the loss to six hundred dollars. "For the first time in the annals of Lucan, the old Rescue fire engine worked as was its wont in days of yore when in the hands of the London Brigade."

In between the two attempts upon the Queen's Hotel that spring, the post office building at Whalen's Corners and its adjoining store burned to the ground. In the flat countryside of Biddulph every fire was visible for miles, and when Patrick Whelan, the grizzled old neighbour of the Donnelly family out on the Roman Line, was later questioned about some of the fires which were said to have taken place in Lucan and vicinity, he simply laughed. "There were so many fires in Lucan," he said, "we took no notice of them."

The outbreak of the many fires in and around Lucan in that late spring may have been purely coincidental with another event, at first unnoticed except by a few. It was the arrival home of Robert Donnelly after an absence of over a year. When the authorities learned of his presence, he was arrested by Detectives Phair and Murphy and, although strong expressions of opinion were given that he should be kept in close confinement, the Crown Attorney agreed to his release if bail was substantial. It was set at two hundred dollars and Donnelly found two bondsmen in London tavern-keepers Edward Morkin and John Lewis.

A few days later the stage war broke out into the open again when Tom Donnelly encountered William Walker on the streets of Lucan. Walker swore at Donnelly and accused him of killing his horses. Donnelly gave Walker a beating. Then Thomas Walsh, a London cabinetmaker who had been hired by the Donnellys to guard the stagecoach, was arrested on a charge of carrying unlawful weapons. Upon his person were a breech-loading pistol, a dirk knife eight inches long, and a razor. Asked about his business in Lucan, he replied, "The Donnellys brought me out on their stage, and they pay me to ride with them." Walsh was fined forty dollars with costs or two months in jail.

With matters again threatening to get out of hand, Reeve William Hutchins called a public meeting for June 26 to discuss the suppression of lawlessness in the village. Michael Crunnican, one of the newly appointed Justices of the Peace and a Lucan shopkeeper, was thought to have some influence with the Donnelly family. He was a Catholic and had been a longtime friend. Crunnican was a man of "magnificent proportions and native eloquence" besides, and he spoke for nearly an hour at the meeting. "In conclusion," he is reported to have said, "I don't mane to offind, but what I spake I say and it is from the fulness of me heart, and if I've said anything to yees that I'm sorry for I'm glad of it." There were prolonged cheers. Finally it was decided that Lucan must have a lock-up and a new constable to go along with the new gas lamps on the streets.

The gas lamps had appeared in the village just that year and were considered a marvel when first installed:

Twenty-four lamp-posts and lamps adorn the streets, and a visitor passing up and down the principal streets would imagine themselves in a metropolis. The first time these lamps were lit one of our citizens, in front of whose house a lamp had been placed, waking up in the middle of the night and seeing the glare on the blinds, rushed out of bed, followed by his wife, who alarmed the whole house with her cries of fire.[11]

The efficacy of the lamps in the suppression of midnight prowling was dubious. The Donnelly stagecoach and its equipment and horses were at this time quartered in James Gleeson's stables on Alice Street, adjacent to the Fitzhenry House, then being operated by James Maloney. On the night of July 4, the hotel and Gleeson's stables burned to the ground. Consumed in the fire was Tom Donnelly's second new stagecoach. During the conflagration two fist fights broke out. The first was between Maloney and a man named Taylor, who was one of the men in charge of the fire brigade. Maloney may have questioned the other's competence or earnestness in directing the rescue of the building. The other fight was between Michael Donnelly and a Dutchman named Hocher. The latter may have originally been recruited from near Crediton by the brothers themselves to assist in the stagecoach troubles but who switched sides. In any event Taylor and Hocher got the worst of the exchanges and, after the fire had completed its destruction, warrants were issued for the arrest of Maloney and Donnelly. The former was apprehended and fined but Michael Donnelly disappeared from the village.

Donnelly was still absent five days later when the house which he rented on Alice Street was burned to the ground at two o'clock in the morning. Nellie Donnelly and the six-month-old baby just barely escaped with their lives. Again the fire brigade arrived on the scene but, despite reports to the contrary, failed to save the house. William Porte noted in his diary: "Ben Blackwell's house occupied by Mike Donnelly burned completely."

Flagging the train in Lucan. The old Holy Trinity Anglican Church. torn down in 1909, can be seen in the background. (Stanley)

Nellie Donnelly was not only badly frightened by this experience but was also upset by the rumours that the fire had been deliberately set from within by the inmates. She persuaded her husband to quit the village and make their home elsewhere.

With the final destruction of his stagecoach, Tom Donnelly gave up the carrying trade, and thus ended the Donnelly stagecoach period of Lucan. In London the McMartin Brothers, proprietors of the City Hotel where the brothers had long made their headquarters and had whiled away many an idle hour between stage runs at the billiard tables, marked the simultaneous falling off of the stagecoach and poolroom business by turning the billiard room into "a spot for reading". No place for Tom Donnelly now!

There was little doubt that what had really ruined the stagecoach business was the London, Huron and Bruce Railway, which had by-passed Biddulph Township when the township had refused to pay its so-called "levy" to the railway corporation. The station was established instead at Flanagan's Corners, renamed Clandeboye. During the first month of its operation, as many as seventy-five passengers arrived in London on the train every day, a form of competition the stage lines could ill bear. Furthermore, the *Exeter Times*, a Tory newspaper, decried "the refusal of the Mackenzie Government to allow the mail[s] to be carried as they are in every other part of the country, by the railway...." And the *Advertiser* said, "It is really too bad that as the mails are now conveyed from London by the old stagecoach we

Long John Hodgins with one of the typical stagecoaches of the period. He succeeded to the stagecoach business after the Donnellys, Hawkshaws, Flanagans, et al., had retired from competition.

have to wait three days for a reply to a letter to that city when a few hours would suffice by train...." The mail stage managed to hang on for another year until June 28, 1878, when the London-Goderich mail stage made its last run.

Meanwhile the citizens of Lucan were in gloom. Bypassed by the new railroad, the village had by this time earned an unenviable reputation throughout the entire province. Page's *Historical Atlas of the County of Middlesex*, published in 1878, stated:

The welfare of the place has of late been imperilled by the unfortunate exhibitions of malice which have lately culminated in incendiary fires, which have created a great deal of distrust, and checked for a time the progress of the village.

It is true that the vigour of Lucan declined, and in the next few decades its population gradually decreased until it was less than half what it was in the flourishing stagecoach days of the Donnellys, when about 1,200 souls called it home.

22

POLITICS

Politically, the Donnelly family usually supported the Reform party, as did most of their neighbours in the Catholic Settlement of Biddulph. The rest of the township, but especially the village of Lucan, was a stronghold of the Conservative party. The electoral district of Huron, to which Biddulph originally belonged, was created in 1844. That year the Conservative right-winger Cayley defeated John Longworth of the Reformers, but in those early days it was the Catholics who had voted for the Conservatives while the Protestants supported the Reform cause.

With the coming of Confederation a new riding called North Middlesex was formed. Reformer Thomas Scatcherd very handily defeated William Watson, garnering almost twice as many votes as his Conservative opponent.[1] Even in Biddulph, now decidedly Tory except for the Catholic Settlement, Scatcherd was so popular that he got exactly as many votes as Watson, but it was only after Scatcherd made a public declaration that he intended to give the government of John A. Macdonald a fair trial. It was a popular stance throughout the country as well as in Biddulph.

Scatcherd, who had obtained for William Porte the postmastership of Lucan, was popular with the Catholics of Biddulph. In 1875, for example, he assisted Joseph Fitzhenry financially in getting into the tavern business in Lucan, and it is quite likely that William Donnelly obtained the mail contract from London to Crediton in 1873 through his efforts. But the Member of Parliament sometimes perplexed even his own supporters. "Mr. Scatcherd, M.P., made a speech in the House yesterday," said a Reform newspaper on one occasion, "but we have not been able to decide whether he supported the Opposition or the Government."[2]

The leading Conservative of North Middlesex was Big Barney Stanley. Once his youthful flirtation with Reform principles was abandoned, Big Barney tried to enlist everyone he came in touch with in the cause of "the right partee". The wealthiest man in Lucan, he never ran for any public office other than that of village councillor or school trustee but took a leading role in politics from the beginning. In the attack on Keefe's tavern on polling day in 1857, for example, Keefe's bartender, Michael Ryan, deposed, "I recollect well of seeing Barney Stanley walking backwards and forwards in front of the house," acting as a principal ringleader of the party and inciting the mob to commit violence. In later years Barney Stanley used subtler tactics on the Catholics, forever trying to win them over to the Conservative cause "bekase the right man must be put in, and the right partee must be sustained by a good majoritee."

In the provincial election of 1871 a political meeting was called at the Cedar Swamp Schoolhouse in Biddulph, and Barney Stanley naturally attended with the Conservative candidate in tow. The latter was one Charley Mackintosh, editor of the Strathroy *Despatch*, who arrived "grip sack in hand and scrap book under his arm". Despite the night being dark and the roads muddy, the Roman Liners and Swamp Liners were out in full force for a bit of election fun. When the candidate began to deliver "a rambling discourse" to the assembly a number of young roughnecks, the younger Donnelly boys no doubt being among them, became unruly. "I myself am one of the most liberal of mankind and never view a subject from the standpoint of party," said the candidate nervously. "Why I scarcely know the difference between party names. What is a Tory?"

A voice from the crowd shouted, "A Tory, in Irish, means an outlaw."

The discomfited candidate stated he appeared in the interests of no party, knowing full well the room was filled with supporters of the Reform party.

"Who is he thin?" a voice cried.

"Where does he come from?" another asked.

Thomas Scatcherd, the Reform politician who was so popular that in most elections no Conservative could be found to oppose him.

Bernard "Barney" Stanley, in 1897 (Stanley)

"He's as thin as a whipping post,"a third cried.

"It's thrue for you, but where's his voice?" asked a fourth.

"Troth, thin, he's left it at home under the pillow," came the answer from another of the crowd.

"Spake up, mavourneen," cried others.

Charley Mackintosh plucked up his courage and, "in order to somewhat conciliate the growing dissatisfaction now rapidly assuming the shape and appearance of a ruction", ventured, "You know, boys, that I am almost one of yourselves, for I was born in the north end of London Township, quite close to Biddulph." And he went on to explain that he was editor of a district newspaper, "and in that paper you will find every week a whole column of North Middlesex items."

"What's the name of your paper?" one of the crowd shouted.

"It's the Strathroy *Despatch*. The *Despatch*, gentlemen," replied the candidate.

"By me sowl, thin," cried out another voice, "we'll despatch you."

With that, a general scrimmage broke out, benches and desks went flying, and "maps and stovepipes became inextricably mingled". Poor Charley fled, trying to scramble through one of the seven-by-nine-inch window lights but getting stuck instead, grip sack still in his hand.

"I'll git him out," bellowed Barney Stanley, tugging at the stuck candidate, "bekase I've heerd that where a man can git his head and shoulders, I tell yees the rest of his body will follow."

They pushed in vain until a reporter from one of the London newspapers took hold of Mackintosh by the pantaloons and drew him back into the schoolhouse. The chairman of the meeting, Hugh Benn, finally got the crowd to settle down. "Now, bhoys," he said, "ye have got through wid yer scrimmage. Come and listen to what the gintlemin have to say."

Michael Crunnican, who was a Tory, although Catholic, prided himself upon his supposed influence with the people in the section. He took the platform. "Bhoys, bhoys, and gintlemin," he said, "I want only to be guided by the majoritee of me counthrymin, and I see that the majoritee of yees is so strong in favour of Smith I will go wid the majoritee."

The crowd cheered and quieted down. London lawyer Hugh Macmahon then spoke on behalf of the Reform candidate, James Smith. Macmahon was a good speaker and he knew his audience. He referred to John A. Macdonald, the Big Premier, and Sandfield Macdonald, the Little Premier, and suggested that when the Big Premier pulled the strings at Ottawa, the Little Premier at Toronto jumped. He said of Mackintosh, "When a man comes before you and says he belongs to no party then keep clear of him, for depend upon it he will upon the first opportunity put himself up for sale to the highest bidder." The meeting ended and everyone filed out of the little log schoolhouse, Barney Stanley and his candidate a little ruefully, and the rough farmers of the Catholic Settlement happily and quite satisfied that their original choice was sound. As usual at such meetings, no one on either side was the least bit persuaded by any of the arguments.

In that election, as in the past, the Donnellys and most of their neighbours, both influential and humble, espoused the Reform cause. Among the more active Reformers were Soldier John Atkinson, Hugh McPhee, Andy Keefe, William Toohey, Martin Darcey, and the Ryder family.

In the following year's election for the federal seat, Thomas Scatcherd was again returned unopposed in North Middlesex. Then a government scandal of major proportions erupted in the country. The London *Advertiser* summarized the matter:

> Prior to the close of the session of 1872, a scheme for the construction of a Canadian Pacific Railway was adopted and between that time and the general election, the Government of which Sir John Macdonald was Premier was busy endeavouring to reconcile the conflicting claims of rival companies for the construction and ownership of the line. One of these companies was led by Senator Macpherson, the other by Sir Hugh Allan. The sequel shows that Sir John played the Knight against the Senator with such skill that he wrung from the former no less than $350,000 for use as a bribery fund during the preceding election.... After the elections...the secret of the sale of the Pacific Railway charter leaked out....[3]

Worse still, John A. Macdonald lied about the matter to Parliament and called God to witness his innocence. But it was established not long after that Sir Hugh Allan

> gave over $300,000 to the Government, on the understanding that it would be "recouped" by giving him the Pacific Railway charter, with its bonus of $30,000,000 of public money and its 150,000,000 acres of public land, together with the monopoly of its working for all time....[4]

The government of John A. Macdonald retired in disgrace and writs were issued for a new election.

The Pacific Scandal election of 1874 was relatively quiet in Lucan and Biddulph, for once again the ever-popular Thomas Scatcherd was returned by acclamation. In this election David Glass, the favourite defence counsel of the Donnellys, stood by his principles and forsook the party of Sir John A. But his resignation from the Conservative party earned him the implacable enmity of diehard Tories like Barney Stanley. When Glass was defeated it was reported:

> The election of Crowell Wilson over the traitor Glass in East Middlesex was the cause of great rejoicing in Lucan. Crowds thronged the telegraph office, and when the welcome news arrived, cheers were given and a rush made to the street, where a huge Bonfire was soon made, into which an effigy of slippery Dave (made still more slippery by a coat of oil on the turned coat with which he was dressed) was thrown, speeches were made, and it was not until the small hours that the company separated.[5]

Just as the dust from the federal campaign settled, a provincial election was announced for the following January. A new-fangled innovation, the secret ballot, was to be introduced. The Conservatives nominated cattle drover John McDougall, who was determined to unseat Silent James Smith (as the Opposition scornfully referred to him), who had managed to win the previous two provincial elections. In Lucan, one or two of the Porte boys began to campaign actively for McDougall, and it was thought that he could win if enough of the Catholic Settlement votes could be swung over. The campaign began to look promising for the Conservatives when several of the Keefes, including Andrew, Jimmy, and Robert, were won over, along with the Feeheleys and at least one of the Donnelly brothers. Michael.

During the campaign, Barney Stanley canvassed at Barber's, the Cedar Swamp, and McFall's schoolhouses and at the various taverns. The night before polling he was out on the Roman Line accompanied by that recent convert to Conservatism, Andy Keefe. They called at Quigley's, Ryan's, Jones's and several other households, coming finally to Michael Glass's hotel at Elginfield to sip hot beer and brag about the number of votes they had got that evening.

Michael Sullivan of the Catholic Settlement held possession of his farm under a lease obtained from his brother-in-law, William Casey, totally unaware that the Canada Company had long before taken steps to void it for default of payment. No payment had in fact been made under the lease since it had been first taken out years before. When the Canada Company took proceedings to evict Sullivan as a trespasser, he went to Robert O'Neil of Lucan and promised to support McDougall in the election if he would help him get the deed to his farm. O'Neil arranged a mortgage with old William Thompson, went to the Canada Company offices in Toronto, and came back with Sullivan's deed. Sullivan thereupon began to tout McDougall among the Catholics as "a good liberal man". Many of the Catholics were asked to change parties. Sideroad Jim Ryder, for example, was approached not only by Sullivan but also by Andy Keefe, Mick Feeheley, and James Keefe. Although some of the Ryders wavered, Sideroad Jim insisted he would continue voting for Reformer Smith.

Cattle drovers always treated generously. This is how the best deal was made in the cattle trade, and politics was not much different. At least so thought John McDougall, the Liberal-Conservative. "I can drink a hundred times a day and not get beyond my depth," McDougall declared. "I think I was in every tavern in Lucan."

When the great day of polling arrived, vehicles were rounded up from all quarters to carry voters to the polls. William Shoebottom, a livery-stable keeper in Lucan, had six vehicles and horses out in and around Lucan. "A commercial traveller in the town," he said, "could not get away because he could get no conveyance." And Michael Donnelly was also employed to drive voters to the polls. On this occasion at least, Michael was

strongly influenced by his friend George Porte, who so actively supported McDougall. Young Porte himself was out on the Roman Line driving voters to the polls early in the morning. For the convenience and comfort of the electors, someone (Barney Stanley was suspected but it was never proved) had thoughtfully ensconced a bottle of whiskey in Porte's sleigh.

Barney Stanley attended the polling at the Cedar Swamp Schoolhouse at that election. One of the Ryders came to him there and said, "Mr. Stanley, I will support who pays me."

But Stanley claimed he said to the man, "Don't come to me, Ryder, go and see whoever employed you."

"But I am still owed something for the last election," Ryder protested in vain.

Despite the fact that the Catholic Settlement threw its votes to Smith by eighty to forty-three, Lucan as usual voted overwhelmingly for McDougall, and the Conservatives were jubilant when he won. They celebrated the victory:

A cord of wood was placed in the street and one of our business men rolled a barrel of coal oil out of his shop and placed it on the street and tapped it....[6]

But the Reformers, proving to be sore losers, contested the election in the courts, claiming that McDougall had "floated into Parliament on whiskey". John Harrison gave evidence at the trial:

I shook a little money at Atkinson and said, "Here's election money;" it was bribing times....[7]

Another witness said he overheard Harrison promise to vote for both parties. But the challenge failed and the result in Lucan was

another drunk, bonfire and night of excitement over the McDougall protest. Our informant tells us the boys burnt up most of the new pound which cost the village nearly $50.[8]

With political excitement in Biddulph and Lucan stirred up as it had not been for years, the pot was kept boiling when the popular M.P. Thomas Scatcherd dropped dead and a by-election was required. His brother, Colin Scatcherd, was put forward as the nominee of the Reformers, much to the disappointment of a man named Waters, who immediately announced he would run as an independent. Party supporters finally persuaded him to withdraw but the ranks had broken. The Conservative standard-bearer was a Mr. Levi. The polling took place in June 1875, with complaints by some that "the ballot system renders it impossible to get any news from the seat of war until all is over...." Although the Conservatives made a strong push, the Reformers came through with Colin Scatcherd winning. Lucan and Biddulph voted true to form: Scatcherd carried the Catholic Settlement by 71 to 28, but Biddulph as a whole was against him 263 to 159 and Lucan by the wide margin of 114 to 41. One Lucan villager was said to have recorded his name and the number of his Orange Lodge on the ballot! The Reformers, however, were subdued in victory, for Colin Scatcherd's majority of 177 was in strong contrast to his late brother's winning margin of 731 when he had last run opposed nine years before.

Bernard Stanley continued to cultivate the Catholic vote of Biddulph. On July 5, 1877, he attended the Catholic Picnic at Collison's Grove near St. Patrick's Church, which was held annually under the auspices of the young ladies of the parish.

> The usual games and sports enlivened the day. But the crowning feature of the exercise was the sharply contested election between Bernard Stanley, Esq., J.P., and the Reeve, Mr. William Hutchins, as to who should become the recipient of the silver-headed cane. The votes were valued at ten cents each. After a most exciting contest Mr. Hutchins came off with a majority of one hundred votes.[9]

Stanley's hero, the illustrious but corruptible John A. Macdonald, himself made a foray into the district in the fall of 1877 when he visited the village of Brecon[10] and drove by coach to Ailsa Craig. The London *Advertiser*, a Reform newspaper, called the visit "a broad farce" when the weather failed to co-operate and the parade ended up "a baptism of mud". As to Macdonald's speech, the journal reported,

> during the course of his address he believed he would soon recover from the "temporary wave of obloquy which had followed one fault – the Pacific Scandal"....[11]

During these years of politicking, the Donnellys generally followed the lead of the Portes, who, although Conservative in principle, followed the Scatcherds as a personal matter. Thus the Donnelly family generally supported the Reform cause, not only because of the Porte influence, but as members of the Catholic Settlement, which was solidly Reform.

But by 1877 Will Donnelly was well out of stagecoaches and politics. In the fall of that year, he purchased "for a large amount" a stallion of local renown from Willie Taylor and went into the horse-breeding business. The following year, when Thomas Hodgins sold the much-admired stallion called Jack's Alive to Mr. Downie of Mosa Township, Will purchased the horse from him for $500. Jack's Alive proved a popular sire in Donnelly's hands, and he once boasted that within two years his horse-breeding business was worth $4,000 per annum. It was a healthy income for those times.

Michael Donnelly also retired from stagecoaching and politicking and got a job with the Grand Trunk Railway as brakeman, travelling up and down the line which ran through Lucan. He was said to be "a favourite with the boys" at Ailsa Craig. But following the burning of his house in Lucan, Mike Donnelly moved to St. Thomas, where he obtained employment with the Canada Southern Railroad which ran from Detroit to Buffalo. Besides the danger inherent in railway work, the society of the railroad was not exactly of a refined sort. It was, in fact, not much better than in Lucan. One newspaper item serves as an example:

> A brutal kicking affray occurred on Monday last, at St. Thomas. It appears several parties were around drinking at the hotels, among the number being Jack Eustace, of Southwold, and Edmund Burke, fireman of the C.S.R. Eustace was talking about his fighting qualities, and boasted there wasn't a man in St. Thomas who could put him on his back....[12]

The incident was typical of the railway crews with which Michael Donnelly worked, his own being the construction gang on the gravel train of the C.S.R. Mike soon established his physical prowess. In any fisticuffs, either threatened or actual, between his own and the other crews he acted as a kind of champion of his men. He settled easily into the urban life of St. Thomas. Moving his family into a house on Fifth Avenue in the east end of the city, he joined the Independent Order of Foresters and regularly attended Father Flannery's local Catholic Church.

Robert Donnelly's attempts to settle into domesticity met with less success. As a result of his frequent visits to his sister Jenny in Glencoe, a double connection with the Currie family was made when Bob forsook celibacy and married Annie Currie, sister-in-law of Jenny. Notwithstanding this, he still spent much of his time at his parents' home in Biddulph with his brothers John and Tom. The latter two, following the demise of the stagecoach, had gone back to farming the land on the Roman Line but still found plenty of time for fun.

LAMBS

When Michael Crunnican was appointed one of the three new Justices of the Peace for Lucan, it was said that he "was born for the express purpose of wearing the woolsack [for] his portly form, elegance of style and jovial countenance make him the beau ideal of a justice dispenser… and should the guilty be given the privilege of selecting their judge, Squire Crunnican will be their man." The dubious compliment proved prophetic. Especially so when the peace of Lucan, despite its new magistrates and gas lamps,[1] had still to contend with Tom Donnelly and his companions, including the likes of Tommy Ryan and the young Keefes, Hogans, and Feeheleys.

Tom Ryan, a nephew of Mrs. Robert Keefe of the Roman Line, was orphaned at an early age and lived out of a trunk, often making his home either at the Donnelly homestead or at Will Donnelly's. In the summer of 1876, Ryan was with a group whiling away a Sunday afternoon picking berries, practising shooting, and throwing the shoulder stone in front of Darcey's gate on the Roman Line when Ryan accused James Carroll, son of Mick Carroll, of hitting him with a stone. When Carroll denied it, Ryan chased him home, taking a couple of shots at him as he fled. This caper landed Ryan, at the tender age of sixteen, at the Assizes and forever endeared him to Tom Donnelly and Company.

The father of the Hogan boys, too, had died when they were youngsters. Mrs. Hogan later married a well-to-do bachelor of the Catholic Settlement named John Regan, but the marriage proved tempestuous, especially when on occasion the boys would beat their stepfather. They were well known for their violent propensities. James Hogan, for example, once entered the house of John Harrigan, who was obliged to lay an information that Hogan

did beat this informant by striking two blows with his fist also threw the informant down on the floor twice and used threats, such words as that he would take the life of this informant….[2]

As for the Feeheley brothers, they were born and lived just three lots up the Roman Line from the Donnellys. They grew up to be rough-and-tumble fighters of note, "of a most forbidding appearance", once described as "a pair of white elephants …of mammoth figure and herculean proportions". Referred to in the press as "the notorious Jim Feeley", the older brother was a "very powerful and muscular" individual, while his younger brother was only slightly less formidable. They were the sons of old Mick Feeheley, who was a crony of Jim Donnelly, Sr., from the early days of Biddulph but who, on more than one occasion, cautioned his sons against associating with Tom Donnelly.[3] "He is bad company," he warned them, "and will only get you into trouble." Despite the parental warning, Jim Feeheley and Tom Donnelly became inseparable companions. "I know no one I liked better than Tom Donnelly," said young Feeheley.

In the fall of 1877 Jim Feeheley, in a brawl in one of the suburbs of London, was stabbed several times in the bowels and kidneys before clubbing his antagonist into submission. Feeheley had no sooner recovered from his encounter than he tangled with Hugh Toohey of Biddulph, an old foe of the Donnelly boys, blackening both of Toohey's eyes. When Toohey charged Feeheley with assault, the case came up before Squire Michael Crunnican of Lucan. "Can't yeez settle it between yeez?" implored the portly J.P. And it was, in the end, Crunnican's naturally conciliatory nature and his reluctance to displease anyone that led him into difficulties.

Other close companions of Tom Donnelly after he had given up stagecoaching were the younger Keefes – Daniel, James, Patrick, and Thomas. They fought many of their battles for Donnelly and his brothers and suffered for it, such as the time that Dan Keefe served six months in jail for an assault on James Toohey arising out of the Maggie Thompson affair.[4]

With the likes of Tom Ryan, the Feeheleys, the Hogans, and the Keefes, to say nothing of the Donnelly brothers, roaming the streets of Lucan, there was reason enough for the good citizens of the place to stay indoors after nightfall, despite the new gas lamps. In 1877 incidents such as the following were common:

> An attempt at highway robbery was made last night in the neighbourhood of Lucan, the victim being Mr. John McNee. Three masked men set upon him as he was travelling along, but he was fortunately able to drive them off without the accomplishment of their designs.[5]

The Lucan authorities soon decided that Lucan must also have a lock-up, and it was quickly ordered.

The Lucan lock-up, completed in August that year, stood on William Street beside the Orange Hall. On the ground floor it housed three tiny, narrow cells along with the fire engine. Upstairs was a room, twenty feet by thirty feet, called the Lucan Council Chamber. Just before the opening-day ceremonies, an anonymous wag wrote over the door of each cell the names of proposed and probable occupants. "He made some very close hits," it was said, and in all probability the names inscribed were those of Tom Donnelly, Jim Keefe, and Jim Feeheley.

With completion of the new Lucan lock-up, it seemed only appropriate for the village fathers to hire a new constable with sufficient nerve and muscle to fill it. Advertisements were circulated for the position and the bill was soon filled by the large frame of one Samuel Lount Everett. Sam Everett came from the environs of Hamilton and had been a policeman by occupation until caught and convicted of manufacturing "spirituous liquors without a licence". Lucan hired him from August 1877 for a period of one year, setting his salary at $400. It was a healthy figure considering he could augment it by constable fees: 25 cents for serving a subpoena or summons plus mileage, and $1.50 for the arrest of each person on a warrant.[6] Lucan seemed to afford plenty of opportunity for an enterprising constable to earn extra pocket money.

One of the first persons arrested by the new Lucan constable was Jim Keefe. Keefe had returned home after an absence of about a year, following the Joe Berryhill fight, and like Jim Feeheley he travelled quickly from trouble to trouble. First came a small fight with Henry Collins in Lucan, for which he was arrested and fined two dollars. Soon after, Keefe was charged with maliciously damaging a buggy of Joseph Percival of London Township and causing an accident in which Mrs. Percival was injured. Then he was arrested again for fighting with another Lucanite, the result of which was reported:

> The penalty attached to blackening a man's eye has been carefully computed by Squire Stanley, of Lucan, and the celebrated Jim Keefe has had to figure to the tune of $9.50 for placing a "shanty" over the left eye of Tom Robinson....[7]

A little while later, Keefe discovered that the whole exercise of "leg bail" for a year was frustrated when he was arrested on a charge of aggravated assault on Joe Berryhill the previous year. For good measure, he was also charged with assault upon a constable for his part in the Fitzhenry Hotel fracas, although the Grand Jury threw out the

Bob and Tom Donnelly, about 1876 (J. McIlhargey)

latter charge. The Berryhill trial took place in the middle of December. Will Donnelly gave defence evidence and after the trial boasted that his testimony was so convincing that the jury was out only ten minutes before bringing in a verdict of Not Guilty.

Then there was Keefe's Flynn caper. John Flynn had hired a rig from McFalls' livery stable in Lucan and was entering a house in Biddulph when he met Jim Keefe and John Cavanagh on their way out. When Flynn came out again, he found his rig and horses gone, and he eventually learned they had been driven wildly about the countryside by Keefe and Cavanagh and then abandoned. Flynn laid charges, but on a Sunday before the hearing, Jim Keefe's brother Patrick heard that Flynn was attending St. Patrick's Church; meeting him on the front steps after the service, he kicked him into insensibility. For this assault Patrick Keefe was fined three dollars by Justices of the Peace J. D. McCosh, William Stanley, and Michael Crunnican, a penalty considered totally inadequate by many Lucanites. The theft charge against James Keefe fell through when Flynn was prevented, because of his injuries, from attending the trial, but he laid a fresh charge. To scare him off this time, Keefe intimated that a suit for malicious prosecution would be instituted if Flynn persisted in proceeding. Flynn refused to withdraw the charge until one day as he sat with his back to the window in the rear of the Queen's Hotel a half-brick was thrown at his head.

Flynn fell forward off his chair, falling on his face on the floor, the blood gushing in a stream from the ghastly wound. He soon, however, staggered to his feet and exclaimed, "I'm shot! I'm shot!"[8]

Finally learning his lesson, when the new charge came up at the Fall Assizes, Flynn was not available to prosecute and Keefe and Cavanagh "were bailed to appear to answer the charge when called on, tantamount to a dismissal."

During his first few weeks in Lucan Constable Sam Everett earned plenty of pocket money. After his arrest of Keefe in August, he ran in a couple of boys in the village named Robert Young and Richard Thompson for being "drunk and dis-

orderly". The next arrest was far more serious. It was for murder, the suspects in the case being James Hogan and his mother, Mary Regan. One of the papers chortled that the new constable "effected their arrest with considerable adroitness", while another crowed, "Constable Everett is just the man for Lucan." It appears that James Hogan gave his mother and stepfather a piece of salt pork which Mrs. Regan cooked up for her husband. Shortly after eating it, Regan died, and when a cat was fed some of the pork it, too, died. Dr. Thomas Hossack was called to the house just in time to see, in Regan, the classic symptom of strychnine poisoning – the body arched in agony – take effect. When the doctor told Mrs. Regan he thought the old man had been poisoned, Mrs. Regan threw up her hands and said, "Some people might be bad enough to say so."

The state of Lucan lawlessness, blamed time and time again on the local magistrates, was exemplified by the Regan case. "They are afraid to do anything," it was said of the Lucan J.P.s, and Dr. John Gunn, coroner from the neighbouring village of Ailsa Craig, wrote the Crown Attorney:

A person was ready to swear an information charging both Mary Regan and her son Hogan with the murder. In fact he had the information drawn up but could not get a single magistrate in the village to take the information. They are perfectly useless in any case that requires immediate...action and I am sorry to be compelled to say that the Magistrates of Lucan are more ornamental than useful to the furthering of justice.[9]

Squire William Stanley retorted that "if Coroner Gunn had applied to me first I would have issued the warrant, but I do not believe in Squire Crunnican shirking his duty and shifting hard cases over on me."

The Regan murder case was the occasion of the first falling-out between Sam Everett and Michael Crunnican, J.P. When Crunnican failed to act, Everett and the coroner applied to William K. Atkinson, a J.P. of Ailsa Craig, who issued the warrants on which the arrests were made. The ill-feeling between Crunnican and Everett was intensified when the case of James Feeheley, charged with assaulting Hugh Toohey, came before the Lucan magistrate. Crunnican was approached by the defendant's father, Mick Feeheley, and for the sake of their long-standing friendship he agreed to try settling the case. "I'll fix it all right with the constable," Crunnican assured the old man and spoke to Everett about young Feeheley. "I tell yeez," he said, "I've known him since he was that high. He's a daicent young man and if it wasn't for the liquor he's quiet as a lamb. Can't yeez settle it between yeez?"

Everett, having had the job of arresting Jim Feeheley, was indignant at Crunnican's characterization of him as a lamb. Even when Toohey was persuaded to withdraw the charge, Everett insisted on payment of the costs. When old Mick Feeheley thereupon complained to the Crown Attorney that they were excessive, the constable grew even more furious. He fumed about the village and repeated with great embellishments the story of Crunnican's thwarting of the course of true justice. Soon the entire village was mockingly referring to Feeheley, Keefe, Donnelly, and the others as the Lucan Lambs.

The Lucan Lambs were at first over-awed by Sam Everett's aggressive approach to his duties. The new constable, it was soon apparent, would not hesitate to wade in with elbows flying and handcuffs at the ready whenever the *argumentum fistscuffum* broke out in the village. Furthermore, he could match "the bhoys" any time in extravagant and colourful language, a necessary attribute to anyone who pretended to patrol Lucan's sidewalks and bar-rooms. On the other hand, Sam Everett's apparent firmness with the Lucan magistrates endeared him to a large segment of the law abiding citizens of the place. They hailed him as a kind of saviour.

> These Biddulph "lambs"…have for years kept the community in a uproar, and they now and to their terror have a "lion" to deal with[10]

said one of the editors, who went on to say that the hitherto magic phrase "'Can't yeez settle it between yeez?' has lost its charms, and the expression is no longer potent in Lucan."

On the part of William Porte, however, the new constable was the recipient of an almost immediate animosity. Perhaps the postmaster was envious of Everett's salary, the post office yielding only $334 that year. More likely it was simply a clash of opposite personalities. The scholarly little postmaster with a taste for culture was quite a contrast to the burly constable of coarse manners and even coarser language. Porte was soon sniping at Everett through the anonymous columns of the *Parkhill Gazette*, where he wrote one day: "Chief Constable Everett was in such a profound state of *coma* as to be unable to navigate,"[11] and suggested that the cause of it was the constable's weakness for "Bob McLean's forty rod and the Queen's tangle leg", two of Lucan's favourite alcoholic mixes. Everett vowed to take revenge, and in addition to instructing a lawyer to institute a suit for libel against the newspaper he wrote the Post Office Department demanding an investigation of the post office at Lucan.

The crafty Everett also kept a sharp eye open for Porte's own weakness for "a touch uv the crathur". One day he found the wee postmaster had indulged in the grog a little too freely, and he dragged him, kicking and screaming, into the village lock-up. William Stanley fined Porte one dollar for being "drunk and disorderly". "It was generally admitted," reports said, "that Everett on that occasion exceeded his duty in the manner in which he ran him in." This act of high-handedness earned Everett the Lucan postmaster's implacable and undying hatred, and the constable and the postmaster feuded verbally for years thereafter. Everett later claimed that Porte had caused much of the trouble in Lucan by encouraging the Donnelly brothers in their wild ways. "If you have a particle of Irish in you which as been transmitted to you by your parents," Everett claimed that Porte had exhorted the Donnellys, "you will come on or send somebody to shoot the man." And, Everett claimed, Porte told the boys: "The fire bug must bite him to learn him something."

With Sam Everett in charge of Lucan, Tom Donnelly and his friends spent more time in the village of Granton. At that time it had a population of about two hundred and boasted three stores, two hotels, two churches, a grist mill, a sawmill, a barrel factory, at least one bootlegger, but no lock-up. Soon the people of Granton were scandalized at "those terrible Lucan oaths" heard more and more on their streets. Wrote James Grant, a village father, local Justice of the Peace, and the leading citizen of the place: "Our village is infested with a few drunken vagabonds [and] although every person wishes them away, no one can be got to make information. Can I as a J.P. summon such parties before me and fine or confine them upon sight as I very often see them in that state and have received abusive language on the spot...?" Grant concluded the letter to the Crown Attorney by asking "in what way a lock-up could be got".

Any suggestion of lawlessness in and around Granton at this time was naturally blamed upon the Donnelly Gang. A favourite prank was to take out horses and run them up and down the concession lines into exhaustion, as Keefe and Cavanagh had done with Flynn's rig. In November 1877, a couple of horses of John McIlhargey, who lived near Elginfield, were found one morning near James Hawkins' blacksmith shop at Garrett's Corners on the south boundary of Biddulph "in a very muddy and exhausted condition...on each horse...a bridle, the reins of one being thrown over the neck of the other". The following week witnessed another incident:

On Thursday night, November 29th, about or after midnight two horses were taken from the stable of Mr. T. C. Hodgins, proprietor of the Granton sawmills, and judging from their appearance were ridden several miles and turned loose....[12]

Earlier, a bolder horse-prank was reported:

Mr. John Hodgson, painter, of Carlisle, takes this opportunity of denying the statement made by certain parties that he had ran his mare at the Ailsa Craig races... Mr. H. informs us the animal was taken out of his stable without his leave, and that he does not believe in, nor is he an advocate of, horse racing.[13]

Meanwhile, rumours circulated in Biddulph that "the respactable Mr. Mick Carroll" of the Roman Line was in possession of damaging testimony which he intended to give in court against James Hogan in the Regan murder case. Shortly after, the barn and outbuildings of Carroll's farm burned to the ground at two o'clock in the morn-

ing. Carroll said that the fire had been deliberately set and blamed the Donnelly Gang, but he laid no formal charges. The Regan murder case continued to drag on when the pathologist from Toronto took sick and was unable to attend the trial. Hogan and his mother were let out on bail, with William Donnelly standing as one of Hogan's bondsmen. [14]

Following the Carroll fire, a number of other burnings took place in Biddulph, the origins of which seemed to be spite of one form or another. First, Richard Reycraft on the fourteenth concession lost his outbuildings valued at $2,000, with insurance of only $1,200. Reycraft said that it was arson and that he was going to sell out and leave the district. A short while later

The barns of Mr. John Herbert, Biddulph, were fired by an incendiary, and a large amount of grain and crops, together with buildings, destroyed.[15]

John Herbert lived between Lucan and Clandeboye and his son had married a daughter of Ted Crowley, former partner of the Flanagans in the stagecoach enterprise. Herbert was bitter about losing his three large buildings, which were "of a superior kind", and he had suspicions about who set the fire, for he discovered footsteps in the snow leading from the road to the barns. Moreover, it was said,

Herbert has had some law suits and difficulties with some of his neighbours lately, and it is rumoured this may have something to do with the outrage.[16]

A few weeks later the neighbour with whom Herbert had been having difficulties was identified after a fashion when he, too, suffered a misfortune:

Mr. William Haskett's frame barn, new reaper, gang plow, sulky rake, and other implements were destroyed by fire Saturday night. There is no doubt about how the fire originated, as the tracks of horses could be discerned around the building.[17]

The account ended by stating that "Mr. Haskett will be a heavy loser as his insurance had just run out." It is a wonder that insurance companies were still willing to do business in Biddulph.

Early in December Jim Keefe ventured back into Lucan and was promptly arrested by Sam Everett,

The Elginfield Hotel. In 1877 this hotel was operated by Michael Glass and invaded by Tom Donnelly and company.

this time for brawling with James Scilly. The combatants were fined by William Stanley for breach of the peace.

Kept at bay in Lucan, Tom Donnelly and Company frequented instead the taverns of the neighbouring countryside. Shortly after Christmas 1877, the gang invaded the big brick hotel built by William H. Ryan at the Elginfield Corner, then being operated by Michael Glass and called the Union Hotel. The event was duly reported:

A few of the natives deliberately took possession of Glass' Hotel, Elginfield, London township and commenced a fearful scrimmage. Poor Glass had no chance whatever.
The table and punch was upsot,

An the row it commenced in a minit, sure.
Niver a taste of shtick had he got,
So he picked up a piece of the furniture.[18]

The invaders "soon made splinters of all and sundry the bar furniture", the report continued, and the poor proprietor was forced to flee his own premises which were left a shambles. He made his way to Lucan, where he applied to Squire Stanley "to send Everett, the constable" in quick dispatch before his hotel was flattened. Stanley replied that Glass himself was a magistrate fully capable of calling out his own constables, if he had any, and that he had enough to do to keep peace in the village without worrying about the rural environs. Glass went away complaining about the lawlessness of the countryside and the cowardice of the Lucan magistrates.

> Glass gives the names of three of the "lambs" with whom probably our readers are already familiar – Donnelly, Keefe and Feely. He says the way they "cleaned out his decanters and tapped his bottled ale wud make any man shed tears." During the row Mrs. Glass with a poker, and Mickey, with an axe handle, did all a properly constituted landlady and an able bodied hostler could reasonably be expected to do, but alas! the good woman was bowled down like a nine-pin, and Mickey retired howling "wid a shanty over his eye".

Constable Everett's next encounter with the Lucan Lambs came not long after, in January 1878, when Tommy Ryan went swaggering through the village like Jim Bowie, waving a "huge dirk-knife" and challenging all and sundry. But Everett pounced on Ryan and dragged him into the Lucan lock-up without further ceremony. The village soon buzzed with rumours that Ryan's friends were vowing to "spring the prisoner" at the first opportunity. Determined to frustrate them, the constable remained on guard at the lock-up with shotgun at hand until finally, at three o'clock in the morning, he deemed all safe. Then he quietly slipped out the door and made his way home to bed. Ryan's friends, however, had been watching the building from a nearby house and shortly after Everett left, they crept out.

> With jimmies, crow-bars and other burglar tools the "Biddulph and Lucan lambs" soon made a hole sufficient to run a wheelbarrow in, and in a very short time Tom Ryan was a free man.[19]

The next morning the Donnellys, Keefes, and Feeheleys swaggered about the village gloating and chuckling. They made sly remarks about the hole in the lock-up, urging everyone to go down and see the draughty little jailhouse. Sam Everett had suffered his first defeat at the hands of the Lucan Lambs.

24

NED RYAN

When, in far-off Rome in February 1878, Pope Pius Xl died,

> The bells of St. Patrick's church, Biddulph, tolled all day Saturday and Sunday in consequence of the death [and] the interior of the church was draped.[1]

One of the many pilgrims who made the long voyage across the ocean to pay homage to the new head of the church, Pope Leo Xlll, was a humble parish priest from Quebec, Canada – Father John Connolly. His destiny would soon be linked to the Donnelly family of Biddulph and Lucan.

In March Edward Ryan, usually called Ned, was robbed on the streets of Lucan, and the men accused of committing the crime were Tom Donnelly and Jim Feeheley.[2] Ned Ryan lived originally on the Swamp Line of Biddulph on the old Ryan homestead. In 1874 a mysterious fire burned down his barn, containing grain and implements, and although he managed to get his horses and harness out of the burning building, he was so hard pressed, he said at the time, that he could not even save his coat. While his loss was $700, the insurance company paid $500 of it and the township refunded his taxes for the year, so, all in all, Ryan was quite well satisfied with the results of his fire. Then, in the winter of 1877-78, Ryan bought Thomas Casey's old place on the Roman Line, close to the Donnelly farm, selling his own farm to brother-in-law Patrick Nangle. Thus it was that on March 5,1878, Ned Ryan made the trip to Lucan, which he had been planning ever since he received the balance of the cash for his old farm from Nangle shortly before. The purpose of the trip was to purchase lumber for new frame outbuildings and to have a spree, for Ned was known to "take a bit of a sip" once in a while. The Ryan boys were, in fact, notorious and legendary drunkards.[3] "I have lain in the bush all night," Ned Ryan once admitted on his oath, "with a jug of whiskey."

On his way to Lucan, Ryan happily fingered the eighty-six dollars which he had counted out into a money bag and jammed into his right-hand breeches' pocket. Pausing for a few moments in Martin Hogan's field, he pulled out the wad and counted it again to make sure it was all there – one ten-dollar bill and nineteen four-dollar bills. Arriving in Lucan at two o'clock that afternoon, he went first to the bar-room of Walker's Hotel. Tom Donnelly and Jim Feeheley were there. Now the only thing that bothered Ryan about his new farm was that it was near the Donnellys. They were no worse than their neighbours, he told himself, but they had a bad name. The chance meeting was an opportunity for creating a little goodwill.

"Well, boys," said Ryan, "as we're going to be neighbours, why don't we all have a drink together."

"Good idea," Donnelly and Feeheley agreed.

Ryan pulled out a four-dollar bill and they ordered – cherry wine for himself and whiskey for the other two. "Have another round, boys," Ryan said and ordered more drinks.

Tom Donnelly then bought the next round and Ryan got up to leave. "Well, boys," he said, "I've got to go over to Haskett's sawmill and buy some lumber. I'll see you later."

Ryan ordered his lumber, chatted with the proprietor, and counted out the money to pay for his order. Returning to Walker's Hotel he found Tom Donnelly and Jim Feeheley still there. Feeheley then bought a round of drinks, after which the three of them strolled over to McLean's Hotel. Donnelly and Feeheley did not usually drink at McLean's and they took nothing. From McLean's they went up the street to John Cain's Royal Hotel, where again they drank nothing. After about an hour of sitting around, Ryan left his companions and went to Farrell's drug store, where he purchased copybooks for his twelve children, paying Farrell twenty cents for them. Sticking the books in his pocket he sauntered over to the Queen's Hotel just before dark. He met

John Casey there and they treated each other to a drink apiece, whereupon Tom Donnelly and Jim Feeheley walked in, greeting Ryan like a long-lost friend and sitting down beside him. The Queen's was a hotel where Donnelly and Feeheley would drink. "Well," mused Ryan to himself, "seeing that I'm going to live down there in that section, I've got to be liberal with them." Out loud he said to them, "Boys, how about another drink?"

They had another drink, and then it was someone else's turn to treat. "Oh, Ned," Tom Donnelly said, "I'm a little short of money. Could you lend me a dollar?"

Ryan hesitated only for a moment. "Why, sure, Tom. Here," he said and handed him a dollar bill. "And here's the loan of a quarter for you, Jim."

"Let's have another round, Mr. Falls," cried Tom Donnelly. (They always referred to the proprietor, Alex McFalls, as "Falls".)

It had now got dark outside but the revelry and the noise in the bar-room of the Queen's Hotel continued. Other patrons had come in until there were about a dozen people in the room, including a man named Coursey and Simon Young. Someone was telling stories and the others were laughing. Tom Donnelly began to make a bet with Coursey and they bantered about the size of it while Ryan kept getting more and more intoxicated. Draped drunkenly over the counter, he roused himself when he heard the discussion of money, and fumbling for his bag he reached in and pulled out a fistful of bills. "Here," he blubbered, "I've got more to bet than any of you."

They all looked at the money and laughed. "No bet, no bet," Coursey laughed. "The bet is quashed."

Alex McFalls scowled and called out, "Ryan, you better let me have that money and count it for you or you'll lose it."

"Oh, it's all right," Ryan muttered and stuffed the money back into his pocket.

"The damned fool!" thought McFalls to himself. "He's the worse of liquor and will lose it sure."

McFalls shrugged his shoulders and left the bar-room after more drinks were ordered. Ned Ryan was too drunk to remember whose turn it was to treat. "Boys, boys," he finally called out to

Alex McFalls, proprietor of the Queen's Hotel in Lucan in the late 1870s

his companions, "Tom Donnelly. And Jim. It's getting late and it's time we got started home."

"Hold on, Ned," they laughed back. "There's time enough. Let's have another treat."

"But I must get started home," Ryan insisted. "It's late."

"All right," they finally agreed. "Let's go home."

As they took leave of the others, all three of them seemed pretty well intoxicated. "Donnelly wasn't extra sober and Feeheley wasn't extra drunk," said Simon Young. The way Ryan himself put it was, "I might was a little hazy."

The three of them wavered along until they came to Alice Street and had gone about ten yards along this thoroughfare when Feeheley said, "I've forgotten something. I must fetch it and I'll be right back. "

He turned and was quickly lost in the darkness. "Don't be long," called Tom Donnelly after him, standing on the right side of Ryan. "Hurry up, and we'll go easy."

Donnelly then flung his arm in a friendly way across Ryan's shoulders and they continued walking slowly. They had reached a point about opposite the house of Reeve Thomas Dight when suddenly someone came up behind Ryan and grasped him tightly around the body, pinning his arm to his side. Ryan was sure it was Jim Feeheley. He struggled but could not break free. As soon as he was taken hold of from behind, Ryan said, Tom Donnelly reached for his breeches pocket with the money bag in it.

Before Ryan could cry out for help, Donnelly brought his other arm up around his throat and choked him. Then whoever had grasped him from behind flung him to the ground, and although he lost consciousness he remembered that as he fell Donnelly's hand was still in his pocket.

When Ned Ryan regained his senses he found Simon Young and Mike Gleeson standing over him. The two boys tried lifting him but he was too heavy. They ran off to get John Nevills, a villager who was related to Ryan by marriage. Other passers-by, including Joseph Lynch, the village auctioneer, William Rollins and his wife, and John H. McRoberts, came along and stared at Ryan lying in the gravel. McRoberts went to fetch the constable.

"The man's dead drunk," said Everett when he arrived on the scene a few minutes later.

The constable tried to rouse him and Ryan opened his eyes but said nothing. When Everett tried to get him on his feet Ryan could barely stand.

"Come along, fellow," Everett said, "it's the lock-up for you."

But John Nevills arrived with Simon Young just then and piped up, "Oh, Mr. Everett, this man is Edward Ryan. My wife is a niece of his. He's been on a spree today but if you release him to me I'll take him home and take care of him."

The constable readily agreed. Young and Nevills

got on either side of Ryan, helped him over to Nevills' place, and took off his boots.

"Ned, do you have any money about you?" Mrs. Nevills asked him.

Ryan half growled and half blubbered in answer, "The money's all right." He staggered and fell as he tried to remove his coat, and then vomited.

"It's no use talking to him about anything," Nevills said. "He's too drunk. Let's get him to bed. But Simon, just wait a minute while we search his clothes. I want a witness."

They then looked through Ryan's pockets and found a dollar bill and some loose change but nothing more, except the copybooks for his children.

The next morning when John Nevills called Ryan for breakfast between five and six o'clock,

Ryan immediately missed his money. "Those buggers!" he thought to himself, trying to remember the details of the night before. "They stole my money. However, I am going to be living close to where Donnelly and Feeheley live so I better not get too harsh about it until I see them and have a talk about it." To Nevills he said simply, "I lost some money last night but I know who's got it."

Ryan ate breakfast and then went down to the main part of the village, where he inquired after Donnelly and Feeheley. Someone said they had taken the train to Granton. Ryan hired a horse and buggy and drove to Thomas Culbert's hotel in Granton, where he asked the proprietor if he had seen Donnelly or Feeheley.

"They're upstairs," Culbert replied.

Beech Street, Lucan, looking toward the spot where Ned Ryan claimed to have been robbed by Tom Donnelly and Jim Feeheley (J. Bilyea)

Reg. vs. Donnelly
Statement of Edward Ryan

On the 5th March 1878 I was in the village of Lucan in the afternoon. I had on my person $83.00. I paid $6.00 and some cents for lumber out of that amt – I spent some money in treating over $1.00 perhaps. I lent one Thomas Donnelly $1.00 and James Feely 25¢. I had the balance of the money on my person excepting 20¢ pd for two children's copy books. I met Donnelly & Feely in Lucan that afternoon & we had a few drinks together – I drank only ginger wine perhaps 10 glasses – I had the money remaining after above sums were deducted in a money bag in my right hand breeches pocket – I had taken out the purse showing the money to Donnelly & Feely between 8 & 9 o'clock on the evening of that day. After we had got a few yards from McFalls hotel Feely said he had forgotten something & shd go back. Donnelly sd to him do not be long. Donnelly then walked along at my side with his left arm thrown across my shoulder – When he had proceeded in this manner about 50 rods from McFalls' some one came up behind me and threw his arms around my body pinning my arms – Donnelly then put his right hand in my pocket – I struggled and shouted – Donnelly then took me by the throat with his left hand. I was thrown on the ground and Donnelly took the money out of my pocket and as I still continued shouting and struggling I was choked until I became insensible – On the following morning I followed Donnelly & Feely to Granton & tried to get my money back. I could not see Donnelly but saw Feely. I laid an information against Donnelly on the evening of the 6th March 1878 – Donnelly was arrested sometime in April 1879 – Donnellys brother offered me his father's note for the amt – for half the money if I would settle – I was threatened if I dared to proceed and my barn was burned down last September (1878).

(UWO)

William "Wild Bill" Hodgins, the Lucan constable (V. Pybus)

"Tell them there's a man wanting to see them," Ryan said.

The landlord went upstairs and Jim Feeheley soon came down and greeted Ryan, who came right to the point. "Jim, you and Donnelly were fit to rob me last night. I can't afford to lose that much. Now you just give me back whatever you have left of it and I'll go home and say nothing more about it."

Feeheley's expression turned into an icy glare.

"I never took your money, Ryan," he said. "You just get the hell out of here before I beat the hell out of you."

Feeheley's tone of voice told Ryan it was useless to remonstrate. He returned to Lucan, had a couple more drinks, and went to see Sam Everett. He had been pretty drunk the night before, Everett advised him, but if he still wanted to press charges

he should see a magistrate. Squire McCosh was available and Ryan had warrants issued against Tom Donnelly and Jim Feeheley for robbery. He returned home that evening a sadder and poorer man.

Within a day or two Constable William Hodgins of Lucan rode out to the Donnelly farm with the warrant for Tom's arrest. Tom met him in the yard before he could even dismount and asked him what he wanted. When Hodgins told him, he went quickly into the house. The constable dismounted and was about to tie his horse up to the fence when Tom reappeared with a long gun which he raised to his shoulder and pointed at Hodgins' head.

"You son of a bitch," he threatened, "I'll blow your brains out if you don't get the hell out of here."

Then James Donnelly, Sr., came out of the house.

He said nothing to his son but spoke calmly and quietly to Hodgins: "Don't worry yerself, he's not goin' to shoot ye. But ye betther not think uv tyin' up the horse."

William Hodgins said later that his horse was a wild and temperamental stallion, and on reflection he considered it might act up if left tied up at the fence while he made the arrest. Hodgins got back on his horse and returned to Lucan. Constable "Wild Bill" Hodgins, as he was called ever after, would not go back to the Donnelly homestead to arrest Tom Donnelly, and neither would any of the other constables.[4] Word soon drifted back to the Donnelly farm that so long as Tom Donnelly stayed away from Lucan, he would not be bothered by any of them.

Ned Ryan later claimed that some time after the robbery John Donnelly came to him. "I'll give you my father's note for half the money, if you settle the case," John Donnelly told him. "If you go ahead, well, you might get some bad luck."

Ryan refused to settle for half the amount, and during that entire summer Tom Donnelly and Jim Feeheley stayed away from Lucan. Toward the end of the year they both left the district and went to work in the Michigan lumber camps. But before they left, in September, Ryan's barns burned down, and the door of his house was broken in with a stone during the night.

TWO YEARS

Shortly after Ned Ryan lost his money, there was more excitement in Lucan; someone took a potshot at Sam Everett. This is the way Everett described it:

On the night of the 18th March about twenty minutes

or a quarter to twelve I was going home. As I was between my gate and my house I heard the snap of a gun or pistol...and saw the flash of the cap. The gun held fire for three or five seconds followed by report of the gun. I looked steadily at the person who held the gun over a pole that stuck out of a pile of wood. The person that held the gun was Bob Donnelly....[1]

The woodpile was some fifty feet away from Everett when the shot was fired. Bob Donnelly must have been either a poor shot or a charitable man, for the bullet missed its mark. Everett ran toward him, but on reaching the spot where the gun had been fired he found only the tracks of stockinged feet in the snow. Everett fetched Malcolm McIsaac, a near neighbour and a friend of Patrick Flanagan, the old foe of the Donnelly family. Together the two men followed the tracks which led through the yard of William Stanley's large grist mill and across several ploughed fields, seemingly in the direction of Cornelius Carty's place.

The news of the shooting caused a great stir among the Lucan populace. What was the place coming to, they asked, when the village constable could be shot dead in his tracks? The citizens became so edgy that a day or two later the London *Advertiser* reported:

The big joke of the season came off at Lucan, [when] the ventriloquist in Cool Burgess' troupe got under the bed and sounded *fire*. The lawyer and the banker who slept in the adjoining rooms, hearing the cry, as they supposed, coming from the street, ran in all directions, the former pounding the doors opposite, with a view of awakening the McCosh Brothers, and the latter making his way to the bank, in order to stand by the vaults in case of emergency.[2]

Sam Everett took a week to mull things over. It seems that his identification of Bob Donnelly as the man who had shot at him was shaky. The cagey constable told no one at first, but let out hints that he was "fully persuaded that the individual who fired the shot was one of the gang" who had rescued Ryan from the lock-up not long before. Finally, exactly one week after the shot was fired, Sam Everett arrested Bob Donnelly on the charge and deposited him in the Lucan lock-up. William Porte accused Everett of trying to blackmail Donnelly before the arrest and of only going through with it after the blackmail attempt had failed.

For the next three or four days the excitement in the village remained high. The brothers and friends of the prisoner skulked about the streets muttering dire threats against Everett, the other constables, and the magistrates. Extra guards were posted around the jailhouse, among them Constable Wild Bill Hodgins, still smarting from his ignominious attempt to arrest Tom Donnelly.

Young Tommy Hines, brother-in-law of Mike Donnelly, was delegated to visit Bob in the lock-up and give him some advice, for while Bob may have been the handsomest of the Donnelly boys, he was definitely not the brightest. It was said that while he bided his time in jail, he appeared quite confident of being able to prove his innocence and was heard to say, "Everett could not possibly have been able to identify me because I was wearing a mask at the time."[3]

It was Tommy Hines' task to persuade him to rely on some other defence. Shortly after the visit, however, young Hines was arrested and charged with "tampering with the prisoner". He was remanded for three days by Justices of the Peace William Hutchins and William Stanley, of Lucan. Finally, James Donnelly, Sr., came to the village and rounded up a villager named Maguire to stand with him as bondsmen upon the release of young Hines.

The same two magistrates, augmented by the presence of Michael Crunnican, then heard the evidence against Robert Donnelly on Wednesday, March 27. In addition to Everett's testimony, there was said to be evidence by Wild Bill Hodgins that Bob Donnelly had confessed to the crime while in the lock-up. The magistrates committed Donnelly for trial on a charge of shooting with intent to kill.

As the news of the alleged confession and committal made the atmosphere of Lucan even more tense, the magistrates ordered the prisoner to be taken to London forthwith to be tried at the Assizes then in progress. All of the available constables in and around Lucan were rounded up, and under heavy guard Bob Donnelly was loaded into a carriage and driven to the Clandeboye Railway

Tommy Hines, Michael Donnelly's brother-in-law (C. Andrewes)

Station. Just as the conveyance reached the station, however, the train drove off and the prisoner had to be taken back to the Lucan lock-up.

The constables, wary of a possible assault on the building, prowled about. Wild Bill Hodgins was poking around the railway tracks not far from the rear of the lock-up when suddenly John Donnelly jumped out of one of the cars brandishing a pistol.

"You son of a bitch. Hodgins," he declared,

pointing the pistol at the other's breast. "I'll teach you to swear false against Bob. I ought to blow the heart out of you."

Bill Hodgins was the same age as John Donnelly and had known him since boyhood.

"Jack," he said quietly, "you haven't got the nerve to shoot."

The constable knew that the Donnelly brothers were basically fist-men, not gun-men, and that of all the brothers John was the least likely to take unfair advantage of an old friend. John hesitated and Hodgins used the opportunity to give his opponent an honourable way out.

"If you want to try your muscle," said Hodgins, "I'll meet you over at the back of Jackson's foundry."[4]

John Donnelly lowered his pistol. "I'll be there in half an hour," he said and walked away.

The news of the impending "pitch battle" quickly spread through the village, and by the time the combatants arrived at the appointed spot there were almost a hundred spectators present. The fight began, and was by all accounts a "terrific rough-and-tumble" encounter between the two well-conditioned and well-muscled men, in the best Lucan and Biddulph tradition. "For a space of thirty minutes" the two men "pounded each other in a brutal manner". With guttural grunts they grappled, thumped, and thwacked away until both were fairly exhausted.

At one point during the fight a lumber merchant of the village, William Henry Atkinson, came along. Scandalized at the proceedings, he attempted to stop the fight, but another of the Lucan constables, John Bawden, stepped forward. Bawden was a close friend of Wild Bill Hodgins and knew that he could hold his own in the contest with Donnelly, for when aroused he was a formidable fighter.

"Hold! Hold!" Bawden bawled out when Atkinson attempted to interfere. He brandished a pistol in the air and waved the lumber merchant back. "Nobody interfere. Fair fight! Fair fight!"

The struggle continued. Finally, one of the combatants – in all probability it was John Donnelly – cried "Enough!"

Sam Everett waited until the din of battle subsided. Then he moved in and charged each of the two fighters with assault and breach of a village by-law prohibiting fighting. Bawden was also charged with a minor offence. J.P. William Stanley meted out the punishment: Hodgins, the apparent winner of the physical contest, was fined five dollars, Donnelly was fined four dollars, and Bawden got off scot-free. Donnelly and Hodgins were each fined one dollar under the by-law.

On Friday of that week Bob Donnelly was transported to London without incident, but the Lucan lock-up was not empty for long, for one of the London newspapers reported:

On the 29th instant one of the Lucan lambs went around with a drawn bowie knife daring anyone to arrest him. Before he was aware of it he was pounced on by one of the constables and placed in the Lucan lock-up.[5]

Bob Donnelly arrived in London in time for the Grand Jury to find a True Bill against him. David Glass, again retained as defence counsel, immediately applied to have certain defence witnesses subpoenaed, and the case was set down as the last one to be heard at the Spring Assizes for Saturday, March 30,1878, before Mr. Justice Adam Wilson, one of the kindlier judges on circuit.

Many of the Donnelly family attended the trial. It was held in the City Hall Council Chambers because the venerable Court House on the banks of the Thames River was then being renovated, with a tower being added to the front door. Constable Sam Everett's story had changed slightly since the time of the shooting. Everett now stated that on the night in question he had knocked at the door and when it was opened by his housekeeper he had stooped to fondle his watchdog. It was then he heard the snap of a gun cap, the shot, and the slugs enter the door casing above his head. His evidence was followed by that of George Gear, the painter who had been shot in the leg the year previous while guarding the goods of Barney Stanley. Gear swore that he had seen the prisoner on the night in question in the village with a gun under his overcoat. As for the alleged confession, it turned out to be an incriminating statement overheard by William Hodgins.

"If the gun had not hung fire," Bob Donnelly

Justice Adam Wilson, who sentenced Robert Donnelly to two years in Kingston Penitentiary

All during the trial the prisoner maintained a cool and easy demeanour, turning his eyes to different parts of the courtroom, as if looking for someone and not caring in the least whether or no he found him.... He frequently broke out in a broad smile, as though it were an excellent piece of fooling gotten up especially for his entertainment.[6]

For the defence, James and Johannah Donnelly and their son John came to court prepared to substantiate the defendant's alibi.[7] Bob Donnelly was at home on the night in question, they testified, and could not possibly have fired the shot. Three other alibi witnesses were produced.

It was late in the evening when the last witness was heard, but Mr. Justice Adam Wilson was anxious to complete the Assize list and proceeded to charge the jury, notwithstanding the late hour. He told them it came down to a matter of credibility. One side must have lied and it was up to the jury to decide which. It was 11:20 p.m. when the jury retired to consider the four counts facing the prisoner. They were:

1. That he did shoot with intent to kill and murder;
2. That he did shoot with intent to maim;
3. That he did shoot with intent to disable;
4. That he did shoot with intent to do grievous bodily harm.

A few minutes before midnight the jury returned with its verdict: Guilty on the first count.

"You find the prisoner guilty on the first count," said the Judge as he was recording the verdict, "which specifies that he shot with intent to kill and murder."

On hearing these words one of the jurymen, S. H. Craig, looked startled and rose from his seat. "There is a mistake," he said. "We only found Donnelly guilty of shooting with intent to kill, my Lord. Murder was not mentioned."

The Judge tried to explain the various counts, but the jury would have none of it, insisting that the word "murder" had not been intended to be used. The Crown Attorney finally got up and said he would be happy to accept a verdict of guilty of any of the four counts in the indictment.

"Well," said Mr. Justice Adam Wilson, "if the jury find that the prisoner shot with intent to kill,

was reported by Hodgins to have said, "the shot would have torn Everett's heart out."

The evidence was, on the whole, pretty damning. But it appears that Robert, who, unlike some of his brothers, was facing a jury for the first time, had apparently been coached on his demeanour for the occasion. His brother Will advised him to appear confident at all times and especially unconcerned when damaging testimony was given. The trial spectators were therefore puzzled when they observed the prisoner in the dock.

they should have no difficulty in agreeing that he shot with intent to do grievous bodily harm."

The jurymen then whispered among themselves for a moment and agreed to bring in a verdict of guilty on the fourth count. The Judge was in the process of recording the verdict when the clock in the court-room struck twelve midnight. This prompted defence counsel David Glass to rise.

"I wish Your Lordship to note that the verdict was rendered after twelve o'clock," he said.

The Judge looked up sharply. "Well, if you wish the jury locked up over Sunday, I must order it to be done."

"I don't wish that," Glass hastily answered. "I will withdraw my objection."

"I don't know that I have the power to allow it," Mr. Justice Wilson replied. "I cannot permit such a circumstance to be taken advantage of by the prisoner afterwards."

"Oh, the prisoner will not take advantage of it, my Lord," Glass assured the court.

"I am not so sure about that," the Judge replied. Then, turning to the sheriff, he said, "Mr. Sheriff, can you tell me what time it is?"

"It is about three minutes after twelve, my Lord," the official replied.

"Then," said the Judge, "I will leave the jury in your hands till nine o'clock Monday morning. Keep them together, and if they desire to go to church you can detail a constable to attend them. Give them all reasonable comforts."

The jurors filed quietly out of the courtroom, casting rueful glances at Glass. The following Monday morning the ritual of obtaining the verdict was again gone through, and the jury brought back the same verdict of Guilty of shooting with intent to do grievous bodily harm. David Glass asked the judge to defer sentencing until affidavits could be obtained as to the prisoner's previous good character. But the judge stated he had to be in St. Thomas the following morning and could not wait, whereupon Glass made submissions as to sentence, stating as his chief point that the prisoner had never previously been charged with any serious criminal offence.

"Do you have anything to say before sentence is passed upon you?"

"No," Bob replied.

Justice Adam Wilson then spoke in somewhat the following words:

In passing sentence upon you I observe that it is true that no criminal charge of a serious nature has previously been brought against you, but still it seems from the evidence that you have been infected with the spirit that seems to be the bane of the neighbourhood of Lucan. Now I believe that there are some good points in the family of which you are a member. I have no doubt that the Donnelly family are generous, warm-hearted, and would make warm friends. But there is no doubt and it is also true that they make bad enemies. I do not wish to refer to any distressing family matters but I can not help referring to the fact that your father was once under sentence of death. And I can tell you, Robert Donnelly, that had the shot in question in this case taken effect and killed Constable Everett, that you would most assuredly have been hanged. I wish, however, to intimate to you in the kindest possible manner that I assure you that the sentence which I am about to mete out is the lowest possible sentence that the law allows, in the sincere and earnest hope that it will prove of benefit to you and lead you seriously to reflect on the enormity of the crime and the serious results that it might have entailed. For the crime of which the jury has found you guilty I sentence you to two years in the Penitentiary. [8]

The prisoner was stunned. As soon as he recovered from the Judge's words, Robert Donnelly's cool demeanour gave way to hostility and resentment. When taken back to the anteroom beside the makeshift court-room, he lost his temper, threatened to escape, and vowed vengeance against his enemies. Once again rumours began to fly that an attempt would be made to rescue the prisoner as he was being removed to the County Gaol. The constables took the rumours seriously.

A large number of city and county constables... surrounded him, and any effort looking to a release would have resulted disastrously to the parties attempting it, [9]

it was reported. The city newspapers cited the case as an argument in favour of establishing an Ontario provincial police force.

A man would scarcely care to be shot at often for the salary Constable Everett receives, and there would be less danger of such an occurrence were the force Provincial instead of local.

On April 2 a great crowd thronged about the platform of the Great Western Railway in London to see Robert Donnelly off for Kingston. His father gave him some kindly words of advice about living in the penitentiary. Then the prisoners, bound in chains, boarded the train and were off. Although the crowd was orderly, the London *Advertiser* sniffed:

> We expect to see it telegraphed abroad that there was a great riot.[10]

Robert Donnelly had no sooner left for Kingston than stories began to surface that the evidence upon which his conviction was obtained had been fabricated. The Lucan lawyer, William McDiarmid, who knew both the accused and the prosecution witnesses at first hand, believed so and informed the Crown Attorney accordingly. Repercussions of the Donnelly case at one of the Lucan Council meetings held in June "caused talk in the streets", and prompted one indignant taxpayer to write:

> It was moved by W. Stanley, seconded by S. Gibson, that the law firm of Becher, Street & Becher be paid the sum of $20 for services rendered the Crown Attorney in the matter of the Queen vs. Donnelly. Moved in amendment by W. H. Hutchins, seconded by J. D. McCosh, that the account be not entertained, Mr. McRoberts voting for the payment of the account.... I have yet to learn if Mr. Hutchinson, the Crown Attorney, is incapable of attending to his own business in the matter of Crown prosecutions, or if the ratepayers of the municipality will quietly submit to have their hard-earned money squandered in this manner...the payment of any such money being illegal....[11]

26

COUGHLIN

In the federal election held in the summer of 1878, the Conservatives made a spirited comeback on the strength of John A. Macdonald's protectionist National Policy. The campaign in the Catholic Settlement of Biddulph was particularly hard-fought. Many of the Catholics changed their politics at this time, with those remaining loyal to the Reform party pouring scorn upon the turn-coats, sometimes by means of horse pranks. The animals of Jeremiah McDonald, James McGrath, Andy Keefe, Ned Ryan, and James Harrigan all suffered for this reason. Jackson's horses were taken out two or three times.

It was not just Big Barney Stanley's blandishments or the redoubtable John A. that brought many of the Catholics over to the Conservatives. The latter had been surprised and delighted at the success of McDougall in the provincial campaign of 1875. When the federal election was called, they were determined to repeat it and to this end again chose as candidate a cattle drover. He was Timothy Coughlin, of Stephen Township, and for added measure, he was a Roman Catholic.

The campaign was as usual a long one, waged over a period of several months and carried on at the accustomed level of scurrility and name-calling. When Coughlin was labelled "a successful farmer" by his supporters, the London *Advertiser* counter-attacked:

> As a matter of fact his farm is one of the most poorly managed in the country. For the last ten years he has tried to raise an orchard...[but has] not half a dozen fruit-bearing trees yet. The trouble was that he could never keep his gate hinged, and his orchard and lawn were comfortable pastures for cattle and hogs....[1]

But the arch-Conservative of Lucan, Barney Stanley, was very sanguine of Coughlin's chances with the Catholic voters of Biddulph. Big Barney scuttled about fomenting rumours that it was the dour Prime Minister Alexander Mackenzie who was raising the Fenian cry and for that very purpose had paid agents in the States. "Bekase I tell yees," he would spout, upon managing to buttonhole one or other of the Catholic farmers, "it's all done just to turn the orange vote in their own favour. Now mind what I'm telling yees."

The candidate himself had the discomfiting habit of beginning his public speeches by denying that he was Barney Stanley's candidate. The opposition belittled Coughlin as a simple cattle buyer not well enough versed in the affairs of state to make a good Member of Parliament, and religious bigotry was openly evident.

At a recent Orange celebration in Goderich, our friend Reverend Mr. Walsh, late of Centralia, in the course of his address, stated that Roman Catholics should not be sent to Parliament, and that Orangemen should not, upon any consideration, vote for anyone acknowledging the authority of the Pope....[2]

And when a leading Conservative let slip that Coughlin was "an unfortunate selection", the Reformers seized upon it and trumpeted it about the countryside. But the true temper of the day was heard in the observation of a little old lady on the town line who said of Coughlin, "Troth, thin, there's no harm in the bye."

At the McGillivray Town Hall on September 15,[3] 1878, Barney Stanley made one of his many typical speeches on behalf of Coughlin:

Gintlemin! Farmers of McGillivray, yees are ruined

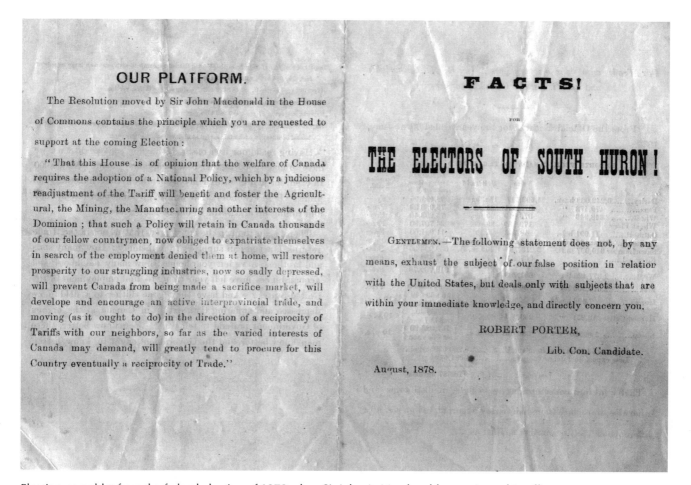

Election pamphlet from the federal election of 1878 when Sir John A. Macdonald was returned to office

by Mr. McKinsey, and his free trade. Ivery market in the country is filled wid Yankee horses, cattle and hogs. Yees are losin' fifteen cints on ivery bushel of barley ye sell, and yees can't git over half price for yees pays and oats, bekase millions av bushels av Yankee corn comes into the country not payin' a cint av duty.... This is what Sir John will do for yees whin he gits in. Bekase I tell yees ye'll have chape tays and sugars, now mind what I'm tellin' yees....[4]

Big Barney was soon boasting that he held five hundred votes, both Orange and Green, under his thumb and the boast seemed well founded. A leading political activist of the Biddulph Catholic Settlement was Andy Keefe, who, up to the time of the McDougall campaign, had been a staunch Reformer but was now campaigning actively for the Conservatives. Many of the other Catholics seemed to be following Keefe's lead.

Patrick "Grouchy" Ryder was one who switched. One morning, shortly after indicating he was going to support Coughlin, Grouchy Ryder entered his stable and could hardly believe his eyes. There standing in its stall was one of his best horses, but in place of its fine bushy tail was a bare stump, clipped short and almost clean-shaven. Tied to this shameful stump was a placard with the mocking letters: "VOTE FOR COUGHLIN". Grouchy Ryder almost choked with apoplexy at the disgraceful outrage thus perpetrated on his dignity. "It's those damn Donnellys!" was Ryder's opinion, and he vowed to wreak his vengeance upon them.

Stanley Hall, the large and pretentious home of Barney Stanley, which still stands at the north end of Main Street in Lucan (Stanley)

150   *The Donnelly Album*

It was well known that the Donnelly Gang continued to support the Reform candidate, the sitting member, Colin Scatcherd. Scatcherd's popular but late lamented brother had during his lifetime held the respect and loyalty of the people of North Middlesex, both Reformer and Conservative alike. But his brother Colin was in a different category. He had not the common touch, was but a pale imitation of his dead brother, and, being in poor health besides, seemed susceptible to defeat. Nevertheless, William Porte remained loyal to the Scatcherd family, as did the Donnellys. To them, loyalty took precedence over everything. It was said they would stick by a man through thick or thin provided the sentiment was reciprocated, but by the same token, a betrayal was never forgiven.

The Tory editor of the *Exeter Times* was outraged at the election prank on Grouchy Ryder:

To put a stop to such acts as this, the Township Council should offer a very handsome reward for the apprehension of the perpetrators of the act, and hand them over to the hands of justice, and if justice would not act properly by them by sending them to penitentiary for one thousand years, they should be handed to a vigilance committee, who would hang them to a telegraph pole, after torturing them for a few days. It is worse than treason that such scoundrels should go unpunished.[5]

Another farmer of the Catholic Settlement who switched political loyalties to the Conservatives, and as a result had pranks visited upon him, was James Maher. One morning Maher, too, found the tails of his horses on the stable floor. Not only was Maher an old enemy of the Donnelly family but he was, besides, an old friend of the new candidate, Coughlin, for his family and the Coughlins had been neighbours in Stephen Township years back. Maher was convinced it was the Donnellys who had perpetrated the deed, considered a most heinous and abusive insult evoking the deepest anger in its victims and their sympathizers. Another editor raved about one such outrage:

We prophesy for the wretch that did this that he will find himself addressing a vast crowd some day when the platform will be kicked from under him....6

Another victim was Patrick Dewan. Dewan had established himself as a grain buyer in the Granton district in 1874 and, as a prominent member of the Biddulph Catholic Settlement, was elected a councillor of the township. By 1877 he was doing such a thriving business that his storehouse had burst. One night during the election campaign of 1878, Dewan was wakened in the middle of the night by stones smashing in his windows. He jumped out of bed, pulled on his pants, and ran out to check the horses. He had feared something like this when it became known he was going to support Coughlin. Out in the stables he found staring at him the bare rump of one of his best horses, its tail lying on the floor. Dewan was indignant. As he returned to the house he heard the sound of tittering voices mocking him in the darkness.

"You'll pay for this. I know who you are, you cut-throat vagabonds," he cried out in frustration

Patrick "Grouchy" Ryder, a sketch by Robert Harris made in February 1880 (PEI)

and rage. "I'll have you up for this. I know it's you, Tom Donnelly, and your friends. I swear I'll prosecute you."

The voice came back from the dark in attempted disguise: "You try it, Dewan, and you won't live to finish it, for I'll cut your black heart out."

While the Lucan constables blamed the people for being afraid to come forward and give evidence, the people blamed the local magistrates for refusing to do their duty when the obligation was plain. The magistrates more or less agreed. Said William Stanley:

The Donnellys were the terror of the township.... Although the boys were often arrested on various charges it was very difficult to secure a conviction. In fact, it was impossible to get evidence, as the people seemed to fear that if they swore against the Donnellys their barns would be burned down, or they would be made to suffer by other depredations. This fear at last reached some of the magistrates, and they declined to receive information against any member of the family.[7]

With Tom Donnelly and Jim Feeheley keeping out of Lucan that summer, things were relatively quiet in the village, enlivened only by the feud between William Porte and Constable Sam Everett. The postmaster kept a pet crow which he called Grip after the popular political cartoonist Bengough, and he tried mightily to teach it to cry foul epithets at the sight of the town constable, but the crow would not respond. Although the libel suit instituted by Sam Everett against the *Parkhill Gazette* was eventually withdrawn, the post office inspector made an investigation of the Lucan post office none the less. Porte passed the examination. But new reasons for hatred between the two cropped up during the election, since Everett happened to be a Grit. Porte supported Scatcherd for personal reasons but was no Grit. He vowed he would be the cause of Everett's dismissal and railed against what he called the constable's grossly excessive salary of "$1 a day and stealings". When Everett's contract came up for renewal in July, the Lucan Council held a noisy session with strong objections being made by the Porte faction to Everett's reappointment as

constable "and street commissioner". They said Everett had failed to repair the sidewalks, that he had "his hands full looking after the 'lambs'", and that he took a mid-day nap in the livery stable on the Main Street every day to sleep off the effects of excessive imbibing. Everett's supporters, on the other hand, claimed that

for keeping the "lambs" in order his equal could not be found in the Province. The high constable may be demonstrative, and probably at times too zealous, yet when we take into consideration the arduous task he was undertaken to accomplish we should overlook his petty failings.[8]

Dispassionate observers of the Everett–Porte imbroglio remarked that "Whiskey had too much to do on both sides of the case." Or, they said, "It is a pity that men of intelligence should allow themselves to be so far degraded by drink as...to shoot off their mouths at such a rate and make such asses of themselves." Everett was rehired for another year.

Despite this setback, Porte continued his attacks on the constable. Through the columns of the *Exeter Times* he complained bitterly that Everett was not doing his job. Thomas A. Edison's "remarkable scientific discovery" was barely known, but gas lamps were the latest marvel of the age. Porte complained, however, that they were no use whatever if "the street commissioner" did not light the lamps. He alleged that Everett used profanity in public, harassed young ladies promenading on the Lucan streets, and often "smelled like a freshly tapped whiskey barrel". He wrote:

Would you allow me to ask the three imbeciles who rule the present Council board why our streets are kept in Cimerian darkness.... The trio in question were very ready to appoint Mr. Everett as a town officer, and strike his salary at four hundred dollars a year, and perquisites, allowing him the same apparently for no other purpose than making a figure head in front of the Central Hotel, insulting respectable females on the streets, and displaying his powers of Billingsgate in abusing worthy men of our town, the latchet of whose shoes the Hamilton jail bird is not worthy to unloose....[9]

Porte spread stories that Everett would only enforce the law if there was gain in it for himself. When, early in October 1878, someone stole the horse of a butcher named Redmond of Biddulph, Redmond refused to go to Lucan to complain of the theft but went instead to the London authorities. When John Morley, of Whalen's Corners, lost two fat steers one night and reported the theft to Everett, he took the precaution of promising a private reward for recovery of the stolen goods. Everett thereupon quickly went after the thieves and succeeded in tracing one of the carcasses to the London Township butcher shop of William Mitcheltree, who was just in the process of skinning the beast. Mitcheltree said he bought the meat at four o'clock that morning from a man who appeared to be in a great hurry, but he refused to divulge his identity. Everett traced the other carcass to Elliot's butcher shop on Talbot Street in London. But, said Porte, it was only the reward which motivated Everett.

Sam Everett's real troubles began when John O'Donohue charged him with taking his cutting-bar and concealing it in a well. Porte seized on the incident and demanded the constable be dismissed or at least suspended until after the courts had dealt with the charge. Everett laid a countercharge of perjury against O'Donohue which was dismissed by Squire Henry Ferguson, who ordered Everett to pay $13.60 in cost. The Grand Jury later threw out the bill against the Lucan constable on the charge of theft, but he remained embroiled in the case for weeks.

During the federal election of 1878, the great Northwest of Canada was opening up for settlement and the departure of several families from Biddulph was noted, including the Sam Blackwell and Davis families. John Davis of the fourth concession of Biddulph had packed up his wagon, team of horses, ploughs, harrows, wife, children, and "a few thousands in cash" and left for Manitoba by way of "the Dawson route", but had suffered great hardships along the way. The *Exeter Times* tried to turn the matter into political grist:

...John Davis and his wife with twelve children, British by birth and British by feeling, are treated worse than cattle, and half starved, because a lot of disloyal men who have accidentally acquired power in Canada must show the gratitude of their Yankee allies who are strongly suspected of assisting them into power by debauching the electors.[10]

The supporters of Colin Scatcherd, the Reform candidate, must have sensed the tide turning against their candidate, for they felt compelled to churn out the news that Colin Scatcherd's

return for North Middlesex may be regarded as certain. Even Biddulph, that stronghold of Toryism, will give him a majority And on the celebrated Roman Line several respectable farmers are openly advocating his return and that without any solicitation whatever as yet on the part of Mr. Scatchered.[11]

The vote was very close, but it came out for Coughlin and Conservatism by a narrow margin of seven votes. In the country at large, Sir John A. Macdonald's National Policy of high tariffs carried the day.

The Reformers of North Middlesex were overtaken by despair and dejection. "We are at a loss to account for the midsummer madness that appears to have seized the electors," lamented the London *Advertiser*. In Lucan the triumphant Conservatives held a great victory celebration in the centre of the village. A platform was erected at the corner of Main and William streets from which the 26th Battalion Band entertained a crowd of 1,500 to 2,000 persons. The music was interspersed with speeches by Barney Stanley, John Carling, John McDougall, M.P.P., William Stanley, the reeve of Lucan, and the victorious candidate himself, Timothy Coughlin. The audience consisted of not only Conservatives but "Reformers who assisted them in securing the recent victory".

27

CARROLL

Towards the end of 1878 a petition was circulated praying for the liberation of Robert Donnelly from Kingston Penitentiary on grounds that the evidence on which his conviction had been obtained was false. Some of the residents of the Catholic Settlement refused to sign it. Reports then went around that Will Donnelly and his brothers vowed to get even with certain Biddulphers

> for refusing to sign a petition for the liberation of Bob, and refusing to be driven to the polls by him and his gang, to vote at their bidding for the Grit candidates. [1]

It was no coincidence that those refusing to sign and those who had switched political loyalties were usually the same families. Among them could be counted the Mahers, Ryders, Carrolls, and some of the McLaughlins.

Timothy Coughlin, the new Member of Parliament for the riding of Middlesex North, came from the Township of Stephen in the County of Huron and more particularly from the Catholic settlement which had taken root there. One of the early pioneers of that community was Roger Carroll, relative of "the respactable" Mr. Michael Carroll of the Roman Line of Biddulph. As a result, Timothy Coughlin had known the eldest of Roger Carroll's boys, James, from the time that the latter was a small boy and once gave evidence of James Carroll's good character. Barney Stanley did, too, and the latter was offered by Carroll as a personal guarantor on one occasion.

The Carrolls were a proud clan. Six miles east from Borrisokane in Tipperary, Ireland, is Knockshigowna, a splendid hill commanding a magnificent view of the countryside, and known in Irish

James Maher, Sr., James Carroll's uncle, a sketch by Robert Harris (PEI)

folklore as the supernatural home of the fairy queen who guarded the fortunes of the celebrated O'Carrolls of Eile, who ruled that land in ancient times. The head of the clan fought at the Battle of Clontarf in April 1014, and his descendants resided at Birr, while Leap Castle was another of their fortresses. [2]

James Carroll, born in the Township of Stephen in Canada to Roger and Catherine Carroll, was but a humble member of the widespread Carroll clan, but he carried the name with pride and felt keenly the responsibility that was associated with it. The family had come out from Borrisokane, Tipperary, about the year 1850. When they settled in Stephen Township in the Huron Tract, a brother, Bartholomew Carroll, picked out a homestead near by and married Catherine Farrell. She may well have been a sister of Patrick Farrell, the enemy and eventual victim of James Donnelly. There were other connections between the Carrolls of Stephen and the Catholic Settlement of Biddulph. James Maher, who lived opposite the Carroll homestead in Stephen Township in the early days of the settlement and was the uncle of Jim Carroll, later moved to the Roman Line of Biddulph. He married Ellen Cain, most of whose family seemed always to be on bad terms with the

James Carroll, a sketch by Robert Harris (PEI)

Donnellys. An aunt of James Carroll was married to Jeremiah McDonald, who lived in Biddulph near St. Patrick's Church, and at whose humble log house the early missionary priests to the settlement said mass.

The Donnellys first came to know of the existence of James Carroll when he returned from the United States in the summer of 1878. Carroll was then twenty-six years old and had been absent from Canada for eight years. His leaving home had been unhappy. It all started when his mother died leaving her husband, Roger Carroll, with a large family. Besides James, who was the eldest, there were other children – Edward, Catherine, Ellen, William, Michael, and Margaret, the last only a small child at the time of her mother's death. James Carroll was in his mid-teens when his father remarried, and in due course two more children were born of this union, Hannah and Martha.

The children of the first marriage did not get along with the second Mrs. Carroll. In the fall of 1869, James and Edward left their home to make their fortune in the Michigan backwoods. The older girls also left as soon as they could and took positions as domestics in London. Not long after, Roger Carroll took sick. Unable to continue farming the old homestead of fifty acres and the addi-

tional sixty-six acres he had acquired from the Mahers across the road, he rented the farms and in 1872 moved into a small house in Petersville, a suburb of London. Catastrophe again struck the following February when Roger Carroll died. Immediately the remainder of the first Carroll family dispersed. Michael departed the household on the day of his father's funeral and William left within a day or so after.

James Carroll was unable or unwilling to return home from Michigan for the funeral of his father. He proved to be a reliable worker, assuming responsibility easily, and was eventually made foreman of a gang of labourers on a railroad construction crew. Carroll was so well thought of, it was said, that when the work on the line was completed he was the last of the foremen to be let go. Eventually, however, the unwholesome living conditions of the construction camps conquered his constitution and he was struck down with a severe attack of "the dumb ague", from which he claimed his body did not fully recover for several years. To regain his health he returned to Ontario. James Carroll immediately looked up his brothers and sisters and found William and Michael with their uncles in Stephen and the girls in London. One of them was a housemaid to the family of Mr. Jeffery, a director of Molson's Bank, London. James Carroll also renewed acquaintances with his two uncles and aunt in the Catholic Settlement of Biddulph.

Carroll arrived just in time to lend a hand in the election campaign of his family's old friend and neighbour, Timothy Coughlin. His assistance in helping to persuade many of the Catholics in Biddulph, including his uncles James Maher and Jerry McDonald, to switch from the Reform ticket earned him the lasting gratitude of Barney Stanley. In turn, Carroll consulted Stanley respecting a private affair, the estate of his late father. It seems that his two uncles in Stephen, John Dolehay and Bartholomew Carroll, had not been doing their job properly as executors of Roger Carroll. It is true the two uncles had interpreted the last will and testament of Roger Carroll to mean that the four eldest children, James, Edward, Catherine, and Ellen, were not entitled to share in the estate because they had not been specifically named in the will. But the executors had consulted a lawyer on the subject and besides, they had sheltered the two youngest boys of the deceased despite their rather delicate physiques and their disposition to prefer school over farm work.

James Carroll was determined to set things right within his family. He gave warning to his uncles, the executors. "I told them they had not acted properly under the Will," he said. "And that the children were all entitled to the rents.... I told them there would be law over it."

James went to see the Carroll homestead in Stephen, where he had been born. The old house, log barn, log stable, well, and granary still stood on the old place, all of them evoking memories of his childhood and his poor dead mother. Determined to get the farm back, he asked his uncles to hand it over, but they refused.

"You will curse the day you were made executors," he told them in a wrath. "And if we cannot get the place by fair means we'll get it by foul."

Even when he was well disposed, James Carroll was said to have "a rather dogged, morose and unprepossessing appearance", with a cruel face, and eyes that were "small, dark and restless, and very seldom look a man straight in the face".

James worked up a fierce indignation against his uncles and began to harass them. Rumours were heard around Stephen Township that "it would not be very safe to take the place" and that "the man that had nothing to do with [the Carroll farms] was best off." The uncles alleged that Carroll wrote threatening letters to them and intimidated anyone who showed an interest in leasing either the fifty-acre homestead farm or the sixty-six acres across the road. "I got afraid to have anything to do with him," said John Dolehay after a while.

The next thing Carroll did was to remove his two younger brothers from Stephen Township and away from their uncles. He found the boys positions in Biddulph Township, where the family was more favourably received, first at Martin Darcey's. Michael Carroll, "a stout kind of boy" worth about four dollars a month as a hired man (although John Dolehay found him "not very fond of work"), later hired out to John Cain. After a

time, William Carroll also left Martin Darcey's and worked with various farmers throughout Biddulph, including William Thompson and Michael Feeheley. James Carroll himself went to live in Biddulph Township, usually staying with his Uncle James Maher on the Roman Line. Carroll considered himself a person far superior morally to the Donnellys. The election pranks of 1878 visited upon his Uncle Maher were only the latest in a long series of compelling reasons for the hatred Carroll felt for the Donnellys. In Carroll's view they were land-grabbers, murderers of his family, jail-birds, and thieves, who brought notoriety and disrepute to the Catholic Church by marrying outside it. Carroll, on the other hand, had a sense of respectability about him. After a day's work, he would change from his woollens to a white linen shirt, for "he wanted to go up to Lucan decent and respectable." Even in his later years his dress was conspicuously neat. "He was strange both in dress and manner," it was said of him, while the Donnellys would speak of him as "that queer fellow".

Soon after arriving in Biddulph, James Carroll added to his natural narrow-mindedness a cloak of indignation at the evil elements in St. Patrick's Parish. Donning a mantle of righteousness concerning the secular affairs of the Catholic Settlement, he soon determined to rid the township of the Donnelly family. During the campaigning in 1878, a raising was held at the farm of a man named Powe in the Catholic Settlement. Tom Donnelly went to the raising, as did James Carroll. There was much bantering between the supporters of Scatcherd and those of Coughlin, and, as often happens in politics, the good-natured exchanges became more and more heated, soon turning into bickering and the hurling of insults. Carroll, the champion of Coughlin, stated in a great loud voice that the Scatcherd supporters were not always within the law and that any man who attempted to shoot down a constable in cold blood deserved to get twenty years in Kingston, not just two. Tom Donnelly's reaction to this gratuitous attack on his brother was relatively mild at first. He told young Pat Keefe he thought Jim Carroll was "a queer fellow". Donnelly and Carroll exchanged a few insults .

After the raising, Tom Donnelly told John and

Will about the row he had had with Carroll. A short time later Will Donnelly told Ned Maher, "That Carroll is a queer fellow. What business is it of his what kind of sentence Robert got?" Will Donnelly went on to intimate that Carroll's big mouth would get him into bad trouble in the future if he did not learn to keep it shut.

Shortly after this James Carroll got into an argument and then a fight, described as "one of our usual donnybrook rows", with a friend of the Donnelly boys named John McLaughlin, outside the Ontario House in Granton. Casualties included the window of Christopher Webb's store, which stood beside the hotel, McLaughlin's pocketbook, to the extent of the one dollar fine that was levied against him in the ensuing assault case, and the edge of Jim Carroll's pride.

At the same court in which Carroll prosecuted McLaughlin, Pat Keefe was fined a small sum for assaulting John Flynn on the front steps of St. Patrick's Church. During the proceedings

...A disgraceful scene took place in the Temple of Justice, Lucan, between Constable Everett and Squires Stanley and Crunnican. It appears Everett refused to read the warrant for the arrest of P. Keefe to the prisoner previous to his being locked up. When at last compelled to do so, Everett is said to have used abusive language to the Bench for which they ordered his arrest for contempt of court, but no constable could be obtained to act, and finally the court broke up in confusion.[3]

It is likely that Will Donnelly was in court that day coaching Pat Keefe on the niceties of legal procedure. James Carroll was indignant at the manner in which the law was apparently being flouted by the Donnellys and their friends, to whom was attributed the frequent stealing that had continued to take place in the village and the township. Carroll himself was of the class of men who "would sooner burn at the stake than touch a cent's worth of property that was not his own".

On Saturday night, October 12, 1878, Tom Donnelly and James Carroll met again at an auction sale in Biddulph.

"Look here, Donnelly," Carroll demanded, "I hear there have been threats made against me."

"What threats?" asked Tom Donnelly.

"You know what I mean," replied the other. "There have been threats made against me and I've heard it's the Donnelly gang that's made them."

"Go to hell, Carroll," Tom Donnelly said scornfully. "What is it you want, fight?"

"Never mind fight," said Carroll. "But I'm telling you your brother Bob can thank his damn luck for such a light sentence for the shot he took at Everett."

"Just mind your own business, Carroll," Tom Donnelly said.

"Breaking the law is everybody's business," Carroll went on. "You and your brothers are a disgrace to their church and to their priest. You have no sense of decency about you. There's your brother John, a married man, I hear, but where's his wife?"

"You mind your own damn business," answered Donnelly. "You think you're too damn smart. Is it beat you want?"

Carroll was carried away with his own bravado. "I'm not afraid of you, Donnelly. I can lick you. I can lick all of the Donnellys."

Tom Donnelly just scowled. There was no doubt that Carroll was up to something.

OCTOBER

The day after the sale was Sunday. Tom Donnelly told John about his encounter with Jim Carroll, and the more John Donnelly thought about it, the angrier he got. Later that day John was strolling up the Roman Line towards Keefe's when he happened to meet young Pat and Jimmy Keefe in company with Jimmy Maher.

"Where's your cousin Carroll?" Donnelly asked young Maher.

"Who?" asked Maher weakly, probably knowing full well who it was Donnelly meant.

"Jim Carroll, that big fighting man," said John Donnelly.

"He's over at his Uncle McDonald's today," Maher replied.[1]

John Donnelly continued: "I just want to ask him in a civil way what he was saying about our family. He was shooting his big mouth off about Robert the other day, and the rest of our family. Well, you can tell him for me, if it's fight he wants I'll make his big head soft."

Young Jimmy Maher could hardly wait to deliver the challenge. Carroll fumed when he heard it and brooded about it the rest of the day. The next morning he set out from his Uncle Maher's and

James Maher, Jr., a sketch by Robert Harris (PEI)

walked south along the Roman Line. James Carroll was at this time the local agent for the Thompson and Williams' Manufacturing Company of Stratford, fabricators of farm implements, and in that capacity was ostensibly going to pick up, from a farmer on the Roman Line, some notes in payment of a milling machine he had sold him. But, knowing he would have to pass the Donnelly place on the way, he had taken the precaution of putting a brand-new revolver in his pocket.

Between eight and nine o'clock on the morning of October 14, 1878, heading toward the Donnelly farm from the opposite direction were Will and Norah Donnelly. They were returning from a few days' visit with Mike and Nellie Donnelly in St. Thomas. Their buggy paused only briefly at the gate. There they greeted Johannah, who was out at the roadway milking one of the cows, and as they continued up the lane towards the house they could see John Donnelly ploughing in the front field near the new frame schoolhouse. When John saw them he left the horses standing in the field and walked to the house. Norah went in, the two brothers chatted for a minute or so, and John was about to go back to his ploughing when he saw Tom coming toward them from the direction of the schoolhouse.

Tom had been working his father's outlying twenty-five acres across the road and had also been ploughing when he noticed James Carroll approaching. Dropping the reins of the horses immediately, he loped with his great stride across the road and fields to his brothers. Tom began right in to tell Will about the row he had had with Carroll at the auction sale.

"That Carroll is looking to make trouble for us, Will," he said. "Maybe we should give him some right now." Tom jerked his thumb toward the schoolhouse. Only Carroll's head was visible above the five-foot board fence which enclosed the Donnelly School plot. When he came into full view he was stepping along smartly. Although seemingly looking straight ahead, he was quite well aware of the three Donnellys near the house. Tom stooped and picked up two field stones, one in each hand.

"Now, Tom," Will admonished, "don't be

fighting every day of the week. Put down those stones and leave that fellow alone. It's not fight he wants, it's law."

Tom scowled and slowly let the stones drop. He always listened to Will. Still scowling at Carroll, he walked over to the front door of the house like a petulant schoolboy and sat down on the two large logs which formed the front steps, facing the roadway.

As Carroll came closer John Donnelly called out, "Hey, Carroll, I want to talk to you."

Jim Carroll glanced up but kept walking. Donnelly called out a second time.

"Hey, you big fellow, I want to talk to you," he said, the words "you big fellow" dripping with scorn and sarcasm.

"I don't want to talk to you," Carroll called back. "I have too much respect for myself." Then Carroll remembered the threat to "make his big head soft" and angrily added, "What were you saying about me yesterday to Jimmy Maher?"

John replied boldly, "Nothing I wouldn't say today, Carroll. And what, I want to know, were you saying about me to my brother Tom here on Saturday night? Just watch your big mouth or I'll fix you."

Carroll had now almost reached the gate at the end of the lane. "You come out and do it," he challenged.

John Donnelly began to move. As Carroll saw him coming, he suddenly noticed, for the first time, Johannah Donnelly crouching beside the cow she had been milking near the farm gate and only a few feet away from him. If looks could kill, Mrs. Donnelly's scowl would have struck him dead on the spot. With John Donnelly descending upon him and his two brothers lurking in the background watching his every move, not to mention the old lady scowling at him but a few feet away, James Carroll quickly sensed his vulnerability.

"Meet me at two o'clock over at Whalen's Schoolhouse," he called out, "and I'll fight you."

The Roman Line where James Carroll confronted the Donnellys in October 1878, as sketched by Robert Harris in February 1880 (PEI)

But John kept loping across the field without a pause. "Why go to Whalen's and have a mobbing?" he asked. "Let's have it out right here and have no more about it."

"I'm not afraid of you," Carroll replied. "I can lick you and all the Donnellys."

Those were fighting words. John Donnelly was only about forty or fifty feet away now and he made a rush at Carroll. Only the split rail fence about fifteen or twenty feet from Carroll separated them. As Donnelly was about to bound over it, Carroll stuck his hand into the left-hand side of his coat and pulled out the gleaming new pistol.

"You son of a bitch," he said, taking a step forward to the edge of the ditch at the roadway, "come one foot further and I'll blow your brains out!"

John stopped short. For a moment no one moved and then his mother, who had been stating intently at the unfolding scene, spoke quietly: "John, go back to yer work and don't mind the blaggard." She then looked directly at Carroll and spat out, "Ye blaggard thieving son uv a bitch!"

Incensed by the old lady's language, Carroll took a step or two toward her and waved the muzzle of his pistol to within about three feet of her fiercely scowling face. "I would just as soon shoot you as him," he said.

When Tom Donnelly saw Carroll brandishing the gun at his mother, he bounded off the front steps and raced toward them, stopping only momentarily to pick up a hefty, fist-sized field stone .

Back on the roadway the old woman spoke again to Carroll. "Go away and mind yer own business," she said. "We want nothing to do wid ye."

Jim Carroll lowered the pistol, glanced at John Donnelly standing motionless at the fence, and then with one eye cocked to Tom descending quickly upon him he stepped back from the edge of the ditch and began to walk quickly down the road. Tom, cursing and swearing all the while, cut across the field to head him off. When he got within range of Carroll he flung the stone at him; it missed its mark. Donnelly cursed and swore again, saying he would kill Carroll, and stooped to pick up two more stones. Will had followed his brother part of the way towards the road, and now he and John stood back and hissed encouragement at Tom.

"Go out there, Tom, and give the son of a bitch the threshing of his life. Come on, Tom, give it to him."

Tom Donnelly had reached a point opposite Carroll in the roadway when the latter cried out, "You come out on the road and I'll shoot you!"

Donnelly stopped and Carroll scuttled past. He was not exactly running but was walking as fast as he could. When he had gone a short distance, Tom Donnelly jumped over the fence and flung one of the stones after him. It missed, and he flung the other, but Carroll was now out of range. Donnelly then shouted after him calling him a thief, a coward, and other "impolite names". His brothers joined him on the roadway, flinging stones and insults. Tom Donnelly challenged Carroll to a fight over at John Cain's place but Carroll made no reply.

James Carroll went immediately to London and laid charges of assault against Thomas, William, and John Donnelly. Constables Hodge, Pope, and Moore of London went out to the Donnelly homestead and arrested John Donnelly. Will was also picked up, but Tom had disappeared. The two brothers were taken to London and bound over for their trial before Justice of the Peace John Peters. Not to be outdone, John Donnelly went to Lucan the following day and there counter-charged James Carroll that he "did point a revolver at me and threaten to shoot me".[2] Carroll was arrested on this charge and taken to London. After giving bail, he laid a new charge against Mrs. Donnelly alleging that

Judy Donnelly did unlawfully assist and act as accessory to commit an assault on said informant; also did use abusive and improper language.[3]

The Donnellys then laid a new charge of assault against Carroll. The charges laid in London were heard first. Justice of the Peace John Peters found William and John Donnelly guilty, and in addition to fining each of them three dollars he required them to enter into peace bonds. The case against Mrs. Donnelly was heard in London on the morning of October 21. In this case the J.P. reserved his decision for twenty-four hours to think the matter over, and the next day found Mrs. Donnelly guilty and fined her one dollar and costs. The Donnellys gave notice they intended to appeal the decision. Carroll was convicted and fined twenty dollars and costs, and he, too, appealed.

The parties seemed to spend all their time going from court to court, for the counter-charge against Carroll was heard in Lucan on the afternoon of October 21. For this trial James Carroll took the precaution of monopolizing the entire legal talent of Lucan by retaining its only practitioner of the legal arts, William McDiarmid. This legal luminary confounded both the Donnellys and his client at the conclusion of the case for the prosecution by pleading that there was no evidence that Carroll's pistol was loaded and therefore the charge was bad! Confronted by this brilliant legal manoeuvre, the learned magistrates, James D. McCosh and Michael Crunnican, felt they had no alternative but to dismiss the charge. The appeals were set down for the December Sessions of the Peace. Carroll was tried on December 9, 1878, before Judge Davis, and John, William, and Johannah Donnelly all gave evidence – Tom being still away from home. A. Robinson, foreman of the jury, announced a verdict of Not Guilty. The conviction of Mrs. Donnelly was also upset on appeal, and the costs against Carroll were taxed at $16.94. It was not a clear-cut victory for either side but the cases proved one thing: James Carroll had staying power.

WOLFSKIN

The Donnelly family were fairly devout Roman Catholics, attending church as regularly as most of their neighbours. The boys probably went as often as the young Keefes – "once every two or three months". And they had always got along with the parish priests of St. Patrick's. Father Peter Crinnon had been especially kind to Mrs. Donnelly during the dark days when her husband had been under sentence of death. He helped to collect signatures for the many petitions of clemency. The family never forgot his kindness. Later priests of St. Patrick's included the popular Father Joseph Gerrard, through whose efforts the grand new brick church was built, and Father Bernard Lotz, who ministered there from 1876 to 1879 and who, although he "did not have the Irish", was also well liked. "Two of the finest clergymen I was ever acquainted with", Will Donnelly described them.

Father Lotz departed in the winter and was succeeded by Father John Connolly. Unlike his immediate predecessor, Father Connolly was thoroughly familiar with the Irish ways and manners, being a native of Ireland, as betrayed by his speech. He was, in 1879, a mature man in his fifties, with a pleasant face and iron-grey hair, a little taller than average but well built. He was a sound administrator, or at least so thought Bishop John Walsh of the Roman Catholic Diocese of London, who had chosen him specifically to quell the troubled parish of St. Patrick's. It is likely, in view of the unrelenting notoriety which the Donnelly family in particular continued to attract since the famous Donnelly Assizes in 1876, that the good bishop warned Father Connolly that "their reputation was not good."

Father Connolly celebrated his first Sunday Mass at St. Patrick's on January 19, 1879. Elevating his tall and sturdy frame into the pulpit to address his new congregation, he said he had heard a great many terrible things about the people of Biddulph – that there were men there bad enough to fight at bees and to knock a man down, bad enough to maim horses and to burn down buildings, and, yes, bad enough even to kill a fellow man. He had been quite content in his former parish in Quebec but had heard the call of duty. Having just come back from a trip to the Eternal City, he was filled with renewed inspiration to carry out God's will through the Holy Mother Church and had answered the bishop's call to come to St. Patrick's and lead the people there by the hand of God. Yes, he continued, there were hard cases in Biddulph, but he believed that every Irish Roman Catholic in the settlement would get behind him to stop the bad work, and to stop the bringing of disgrace and shame down upon the religion of their fathers and upon their parish. And, to this end, the first thing he proposed to do was to make a visit to every household of the parish in order to meet each and every one of his flock.

The next few weeks saw Father Connolly, bundled up in a huge wolfskin coat given to him as a farewell present by his grateful parishioners in Quebec, being driven by one of the altar boys, the young son of Stephen McCormick, in the family's cutter up and down the lines of the Catholic Settlement of the township. Up the Roman Line to the Nangles, Collisons, McGraths, Hogans, Ryders, Caseys, Tooheys, Ryans, and Cains he rode, stopping at each house just long enough to meet the farmers and their families, exchange a few words, and give them the blessing. Eventually the priest reached the Donnellys' storey-and-a-half log house. None of the boys were at home, and the priest had to content himself with speaking briefly to Mrs. Donnelly.

"I have heard about your boys' bad doings," the priest told her, "and that they are hard cases. They should change their ways or I shall straighten them myself."

Mrs. Donnelly was taken aback. "Father Connolly," she protested, "there are worse than my bhoys in the neighbourhood. But the biggest crowd is agin us and shure it's meself and me bhoys whot are parsecuted."

To change the subject, Johannah Donnelly introduced to the priest her husband's niece Bridget. Bridget Donnelly was twenty-one years old, a comely girl just lately arrived from Bornsokane, Ireland, and Father Connolly seemed eager to talk to her about the Old Country. He asked her about conditions there and Bridget recounted the hardships of their people and how overjoyed her father had been to hear from his brother James after so many years of silence. She told him how happy her entire family was at her prospects in the New World.

Father John Connolly (*The Globe*)

St. Patrick's Roman Catholic Church, Biddulph

The enemies of the Donnelly family somehow thought of Bridget's entry into the family as in some way indecent, with snide remarks and rude jokes being made and old Donnelly being referred to as "Old Decency". But for her part, Bridget Donnelly was happy to come to Canada, and shortly after her arrival she wrote her brother Michael in Dublin telling him of the family's kindness to her. She was almost exactly the same age as Mr. and Mrs. Donnelly's daughter Jane and was a welcome addition to the predominantly male household.

From Donnelly's place, Father Connolly dropped in briefly to see the scholars at the Donnelly Schoolhouse and then continued his visitations to the Whalens, Thompsons, Ryders, McLaughlins, Feeheleys, Carrolls, and Keefes, and so on down the line. In due course he came to the house of James Maher. Here, according to Will Donnelly, Maher seized the opportunity to relate to the priest in great detail the entire past troubles of this part of Biddulph Township, all as seen through the eyes of the enemies of the Donnelly family. For two long hours the priest listened to the lurid litany of evil deeds: the thieving, the threats, the clipping of horses' tails, the burning of barns, the deaths by violence. And who was at the centre of all this devil's work? Why, had not old Donnelly himself been sentenced to hang for the murder of poor Pat Farrell over twenty years before? Had he not been saved from the gallows only by the kind graces of that saintly man, Father Peter Crinnon, who sent petition after petition to the government? And had not the family betrayed the good priest by bringing shame upon the parish with their unending criminal activities? Had not Jim Donnelly, the son, and his brother Jack both served time in the Central Prison a couple of years back? And shouldn't Will Donnelly himself have been there with them except for his playing sick and fooling the authorities? Had it not been necessary to call out the Lucan Volunteers after the fierce riot at Fitzhenry's tavern in Lucan three years before? Was not Bob Donnelly serving time in Kingston that very moment for trying to murder in cold blood a constable of the law ? No, it was not necessary to invent stories about

the Donnelly family. Of the eight males, fully half of them were convicts. Blacklegs!

And who was the leader of this frightful pack? Why, it was none other than that old she-wolf herself, Mrs. Donnelly. Forever lurking in the background, urging her boys on, or even getting into the thick of things herself, had she not just last fall gone to law herself against James Carroll, who had worked so hard to get elected to Parliament Mr. Timothy Coughlin, as upright and righteous a man as ever walked the earth, and a Catholic besides? Like the rest of them, the old lady would swear a decent man's life away without hesitation. And then there was that spawn of a devil, Will Donnelly, the cripple. Now old Maher did not believe it for an instant, mind you, but it was whispered often enough by the old grannies of Biddulph that Old Cloven Foot himself had the power to leave his mark on his chosen instruments willing to carry out his evil work. Father Connolly left Maher's musing on the lurid revelations with which the man had filled his head.

A short time after this, when the priest was hearing confessions, he learned that there was in the parish a secret faction of some of his people. Bound together by an oath, a small group of men had banded together, ostensibly to protect themselves from the depredations of a gang who infested the township and respected no laws. Secret societies of this sort were a tradition among the Irish peasants and the bane of their priests, who in most instances strenuously opposed them.[1] But there were exceptions, and perhaps this was a special case. Had not the saintly Father Nicholas Sheehy himself been martyred in such a cause when at the head of such a secret society in Ireland over a hundred years ago? Executed by the authorities on March 15, 1766,[2] at thirty-eight years of age, Nicholas Sheehy was hanged as a traitor to the British Crown, his body drawn and quartered, and his severed head displayed atop the jail wall of the assize town of Clonmel for many years after, as a warning to other would-be traitors.[3] To the Catholics whom he had served as parish priest, Father Sheehy was a martyr and a saint, but to the authorities he was the outlaw leader of a secret society known as the Whiteboys.[4] Father of Confederation Thomas D'Arq McGee chronicled the fate of the enemies of Father Nicholas Sheehy in his *Popular History of Ireland*:

...They met deaths violent, loathsome and terrible. Maude died insane, Bagwell in idiocy, one of the jury committed suicide, another was found dead in a privy, a third was killed by his horse, a fourth was drowned, a fifth shot, and so through the entire list. Toohey was hanged for felony....[5]

Toohey was also, according to McGee, a "convicted horse stealer" and had given testimony in the prosecution against Sheehy. One hundred years after his death the memory of the priest continued to live in the hearts of his countrymen, for in 1867, just a matter of months before the assassination of McGee himself in Ottawa, the military commander in Tipperary called out the troops to prevent the erection of a memorial over the grave of Sheehy.

With these thoughts running through his mind and struggling with his conscience and sense of duty, Father John Connolly continued his visitations throughout the parish. Whenever the opportunity arose, he inquired as discreetly as he thought necessary about the Donnelly family. Yes, it was true they had a bad reputation, many of the Biddulphers had to admit, even their acknowledged friends could not deny that. But, some maintained, part of it was undeserved. For example, was not Bob Donnelly wrongfully convicted of the shooting at Constable Everett on false testimony? Why, Sam Everett himself had gone to London not long before and made affidavit that this was so.

In the winter months of early 1879, Father John Connolly was not the only spiritual adviser travelling the Biddulph roads and thinking about the Donnelly family. The Reverend James Donaldson, an itinerant Presbyterian minister, on his previous visits to Lucan in 1874-75 had always preferred to travel from London via the Donnelly stage and return via the Hawkshaw or Mail Line. On this occasion he came by the Grand Trunk from Parkhill and was departing via the London, Huron and Bruce from Clandeboye, taking Hawkshaw's Omnibus Line for the short trip from Lucan to the station. On

the way he chatted amiably with the driver, young Hawkshaw, who remembered the minister from his earlier visits.

In the course of the conversation, the man of the cloth happened to say, "Whatever happened to the Donnelly boys who used to run the stagecoach line from London?" When Hawkshaw made no reply to this, the minister added, "I liked those Donnelly boys."

Young Hawkshaw then replied, "You do not know them, sir. They just put on appearances to deceive strangers. The truth is they are a bad bunch." Hawkshaw went on to call the family many uncomplimentary names and concluded, "I once thrashed one of them, the second from the youngest, and I will thrash him again."[6]

"But they had a good line," said the Presbyterian minister. "I always took their coach whenever I could, though I knew it offended some of my own congregation in Lucan."

Young Hawkshaw's handsome face flushed red, and he answered with vehemence, "The Donnellys have been run off the line at last. They are a bad lot, and the people are bound to get rid of that family some way or another, and that before too long!"

"What? How's that?" asked the other, surprised at the depth of Hawkshaw's emotion. "But surely you do not mean that, or you would not speak so to strangers."

Hawkshaw thereupon fell silent and would say nothing further during the rest of the short trip to Clandeboye Station.

In due course Father Connolly came to the home of Will Donnelly, who was living at the time in the neighbouring township of Usborne. It was a cold, wintry day and as usual the priest was wearing his long wolfskin coat. William Donnelly kept a watchdog at his home. "It was a large dog," said Donnelly, "and pretty wicked." When the priest alighted from the buggy and entered Donnelly's yard, the dog took one look at the coat and rushed to attack it. Father Connolly cried out for help, but Norah Donnelly was the only one home at the time. Not only was she in a fairly advanced state of pregnancy but she was slightly deaf, and by the time she had been roused to open the door the priest was frantic. She shushed the dog down and

Father Connolly scampered through the doorway. But, never having seen him before and with his clerical collar under the wrappings of his huge coat, Norah Donnelly failed to recognize the man as the new parish priest.

"Who are you and what do you want?" she asked him.

"I am the parish priest of St. Patrick's," he replied testily, "and I am looking for Mr. Donnelly."

When she informed him her husband was not at home he left, in a vile temper and admonishing her to keep her mongrel from tearing off his clothes as he departed.

In his sermon at church the following Sunday, Father John Connolly made the first of many allusions to the Donnelly family. Although such references were almost never by name, there were few parishioners who did not know exactly about whom he spoke. He began by saying there were certain people in St. Patrick's Parish whose manners and hospitality left much to be desired.

"Why, I went to a certain place this past week," he related, "where the dogs were ready to eat me up. And if this were not enough, the people of the house were so ignorant that they did not even recognize me as a priest. Now in the parish where I came from such a thing would not have happened. There, whenever I visited any of my flock, they immediately fell upon their knees and offered up a prayer. People here in Biddulph have not done this."

The young McCormick, who had been driving the priest in his father's cutter, had witnessed the entire incident between the priest and Will Donnelly's dog. The boy naturally told his father about it. Soon after, Stephen McCormick met Donnelly and related to him the sermon about the dog and the wolfskin coat. "Judging from the way he spoke at church," McCormick said, "I fancy, Will, that Father Connolly's mind has been poisoned against your family. My boy tells me, too, that he stayed over two hours in conversation at Maher's."

A few days later Will Donnelly was visiting James Powe, an old friend on the tenth concession of Biddulph, when Father Connolly drove into the yard. As the priest clumped the snow off his boots, James Powe and his wife Margaret greeted him at the door of their log house and then turned to introduce Will standing inside.

"Oh, Father Connolly," they said, "this is Mr. Donnelly."

The priest stepped forward to greet the other but in the act of doing so, he made a brief quick glance down at Donnelly's clubfoot. "Oh, yes, you're William Donnelly," he said. "Well, I am glad to meet you. I was over at your place the other day but you were away from home."

They talked innocuously for a few minutes about the priest's coming to Biddulph, with only a vague and fleeting reference to the past troubles of the township, and the priest concluded by saying, "Well, I certainly hope that things will be better in Biddulph in the future. I intend to lay a good foundation with this end in view." He then left.

On his way home that night Will could not help feeling uneasy. The new priest had certainly seemed affable enough towards him, but he could

Will Donnelly

not suppress his resentment at the glance he had taken at his foot. He knew he had been talked about. It was as Stephen McCormick said, thought William Donnelly, the enemies of their family had got to the priest first, and the latter now believed that they were at the root of all the trouble in Biddulph.

Other incidents soon confirmed Will's suspicions. Shortly after, in the middle of February, a funeral service was held at St. Patrick's Church for Maria Nangle, the wife of Andy Keefe. Many of the villagers of Lucan – including some Protestants – attended the funeral, and during the service the bells from the cutter of one of the prominent Protestants were stolen. Keefe's friends were dismayed and chagrined at this act of rudeness. Will Donnelly claimed that everyone knew who the culprits were – young Jimmy Maher and Jack Darsey – yet Father Connolly made no reference in any of his sermons to this particular "depredation" committed under his very nose. Then, about this time, a family fight erupted in one of the numerous Toohey households, in which one of the young Tooheys broke his father's ribs. "Father Connolly never mentioned this from the altar," said Will.

Again, after the Keefe funeral Will Donnelly hired a servant girl to attend to his ailing wife, who had suffered a miscarriage. On the evening of Friday, February 28, three heavily muffled men suddenly burst into the home, pushing Will Donnelly into a bedroom and trussing his hands to the bedstead.

"What do you want?" Donnelly asked them.

"We know you've got $400 in the house," one of the men said, "and we want it. And if we don't find it we'll burn the house down."

"There's no money here," Donnelly replied.

"We'll see about that," was the answer, and one of the bandits fired two balls from a revolver just a couple of inches over Donnelly's head.

"I tell you there is no money here," he insisted, but while the man with the gun levelled it at his head, the other two ransacked the house, including the women's room where the two females set up a great shrieking. The intruders opened a trunk and found a pocketbook containing $134, the proceeds of some sale notes Donnelly had recently collected, but in the commotion they missed $35 on a stand at the head of the bed belonging to the servant girl.[7]

Father Connolly's failure to mention this "depredation" also helped to convince Will Donnelly that the priest had turned his face against his family. The enemies of the family, on the other hand, claimed the entire story was concocted out of Will's fertile brain for the purpose of deflecting suspicion from the very gang of which he was leader .

Another depredation took place near Biddulph in February, when the house of Ellen Fogarty, whose house had been raided in the attempted abduction of Maggie Thompson several years earlier, was raided again, this time by two masked men who tried to smash in the kitchen door with an axe. But the brave woman, watching for an opportunity, seized the axe head when it came splintering through the wood. Taking hold of it, she pulled it through and then fired a revolver through the hole, hitting one of the robbers in the thigh. They ran for their lives. Mrs. Fogarty claimed she recognized one of the men as being either of the two youngest Donnelly boys, and she went to Lucan and reported the incident to a village magistrate. He advised her to pay Everett fifty dollars and he would "hunt the case up for her". The matter was dropped when Sam Everett informed the lady that Bob Donnelly had been in jail for almost a year, and Tom Donnelly had not been seen in the parts for several months and was last reported in the lumber camps of Michigan.

30

ARREST

The petition to the new Governor General of Canada asking Her Majesty to grant a pardon to Robert Donnelly, on grounds of his wrongful conviction in the Everett shooting case, was signed by many respectable persons. From the London legal fraternity the signatories included David Glass, the defence counsel in the case; his brother William, the Sheriff of the County of Middlesex; Edmund Meredith; and William R. Meredith, one of the most respected members of the bar in the province and Leader of the Opposition in the provincial Legislature. Bishop John Walsh was reported to have signed the petition, as well as John McDougall, M.P.P. for North Middlesex, whom Michael Donnelly had assisted in his election campaign. Among Lucanites who signed were Dr. Thomas Hossack, John Bawden, Sylvanus Gibson, James D. McCosh, J.P., William Matheson, Wesley Orme, John Fox, James Watt, and William Porte.

While rumours floated around that some of the signatures were forgeries, many well-informed persons were of the opinion that the conviction against Donnelly had indeed been obtained by doubtful testimony. William McDiarmid, the Lucan lawyer, characterized the prosecution witnesses as perjurers. The complainant himself, Samuel L. Everett, had come around to the belief that the evidence had been falsely obtained, and the Lucan constable even went so far as to swear an affidavit in London to that effect. Everett's action showed a remarkable change in his attitude toward the Lucan Lambs, whose favour he now curried, for Everett had need for allies.

The Lucan village elections in December 1878 were apparently fought on the issue of whether or not to retain Everett as village constable.[1] During the brief campaign, it was brought out that the policeman had

> acquired the happy art of smiling and bowing to the toll gate keepers and pronouncing the word "Minister" with an unction that would do credit to an archbishop[2]

in order to avoid paying toll. On the other hand, his supporters claimed that he was "the only peace officer that ever attempted, and that successfully, to put down with a strong hand open violence, incendiaries and midnight rapine." But the anti-Everett forces, fuelled by the spite of the Lucan postmaster, won the election. When the

new Council met in January they held "the general opinion...that Everett...should be discharged..."[3] Everett, however, refused to go quietly. He pointed out that the previous Council had hired him for a full year and refused to resign unless he were paid a bonus for retiring early. The Council decided to drop the matter for the time being.

When Father John Connolly arrived in Biddulph early in 1879, he heard of the petition for the pardon of Robert Donnelly and deemed it a good opportunity to gain favour with the family. The priest wrote to an influential friend in Quebec, a government Minister, and also spoke to the local Member of Parliament, Mr. Timothy Coughlin. The latter soon disabused the priest of any friendly notions he might have entertained for the family, pointing out that many of the people in Biddulph, and especially within St. Patrick's parish, had refused to sign the petition. He may have related the fact that a previous pastor of the parish had sent petitions saving James Donnelly, Sr., from the gallows, but the family repaid the favour by supporting the Reform party in the last election, while many of their neighbours had seen the light and supported the Conservative candidate – who happened to be Coughlin himself. Coughlin may also have pointed out that since the imprisonment of Bob Donnelly and the disappearance from the district of his pugnacious brother Tom, the village of Lucan had been relatively quiet those past six months. No, certainly, the Donnellys were not deserving of help.

Later in the spring, the standing of Constable Everett again cropped up, this time over the question of the new Lucan gas lamps. Sam Everett wanted ninety dollars a year extra for lighting them each evening, while some of the councillors believed the job was part of his constabulary duties or, at the very least, of his duties as street commissioner. The lamps, it was said, "contribute largely to the suppression of midnight rowdyism" and thereby lessened the constable's duties. One Lucan lady considered them such a boon that she was moved to write:

> Lucan, sweet spot, thy memory entwines,
>   Around my heart I bind thee still,

E'en while I write a street lamp shines,
    Beside the lock-up near the mill.
Tho' fire and torch around thee burn,
    Tho' lawless bands at midnight rove,
My fondest thoughts still to thee turn,
    Thy grassy lanes still claim my love.[4]

On Sunday, March 30, a drunken row took place on the main street of Granton. It was a kind of homecoming party for Tom Donnelly. The party took place in Granton because Donnelly's friends had warned him to stay away from Lucan, where he would be arrested immediately upon setting foot in the village on a warrant still outstanding. And, besides, there were five or six constables in Lucan now, including one, George Shoebottom, who had been appointed toward the end of the previous April. He was a wagon maker, standing "six feet one in his stockings, fighting weight 225 pounds". When appointed, it was said he seemed "just the individual to deal with the 'Lambs' [but] the only fault is he presents too much surface for buckshot."[5]

On the other hand, Tom Donnelly was told, Sam Everett's loyalties were shifting. He was kept under constant attack in the columns of William Porte, who called the constable

an adventurer, whose standing post for Lucan is the body of the jail where he had been previously incarcerated for making clinch whiskey....[6]

The most dangerous of the other Lucan constables now seemed to be Wild Bill Hodgins, also known as "Betty's Bill" after his mother, Betty Dobbs Hodgins, a strong-willed woman whose husband had died while crossing the ocean, leaving her to raise their three small children alone. Hodgins was a carpenter and stonemason of Lucan and a proud man. He had come out of his fight with John Donnelly with honours, but his failure to take Tom Donnelly had rankled ever since the story got out of his being driven off the Donnelly place. He vowed to take Donnelly yet if he got the chance. The opportunity came on Thursday, April 3, 1879, when Hodgins heard that Tom Donnelly was in Ailsa Craig. He hopped the next train, and there met and apprehended Tom Donnelly. The arrest was quite a simple affair. This time it was Hodgins who held

William Hodgins, the Lucan constable, in his later years (V. Pybus)

a gun at the breast of Tom Donnelly, who was thereby persuaded to accompany the constable quietly back to Lucan and stand bail before one of the magistrates. The warrant on which the arrest was made was on the old charge of robbing Ned Ryan over a year before. As soon as Donnelly was safely lodged in the Lucan lock-up, rumours floated around the village that he would also be charged in the shooting at Constable Everett, which had also taken place a year before. When the second charge was disclosed, however, it turned out to be the old charge of assault laid by James Carroll, arising out of his confrontation with the Donnellys in October.

Tom's arrest, in the eyes of his captor, restored his standing with his fellow constables in Lucan. But Hodgins also retained in his possession the warrant for the arrest of Jim Feeheley on the Ryan robbery case, and he was determined to arrest him if he returned home as expected. Meanwhile, Sam Everett was plainly jealous.

On the evening of the day of Tom's arrest, both Everett and Hodgins were in the Queen's Hotel. William O'Neil, a friend of Hodgins, thought to have a little fun with Everett and asked him, "Hey, Sam, what will Tom Donnelly's case amount to?"

"Donnelly is going to be discharged," Everett replied scornfully, speaking loudly enough for Hodgins to hear him in the adjoining lounge. "It was a very foolish thing to bring him in. Why, I could have arrested Tom Donnelly many times if I had wanted to, but there are some around here who want to make a big name for themselves by running him in."

At these words Hodgins stepped smartly into the bar-room brandishing his constable's cudgel.

"Are you referring to me?" he asked, looking directly at Everett.

"Yes," replied Everett.

"That's a lie, Everett," Hodgins declared. "I arrested Donnelly because you were afraid to."

It was Everett's turn to get angry. "You talk like a fool, Hodgins," he shot back. "I have arrested Tom Donnelly before and I could do it again if I wanted to."

"You?" said Hodgins mockingly. "Why, you don't dare arrest Tom Donnelly," and then added with dripping scorn, "Go away, Everett, you're too big a man for me to quarrel with."

But Everett's pride was stung. "You're a liar!" he shouted at the other.

"And you're another!" Hodgins shouted back.

Everett sprang up and shook his big fist in Hodgins' face. "You're a lying son of a bitch!" he yelled so loudly that young Hugh Toohey, who lived in a room of the hotel, jumped out of bed and ran downstairs to see the row.

The provocation proved too much for Wild Bill Hodgins; he took a swing at Everett with the baton but failed to connect because the other constable seized hold of him and pulled him close. But young O'Neil, who had started the argument, ran up to Everett and began pummelling him from the side and rear and Everett turned, releasing his grip on Hodgins. O'Neil fled the room with Everett after him and the fight thus ended.

Two days after Tom's arrest, John Donnelly went to see Father John Connolly and asked to go to confession. The priest refused him. "You are trying to compromise me," he told Donnelly, "for you are going to tell an untruth to save another, and I will not be a party to a bad confession."

"But Father Connolly," replied Donnelly, "you will not hear my confession but you willingly hear stories brought to your ears by the enemies of our family."

"Yes," the priest answered heatedly, "and the things that they have told me have kept me from sleeping at night!"

The priest's refusal to hear his confession cut John Donnelly deeply. He never forgave him. "Father Connolly is a fine man," he told his brother Will bitterly, "but he should first find out whether stories are true or not before following them."

What was the untruth which Father Connolly anticipated John Donnelly was going to confess to? The priest felt that it related to the robbery of Ned Ryan or the shooting at Sam Everett, and that Donnelly intended to give information absolving his brother but implicating others. According to this version of the plot, which came to the ears of the priest, the finger was to fall on the absent James Feeheley.

The trial of Tom Donnelly for robbing Ned Ryan came off in Lucan on Monday, April 7. A great storm, said to be the heaviest within memory of the oldest settler, had swept the district a day or two before, and the streets of Lucan were choked with snowdrifts "fully twelve inches on the level on Saturday". But the warm April sun came out and by the day of the trial much of the snow was turned to water, cutting great ruts through the streets which abounded with mud holes. Despite the difficulty which the storm had caused in travel, when Justice of the Peace Michael Crunnican heard that the Donnelly case would be coming up on Monday morning he arranged for urgent busi-

W. K. Atkinson, the Justice of the Peace from Ailsa Craig who was summoned to Lucan when the local magistrates refused to act (Page)

Jim Carroll, a sketch by Robert Harris (PEI)

ness to take him out of town. James D. McCosh, a more conscientious magistrate, suspected that the others would also attempt to shirk their duty, and he telegraphed for W. K. Atkinson of Ailsa Craig to come and assist him in the case.[7] Upon his arrival, Atkinson suggested they issue written invitations to each of the other Lucan magistrates. Crunnican thereupon feebly explained he had urgent business out of town, while William Stanley refused outright to sit on the case. The reeve of the village, William Hutchins, and Patrick McIlhargey, however, put in their appearance and took their seats on the judicial bench.

Court was held in the Lucan Council Chamber room above the lock-up. The room was crowded, what with the four magistrates, the prisoner, the complainant, the witnesses, and numerous interested parties. Among the witnesses were were Alexander McFalls, proprietor of the Queen's

Hotel, Simon Young, Constable Sam Everett, John Nevills, and John Rollins. Among the interested parties were Will Donnelly, James and Thomas Keefe, and James Carroll. When court opened, Carroll stood up and addressed Atkinson, who appeared to be the magistrate with the most authority, and asked to speak for Ryan. Permission was granted and Carroll then requested that the case of Tom Donnelly be adjourned, as Ryan wanted to get a lawyer. Will Donnelly, speaking for Tom, then stood up and said that the case had been postponed for that purpose once before, that Ryan had had plenty of time to retain counsel, and that the matter should proceed. The adjournment was refused and the court ordered the witnesses to be heard.

The reporter for the London *Advertiser* described the testimony for the prosecution as "absurd and contradictory", and the magistrates de-

170 *The Donnelly Album*

A certificate of the magistrates as to the acquittal of Tom Donnelly on the charge of robbing Ned Pyan, April 8, 1879 (UWO)

cided to dismiss the charge. Court was then adjourned to two o'clock in the afternoon. James Carroll was visibly angered at the result and told Ryan in a loud voice that, because the case had gone on without his consent, the adjudication had been improper and that the matter should not rest there. Will Donnelly, again acting the lawyer, thereupon requested the Justices of the Peace to issue a certificate of the dismissal of the charge against his brother, and this document was duly drawn up and signed by the magistrates. James Carroll was livid.

31

COMBAT

The crowd spilled out into the muddy street. Trial by judge gave way to trial by combats when surro-

gates for the principals, Tom Keefe for Thomas Donnelly and Jim Carroll for Edward Ryan, decided to re-try the case in rough-and-tumble. Not long before, Carroll's Uncle Maher had met Tom Keefe on the road to Lucan, and notwithstanding that Keefe and Maher were related, or perhaps because of it, the two argued about Keefe's close association with Tom Donnelly and how it would bring shame to the family. Keefe told Maher to mind his own business, words led to blows, and finally Keefe knocked Maher down and kicked him severely about the head. Jim Carroll was indignant at Keefe's treatment of his Uncle Maher. Carroll made his home with the latter and rented a thirty-acre slip of his own beside Maher's farm. When Tom and Jim Keefe jostled past Carroll on their way out of the lock-up building after the trial, it took only an insult or two before Carroll and Keefe came to grips. At the corner of Main and Alice streets they were soon rolling in the spring mud, pounding and scratching each other like wild beasts, while the Donnellys and others shouted encouragement to Keefe from the side. They fought, literally, with tooth and nail. At one point Keefe got Carroll's nose between his teeth and almost tore the end off.

Wild Bill Hodgins heard the din of battle from up the street and pushed his way through the excited crowd. When Sam Everett saw Hodgins interfere, he bellowed a volley of oaths at his fellow constable, telling him to stay out of the fight. But Hodgins managed to drag Keefe off the now hapless Carroll and clamp a pair of handcuffs on him. He pushed Keefe back along William Street to the lock-up and shoved him inside and into one of the three tiny cells.

About half an hour later, Tom Keefe, still scraping the mud off his clothes, was astonished to see Hodgins push none other than Constable Sam Everett himself into one of the other cells. It seems that immediately after confining Keefe, Hodgins had gone to Magistrate McCosh and sworn out a warrant against Everett for using abusive language contrary to a village by-law. He met Everett walking towards him on the sidewalk, in company with W. K. Atkinson, the Ailsa Craig J.P., and his brother, Harry A. Atkinson, the Lucan lumber merchant. Hodgins attempted to arrest Everett, but Sam shoved the other off the sidewalk, tearing his shirt in the process. This so angered Hodgins that he pulled out his constable's baton, rushed at Everett, and began to beat him over the head. W. K. Atkinson was startled at such goings-on between the two Lucan constables, and he advised Everett to give himself up quietly. Everett was only too glad to comply.

With the restoration of peace in the streets of Lucan, court was reconvened at two o'clock. The first case called was The Queen versus Thomas Donnelly, charged with assault and the use of threatening language on the complaint of James Carroll the previous October. While giving his testimony, Carroll was obliged to clutch a handkerchief to his nose, which was still bleeding from the wound inflicted by the teeth of Tom Keefe. The court remanded Donnelly for trial before John Peters, a London J.P., but allowed his release on bail. The next case was The Queen versus Thomas Keefe on a charge of assault, the subject matter of this investigation being plainly evident on the face of Jim Carroll. On this charge the prisoner was remanded for trial before Squire James Daniel McCosh of Lucan at three o'clock the next day.

The next case called was The Queen versus Samuel Everett, charged by Constable William Hodgins with using abusive language. But when Hodgins went to fetch the prisoner, much to his embarrassment he discovered that Everett had in his possession the only set of keys to his own cell! He refused, moreover, to deliver them up and Hodgins was forced to go back upstairs and sheepishly report the dilemma. It caused great consternation on the bench. One magistrate suggested they leave Everett in the cells and starve him out, while another said, "Let's burst the lock and whatever damage is done he will have to pay for it." Finally Reeve William Hutchins stalked down to the cells and demanded that Everett turn the keys over to him as chief magistrate of the village. When Everett still refused, the reeve ordered the lock smashed. Hodgins got a heavy hammer and broke the lock, and Everett was taken upstairs. The hour was now late, for Everett had been in jail six hours during all the deliberations, and the magistrates decreed he should stand trial the following day at one o'clock before McCosh and Hutchins. Court then adjourned.

Reeve Hutchins was scandalized at Sam Everett's obstinacy in the matter of the lock-up keys and called a special meeting of the village council to deal with it. But the teapot of Lucan politics brewed a little tempest when the reeve proposed that someone make a motion censuring the constable for his conduct. While Hutchins had beaten William Stanley for the reeveship the previous January by the handy margin of thirty-seven votes and was popular with most Lucanites, the rest of the council formed a clique against him. No one offered to move the motion. Hutchins thereupon resigned and the meeting dissolved in acrimony. At the next meeting of council the following Monday evening, the remaining councillors passed a motion accepting the reeve's resignation and then dismissed Samuel L. Everett as town constable! The council issued a warrant to the village clerk empowering him to call a new election for reeve, and William Porte, James D. McCosh, and William Stanley were nominated for the position. Porte and McCosh declined and Stanley accomplished by inside politics what he could not do at the polls and was declared the new reeve of Lucan.

In the meantime the Donnelly family, in retaliation for what they believed was the unjustified dredging up of old cases against Tom, in turn resurrected charges against James Carroll. Before Justice of the Peace James Owrey, of London, Carroll was charged with drawing a pistol on Johannah Donnelly. When two London constables, Charles Pope and William Hodge, went out to Biddulph on April 10, 1879, to arrest Carroll, they found him at the home of his Uncle Maher, still nursing his injured nose. They showed him the warrant, and Carroll studied it for a moment.

"I am perfectly innocent of this charge," he declared. "I did not draw a revolver on Mrs. Donnelly."

If the charge were taken literally, Carroll was right. He had drawn the pistol on John Donnelly, not the old lady, and had only pointed it at her afterwards. It seemed that Carroll had learned a trick or two from the shrewd legal eagle, William McDiarmid.

James Maher then said, "It's too bad that people should be pulled about the country by such characters as the Donnellys. Why, they would swear any decent man's life away. Something, a society maybe, will have to be got up to stop them or get them out of Biddulph."

Carroll added, "Tom Donnelly beat the law again the other day on the Ryan robbery charge, and now all the constables around here will be afraid to arrest him. But I swear, if necessary I am going to get myself appointed a special constable and arrest him myself."

Carroll was taken to London and released on bail. Then followed a series of counter-charges, arrests, and counter-arrests. Carroll laid a fresh charge before John Peters, J.P., against Thomas Donnelly for assault and threats arising out of the October encounter. When Donnelly was arrested on this charge and remanded on bail, he in turn laid a counter-charge against Carroll of pointing a revolver and threatening to shoot him arising out of the same incident. Catroll was again arrested, this time by Constable Pope.

In the meantime the charge preferred by James Carroll against Tom Keefe of assaulting, biting, and wounding him on April 7 came up. Not to be outdone, Keefe had laid a counter-charge against Carroll in identical terms, and Carroll was arrested on this warrant by Sam Everett. Carroll then laid an information against both the Keefe brothers, Thomas and James, with threatening an assault, and on this charge the Keefes were arrested and gave bail to appear before Squire John Peters in London.

Some of these cases came up before Peters on April 14. Tom Donnelly and Tom Keefe retained

A Lucan street scene, boxers in front of the Queen's Hotel (Stanley)

Edmund Meredith to act for them, while James Carroll hired a relatively new London lawyer, John J. Blake, a brother to Michael Blake of the Catholic Settlement. Michael Blake had taken over Pat Mooney's old farm, and had a sister, Ellen Blake, who sometimes taught at the Donnelly Schoolhouse. The charge against Tom Donnelly was dismissed. Donnelly's lawyer applied to the court for payment of the costs, but the J.P. refused. In the next case the position of the parties was reversed, Donnelly being the complainant against Carroll, with Blake defending and Meredith prosecuting. Blake made a preliminary objection that the charge had not been laid within three months as required by law. The report of the case goes on:

> Mr. Meredith said he intended making it a charge of common assault, and amended the information for that purpose.
> Mr. Blake then objected that the information should have been laid within three months in this case also, and quoted the statute on that point.
> Mr. Meredith contended that this provision did not apply to common assaults.[1]

Without ruling on the point, the magistrate decided to hear Donnelly's testimony in the case. Carroll then stated that he had drawn the revolver in self-defence. Jeremiah McDonald of Biddulph, who was married to Carroll's aunt, also gave testimony in the case, stating, "I have known the Donnelly family for twenty years past, and from their reputation I would not believe any of them on oath ."

John Peters reserved judgment in order to consult with the Crown Attorney on the legal point raised by Blake. On the charge which James Carroll had laid against James and Thomas Keefe of threatening an assault, the Keefe brothers were put on their bond to keep the peace in the amount of $100 personally and two sureties of $200. In the next case of Tom Keefe charged by Carroll with "assaulting, biting, tearing and wounding", Mr. Meredith stated that he had only just been retained by Keefe and had not had sufficient time to prepare the case, and it was postponed until April 21.

The next day the same parties appeared in Lucan before Magistrates James D. McCosh and W. K. Atkinson. For his assault upon James Carroll, in which Carroll's nose was mutilated, Thomas Keefe was fined $10. The case of William Hodgins versus Sam Everett for abusive language and assault was heard with Squire Patrick McIlhargey added to the bench. The magistrates in this case reserved their decision.

Back in London on April 21, Squire John Peters, having consulted with the Crown Attorney, gave judgment in the case of Donnelly versus Carroll by dismissing the charge. Carroll's case against the Keefe brothers was compromised by Keefe's agreeing to pay all of Carroll's costs, including those of the lawyer, John J. Blake, in return for a withdrawal of the charge.

While all these troubles were brewing in Biddulph, miles away in St. Thomas Michael Donnelly was making a new life for himself and his family. On April 12, 1879, Nellie Donnelly gave birth to a son. He was baptized James Michael Donnelly.[2] Mike Donnelly was quite popular with his neighbours in the east end of St. Thomas, among them the Marrs brothers, David and James, who also worked on the cars of the Canada Southern Railroad. James Marrs was particularly fond of Mike, and they often referred to each other as "Neighbour". Donnelly's job on the railway required his absence from home for several days at a time, during which the crew of the gravel train with whom he worked boarded at Slaght's Hotel in Waterford. A great rivalry existed between the gravel train crew and another gang of men of the same railroad, who lodged at Best's boardinghouse in Waterford.

Being a young man of powerful physique and audacity of character, Michael Donnelly soon established a dominance among his fellow workers on the gravel train crew. "A fighting character" he got to be known as, while Freeman Slaght, the Waterford hotel proprietor, and his son Charles even went so far as to refer to him as "a desperate character and the bully of the road". And it is true that the Hamilton detective Hugh McKinnon considered Mike to be one of the most dangerous of the brothers. But by his co-workers, men like James Muir, who was fireman of the gravel train, and Robert Brooks, who joined the construction crew in July of 1879, he was well liked and considered "a good-hearted fellow". Brooks thought Donnelly to be "a pretty good man [who] used the boys well".

"He was a good fighter," said James Marrs of his neighbour and fellow worker, "but as a bully I never saw him have a row...." However, even Marrs conceded that Michael Donnelly "would not allow himself to be run on but would fight if he was put upon."

Michael Donnelly began boarding at Slaght's Hotel in Waterford in November 1878. About a year later, in October, a man named William Lewis joined the construction crew of the Canada Southern. Lewis, whose name may have once been Louis, was apparently a Frenchman, and an aggressive,

abrasive kind of man, who went to live at Best's boardinghouse along with one Robert Greenwood. One day about a month after Lewis's arrival, James Muir had a bad day at work. Although he was an experienced fireman who had had four years of the same work in Detroit, for some reason on this day he backed up the gravel train too far and just missed injuring a gang of labourers working in the pit. Among them was a car-repairer, James Brown, and a sidekick, Robert Greenwood. They were angry at what they believed to be Muir's carelessness, and when the boss of the construction crew, Tom Tremellon, berated Muir for wrecking part of the train, the labourers who had been imperilled joined in. Michael Donnelly came to Muir's defence, and he and Tremel-

Waterford. Slaght's Hotel stood to the left of the building under construction in the centre of the photograph.

lon had a heated exchange of words. Greenwood got into the argument and Donnelly slapped him down.[3]

William Lewis was not at work that day, but said later that if he had been on the train, he would have knocked Muir into the pit and threatened to kill him. And as for Donnelly, Lewis said, "Greenwood, if Donnelly slaps you again, you tackle him and I'll fix him."

32

KELLY'S HORSE

In the June 1879 provincial election, the Maher-Carroll-Toohey faction was decidedly in the camp of Conservative John McDougall, and the Donnellys were just as decidedly on the side of the Reform standard-bearer, John Waters. Father John Connolly sided with McDougall. The newspapers echoed the din of the campaign:

In Thursday's *Free Press*, there appeared a letter signed "Biddulph", in which ... an endeavour is made in connection therewith to influence the Catholic electors of this locality against Mr. Waters, and to make a little capital for the Tory candidate.... "Biddulph", if he lives in Biddulph, will remember that no Reformer was engaged three years ago in the dastardly work of breaking into Catholic houses in Biddulph in the night, and compelling the inmates – women and girls – to get up in their night-clothes, in order that these marauders might, under the pretended sanction of the law, search for a Catholic offender. The treatment of Catholics above described, was reserved for the Orangemen, whose champion John McDougall is....

A REAL BIDDULPHER.
Biddulph, April 27, 1897.[1]

The last time McDougall had run, Michael Donnelly had worked for him on election day, but Mike was no longer living in the riding. His brothers in Biddulph all supported Waters, who seemed to be gaining so much ground that Big Barney, the Tipperary Roarer, grew worried. At one Lucan meeting

...Barney Stanley at the close of Mr. Waters' speech, asked for some explanation as to the hundreds of millions of dollars which he claimed the Government collected for tavern and shop licences, asserting with his well known recklessness and want of truth, that the Government retained it for a corruption fund and that all fines collected for infractions of the law were paid for by the whole community, and not by those who broke the law...all of which came directly out of "Yees poor farmers" pockets...![2]

Mr. Waters, the obviously biased report of the *Advertiser* continued, "made a short but effective reply and the meeting was closed by three cheers for the Queen." The following week Waters was reported to have held a "very successful...large and orderly" meeting in Granton.

On the evening of Monday, June 2, the Conservatives held a meeting at the Donnelly Schoolhouse, a new frame building just about a year old. Barney Stanley had circulated word that Mr. Fraser would be at the meeting, and everyone thought he meant the Honourable C. F. Fraser, who was at the time a prominent politician. Among the luminaries who came were the Leader of the Opposition at Toronto, Mr. William Ralph Meredith, as well as the candidate himself, John McDougall, the man who "floated into Parliament on whiskey". The teacher and chairman, Stephen J. Patton, called to the podium Mr. Fraser, who said he was an Irishman and felt proud to meet his countrymen. But the crowd grew unruly when they discovered he was not C. F. Fraser but J. H. Fraser, an ex-M.P.P. He said his grandmother and the mother of John Martin, the distinguished Irish patriot, were near relations who lived in the same county in Ireland, which seemed to mollify them. The others also spoke but, "as they had all the meeting to themselves," sniffed the London *Advertiser*, "of course they pronounced it a great success . "

Other usual functions were held at the Donnelly Schoolhouse in that summer of 1879. From the

In 1879 James and Johannah Donnelly attended mass at the Donnelly Schoolhouse, where it was said by Father Connolly at this altar.

earliest pioneer days of St. Patrick's Parish, it was the custom for the parish priest to say mass and hear confessions at the two outlying schools in the Catholic Settlement, to enable the older and feebler parishioners "to go to their duty". Father John Connolly held church at the Donnelly Schoolhouse, an altar being kept there for that purpose, during the summer of 1879, and James Donnelly, Sr., his wife Johannah, and young Bridget Donnelly attended mass there, but the boys did not go.

At the height of the election campaign, on Saturday night, May 10, 1879, the stables of James Kelly, a Catholic farmer living on the Swamp Line of Biddulph about a mile south of Whalen's Corners, were entered surreptitiously. Whoever it was extracted Kelly's horse and rode it up and down the concession lines into exhaustion, leaving it on the road where Kelly found it next morning in a broken condition. He told one of his neighbours about the outrage, the neighbour told another, and by the time of church service at St. Patrick's that morning everyone knew about it. Father Connolly was informed, probably by the Mahers, and immediately made up his mind to do something.[3]

That very day, after lunch, Father John Connolly drove over to Kelly's place. "Do you know who took the horse out, Mr. Kelly?" asked the priest.

"No, Father," replied Kelly, hesitating slightly, "I do not."

"You do know, Mr. Kelly," the priest said, "but you are afraid to tell."

"But I could not tell who it was, Father Connolly," the man insisted, "bekase I see'd no one take it out."

The priest then said, "This is Tom Ryan's work."

Tom Ryan had lived all his nineteen summers in Biddulph. He had a knack for getting into trouble, partly because of his admiration of and close association with the younger Donnelly boys. Young Ryan was working as hired man for Michael Powe, on the Swamp Line just a mile south of Kelly's farm.

"I don't know if it was Ryan or not, Father," Kelly told the priest.

The priest left, saying he would find out about it, and drove his buggy toward Powe's. On the road he met, strolling down the Swamp Line, several young fellows, among whom were Jim Toohey, Jr., and young Dennis McGee.

"Is Tom Ryan among you?" the priest asked them sharply.

"No, sir, he isn't," one of the boys answered.

"Well, then," continued the priest in the same tone, "do any of you boys belong to the gang?"

The boys raised their eyebrows and glanced at each other self-consciously at being thus questioned by the parish priest.

"No, sir," one of them at last spoke up. "We don't belong to any gang, Father."

The priest left the boys and continued on to the farm of Michael Powe, a large-sized Irishman with fiery red hair and whiskers. He and his wife greeted the priest, who asked them whether Ryan was at home. They said he was not.

"I want to talk to him about the taking out of Kelly's horse," he told them before departing. "And I want you to tell him he is to come down and see me."

When Ryan arrived home later that evening, his employer gave him the priest's message. Getting mixed up with the parish priest was a serious business, Ryan thought, and he had better get help. The next day being Monday, he asked Powe for the day off and went to see Will Donnelly at Whalen's Corners to obtain his guidance.

"Will, Father Connolly is blaming me for the taking out of Kelly's horse and he wants to see me about it," he said. "I would sort of like to clear myself."

"Well," asked Donnelly, "can you?"

"Yes, I can," the young fellow replied. "Half a dozen respectable people can vouch for my being elsewhere last Saturday night when Kelly's horse was taken out. But you know, Will, I'm kind of shy about talking with the priest. Would you come with me?"

"Sure, Tom," Donnelly said, "I'll go with you." The two of them drove into Lucan. When they learned that earlier that day Father Connolly had taken the train to St. Marys, William Donnelly got a pen and paper and sat down to write the priest a letter concerning the affair of Tom Ryan and Kelly's horse. It went:

May 12th, 1879

Revd. Father Connolly,
Dear Sir, —

I have been informed that yesterday evening you were down the Cedar Swamp Line and openly accused Thomas Ryan of taking out Mr. Kelly's horse last Saturday night. I am also informed you asked different parties if their name was Ryan, and if they belonged to the Gang. I would like very much for it to be explained to me what Gang was referred to. I do not wish to offend but it is my humble opinion, dear Sir, that it appears your sole object is getting our family out of Biddulph, and it seems strange indeed to some that the deeds of some of the people of St. Patrick's are quietly smoothed over while our supposed deeds are talked about. At Mr. Andy Keefe's wife's funeral you may recall, sir, some parties stole the bells off a respectable man's cutter but you never drove around the lines looking up that, or ever spoke of that in the church. No, but the whole cry seems to be Banish the Donnellys.

I wish your Reverence to take note that said Thomas Ryan and I called on you this day and proposed to give satisfactory proof of the complete innocence of said Ryan and that being unjustly accused when being innocent it is intended to lose no time in going to London and instituting action against the proper parties.

Now, sir, this is to inform your Reverence that should you still desire to do so then you are able to come and see the said Thomas Ryan at any time at the residence of Mr. Michael Powe, and the writer will receive you at his own house also at any time you may find it convenient to call.

I remain, Sir, ever
Your humble servant,
WILLIAM M. DONNELLY.[4]

William Donnelly and Thomas Ryan then drove by the priest's house and left the letter with his housekeeper, Mrs. Thomas Carroll. Father Connolly was not at all pleased when he read its contents. He considered its tone insolent in imputing misconduct to him. The veiled threat of legal action aroused the deepest anger and resentment. He brooded on the letter the rest of the week and on the following Sunday, May 18, preached his sermon on it. First he spoke about the taking out of Kelly's horse. Upon the man who had perpetrated this foul deed, he told his congregation, a curse would fall, and the grave was open for him. "Mark my words, people of St. Patrick's Parish," the priest harangued them, "inside of one month the guilty party will be a corpse."

The priest then told his congregation that he had received a threatening letter from two parties who had come to his house. One of them, he said, was a well-known man in the neighbourhood, a man who was the leader of a family and the leader of a band of men who set at defiance all respectable and law-abiding citizens of the community. He said that from the stories he had heard of this person, he considered him a desperate character, and he would not be at all surprised if there was an attempt made by this man and his gang to waylay him. But, he continued, he was not afraid of this man, no matter what threats were made against him. He did not care if he got a bullet put through his heart, he said, for he knew his spiritual duty and would let no one stand in the way of his doing it, least of all the likes of the man who had sent him that disgraceful letter. "I consider," he said, "that this letter came from a man who is too smart. It would be a good letter to send to a politician or to a newspaper editor, but not to a priest."

Father Connolly then alluded to the efforts he had made in trying to obtain the release of Robert Donnelly from the penitentiary, and how such efforts had not been appreciated by the family. "I will have nothing more to do with them," he concluded.

After church, in conversation with his parishioners Father Connolly was told by some of them, who were perhaps eager to play up to his overwrought emotions, that William Donnelly had threatened to drive the priest from the country. It added fuel to the fire, and Father Connolly continued to brood for days over the letter, the rumours, and the events surrounding them. Over and over he turned in his mind the knowledge obtained through the confessional that a sworn faction existed within the parish. Finally he decided to take action. He would form his own society for the purpose of obtaining the co-operation of his parishioners in the elimination of the depredators of the parish by ensuring they were caught and punished for every crime committed in Biddulph from that time on.

By means of discreet inquiries, Father Connolly learned that the brother of Michael Blake, one of his parishioners, had but recently been called to the bar and was practising law in London. The lawyer's name was John Joseph Blake, and he had for a time worked on the boats on the Great Lakes before abandoning the sailor's life for the bar. Father Connolly wrote to Mr. Blake in May. He asked the lawyer's advice as to the legality of forming a kind of society or vigilance committee for the discovery and putting down of crime within the parish. He said in the letter that he had great hopes of the Donnelly family's joining such an organization and thereby ending the depre-dations that had plagued the district for so many years. Mr. Blake replied, advising the priest that so long as the society was merely the common agreement of a number of citizens to assist one another in the detection of crime and the recovery of stolen property, and was merely to aid in the enforcing of the law, then such an organization would be perfectly legal.

In the meantime on June 5, 1879, the provincial general election came off and, in the riding of which Biddulph and Lucan formed a part, McDougall was defeated and the Reformer, Waters, elected. The polling in Biddulph and Lucan alone, however, went as follows:

John J. Blake, the London lawyer who was the legal advisor of the Biddulph Peace Society and brother of one of its leading members, Michael Blake (Provincial Archives of British Columbia)

	Division	Waters	McDougall
Biddulph	1	24	127
	2	37	101
	3	67	60
	4	33	105
		161	393
Lucan	1	19	58
	2	12	73
		31	131

While in the Catholic Settlement, Division 3, almost half the Catholics had swung over to the Conservative candidate, McDougall had not held strongly enough in the rest of the riding, and the seat went back to the Reformers by a margin of 232 votes.

During the election campaign, Sam Everett's feud with William Porte and the Lucan Council had come to a climax. When Everett appeared on the charge of assault laid by William Hodgins on April 15, 1879, before Justices of the Peace James D. McCosh and Patrick McIlhargey, he felt he was unjustly dealt with when McCosh wanted to acquit the constable but McIlhargey preferred to convict. They finally agreed to consult the Crown Attorney. He suggested dismissal of the charge but, the advice notwithstanding, Squire McIlhargey insisted on a conviction and Everett was fined $2 and $5.40 costs "or twenty days". Everett lost on other fronts also when the Village Council suspended him from the job of Chief Constable after Reeve Hutchins' resignation. William Porte's revenge on his old enemy seemed so complete that he could not contain himself and wrote the following missive for the Exeter Times:

Everett's Soliloquy

To be or not to be? that is the question;
Whether it is easier for a town constable
To light lamps and repair sidewalks
Or to take up arms against the Council,
And by bullying, gag them to light, to mend
No more; and with an oath to say I end
The row and the dozen jobs the Council
Would have me do, – 'tis a consummation
Devoutly to be wished. To swear, to bully;
To bully, perchance to fight – ay there's the rub –
For in that fight what knocks may come
When we have the other constable's club across our pate,
Must give us pause; there's the respect that
Makes bullies take water;
For who would bear the knocks of Betty's Bill,
The Council's jeers, the whole town's contumely,
The pangs of despised bullyism, the law's delay,
The insolence of small boys, and the spurns
That a caged bully of the worthy townsman takes
When he himself might lift his club
And lay the other fellow out?
But that the dread of something mighty strong
The undiscovered muscle in Bill's right arm
From whose stroke I might not again arise,
Makes me rather bear the welts I have

Than rise up others I know not of;
Thus determined pluck makes a coward of me,
And then my affected hue of courage
Is sicklied o'er with the shadow of the lock-up,
As I take a cell I once was wont to give.
But when once more I'm out again
I will quietly slink away,
And lose the name of constable.[5]

Sam Everett refused, however, to slink away. He stayed in Lucan seeking his own revenge, with his first opportunity coming against Squire McIlhargey. It seems that Patrick Keefe had got into trouble again, having been charged on the complaint of one William Thorpe, but Keefe, in the tried and true methods of the day, had gone to Squire McIlhargey and made affidavit that the charge was laid "for the purpose of extorting money and for no other purpose". The making of such an affidavit had in the past been an effective defence against a charge, but the practice had been abolished by statute five years previously because of frequent abuse. Upon pain of penalty of as much as fifty dollars or three months, it was made unlawful to administer such an oath. Everett promptly laid a charge against McIlhargey under the statute, and the magistrate was convicted and fined five dollars.

Next, Everett appealed his own conviction of assault and laid a counter-charge of assault against Constable William Hodgins. The case was heard by both the senior and the junior county judges, William Elliot and Fred Davis, who invited the two Catholic magistrates from Lucan, McIlhargey and Crunnican, to occupy the Bench beside them. Everett won the appeal and his conviction was overturned. Thus encouraged, Everett pursued his vindication further, and at the next regular meeting of the Lucan Council he submitted a bill for three months' service for the unpaid portion of his annual salary. Council refused to pay and Everett sued. Judge William Elliot, in the course of giving judgment in this case, said:

It would seem from the evidence that there has been much lawless violence in Lucan, and that he who fills the office of the village constable has no easy task to perform. If that task could be performed, as I think it could, without the use of coarse language which by one or more of the witnesses was imputed to the plaintiff, so much the better. But as the world goes, it may not be found very easy to get a man of a refined mind who will engage to do the kind of work which seems to fall to the lot of the constable of Lucan.[6]

The Court upheld Everett's suit and awarded judgment in his favour.

Sam Everett continued to live in Lucan. When later that year he stood up as one of Tom Donnelly's bondsmen, this action did not at all please the Donnelly family's old enemy, James Maher. He met Everett in Lucan shortly after, and the result was that Everett charged Maher with using abusive and improper language towards him and had him hauled up before Squire John Peters in London. James Maher's attitude to Sam Everett illustrated the determination the Maher faction had by this time formed, to isolate the Donnellys and in one way or another get them out of the township.

SOCIETY

On Sunday, June 15, 1879, having heard from lawyer Blake, Father Connolly announced to his congregation that he had decided to take matters in hand in Biddulph and form a "property protective association". What he asked them to do, he said, was to pledge one another to allow their properties to be searched for stolen property, and to signify such pledge by signing the open book which he had left in the vestibule of the church that morning.

"All those who decline to join this society," preached the priest, "I will consider to be backsliders and sympathizers of the gang which is the cause of the depredations in the community! And let me caution you, that if any of those backsliders and sympathizers take sick, they are not to send for me. Let them send for the leader of that gang, that devil of a cripple, to administer to them. And remember that as Irish Catholics you are duty bound to protect your priest at all times. I will not mention again the disgraceful letter which I have already spoken to you about. I am not afraid. I am ready to do my spiritual duty come what may."

As the rough farmers and their families filed silently out of the church that morning, sure enough, in the vestibule was a small book with a dark cover, a little larger and thicker than a student's copybook and left open at the middle pages. Across the top of both pages Father John Connolly had written:

We the undersigned Roman Catholics of St. Patrick's of Biddulph solemnly pledge ourselves to aid our spiritual adviser and parish priest in the discovery & putting down of crime in our mission. While we at the same time protest as Irishmen and as Catholics against any interference with him in the legitimate discharge of his spiritual duties.[1]

Below these words those of the congregation who could write scrawled their signatures.

Old Pat Whalen could hardly write an "X", let alone his name. "I'm in a haste, Jamey," he said, addressing James Corrigan, "Would ye moind puttin' me name down there?"

Corrigan obliged and inscribed Whalen's name, along with those of several others who asked him to do the same. The signatures, including those signed the following Sunday and the next, eventually filled three pages of the book and came to a total of seventy-eight.

"There are rings within rings," William Donnelly once said about the combination in Biddulph, which was the cause of the eventual downfall of his family. There was truth in the statement, even though many of the members within the rings may not have been aware of their exact limits. It can be argued that the priest's "property protective association" was the outer ring: ostensibly legitimate, a simple declaration of a common lawful purpose, sanctioned by the parish priest, and joined in by almost all the churchgoing members of the parish, including those in definite friendship with the Donnellys. Included among the

St. Patrick's Church, about 1929

latter signatories, for example, were Stephen McCormick, Michael Collison, and Michael O'Connor, and the Powes, Graces, Nangles, and Keefes. The most secret and innermost ring consisted of the families of the blood-feud bent on vengeance, going back to the killing of Pat Farrell: the Farrell-Maher-Carroll-Cain faction. Between these was a whorl of families which for one reason or another were drawn over the years into the inner vortex of hatred. Such families of the middle ring included the Flanagans, Kennedys, McLaughlins, and Ryders.

The crystallization of the middle ring into a definite group occurred at the Cedar Swamp Schoolhouse in the fall of 1879, when meetings there began to be held fairly often. The connection between Father Connolly's "property protective association" and the other rings has always been blurred. While some claimed to have seen the priest in attendance at at least one of its meetings at the schoolhouse, others claimed he had nothing to do with that group. Michael Collison, respected by everyone in the Catholic Settlement, lived near the church and had signed the priest's book. He claimed that when the meetings began at the Cedar Swamp Schoolhouse he was continually tormented to join by those who attended them, but he refused because he believed that the main purport of those meetings was to plot against the Donnelly family, and that the society formed there was different from the priest's. He would have nothing to do with it.

The immediate reason for the commencement of the meetings at the Cedar Swamp Schoolhouse, it was generally agreed, was Tom Donnelly. Those meetings were attended by many, but not all, of those who had signed the priest's book at the church .

"The cause of the starting of the Society," Martin Darcey swore, "was that Tom Donnelly had ordered people not to thresh for one of us."

The series of events giving rise to the Cedar Swamp Society, according to this version, began with Tom Ryder's threshing. In the summer of 1879[2] Tom Ryder had hired a custom thresher named Martin Curtin to bring in his grain. The threshing season was in progress when Tom Donnelly, in company with Mike Toohey, went to

Ryder's farm and, calling Ryder aside, asked him, "Where's Martin Curtin?"

"I think he's in Lucan," replied Ryder. "He broke his machine at my place today and he's had to go to Lucan to get it fixed. But he'll be back tomorrow and you can see him here. What did you want of him?"

"Well, you'll do as well," said Tom Donnelly. "I understand he is going to do Ned Ryan's threshing. I don't want him to go there."

The implication of Donnelly's words slowly sank into Tom Ryder's brain. Donnelly was going to punish Ryan by forbidding his grain to be threshed.

"Now, Tom," Ryder answered slowly, "you'd better take it easy on the man. It's impossible for Ryan to get his grain threshed if Curtin can't go there."

"That's the way I want it," Donnelly said.

Ryder thought for a moment. "I'm opposed to any such thing, Tom," he said finally. "I suppose you know I must make this known."

"That's just what I want," Donnelly said. "To get this thing circulated. Ryan, the son of a bitch, bought a new pair of sewed boots to send me to Kingston with and I'm going to keep his stacks there till they rot on the ground."

Ryder tried once more to dissuade him. "Now, Tom," he said, "you oughtn't to do that. I am against it. I will deliver no such message to Ryan."

"Ryan has persecuted me," insisted the other, "and now I am going to pay him back in his own coin."

News of Tom Donnelly's ban of Ryan's threshing spread quickly throughout the Catholic Settlement. Fear of reprisal was enough to dissuade everyone from helping Ryan, and the ban stuck. When Will Donnelly heard of it, he admonished his brother, "You are doing wrong, Tom." But Tom was determined. "Father Connolly never tried to protect me in any way in this injustice of dragging up this old charge," he said. "Now I am going to torment both Ryan and the priest."

Ned Ryan went to ask Father Connolly for his help in the matter. The priest promised to see what he could do. He drove down the Roman Line and found that the threshers had moved to Pat Whalen's farm across the road, and the boys were there

The priest's book showing the declaration of Father Connolly and the signatures of all those who joined his association

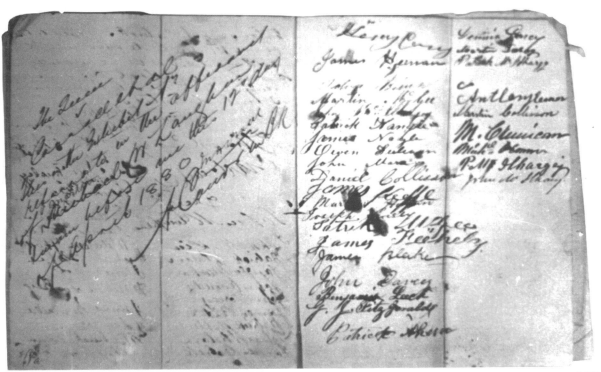

(UWO)

helping as they had always done. Father Connolly approached the threshers, caught the eye of Tom Donnelly, and beckoned him over out of the earshot of the others. They spoke briefly. Father Connolly asked Tom Donnelly who rode Kelly's horse. Donnelly answered that he wondered what concern that was of his, or his family's, or of the priest's for that matter. The priest was annoyed at Donnelly's impertinence, but remembering the original purpose of his journey he asked him, "Would you, as a personal favour to me, allow Curtin to go and thresh Ryan's grain?"

The sudden change of tack by the priest caught Tom Donnelly off guard. He hesitated, bowed his head, scraped his feet, and finally muttered, "I'll ask my brother John and see what he says."

"Fine," said Father Connolly. "He is here, isn't he? Come, let us go find him and I will ask him myself."

They found John Donnelly among the threshers, and calling him aside the priest put the same request to him. Now John was aggrieved by the priest's refusal to hear his confession a few weeks before and nursed a grudge on that account. He nevertheless hesitated at turning the priest down outright.

"I will have to think about it, Father Connolly," he said. "I will give you an answer before Sunday."

The priest left. Sunday came and went, and when John Donnelly did not show up to give his answer the priest felt betrayed. He had believed that his efforts to obtain the release of Robert Donnelly from the penitentiary should have counted for something with the brothers, and he was chagrined at having gone hat in hand to request a favour from them. His heart hardened against them.

Father Connolly had heard plenty of stories against the Donnellys in Biddulph and in Lucan. The stories surfaced again when, in the early hours of the morning of Friday, August 1, 1879, at half past two o'clock, the old Dominion Hotel in Lucan burned to the ground. Old Charlie McRoberts, the proprietor, had given up the hotel business three or four years before and was at this time carrying on a butcher and drover business. The origin of the enmity of the McRoberts family towards the Donnellys is obscure, but it may have been tied up

with the McRobertses' friendship with the Hawkshaws and the rivalry among the local hotels for patronage, in which the McRoberts family lost out. There was no doubt, at any rate, about the enmity felt by them against the Donnellys.

"William Donnelly," said David McRoberts, Charlie's brother, "is always spoken of as leader of the gang that has been troubling the country for years past."

When some of the parishioners of St. Patrick's learned that Father Connolly had been rebuffed by the Donnelly boys, they were angry and chagrined. A vague and uneasy feeling grew up that their priest had been insulted and that the Donnelly family had dared to defy the spiritual authority of the Church itself. Several of the leading men of the congregation got together after mass to discuss the disquieting developments in their midst. The suggestion was made and adopted by general agreement that a meeting be held soon to do something, or there would never be peace in Biddulph.

Many persons attended that first meeting of the society at the Cedar Swamp Schoolhouse on the night of Thursday, August 7, 1879. William Casey said, "I was summoned by men riding around the concession on horse back. The meeting was held late in the evening."

The Cedar Swamp Schoolhouse had been built in 1874 on the northwest corner of the old Harrigan homestead, on the Swamp Line of Biddulph. It was a fine, commodious brick structure, replacing the old log school that had previously stood on the site, and, apart from St. Patrick's Church itself and the priest's house, was the pride of the Catholic Settlement. The building had a front porch, with the interior divided into a large classroom and a small anteroom at the rear. In a central position stood an ancient stove on large flat stones, its cast-iron legs long before knocked off by blocks of wood dumped by the scholars. In one corner of the room stood a tall, bureau-like piece of furniture surmounted by a cross, which was, in fact, an altar. In another corner stood the old desk used by the teachers in the original log schoolhouse. Several of the men who crowded into the schoolroom that evening remembered the colourful old schoolteacher of their youth, Donate Crowe, who had often pounded that same old desk with his heavy ruler and challenged anyone to beat him in a fight.

The schoolteacher at this time was a gentler soul named Peter Bench. He was a quiet and unassuming young man from the Orangeville area, who came to Biddulph at the beginning of 1879, hired at a salary of between $200 and $400 a year, and boarding usually with the Harrigans. During the weeks following that first meeting, Mr. Bench would often ready the old stove for lighting the next morning but would sometimes find that the kindling had been burned up the night before. He wondered at first why the school trustees of Biddulph held so many meetings.[3]

The prime movers in the conversion of Father Connolly's loose "property protective association" into a sworn secret society were – according to William Donnelly – Big Pat Breen, Michael Blake, Pat Dewan, Anthony Heenan, Martin

McLaughlin, John Kennedy, and James Carroll. Most of these men had some pretensions to leadership within the Catholic Settlement. One of them, Patrick J. Dewan, was a member of the township council; others, such as Breen and McLaughlin, were school trustees; while still others were directors of the local agricultural association, which put on the annual fairs that were so much a part of the farming community.

Once the ruddy-faced and rough-hewn farmers of the Swamp and Roman Lines had crowded into the schoolhouse, Martin McLaughlin was elected chairman. Dennis Heenan, better known as "Din" to his cronies, was elected secretary and read to the meeting a declaration or paper containing a brief "set of rules", which were all assented to. The objects of the peace society were "to preserve law and order, and to put down barn-burning, robbery, the cutting of horses' throats and other depredations". According to Michael Blake, more

Cedar Swamp School on the Swamp Line, Biddulph Township. This building was erected in 1874, replacing the original log building on the same site.

186 *The Donnelly Album*

Peter Bench was the teacher at the Cedar Swamp School in 1879-80 when the Biddulph Peace Society was meeting there. (M. Bench)

rules were drawn up: members were to report all depredations; they were bound to prosecute in the courts anyone found committing any depredations; if anyone reported property stolen, all were to turn out to search for it; if a prosecution were launched, it was to be kept secret until the parties accused could be arrested. A special group, known as "the Committee", was set up to hear complaints, meeting in the small anteroom at the rear of the schoolhouse. The Committee consisted of Pat Breen, Jim Carrigan, Patrick J. Dewan, Long Jim Toohey, and Jim Harrigan. Thus began and was constituted the Biddulph Peace Society, as it generally came to be known among its members. It eventually was known by the public as the Vigilance Committee of Biddulph.

34

MARTIN

When asked what went on in the anteroom at that first meeting of the Biddulph Peace Society at the Cedar Swamp Schoolhouse, James Toohey replied, "Martin [McLaughlin] talked of the things that were being done, that if it was not stopped they would have to leave the country." McLaughlin was about nine years older than Will Donnelly but had grown up with him. His family lived on the next farm but one to the Donnellys in the early days, and his brother, William, still lived there in the 1870s. Martin McLaughlin himself was born in Shinrone, near Borrisokane, Tipperary, and had come out from Ireland in 1845 as a small boy with his father. The senior McLaughlin was killed four years later when a tree fell on his head, and young Martin was bound to a trade, lived in the city of London for a year, and spent another year in nearby Lobo Township before his marriage.[1]

McLaughlin was a husky man with a reddish tinge to his hair, a characteristic of some members of the Donnelly family.[2] He was a man of strong opinions, and he had a yearning for respectability within his own community. He bought a farm on the Swamp Line and there raised a family, which in the late 1870s consisted of seven children. His wife was sickly. McLaughlin's younger brother left Biddulph and settled in Iowa near the Missouri border, and Martin McLaughlin visited him there in the 1870s for a period of seven months. In Missouri he heard many stories of the outlawry and desperadoes who flourished during and immediately after the Civil War. It was Jesse James country, but there were many other marauders of lesser fame who had preyed upon the respectable and law-abiding citizenry. Some of them had been hunted down and dispatched by vigilance committees.

During his Missouri sojourn, too, Martin McLaughlin came in contact with other Irish-Catholic families who had originally emigrated from Ireland to Canada but had deserted British dominions for the more open society of the United States. One such family was that of Michael Maher, whose son was now a ship captain who travelled widely. Maher himself had died in Bay City, Michigan shortly after leaving Biddulph. It was Michael Maher who had ejected James Donnelly, Sr., from the south half of the Donnelly homestead in 1856, and the Missouri visit doubtless afforded McLaughlin an opportunity of being refreshed of the old Maher-Donnelly enmity.

By 1877 Martin McLaughlin was serving as school trustee of the Whalen School near his farm. As it was a union school attended by residents of Blanshard, mostly Protestants, as well as the Catholics of Biddulph, McLaughlin felt more than usually aware of representing the Catholic portion of the community and assumed a certain responsibility for the conduct of all the members of his religious persuasion. At one of the meetings of trustees, he overheard some of his Protestant neighbours discussing the numerous thefts in the district, one of the most recent of which had been reported thus:

Martin McLaughlin, a Whalen School trustee a leading member of the Biddulph Peace Society, and its nominee as a Justice of the Peace, a sketch by Robert Harris (PEI)

GRANTON... The barn of Mr. Brooks, who resides on the townline between Blanshard and Biddulph, a few miles from this place, was entered one night last week and fourteen bags full of grain stolen. The tracks of a one-horse wagon were discovered going into Biddulph, but the clue was not followed up.[3]

This theft occurred in early May 1879. "Why had not the clue been followed up?" McLaughlin inquired of his Protestant colleagues.

"Oh," came the answer, doubtless accompanied by a significant glance at McLaughlin and than at the other Protestants present, "once any stolen goods are taken into St. Patrick's parish, they are

lost for good. Nobody dares search for them there."

McLaughlin's always reddish complexion may have turned a deeper shade of red. Just in the manner the farmer had enunciated the words "St. Patrick's parish" would have been enough for McLaughlin to get the point. Stung by the remark, he took it as a slur against his religion, especially because there was some truth in it.

"If you lose any more property," he finally declared to the man, " just call upon me. I will see to it that St. Patrick's parish is searched from beginning to end and the property recovered. And I can procure the aid of at least forty men of the parish to assist me."

A few weeks later McLaughlin purchased a rifle and a shotgun which, he claimed, were "to scare birds from his orchard". About this time Will Donnelly met his old friend at Morley's funeral and thought it strange when McLaughlin stared right through him without returning his greeting. It disturbed Donnelly. One more thing about Martin McLaughlin was that he was brother-in-law to Timothy Carey, in whose field outside Lucan the stage horses of William Walker and Joe Watson had been found butchered, with their tongues slashed out, a couple of years before. This work had been almost universally attributed to the Donnellys.

About 1875 a young, intelligent-looking man of the Catholic Settlement, Patrick Breen, was chosen, at the age of thirty-two years, to be a trustee of the Cedar Swamp School. Three years later Breen was elected a director of the Biddulph Agricultural Society. He, too, became a leading member of the Biddulph Peace Society and took upon himself the guardianship of the morals of the community, as well as its schooling, its fall fairs, and its horse shows. Like Martin McLaughlin, he assumed responsibility for demonstrating to the Protestants of the township and district that the Catholics were equal in every respect to the Protestants and fully capable of filling responsible positions in the community.

McLaughlin acted as chairman at many of the meetings of the peace society, and Pat Breen kept the books, although others also served in those capacities. When William Carroll, the younger brother of James Carroll, came to join the society at the Cedar Swamp School one evening, it was Martin McLaughlin who admonished the young man to say nothing about what he heard there.

Ned Ryan lodged a complaint with the Committee about Tom Donnelly's forbidding the threshing of his grain. There was much heated discussion as to what was to be done. A motion was made to go in a body and lynch Tom Donnelly, and it was only after the mover of it was wrestled into submission that the motion was lost. "We'll be as bad as they are if we allow such a thing," said the opposer, who later resigned his membership.

While some who originally joined later quit the association, there were others who were not allowed to join at all. Young Tommy Ryan's employer, Michael Powe, went to join up, in the belief, he said, that it was founded on the basis set out by Father Connolly in his sermons. When he went inside the schoolhouse, he found the men talking and smoking, and some of them singing. As soon as he was inside, however, John Kennedy approached him with a book and asked him to take an oath. Powe refused to be sworn and was immediately shoved outside.

One of the Hogan boys named Martin, otherwise known as Weston to distinguish him from another Hogan of the same name, happened to pass by between eight and nine o'clock. Hogan had been drinking, and when he saw the lights on at the school and some men at the porch of the front door, he thought to himself, "It looks like they're moving an organ into the school. I'll go and investigate."

By the time Hogan reached the door, the men had gone inside. When he pushed, John Heenan poked his head around the door and tried to hold it shut. But Hogan put his shoulder to the door and pushed his way inside where he found, besides Heenan, four or five others in the little porch.

Heenan said, "Come in. What do you want?"

"I want to go in," Hogan replied, indicating that he wished to enter the main room of the school.

Heenan stood to bar the door. "Will you take your oath?" he asked.

"What for?" Hogan inquired.

From the front of the classroom Martin McLaughlin called out to Hogan through the doorway, "Are you going to join up?"

"What does that mean?" Hogan called back.

"You know what it means," McLaughlin answered. "The book in the church, did you sign it?"

"I did," Hogan replied.

"Come in, then," said McLaughlin.

Hogan entered and looked around the school. It was filled with men, some walking around and others sitting at the scholars' desks. A few of the men gave Hogan dark looks, and one or two muttered half aloud that he should not be admitted. McLaughlin, who was acting as chairman, called for a vote of admission.

"All in favour, to my right; against, to my left," he called.

Everybody moved to the left. Hogan gave a contemptuous look around the room and went out, reporting the occurrence to his friend William Donnelly.

Inside the schoolhouse the business of the meeting resumed. It was proposed that Martin Curtin's threshing machine be guaranteed by the society for twelve months to permit Curtin to thresh Ryan's grain. The proposal failed to pass.

What did the peace society eventually resolve that night? William Casey said on the subject, "We were to keep secret those who were prosecuted for badness until the warrant was executed."

The members also agreed to try to get as many other inhabitants of the community who were not in league with the Donnellys to join the society. One of them approached his brother-in-law, and when the latter objected to having to take an oath, the other tried to explain the nature of it to him. "That's a hard oath," replied the brother-in-law, "when a man is sworn not to speak or keep company in any way with the Donnellys, even though they have never injured me."

Many members of the peace society were closely linked in blood and marriage. James Carroll's mother had been a sister of James Maher, and Carroll's Aunt Ellen was married to Jerry McDonald. William Thompson was married to Mary, the daughter of "the respactable" old Mick Carroll, and was a brother of Mrs. James Toohey. James McGrath and Michael Blake were cousins, and the wife of James McGrath was Rebecca Fogarty, whose father, John Fogarty, was a brother of Ann Fogarty, the mother of William Donnelly's old flame, Maggie Thompson. The Fogartys thus linked the McGraths and the Blakes to the Thompsons and the Tooheys. Margaret Bruin was married to John Quigley. Mrs. James Maher was sister to John Cain, as well as to the wife of Michael Feeheley. William Casey was married to Rachel, a daughter of old Patrick Ryder, who was an uncle of Grouchy Ryder. The wife of Anthony Heenan was an aunt of John Kennedy. Old Timothy Toohey was married to Mary Ryder, while James Toohey had married Sarah, a sister of William and Maggie Thompson. Mrs. James Maher, as mentioned, was a Cain, and Bridget Cain was the wife of Martin Darcey, Jr.

Sarah Farrell, widow of James Donnelly's victim, married Pat Flannery, related to the Cains, and thereby linked the Mahers, Farrells, and Carrolls, as well as the Darceys and Feeheleys. James Carrigan was related by marriage to the Blakes and the McGraths. Michael McGrath, brother of James, was assistant priest at St. Peter's Roman Catholic Church in the north part of Biddulph for a short time, until his transfer in 1879 to Bothwell. James Morkin was married to a Ryder, Margaret, while another Morkin had earlier married a sister of Big Jack Kennedy, forming a link between the Ryders and Kennedys; it was James Morkin who finally sold Pat Farrell's old farm to his brother-in-law, Grouchy Ryder. Another Morkin, Thomas, was married to one of the Toohey girls, sister of James Toohey, and the Morkins thereby formed a further link between the Kennedys and the Tooheys.

In his sermons at St. Patrick's Church, Father John Connolly on more than one occasion called upon God's purging fire to come down from the heavens upon the evildoers of Biddulph. When a fierce thunderstorm swept the district on the morning of Friday, July 11, 1879, lightning struck the chimney of John McCaffrey's house in the village of Lucan, causing it to tumble to the ground and "smashing the cook stove to atoms". To the superstitious, it was a sign of divine displeasure at an unnatural event – the birth of triplets to Mrs. McCaffrey – while to others, it was an omen of darkening clouds over Biddulph. Elderly grannies in the back kitchens of Biddulph gossiped that the McCaffreys were being warned against continuing their friendship with the Donnellys.

And it is true that the Donnellys began to notice that old friends, with whom they had been on visiting terms for many years, now "just passed the time of day" with them. The William McLaughlins, the Pat Whalens, the Pat Ryders, the John Carrolls, the Patrick Quigleys, and the Martin Darceys all remained near neighbours but ever more distant in friendliness.

Following the lead of Will Donnelly after the formation of the Peace Society, the young Keefes as well as the Donnelly brothers stopped going to St. Patrick's Church.

"I didn't feel like going to a church where I was

called a devil and a cripple," said Will Donnelly. McLaughlin and other leading members of the association began to spread the word throughout the township that the Donnellys were to be shunned. McLaughlin's own younger brother, William, who had stayed on the home farm but two doors away from the Donnellys, had always "neighboured" with them, which is to say they assisted each other at threshings and bees. While McLaughlin had six growing boys of his own, a few extra hands could always be used at threshing, and McLaughlin asked Jim Donnelly to send over a couple of the boys as the help was owed him. Donnelly said he would gladly oblige and send Tom and John. But early the next morning, one of the McLaughlin youngsters came to bring word that the boys were not to come. old Jim Donnelly asked why not.

"My father says that he cannot permit them to come," said young McLaughlin. "Mr. Thompson and Mr. Carroll and some others of that faction came to our house last night and said that if any of the Donnellys came to our threshing they would not come."

William Thompson was the Donnellys' next-door neighbour, and Mr. Carroll was Thompson's father-in-law. "Do not neighbour with the Donnellys," they had told William McLaughlin, who had little choice but to heed them.

The Whalens had lived opposite the Donnellys since about 1863, and they, too, had always exchanged help at threshings and had got along well with each other, even though, as Mrs. Whalen said, "The boys would sometimes have a tiff." But Ann Whalen, wife of grizzled old Pat Whalen, also said, "We were not very friendly over the last year." She did, however, continue to speak to any of the Donnellys she met on the road and bid them the time of the day.

The Donnellys became aware of the forces being turned against them and said, "A great many people used to call before the Society was formed, but none after. Lots of people who did not belong to it did not call." The latter, they said, were afraid of those who belonged and did not wish to antagonize them.

"Good and honest neighbours are bein' kep' from visitin' our house," Mrs. Donnelly would sometimes tearfully complain to her husband and her sons. "And they don't be friendly wid us any longer, though I know they still wish us well."

When she blamed the unfriendly attitude of the priest, her husband would reply, "Ye cannot blame the priest for it all, for they are wid him night and day tellin' him lies about us."

That fall James Donnelly borrowed a shotgun from one of the Feeheley boys. When he found it not quite in working order, he got it repaired at Sutherby's blacksmith shop at Whalen's Corners.

"You should get the property insured," his son William also told him. "You've had your barn burned once, and it could happen again."

"Oh, there be no need for it," the father replied. "Ez long ez I be heer, there'll be no one comin' to burn it. An' if I see any o' thim thryin', why I'll shoot thim."

The six sons of William McLaughlin, who lived on the Roman Line opposite Grouchy Ryder and the next farm but one to the Donnellys (P. McLaughlin)

Whenever Patrick Donnelly came home to visit during this time, he urged his parents to move from Biddulph and avoid further trouble and persecution. "You will never have peace while you live in Biddulph," he told his father. But, at his season of life, the old man did not like the idea of leaving the old place, he said, and Johannah agreed with him. In his letters, Pat Donnelly continued to urge his parents to pull up stakes and warned of a premonition he felt of something terrible which would happen if things kept on in the same way. He even took the trouble to write his sister, Jenny, to use her great influence with the old people to get them to leave Biddulph, but it was of no avail.

35

HEIFER

On Wednesday, August 20, 1879, Will Donnelly visited his brother Michael in St. Thomas. Once again he saw Father Flannery, and both he and Norah went to confession and mass. Back in Biddulph on the following Sunday, William and Mary Thompson also attended mass. As they drove out of their farm gate, they counted their cows, and when they returned from church they counted them again. With all the thieving going on in the district, they felt that one could not be too careful. Sure enough, that evening one of their cows was missing. Early the next day both Thompson and his wife went into the bush in search of the heifer, but without success. They did find what appeared to be its track leading across the fence to the Donnelly farm immediately adjacent. It also appeared to the Thompsons that the fence rails had been taken down and replaced, except for the top rail which still lay on the ground.[1]

"It's them Donnellys," they told each other. "They've stolen the heifer."

Mary Thompson thought she heard a cow bawling from over in the direction of the Donnelly farm. The more she listened, the surer she became that it was her cow. It must have been locked in the stable of their neighbours, and although William Donnelly later said she had to have had remarkable ears to be able to distinguish her cow from any other at some fifteen hundred feet, Mary Thompson was one of those infuriatingly superior persons who seldom lost their self-assurance. A hired man of the Thompson's by name of James Kelly used to stay out late at night, and whenever he tried to sneak back into the house at a late hour Mrs. Thompson would say, "I always heard him come in, and told him to lock the door."

The Thompsons had got rid of Kelly long before, and their hired man at this time was James Carroll, nephew of James Maher. They immediately told him of their suspicions, and Carroll accompanied Mary Thompson down the Roman Line to spread the news. They told John Cain, John Darsey, and Long Jim Toohey, all of whom lived south of Donnellys.

"I suspect it's my cow that's on Donnelly's place I heard bawling," she told them. "It sounded very much like my cow."

This evidence was good enough for these men. As it happened, a meeting of the Biddulph Peace Society was being held that night at the Cedar Swamp Schoolhouse having to do with an insult received by the Biddulph councillor, Patrick Dewan, at the hands of the young troublemaker Tommy Ryan. Dewan claimed that he had lately recognized Ryan as the person whose voice he had heard in the night threatening him. Besides, many thefts of pigs and cattle had taken place about this time, and it was believed that young fellows like Tommy Ryan and Tommy Hines, Mike Donnelly's brother-in-law, were used by the Donnelly gang to drive the stolen livestock to the city or other towns, where they could be conveniently and anonymously disposed of.

The meeting to deal with Ryan had been called for Monday night, September 1, 1879. The loss of Thompson's cow was brought up and the discussion continued late into the evening until the members finally resolved to send a delegation to Lucan for a constable and a search warrant. William Thompson, James Carroll, Patrick Dewan, Big John Kennedy, and John Cain were nominated and trudged off to the village, where they rounded up Constable Wild Bill Hodgins and went with him to the house of William Stanley, J.P., at the corner of Main and William streets.

The magistrate listened to their story. He was reluctant to issue legal process, telling them they could not search at night. What they should do, he eventually advised, was to go back and watch the road leading from the Donnelly farm, or, alternatively, they should go and ask the Donnellys for permission to search. If permission was refused, they could come back during the day and get a search warrant. Stanley did issue, however, a warrant for the arrest of Tom Ryan, which was handed to the constable.

The delegation returned to the Cedar Swamp Schoolhouse to report. Although it was four o'clock in the morning, the discussion continued unabated, many of the men grumbling that the society should get magistrates appointed from among themselves instead of relying on the Lucan Justices of the Peace. Several names were put forth, among them William Casey, Martin Darcey, and Martin McLaughlin, and discussion took place as to which of these, from political considerations, might have the best chance of being appointed. The men finally resolved that for the moment they would go to arrest Tom Ryan and then go on to Donnelly's.

The entire gang of some thirty or forty men set out, many of them carrying clubs. One had a rifle. Accompanied by Constable Hodgins, they went first to the farmhouse of Michael Powe on the Swamp Line and got the proprietor and his hired man, Tom Ryan, out of bed.

"What do you want me for?" Ryan asked them.

"For insulting Mr. Dewan here," they replied "and also for stealing Mr. Thompson's heifer."

"What?" reacted Ryan, surprised to hear it.

"And where's the heifer then?"

Don't worry," they replied, "the next thing is to find her."

They looked around Powe's farmyard, and when Powe protested that he had nobody's cows but his own, some of them threatened him with a beating for keeping Ryan against the wishes of

the priest. They called Ryan many uncomplimentary names. Constable Hodgins sensed that things might get out of hand and took Ryan in charge.

"Hodgins treated me decently," Ryan later told Will Donnelly, "not like the rest of those bastards."

From the Powe farm the entire mob headed towards the Roman Line and the Donnelly farm. William Stanley's advice had apparently lost some of its finer meaning along the way, for the men were now determined to make a search of Donnelly's place with or without permission. Among the crowd that morning were James Carroll, John Kennedy, Michael Blake, William Thompson, John Thompson, Martin McLaughlin, John McLaughlin, James Toohey, Tim Toohey, James Maher, Anthony Heenan, James Heenan, Dennis Heenan, John Heenan, William Casey, Patrick J. Dewan, Pat Quigley, John Quigley, young James Ryder, young Patrick Ryder, Edward Ryan, Martin Darsey, John Darsey, Pat Breen, James Carrigan, William Feeheley, John Cain, and several others. Rounding out the crew was Constable Wild Bill Hodgins with his prisoner in tow.

Approaching the Donnelly farm from the north, when they had reached a point in the road just beyond the Donnelly Schoolhouse, John Cain and William Hodgins detached themselves from the main body and with their prisoner continued on to the next farm, which was Cain's. They wanted to get Cain's buggy with which to take Ryan to Lucan. The main body of men, instead of going on to Donnelly's gate, left the road at that point and stole quietly along the north boundary line of the Donnelly farm, marked by a rail fence. As it neared the house the rail fence became a board fence, and a missing board just past the house provided access into the farmyard. One by one the men slipped through the hole.

All was quiet in the farmyard, as it was still only six o'clock in the morning. Besides the large log house with its frame kitchen at the rear, there stood in the farmyard a small milkhouse built of frame a few feet from the northeast angle of the house, a couple of small stables for horses and cattle respectively, both enclosed by a rail fence, a strawstack, and a couple of small sheds serving as granaries. "Some crotches with straw on top" was the way one of the men contemptuously referred to the latter shelters, "what they called granaries." Aside from the house, it is true the buildings were not imposing. Their old and wretched appearance was considered by some of the neighbours a disgrace, even though, as a general rule, farm outbuildings in Biddulph at that time were not the large and imposing structures of later days.

In groups of five or six, the crowd quickly searched all the buildings and enclosures, breaking open at least one door that was fastened. But they found no stolen heifer. One of them pointed at a goose and said it might be a stolen goose, but no one seemed willing to press the point.

Inside the Donnelly farmhouse that morning of September 2 were the usual occupants, James and Johannah Donnelly, and the old man's niece, Bridget. Of the sons, only John was at home, but helping with the harvest that year and sleeping in the same bed with him were young Tommy Keefe and Tommy Hines.

Bridget Donnelly was the first person to notice the intruders out in the yard. She jumped out of bed and, running into the boys' room, she shook her cousin.

"Johnny, Johnny, get up ! There's a lot of men at the barn," she said, rushing then to waken the old people .

John Donnelly got up, dressed quickly, stepped out the back door of the kitchen, and walked toward the stables, where some of the searchers were scurrying about. He saw James Carroll opening a stable door and John Kennedy looking into one of the granaries.

"Good morning, boys," he said, half in greeting and half in surprise, for he was quite astonished at seeing the large crowd.

Standing nearest him was Martin Darcey, who replied, "Good morning."

When John Donnelly saw some of the men coming out of one of the stables, he called out, "Here! Here! What's going on here? What do you fellows want?"

The men stopped in their tracks and turned nervously towards Donnelly, holding their sticks a little tighter in their hands. William Thompson spoke up. "I've lost a cow and we're looking for it."

"Well, you'll not find it here," said Donnelly indignantly. "If anybody has taken your cow it is one of you who's done it."

No one answered him, for in truth they all felt a trifle sheepish making such a bold entry and not turning up the cow. John Donnelly went on, "I say the thief is in your own crowd. Why don't you go and ask the priest who took it? I am sure he would put a curse on that man and you would find your cow before nightfall."

From this it was plain that the Donnellys had been thinking a great deal about Father Connolly's role in the recent events of the community.

"Never mind," James Carroll replied, "we've got the man that took the cow going up there in the buggy."

Carroll pointed in the direction of Cain's farm, where Constable Hodgins could be seen in Cain's buggy with his prisoner, about to embark for Lucan. Donnelly looked and then said, "That's not the man. The curse would fall on you, Carroll. You'd be the first man taken up."

In the meantime Johannah Donnelly had slipped on a petticoat and had followed her son out of the house. As she came to the stable enclosure, her eyes darted from face to face, her dark and bushy eyebrows beetling furiously. When she saw John Kennedy, she hissed at him half under her breath, "You robber!"

She had expected to see Kennedy among such a crowd, for she knew how bitterly he had reacted to Will's marriage to Kennedy's sister. But she was slightly taken aback when she saw young Jim Ryder, the Ryders and the Donnellys having lived near each other for over thirty years without ever quarrelling.

"I'm sorry to see ye among sich a crowd as this, young Grouch," she said.

The entire crowd, still feeling a trifle chastened, turned and began to walk in the direction of the farm gate at the roadway, and John Donnelly, followed by his mother, walked with them. As they neared the house, Jim Donnelly came out, still pulling on his pants as he hastened forward to meet the crowd.

"Good mornin'," he said. "Whot's up wid ye?" Not one of the men answered. The old man looked from one grim face to the next and then inquired again, "Heer, whot might yeez be up to?"

Someone finally replied, "We have lost a stolen cow and we're looking for her."

James Donnelly looked at them. "I'll be damned if ye'll find her heer," he said, not with a little astonishment. "Look for her, thin, if ye think ye can. Go ahead."

The words were spoken in indignation. He pointed his finger. "Theer's a straw stack over theer," he exclaimed. "Go an' turn it over straw by straw if ye will, ye won't find yer cow."

Somebody in the crowd finally answered him, "Oh, we won't have to do that. We've got the thief, all right. There he goes down the road in the buggy now, young Tom Ryan."

The old man saw the buggy retreating down the road. "Well," he said, "if ye have given him the benefit uv the law, that's all whot he wants."

James Harrigan then spoke up. "But you harboured him. We know he lives with you sometimes."

"An' whot uv id?" retorted the old man angrily and turning towards Harrigan. "I hev known his father, and well, too. And I will harbour his father's son."

"You son of a bitch!" Harrigan answered back vehemently. "Little you care about his father or his sisters either!"

The references to Tom Ryan's sisters may well have been an allusion to the well-known amorous proclivities of the Donnelly boys, for many a Roman Line maiden was believed to have taken a tumble in the straw with one or other of the dashing Donnelly boys.

But James Donnelly's answer was short and succinct. "Kiss my ass!" he said to Harrigan.

John Donnelly had by this time walked up and stood beside his father. When the old man made his last retort, James Heenan ran up to the two Donnellys and brandished a stick at John Donnelly.

"This work will be put down!" he exclaimed, "And down we will put it."

"What work?" asked John Donnelly.

"You know what work. Who stole my horses?"

John Donnelly made no reply, and Heenan answered for him. "It was Ryan, that's who," he said.

"It was not," replied Donnelly.

"It was," cried Heenan in a rage, "and I will have satisfaction if it takes twenty years."

James Maher ran up beside Heenan and shouted, "Who shaved my horses' tails?"

"I don't know anything at all about your horses' tails," said John Donnelly.

John Donnelly, from a sketch in the *London Daily Advertiser*

"It was either you or your brother Tom," cried Maher, shaking his fist in Donnelly's face, "and I am bound to have revenge if it takes twenty years."

"That's right, Jim, that's right," yelled the others in the crowd.

"Who stole my discs?" someone then called out.

"Who stole my pig?" cried another voice. It could have been James Heenan.

Inside the house, young Tommy Hines, who was cringing behind the kitchen door, heard the voices in the crowd becoming angrier and more excited and was afraid to step outside.

James Carroll then walked up to the elder Donnelly. "We don't want anything from you," he said. "We have the thief. We just want to show you we're not afraid of you. Why, we could break all your bones right here at your door this morning, and you could not help yourself."

The grizzled old man sneered back into Carroll's pudgy face and replied in a voice containing the most contempt he could muster, "Why, ye young pup, I was a man long before ye could wipe yer ass."

Carroll flushed with anger and replied heatedly, "Hold your tongue, old man, or you'll get a few kicks in the ribs."

But the old man continued to sneer at him. "I've seen the day when I could give ye a few kicks," Donnelly replied, "an' I don't think it wud take much uv a man to do it yit."

Someone else then yelled at Donnelly, "We'll make you keep quiet, or drive you out!"

John Donnelly sworn   I am the son of James Donnelly. I laid the information against these parties. On the morning of the 2 day of Sept '79 I was in the yard of my father's premises about 6 o'clock in the morning. I saw a number of men going towards our stable on our premises, there were between 30 & 40 persons, I think it was James Carrol that went up and opened the stable door. John Kennedy I met at the granary door, he also opened it, I believe. I said to some of the persons What do you want. William Thompson spoke and said I have lost a cow. I told him to go up to the priest and curse the man that took the cow and if the priest did curse the man that took the cow my believe was that "Carrol" would be the man that would be first taken up. Carrol replied, we have the man going up there in the buggy that took the cow. That was Ryan that was arrested. Carrol alluded to Ryan. The parties named in the information, besides others not named, are the ones that I saw on my father's place. My father came out of the house and asked the parties what they wanted. Carrol replied we want nothing but to let you see that we are not afraid of you. Some one then answered and said, We have lost a cow. My father then said if they thought the cow was there they could go and hunt for her. Carrol then went up to my father and asked him how he would like a couple of kicks and we could break your bones now and you could not help yourself. James Heenan said to me, Who rode his horse. Heenan said it was Ryan. I told him it was not. Heenan also said he would have satisfaction if it was for 20 years. James Maher made a lunge up at me and said Who shaved my horses Tail. I told him I did not know anything at all about his horse. Some of the parties clubbed around the pump and took a drink. Others would congregate around our place in groups. They then would move off a piece and then stop and talk together. I then heard John Kennedy (I think) say to the parties when outside the gate, Now fight among yourselves. Some of the parties had sticks in their hands. When James Heenan came up to me he had a stick in his hand he said he would [have] satisfaction if it was for 20 years, John Dorsey told my father to kiss his backside. The parties did not look as though they were looking for anything lost. They showed no search [warrant] to me. My father's land is enclosed (the land mentioned in the information). The parties went into our premises without premission.
Cross ex
My father owns the land. I think it is situated on lot 18 – Tp of Biddulph, 6 Cons. I had heard that a cow had been stolen from William Thompson's. He lives next to our farm. I have not heard of any stealing in our neighbourhood in a year past. I did not know that there was a 'vigilance committee' sworn in to protect the township. I did not know of cattle stolen being near our place. I did not hear of having a stolen cow on our property. These parties came in to my father's place about 6 a.m. in the morning. I saw them when they came around in the back of the house. Most of these parties are farmers. I did not say good morning boys. When I first saw them the parties did not say that they were looking for a stolen cow. I did not tell them that they could go and search. No other person was present. Tommy Hines, my father, my mother, and the girl, were in the house. After the parties spoke to me no search was made on our premises. A door is on our stable I think it was closed. I believe every man that came into our place came to do us harm. When they came to the house my father asked them what they wanted. Bill Thomson said they were looking for a stolen cow. My father told them to go and search for the cow. James Carrol said to my father 'how would you like a few kicks. Some of the parties complained to my father for keeping of Ryan. Dorsey said to my father to kiss his ass. My father replied to Dorsey in the same language. My mother did not mention Jo Kennedy as a robber. Carrol replied to my father when he asked them what they wanted that they wanted nothing but to let you, see they were not afraid of you, but that they had the man that stole the cow.

"John Donnelly"

(UWO)

But the old man merely replied, "Go to hell. I'll stay heer if the divil has the whole lot uv ye yit. Ye kin all kiss my ass!"

And with that James Donnelly turned and walked back into the house with never another look behind.

John Darsey, a large and pale-faced Irishman of some sixty years who had up to this time kept quiet, muttered after the old man that he, too, could kiss his ass. The rest of the men stood around not knowing what to do next. Some of them took a drink from the pump.

John Kennedy's voice was then heard a little louder than the rest, "Come on, boys, we'll go and take a look at brother-in-law's now."

Johannah Donnelly heard Kennedy clearly. As they began to leave one of the men raised his club and vowed aloud, "If we ever come back, we won't go away as peaceable as we are now."

Some of the men began to bicker among themselves as they passed through the gate at the roadway, a few wanting to have it out with the Donnellys right then and there. But Kennedy was the peacemaker. "Boys, boys," he admonished, "go ahead, fight among yourselves if you will."

His chiding quieted them and they continued through the gate and down the Roman Line in the same direction from which they had come. The entire time spent on the Donnelly premises by the crowd was not much more than fifteen minutes.

FIDDLE

As the crowd left the Donnelly farm it split up into groups. Some of the men went to Thompson's for breakfast, some went to Grouchy Ryder's, while others went to Jim Maher's or to Mick Carroll's. At the latter place, a team of horses was hitched to a wagon and Carroll and some of the older men, like Anthony Heenan, rode in it as they started out again. When the entire party regrouped, it continued north along the Roman Line.

The schoolteacher of the Donnelly School on this day was an old Irish gentleman by the name of Thomas Marshall who had taken over temporarily during the short absence of the regular teacher, Stephen J. Patton. A resident of London, old Marshall was not thoroughly familiar with the ins and outs of the factions of the Catholic Settlement of Biddulph. He had gone about half a mile towards the school from Robert Keefe's, where he boarded, when he met the Biddulph Peace Society. His eyes widened with astonishment at the approach on the quiet country road of a "body of men, between forty and fifty in number, having clubs and bludgeons in their hands".

"In the name of God," he blurted at them when they had got within earshot, "where are ye all goin' to?"

"We're looking for a heifer," someone from the crowd answered.

The elderly schoolteacher puzzled over the reply for a moment. "And have ye each lost a heifer?" he asked, wondering why so many men, some of them armed, had to go looking for one cow.

No one from the crowd answered, and the teacher continued, "Men, would ye know it if ye saw it?"

The men continued to trudge along in silence, and he addressed them again: "Would ye not be surprised if the heifer should turn up yit?"

One of the last to pass by finally answered him. "The heifer is killed, we know that. Now we are looking for the meat and we're going around smelling the chimneys to find the scent of it."

The old man chuckled after them. "Well, thin," he said, "bid the divil good mornin' fer me if ye see 'im."

"We've been a long time looking for the chap," one of them called back, and they continued on their way.

After a short piece the Biddulph Peace Society met James Keefe near the gate of his farm, and Keefe, too, was amazed at seeing such a crowd of men on the road at nine o'clock in the morning. Noticing the Biddulph Township councillor, Dewan, among them he addressed him.

"What are ye doing?" he asked.

"We're looking for a stolen heifer," replied Dewan.

Keefe looked incredulous. "I don't think it was stolen at all," he said.

"Well," said Dewan, "we're going to the Town Line, then divide and go through the woods."

Keefe watched the men pass his farm. He noticed a gun in the wagon beside Carroll and Anthony Heenan. The search party continued past the Keefe farms and did not, in fact, make any other searches along the way but continued on to the Biddulph and Usborne Town Line.

In the meantime, as soon as the crowd had left the Donnelly farm, Mrs. Donnelly made up her mind to warn her son William that the search party was intending to pay him a visit. Hitching up her petticoats she set off on foot in a northeasterly direction towards Whalen's Corners. Much of her journey was cross-country, through fields and bush. Crossing the Roman Line she lit out across the outlying twenty-five acres of the Donnelly farm to the rear of the seventh and eighth concessions, through the bush of Michael Powe, across the fields of Thomas Lamphier, down the sideroad to the Swamp Line, and then north to Whalen's Corners, arriving in a great puff at her son's house. Here all was quiet, with William and Norah both at home.

Thus forewarned, William Donnelly was ready for the Biddulph Peace Society. He made up his mind that he would demand their authority to search and tell them that if they could not show a legal warrant he would shoot the first man to enter his gate. He thereupon loaded his guns and waited inside the front door. An hour or two passed without a sign of the crowd. Neither Johannah nor Will knew that the search party not only had stopped for breakfast but had taken the long way around, by way of the Town Line road, to Whalen's Corners. In addition, they had

Will Donnelly, with autograph, taken about 1880 (R. Cunningham)

made a slight detour over to Kinsella's farm on the Town Line, where Pat Quigley was doing some custom threshing. They asked Quigley to bring his machine down to Ryan's place next. Quigley was aware of Tom Donnelly's ban, however, and refused. Some of the men grew angry and threatened to take his machine to Ryan's by force, but others persuaded them to leave Quigley alone and continue on to Whalen's Corners.

When the gang finally made its appearance, Will Donnelly called out to the two women in the house, "Here comes the Black Militia!"

They waited tensely for the search party to approach the house, but about two or three hundred feet away from it the crowd stopped. While they hesitated Donnelly observed that most of them had sticks in their hands, Michael Heenan with a "sliver of scantling", James Heenan with a stick of some kind, and Martin McLaughlin gripping a blackthorn cudgel. No one stepped forward. Perhaps having caught sight of a gleam from the pistol held by Donnelly inside the door they had lost appetite for another confrontation. Will Donnelly, for his part, was a little surprised to see some of the faces among the crowd, such as that of William Feeheley and young Jim Ryder, Grouchy's son.

Finally, two of the men stepped out from the main body, which remained clustered around the wagon, and walked towards Donnelly's house. The two were John Kennedy and William Ryan. When they came to a point opposite the house but still on the other side of the road, they stopped and squatted down on a log which happened to be lying there. They sat, occasionally glancing at the house and then back at the crowd, and sometimes pointing in a certain direction and then another. It was painfully obvious to everyone that none of them had any relish to approach any closer the house of Will Donnelly.

"What are you going to do now, Sitting Bull?" Donnelly called out loud enough for the two men squatting on the log opposite to hear them, and he saw the two shrink at his words. Sensing they had lost all courage, Donnelly quickly laid down his pistol and, reaching for his fiddle, returned to the door with it tucked on his shoulder. He began to scrape out a well-known fiddle march called "Boney Crossing the Alps".[1]

"I thought it was very appropriate for that bunch," Donnelly said later as he gleefully recounted the incident to his friends.

It was a brilliant stroke. As soon as the two heard the fiddle tune dancing across the warm summer air they rose quickly and walked beyond the Donnelly house, soon followed by the rest of the men. Their sullen silence was broken only by the rasping of the fiddle strings and the clattering of the wagon as they passed in front of the little house.

A few of the men turned into the blacksmith shop of Edward Sutherby, which stood close to Donnelly's house. Sutherby asked them what they wanted, and when they told him they were

looking for a stolen cow, the blacksmith laughed at them.

"You're a respectable-looking crowd, indeed," he said. "Why, it would look better if you were at home cutting thistles or ploughing. Well, don't expect to find a stolen cow here in my shop."

The men scowled their blackest looks at the smith before replying. "We mean business," they warned him, "and you can expect other visits from us, too. We might come at any time, perhaps in the dead of night."

They trudged out of the blacksmith shop and set off down the road. When he saw them retreat Donnelly put down his fiddle and stepped outside the door, followed closely by his mother.

"Hey, Quinn," Donnelly called out scornfully after one of them, "are you looking for your mother?"

The allusion was to the family shame of Quinn's mother having been left to die in a poor-house in Ireland, notwithstanding that her son was a prosperous farmer in Biddulph.

Mrs. Donnelly added her piece. "Ye should be ashamed of yerselves, the lot of ye, fer I often took

John Kennedy was a close friend of Will Donnelly until Will married his sister Norah.

the hunger off uv a great many of ye." The appearance of Mrs. Donnelly only made the men glower all the more darkly over their shoulders. Although it was well known she had a heart to match her huge body, she also had a rebuking and scornful tongue to match both. She continued, "I wonder at ye, Martin Darcey, bein' wid sich a gang. Why yer father is the daicentest man in Biddulph."

Relieved to retreat at last out of the range of those scornful voices, the party continued along the Swamp Line until it reached the place from which it had set out many hours earlier, the Cedar Swamp Schoolhouse. It was by this time afternoon. The men dispersed to their farms to ponder alone the events of the day and to catch up on the farm chores.

Johannah Donnelly also returned home later that afternoon, but that evening she was back on the road paying a visit to a neighbour, Mrs. John Carroll, who lived a couple of farms south of the Donnelly place on the opposite side of the road. Mrs. Carroll noticed immediately that her neighbour was in a great passion.

"Is this not a pretty way we are used?" began Mrs. Donnelly.

The Carroll woman had heard of the search made of her neighbour's premises earlier that day. Her own husband was a member of the family of "the respactable" Mr. Carroll. Although for years on fairly friendly terms with the Donnellys, the John Carrolls were well aware of the emotions then in the process of being released along the Roman Line.

"Yes, it is," replied Mrs. Carroll, "if ye do not desarve it."

But Johannah Donnelly hardly listened to her neighbour's reply, continuing angrily, "And young Grouch was searchin' wid the rest of thim." She waggled her finger in the direction of the Ryder farm and harangued the other. "I tell ye, I will go out on the road and meet young Grouch when he passes by in his grand new buggy. I'll put a blush in his face, I warrant, and thin he'll lie back in his buggy."

"Mrs. Donnelly," replied the other woman, "it would be betther if ye did not go out on the road."

Mrs. Donnelly was still angry when she left the Carroll farm. That evening she also visited the homes of Mrs. Pat Whalen, Mrs. Patrick Quigley, and Mrs. William McLaughlin, some of her nearest neighbours, and expressed the same feelings to them about the invasion of their farm by the Biddulph Peace Society. Grouchy Ryder claimed later that Johannah Donnelly had made threats against his son. He claimed that Mrs. John Carroll had told his daughter, Mary Ryder, that Mrs. Donnelly had said that young Grouch would not be riding in his fine new buggy for long.

Late in the afternoon of the day of the search party, an old man named James Quigley, who lived on the Quigley sideroad near the Thompson farm, saw Mary Thompson still looking for her cow in the bush at the back of her farm. Quigley told her he had seen the cow over in William McLaughlin's bush. The bush was next to the Thompsons' on the north side. Quigley went back to the place, and finding the cow there at half past eight that evening, he drove it over to Thompson's, saying, "Here's your cow." There was no line fence separating McLaughlin's property from the pasture from which the cow had disappeared, but for some reason the Thompsons had never thought of looking for her there.

Word of the routing of the Biddulph Peace Society by Will Donnelly's fiddle spread quickly. When James Carroll went to Lucan shortly after, he was taunted so unmercifully by a schoolboy named Edward Dayly that he retaliated with his fists, resulting in his arrest by County Constable Hodge. He pleaded guilty to assault and wounding under provocation and was fined $4 and $8 costs.

The newspapers picked up the story of the invasion of the Donnelly farm and reported it thus:

... A number of the residents to the number of forty banded together and formed a "Vigilance Committee, invested with power similar to Judge Lynch's, for the summary treatment and disposition of all offenders against the property or persons of any one in the vicinity. It is said...that legal advice was given them that their action in this proceeding was perfectly in accordance with law.[2]

The Donnelly family did not believe the latter statement at all and, taking their own legal advice on the matter, decided to sue the members of the Biddulph Peace Society for trespass.

The family was especially perturbed at the participation of young James Ryder in the search. The two families had lived near each other for over thirty years without any trouble, and the outlying Donnelly farm of twenty-five acres now adjoined Grouchy Ryder's own farm without even a line fence between them. "The Ryders are good friends," Will Donnelly insisted, and pointed out that he himself had known Grouchy since before the latter was a married man. A brother of old Grouch was Tom Ryder, at whose wedding celebration the fracas had occurred between the Donnellys and the Lucan constables. And, many years before, back in the early days of the township, Ryder's own father and a brother had arrived in Biddulph with Jim Donnelly himself, and had helped to clear the Roman Line.

But Will Donnelly did not realize that during the Coughlin election campaign the Ryders had changed more than their politics. Patrick Grouchy Ryder was certain that it was Tom Donnelly and his friends who had pinned the derisive election slogan to the bare rump of his horse during that election. As a result, Ryder had quietly changed not only his politics but his factional allegiances in the neighbourhood. He became friendly with James Maher and the Carroll-Cain faction and most of his brothers followed his lead, among them Sideroad Jim, Dan, and the youngest, Tom. After the Coughlin election, only William Ryder remained a steadfast friend of the Donnellys. He soon had a falling-out with the rest of his brothers, quarrelling, in turn, with Sideroad Jim and then Dan. And it is entirely possible that at least part of Grouchy Ryder's animosity against his old friends originated in a long-standing competition for land on the Roman Line. Ryder had eventually acquired the old Patrick Farrell farm and had purchased half the old Maloney farm from poor Dan Clark. But the Donnellys purchased the other half And they seemed to be prospering in the new ventures, such as the horse-breeding that Will Donnelly had taken up. Patrick Nangle told how Martin McLaughlin on one occasion abused him for engaging Donnelly's stud horse.

"You are as bad as the Donnellys if you do it," McLaughlin said.

37

PETITIONS

Young Tommy Ryan was bailed to appear for his trial before J.P. William Stanley on the next Saturday, one of his bondsmen being John Kennedy, Sr. On behalf of Ryan, Will Donnelly retained the services of Lucan lawyer William McDiarmid. On the day of the trial, September 6, Donnelly, Ryan, and McDiarmid were surprised, upon walking into the little courtroom above the Lucan lock-up, to see Father John Connolly among the spectators. Court was called to order, the charge was read, and the defendant pleaded Not Guilty. The complainant Dewan took the witness stand and testified that on the night in question he had heard Ryan's voice, albeit disguised, cursing him and threatening to cut his heart out. Squire Stanley called for the defence and lawyer McDiarmid sprang into action. He ushered his client into the witness box and, at his prompting, Ryan swore that although he might have called Dewan a few uncomplimentary names he did not threaten him. But when Ryan made the denial, an extraordinary thing happened. Father Connolly jumped up from his seat and cried out at the surprised lawyer, "You are trying to make him tell a lie. He has sworn to tell the truth and you are making him perjure himself!"

The interruption astonished everyone and pandemonium broke loose. Defence counsel, defendant, magistrate, and spectators all began to talk at once .

"Order! Order!" cried the magistrate until peace was restored.

When Stanley had collected his wits, he asked the parish priest politely but firmly to refrain from further disruption of the proceedings, and then pronounced judgment: "I find the defendant guilty of abusive language and he is fined three dollars. The charge of threatening is dismissed. Court is adjourned."

Father Connolly was angry as he left the courtroom in company with Dewan. They felt that justice had not been done.

The following day, the parish priest related from the pulpit his version of the trial of Tom Ryan and spoke of the callousness and indifference of the magistrates of Lucan. He said he intended in future to go to all the court trials of his people to see that justice was done in the community. "And if the magistrates do not do justice," he told his congregation, "then I will have them punished."

The priest referred to Tom Ryan's alleged conduct towards Mr. Dewan, not only a most highly respected citizen of the parish of St. Patrick's but a man who, as councillor of the Township of Biddulph, deserved the respect of the people who had duly elected him. He considered the penalty imposed on Ryan disgracefully inadequate. He railed against the magistrates who would permit such an abuse of the law. He denounced those who protected and harboured Ryan, and in particular a certain family who were always sheltering "firebugs and blacklegs". Again, although he did not refer to the Donnelly family by name, every one of his listeners knew at whom the accusing finger was pointed.

Michael Powe was among those who sat and listened that Sunday morning. The words of the priest disturbed him, for Tom Ryan was his hired man. Powe decided he had better have a talk with the parish priest and, going to Father Connolly after church, asked him what he should do about Ryan .

"I want you to discharge him," the priest said.

"But Father Connolly," protested Powe, "I cannot do that. His time is not up, and if I put him away now, I would have to pay him his wages for the whole season."

"How much would that be?"

"Oh, about twenty dollars."

Reaching into his pocket, the priest pulled out some paper money and, counting out twenty dollars, handed it to the surprised farmer. "Here, take it," he said. "Now I want you to drive Ryan and his belongings to Granton Station tomorrow and see him started out of the country. Will you do it?"

Powe reluctantly agreed. He went home, gave Ryan the news and the twenty dollars and told him he would drive him to Granton in the morning. But Ryan said he would have to pick up his trunk from Will Donnelly's, and Powe agreed to take him there first.

The next morning the two drove up the Swamp Line to Whalen's Corners. But as soon as Powe's buggy had pulled up in front of William Donnelly's

William Stanley, brother of Barney Stanley and a Justice of the Peace in the village of Lucan (Stanley)

house, Ryan jumped briskly out. "You go on back home, Mr. Powe," he said laughing, "I'm not going any further. Why, that's the easiest twenty dollars I ever earned in my life."

Will Donnelly liked young Ryan and considered his attempted banishment by the priest an injustice. Ryan's family had been one of the first to settle in the parish and was respectable enough, Donnelly considered, and besides, young Ryan was willing to work for his keep. The next day Donnelly drove Ryan to Lucan and arranged a job for him with a team of custom threshers. But about two days later the boss of the threshing gang was confronted by James McGrath of the Roman Line.

"You had better discharge that young fellow," McGrath said, indicating Ryan.

"Discharge him?" the man replied. "What would I want to do that for?"

McGrath ignored the other's question and said ominously, "How would you like to have your machine burned some night?"

The threshing boss grew angry. "I will not discharge Ryan," he said, "and you just better try your hand on burning my machine. Now get out of here! "

Father Connolly was vexed when he heard that Will Donnelly had found Ryan a job. His next step was to visit the elderly John Kennedy and berate him for having gone bail for Ryan.

"But Father Connolly," protested the old man, "I had a good right to do it. Why, Paddy Ryan, the boy's father, stood for my Joseph when he was christened and a right daicent man he was. And once, when some of that society faction was trying to kill my son in a fight in Lucan, it was Ryan's cousin and his uncle, Bob Keefe, whot saved him. I tell ye, Father, Tommy Ryan is a quiet, harmless boy if he is but let alone."

The priest was surprised at Kennedy's spirited defence of young Ryan and tried a different tack. "What are you going to do with that son-in-law of yours?" he demanded.

"What do ye want me to do wid him?" asked Kennedy.

"He's a devil!" said the priest vehemently. "The biggest devil I ever met, and Ryan is another!"

But the old man simply replied, "Well, Father Connolly, that's where ye and me differs."

The priest went on. "I want you to keep Donnelly away from your house," he commanded.

"I will do no sich thing," replied Kennedy.

"Well, then," said the priest, "if anybody takes sick in your house and you send for me, if I come and Donnelly is here I'll take the patient out in the yard and there prepare him or her for death sooner than enter the house he is in."

Old Mr. Kennedy shook his head slowly at the priest. "I have known Will Donnelly since he was a child and I never saw anything wrong wid him," he said. "He will ever be welcome to my house while I have one. And as for Tom Ryan, I will go his security any time it is needed."

The priest left Kennedy's house in great indignation. On the following Sunday he again harangued his congregation and warned them that no one among them was to hire Tom Ryan. He said there was a man in the township, a devil and a cripple, who had set himself at defiance to the spiritual adviser of St. Patrick's Parish. It was this man who was trying to run things in the township by pulling strings and defying the peaceful and law-abiding citizens. It was he who harboured and brought strangers in to make trouble for the respectable residents .

"I am bound," he intoned, "to do away with all fire-bugs, gaol birds, and blacklegs!"

With the threshing season coming to a close, Ned Ryan's crops stood in the fields rotting. A good crop could yield as much as forty-seven bushels to the acre in Biddulph and, at a dollar a bushel, it would be a hard loss for Ryan unless something was done quickly. His friends appealed once more to the priest, who told them to tell Martin Curtin, then threshing at Dan Ryder's, that he would personally guarantee the safety of his machine. On this basis Curtin was ready to take his machine over to Ryan's, but the next morning it was found broken to pieces. Everyone agreed that it was Tom Donnelly's work.

The Biddulph Peace Society held a meeting that night to discuss the latest outrage. Old Pat Whalen, deciding to see what the society was all about, took the half-hour's walk over to the Cedar Swamp Schoolhouse for the meeting. James Carroll asked Whalen to come again, but it was the old man's only attendance. "We were three or four hours talking on farming affairs," said Whalen.

The farming affairs spoken of concerned the necessity of Father Connolly's having to make good the damage to Curtin's threshing machine. One group was apparently convinced it would be a shame and a disgrace for the priest to have to suffer a loss on account of Tom Donnelly's wickedness. Another group wanted to act on more than suspicion, while a few thought Curtin should bear the loss himself. Dennis McGee related that Dan Ryder stood up at the meeting and said, "No, we ain't going to pay Curtin for this damage. I saw him running away at night after breaking his own machine!" And Dan Ryder went on to explain that when he got up in the night to investigate a noise, he saw Curtin running out of the barn which housed the threshing machine. He reminded them that Curtin lived on the farm immediately across the road from Ryder, that he only rented it, and that, since the lease had expired, he was in the process of disposing of all his stock and effects. Dan Ryder argued that, in the circumstances, Curtin wanted merely to avail himself of the priest's security now that the threshing season was coming to a close.

"The whole thing seemed to be hushed up all at once," Will Donnelly said later, and he again wondered why the priest never spoke of this "depredation" from the altar of Biddulph Church.

The Donnelly family had decided to charge with trespass sixteen of the men, all the family could recall as being among the search party for Thompson's heifer. On a charge sworn in London by John Donnelly before J.P. John Peters, all sixteen were arrested. They were bailed out to appear at their trial, which was set for September 20. The suit caused grave consternation in the ranks of the society. A meeting was called to discuss the strategy to be employed in "the law scrape".

Michael Blake consulted his lawyer brother, John J. Blake, and money was collected at the meeting to defray the legal costs. Said William Thompson of that meeting, which was presided over by Pat Breen, "There was a lot said about the Donnellys."

The society at this time also resolved to get their own magistrates appointed. They felt that if Squire Stanley had only given them the warrant to search when they asked for it, they would have caught the Donnellys red-handed with Thompson's cow. As Dennis Heenan (who could write a good script and usually kept the books) was absent on this occasion, Chairman Pat Breen produced several sheets of paper. He put his name near the top of the first sheet and asked the others to inscribe their signatures below. The following persons signed:

Patrick Breen	James Toohey
John Heenan	John Ryder
P. J. Dewan	John McLaughlin
Michael Blake	Wm . Thompson
John Lanphier	James Barnes
James Ryder	Thomas Ryder
Thomas Lanphier	Martin Darcey
Pat Quigley	Anthony Heenan
Patrick James O'Shea	Patrick Breen
James Harrigan	James Ryder
Philip Kehoe	James Corrigan
Dennis Heenan	Michael Carroll
Dan Ryder	Joseph McCarthy
Wm. Casey	Michael Sullivan
John Darsey	Patrick Ryder
John Morkin	James Shea
James Maher	John Thompson
Patrick Ryder	Timothy Toohey
James Kelley	James Feeheley
John Bruin	William Feeheley
Martin McLaughlin	Ed Sullivan
Jeremiah McDonald	John Cain
Michael Mara	Thomas Kinsella
Daniel Ryder	John Kennedy
Michael Heenan	John Quigley
James Maher	Martin Ryan
Dan McDonald	William Carroll
James Heenan	Patrick Dorsey

On the following Saturday when Michael Blake travelled to London to attend court for the hearing of the Donnelly trespass case, he handed the papers containing the signatures to his brother, who added the following] paragraphs to the top of the first page:

To William Elliot, Esq., Judge of the County of Middlesex, —

The humble prayer and petition of the inhabitants of the Township of Biddulph sheweth as follows: — Whereas, for some time past evil-minded persons of the Township of Biddulph have been violating the laws and acting in such a manner as to endanger the persons and property of the peaceable portion of the inhabitants thereof; and

Whereas from there being but a few constables in said Township, it is difficult and often impossible to have warrants or other process of the local Justices of the Peace executed; and in consequence thereof compelling injured persons to either refrain from taking legal proceedings for the redress of wrongs or go to the expense of laying complaints before the justices of the Peace of the City of London; and

Whereas your petitioners are of opinon that much of the above recited inconvenience would be obviated by the appointment of Jas. Carroll, of the said township, as a constable therein;

Your petitioners therefore pray that the said James Carroll be appointed as a constable in and for this county, and your Petitioners will ever pray, &c., —[1]

Blake then presented the petition to Judge Elliot through the Crown Attorney. In due course an appointment was issued making James Carroll a constable in and for the County of Middlesex. Carroll immediately took the document to the office of J.P. Peters in the Court House, who swore him into office.

38

TRESPASS

The first official act of James Carroll as constable was to swear out an information against Tom Donnelly. The charge was for robbing Ned Ryan on or about March 18, 1878, in Lucan. Carroll tucked the warrant in his pocket. On Dundas Street in front of the Court House on his way out of the office of the J.P., he almost bumped into Constable Charles Pope.

"Hello, Jim, let me congratulate you," said Pope, for the news of Carroll's appointment travelled quickly. "I understand you have been appointed a constable."

They shook hands. The constables of London made it a practice to be friendly with everyone, especially those whom they were called upon to arrest. It was found to be very effective with the Donnelly boys in particular but was said to be part of the reason why the Biddulph brothers were so difficult to deal with by others. Pope and Carroll chatted for a few minutes, recalling the occasion when Pope had arrested Carroll at the instance of the Donnellys.

"Well," said Pope, "you have got into a position to fix them now."

"Yes," replied Carroll, "and I'll be the cause of the family being banished out of Biddulph."

The next day was Sunday and, not being a man to desecrate the Sabbath, Carroll made no attempt to execute the warrant. He went instead to mass at St. Patrick's Church as usual. After church he and his uncle Maher told the priest of his appointment and of the intention to prosecute Tom Donnelly for the Ryan robbery, which had occurred some time before either the priest or the constable had come to Biddulph. The priest appeared satisfied with events. During the course of that Sunday, James Carroll made a trip to Lucan and borrowed from Wild Bill Hodgins a pair of handcuffs, a revolver, and a baton.

Thus suitably armed, Carroll drove the next day to William Haskett's farm where he had heard that Tom Donnelly was helping the threshers. He stopped the buggy in the yard, alighted, walked over to Haskett, and asked to speak to him alone. The two men walked into the granary. Carroll produced his credentials and in a low voice told Haskett he wanted no trouble. Haskett indicated he would not stand in the way of the constable's duty.

The threshing crew, with Tom Donnelly among them, had seen Carroll enter the granary. Tom watched closely as they came out, for he knew that Carroll's coming meant trouble. Carroll strode up to Donnelly, drew his revolver, and waved it at William Simpson who stood next to him.

"Keep back there," he barked harshly, levelling the pistol at Donnelly. "I am arresting this man."

Tom Donnelly, with the muzzle of a gun pointed at his breast, made no resistance. The constable produced his handcuffs and clamped them around his prisoner's wrists behind his back.

"Don't make them so damned tight, will you," Tom said.

Carroll ignored him. "Get into the buggy," he ordered.

"I want you to read the warrant," said Donnelly.

James glanced around at the onlookers. Besides Haskett and Simpson, there was John Kent, several of the Cornishes, and some of the Skinners from neighbouring Usborne. They were all Protestants. Some of the farmers of the Catholic Settlement of Biddulph had nothing to do with Protestants, but the Donnellys had always been among those Catholics who did not shun them, and lately, with so many of their old friends turning against them, they had been looking more and more to the Protestants to "neighbour with". The Protestants, for their part, welcomed them. They were good, strong workers and very handy at a threshing.[1]

Jim Carroll realized the faces turned toward him were not at all friendly and he resignedly pulled the warrant from his pocket and read it out. Then, stuffing the blue paper back into his pocket, he motioned for his prisoner to get into the buggy. When John Kent went to hand Tom his coat, Jim swung sharply toward him.

A map of the village of Lucan in 1878 (Page), with (left) an aerial photograph of the village taken about 1940 (London *Free Press*)

"Keep back or I'll shoot!" he cried out, and Kent stopped in his tracks.

As Tom lifted his foot to climb into the buggy he momentarily lost his balance and his foot slipped. He fell against the vehicle. Carroll pulled the baton out of his belt and waved it over him.

"I'll give you this over the head if you don't get in," he snarled.

John Kent then spoke up: "You may as well kill the man at once while we're all here!"

Jim Carroll turned his scowl on Kent and in a surly tone said, "The revolver is half cocked."

It was obvious to all that Jim was not to be lightly tampered with that day. Tom then jounced himself into the buggy and sat down. Jim got in and seized the horse's reins, and with a smart "Giddyap" the buggy started up at a rapid pace and they drove off Tom at no time made any resistance.

After a long, stiff ride to London, Tom Donnelly was glad to stand before John Peters, who had issued the warrant and who now released him on bail. One of the two bondsmen was Tom's old friend, Jimmy Keefe, while the second was none other than ex-constable Sam Everett!

In the meantime, the defendants charged with trespass on the Donnelly farm came up for trial in London on September 20 before the same J.P. James Donnelly, who had retained Edmund Meredith as counsel, gave evidence for the prosecution, along with John and young Tommy Hines. Questioning the reason for the organization of the Biddulph farmers into a "Peace Society" and the role of the Lucan Justices of the Peace, the magis-

The Main Street of Lucan in 1880 (Composer-singer Earl Heywood from song folio and Dominion LPS 21013 entitled *Tales of the Donnelly Feud*, Canadian Music Sales, Toronto)

trate finally decided to adjourn the hearing to Lucan. He wanted to hear the testimony of William Stanley, J.P., and Father Connolly, P.P. The adjournment was made, much to the chagrin of Meredith, who was loath to travel to Lucan. Tom Donnelly's case was also remanded by Peters for trial in Lucan on the same day, September 27, on the Ned Ryan robbery charge.

On Thursday night of that week, Ned Ryan's barn burned to the ground. Inside the barn was the threshing machine of Patrick Sullivan, who had agreed to thresh Ryan's grain after the society had agreed to guarantee the safety of his machine. Ryan blamed the Donnellys for this fire.

On the day appointed for the trials Lucan "presented a very lively appearance", with the village in an almost festive spirit. "The Vigilance Committee of Biddulph up before Squire Peters" trumpeted the headlines of the London newspapers. In addition to the numerous defendants, and their families and allies, there came into the village the usual Saturday shoppers from many miles around. The taverns, stores, and sidewalks of Lucan buzzed with wild rumours. Will Donnelly was going to shoot the priest! The whole Donnelly family was going to be lynched! The London J.P. in charge of the case was afraid to come to Lucan for fear of a riot!

Finally all the rumours were put to rest, and the now celebrated trespass case was resumed in the little courtroom above the lock-up on William Street. "Upwards of two hundred persons crowded into the courtroom to hear the trial," it was reported, a huge crowd for such a small place.

Eleven witnesses were called for the defence that day, one of them being Father John Connolly. There was no doubt on whose side the priest stood. During additional testimony by John Donnelly, the priest interrupted the witness and contradicted him to such an extent that Donnelly became angry.

"Father Connolly," he said, "if you had attended to your spiritual affairs and not organized this society, the present law business would never have taken place."

When the priest took the witness box he swore that he had come to Biddulph for the express purpose of putting down all crime that was being committed there, and that the men who were charged with the offence then in question were the most respectable members of his congregation. He admitted he was not on friendly terms with the Donnelly boys and stated that he had received a letter from Will Donnelly. At the mention of the word "letter", the magistrate and all the lawyers quickly jumped to attention. "Hearsay! Hearsay!" everyone shouted. No mention of the contents of the letter was allowed, but the priest did manage to convey the impression that it had been a threatening one. He then swore that he had asked his people to form an association to enable them to search each other's premises for stolen property.

"Did James Donnelly, the owner of the land which was searched, ever join the society?" the priest was asked.

"No," he answered.

"Why, then, did the association search his place?"

"I considered these men were justified in searching Donnelly's place," replied the priest, "if they thought the cow was there."

Then came some legal manoeuvring. An objection was raised by the defence that since it was John Donnelly who had laid the charge, it must necessarily fail, because the land was actually registered in the name of James Donnelly, the father! After prolonged argument, the charge was allowed to be amended but, in giving judgment, the magistrate decided, albeit reluctantly, to dismiss the charge. In view of his reservations, however, he refused to award costs against the Donnellys. The Peace Society had won the battle, although the victory was not total.

Squire John Peters then dealt with the other matters before him.

First was the case of Sam Everett versus James Maher, arising out of Maher's swearing at the ex-constable for standing bail for Tom Donnelly. Everett accepted an apology by Maher and agreed to withdraw the charge upon the defendant's paying costs. As for Tom Donnelly, Peters adjourned that case to the following Friday in London.

The next day James Donnelly went to mass at St. Patrick's Church for the first time in many months. The old man felt that the court case had to a certain extent cleared the air between his family and the priest. He was also determined to show his neighbours that he was not afraid of them or of the priest and would continue in their midst despite their hard action in invading his farm without a warrant. That Sunday, September 28, 1879, Father Connolly in his sermon harked back to the alleged theft of Thompson's cow and intoned, "Such business should be put down, and if you are afraid to do it, then I am not."

It is likely the cleric noted the father of the Donnelly boys in the congregation, and perhaps he directed his words at him. Once more he urged his audience to join the society if they had not already done so. But the tone of his remarks was not conciliatory, and more than once he called down the wrath of God upon those who brought shame and disgrace to their church and religion. He prophesied that one day the skies would open and a ball of fire would descend and consume the wicked. Little did he or his listeners realize that within hours they would recall that prophecy with awe.

After mass, Jim Donnelly was greeted warmly by his old crony, James Keefe, and he accepted a ride home with him in his wagon. Many of the congregation watched with silent frowns as Keefe's wagon wended its way back up the Roman Line. Some muttered deprecating remarks about "Old Decency" deigning to come to church after all the trouble he had caused.

On the trip home Jim asked his friend Keefe if he should join the priest's association. Keefe, having heard the railings of the priest all summer, could not bring himself to explain his understanding of the real purport of the priest's remarks. He merely replied to his old friend, "Why don't you ask Will about it?"

That afternoon a brief but violent thunderstorm swept over Biddulph. The double buggy of James Donnelly, which was worth about $150 and had been left standing beside the house, was struck by a flash of lightning. It was "smashed to atoms by the electric fluid [and] not a spoke was left in a wheel." The coincidence was curious but awesome. To the superstitious Irish of Biddulph it was the fulfilment, pure and simple, of the prophecy made by the parish priest that very

morning. For many weeks thereafter every household of the Catholic Settlement echoed the whispered tales of divine retribution invoked from the altar, and its sudden fiery consummation that very afternoon. To be sure, no one had been struck, but without a doubt it was a warning from God Almighty.

ESCAPE

When the Biddulph Peace Society met the following Monday night at the Cedar Swamp Schoolhouse, the supposed divine destruction of the Donnellys' double buggy was alluded to with solemnity and awe. Pat Bennett was at that meeting. He said that Father Connolly arrived at the schoolhouse while the meeting was still in progress and, divine retribution or not, Bennett did not like the way things were being handled. He thought there were two groups, one trying to keep things secret from the others. Among the Committee, as it was called, or inner group of men who gathered in the anteroom at the back where complaints were aired, were James Carroll, Big Pat Breen, Pat Dewan, Long James Toohey, Anthony Heenan, James Harrigan, Martin McLaughlin, James Corrigan, and Big Jack Kennedy. Bennett left in disgust while the meeting was still in progress and while the priest was still there.

At this meeting the members discussed in great detail the successful defence of the trespass case and sifted the testimony given. Someone wondered if John Donnelly could not be prosecuted for giving false testimony. Although he had sworn out the charge of trespass in the first case, it had been admitted at the hearing that he was not even the owner of the lands in question. Was this not perjury? Next to raising a son to the priesthood, it was the fond hope of every Irish Catholic farmer in Biddulph to raise a son as a lawyer for the family. Someone recalled that John Donnelly had sworn in his testimony that permission to search had not been given. Since the court, in dismissing the charge, had in effect ruled that permission had in fact been given, then ipso facto it appeared to the society members that John Donnelly must have perjured himself. Michael Blake said he would consult his brother about it.

Next day, Father Connolly drove up the Roman Line a distance of five miles from the church for the express purpose of speaking to Mr. James Keefe, Sr. The Keefes were a large, influential, and respectable family of Kilkenny Irish, and among the first and leading settlers of the parish. The schoolteachers who taught at the Donnelly School invariably boarded with one or other of the Keefe families. At that very time the current teacher, Stephen Patton, was living at James Keefe's, for he had married one of Keefe's daughters and was present on the occasion of the priest's talk with his father-in-law.

Father Connolly began by rebuking Keefe for daring to carry old Donnelly home from Sunday mass two days previous. The old man was a convicted murderer, said the priest, several of his sons were also blacklegs, and one of them, Robert Donnelly, was at that very time serving a sentence in Kingston Penitentiary. They all deserved to be there, and they were wicked, evil persons, said the priest.

"Even Mrs. Donnelly?" Keefe asked.

"She is a wicked woman," the priest said.

Keefe grew annoyed at the attack on his old friends. "But Father Connolly," he said, "the people who have joined your society are also wicked, for there are murderers, blackguards, and thieves among them. Why, Jim Donnelly and I helped to make the very road you drove up here upon before most of that gang was born. I have always found Donnelly a good neighbour and a warm-hearted friend, and I will carry him wherever I have a horse to draw him."

At this point in the conversation Patton, the schoolteacher, who had always been kindly treated by Mrs. Donnelly, broke into the dialogue and asked the priest why he had such an antipathy towards her.

"She is a bad woman," said the priest vehemently. "She is not worthy to receive the Blessed Sacrament. You mark my words, she will yet die in the ditch!"

In the meantime old James Donnelly had been pondering the words of the priest and of his friend Keefe, and the next time he saw his son William he said, "Will, I believe I will become a member of Father Connolly's society."

"Why would you do that, Father?" asked the son .

"For fear people will say we be afraid o' thim," answered the old man. "Whot do ye think uv id?"

"Do not do it, Father," the son replied. "There are some very decent men in the Committee, but there are three or four in it who would not scruple to do anything to injure you."

"Whot do ye mane, Will?" asked old Donnelly.

"How easy it would be for them to steal something and hide it on your place," the younger man explained. "Then the whole Committee would come and find it and send you up for robbery."

Donnelly took his son's advice and made no attempt to join.

Robert Ross, a "shipper of bones and glue stuff", was a Stratford dealer in animal carcasses who made periodic rounds throughout Biddulph, during the course of which he dropped in to see Big Jack Kennedy. They chatted about the recent trespass trial, the fame of which had apparently reached Stratford.

"I may get burned out," Kennedy told Ross confidentially.

"By whom?" asked the other.

"My brother-in-law has threatened to do it," Kennedy replied. "But if anything happens to my property I will take my gun and shoot him."

Kennedy confided to Ross that the society had decided to bring John Donnelly up on a charge of perjury. "It's a pity that one family should bully and destroy a township," added Kennedy, "but if I catch any of them around my place they will get shot, sure."

James Carroll had been attending to the old Ryan robbery charge against Tom Donnelly.

When the Grand Jury met for the London Assizes in October, John J. Blake accompanied Ryan to the office of the prosecutor in charge of the Crown business at the assizes, Mr. M. C. Cameron, of Goderich. Blake and Ryan apparently convinced Cameron of the justice of their cause, and he included the charge among the list of cases to be tried at the sittings. But as there had been no preliminary hearing, the Crown Attorney for Middlesex required an explanation, and a few days later Cameron wrote to Charles Hutchinson as follows:

Before deciding to present the bill in this case to the Grand Jury Blake and Ryan told me that there had been an investigation before the J.P.'s and that the case had been dismissed – but dismissed because the J.P.'s were afraid to commit Donnelly on account of the well known character of the Donnelly tribe – that it was a very gross case and that justice would be defeated if a preliminary investigation were insisted on. And so I reluctantly submitted the bill, and now it must take its course. From all I can learn they are all a bad lot and a few months in Gaol would do them all good.[1]

The Grand Jury returned a True Bill against Tom Donnelly on Wednesday, October 8. A bench warrant was issued for his arrest immediately, and by ten o'clock that night it was in the hands of Constable James Carroll. An hour later he had set out for Biddulph to make the arrest. Shortly before two o'clock the following morning he dropped in at the Quigley farm on the Roman Line, where a threshing was being carried on. No, Tom Donnelly was not there, they told him, but someone thought he was at home. Someone else told Carroll to watch out, that the Donnellys were getting up a charge against him for pointing a revolver at John Kent on the occasion when Carroll had arrested Donnelly at Haskett's threshing. Another said Tom Donnelly was not home at all, that he was at the Skinners' threshing in Usborne. Still others said he was at his brother Will's place at Whalen's Corners.

With all this conflicting advice, Carroll made a trip to Lucan, where he hunted up Constable Hodgins. The possibility of a counter-charge worried Carroll a bit. Together the two constables went straight to the Donnelly farm. It was about eight o'clock in the morning when they met Mrs. Donnelly at the door.

"What do you want?" she demanded.

"We're looking for your son Thomas. Here is a warrant for his arrest," they said, showing her the paper.

"He's not here," she told them.

"We'll take a look for ourselves," said the constables and pushed inside, where they glanced quickly through the rooms of the house. Tom Donnelly was not there or in the outbuildings, which they also looked through.

The constables then made their way to Will Donnelly's house at Whalen's Corners, picking up one or two of the threshers from Quigley's, where some of them were sitting idle as a consequence of the machine's having broken down. Norah Donnelly answered the door and told them that Thomas was not there. She did not tell them her husband was at the moment in the stable beside the little house. He was in fact in the loft, and from this vantage point he silently watched through a crack in the boards and listened as the constables talked to his wife and then entered the house. Inside, the constables quickly peeked through each of the three or four small rooms of the house. They searched quickly, Mrs. Donnelly noticed, not even taking time to look under the beds. Leaving the house, they then entered the stable and had a quick look around but did not look in the loft.

The men then went next door to blacksmith Edward Sutherby's shop. "What do you want now?" asked the blacksmith. He wondered why the men were always pestering his tenant, for Sutherby was the owner of the house which Will Donnelly occupied.

"We're after Tom Donnelly and have got a bench warrant for his arrest," they replied.

"What for?" asked the blacksmith.

"On a charge of robbery, for robbing Ned Ryan," they answered.

Sutherby knew that Donnelly had already been tried and acquitted of this charge, and he said to them, "Would it not be better for you to let these Donnellys be?"

Carroll answered by looking at the blacksmith

grimly and replying, "You mark my words, I'll have them out of Biddulph if it costs me my life."

The constables stayed about fifteen minutes and then left to go to Skinner's farm in Usborne Township. Donnelly was not there either. They turned back to Biddulph and headed for the farm of James Maher, where they had breakfast, and then made their way once more towards the Donnelly farm. It was by this time eleven o'clock in the morning.

As soon as the searchers had left Whalen's Corners, Will Donnelly spoke to his wife and Sutherby and, after a time, decided to hitch up the buggy and head over to his father's place to warn his brother that they were after him. He passed William Thompson's house shortly before eleven and noticed Mary Thompson, the woman with the fine ears who apparently had just as fine eyes, sitting at the front door of her log house. She was spinning, and she saw him, too. As soon as Donnelly had passed their lane, she stopped the wheel, ran upstairs to the second floor of the house, and looked out through the single window in the attic facing south and directly overlooking the Donnelly farm. She had been keeping a sharp eye on all comings and goings at the Donnelly place ever since losing her heifer a few weeks before. Mary Thompson saw William Donnelly drive up the laneway of his father's farm, alight from his buggy, and walk along a wagon road which ran through a potato field behind the farm buildings. Working out in the potato field were James Donnelly, the father, and two of the sons, Tom and John, along with the niece, Bridget.

Will spoke to Tom about the constables who were looking to arrest him. "Don't let them take you, Tom," he told his brother. "What you must do is deliver yourself up to Sheriff Glass in London."

The Donnelly boys knew they would get fair treatment at the hands of the Glass brothers, William, the Sheriff, and Samuel, his deputy, even though their brother, David Glass, had left London and was no longer available to them as defence counsel.

Will had just walked back to the farmhouse to see his mother when Constables Carroll and Hodgins came along the Roman Line in a buggy.

Stopping at Thompson's gate and looking across the fields, they could hardly believe their eyes, for there in the distance was their quarry, Tom Donnelly. The constables quickly tied the horse to the gate post and lit out after him. After proceeding a short distance up Thompson's lane, Hodgins went over the fence to cut off any possible retreat Donnelly might make by way of the farm laneway. Carroll continued up Thompson's lane and then he, too, crossed the fence. He headed straight for Donnelly through a fall wheatfield. For a few moments a piece of bush and the Donnelly farm buildings obscured his view.

When Tom Donnelly came back into Carroll's sight, he was on the run and going away from the constable. Apparently someone had seen the constable and had warned Tom. Carroll broke into a run and just then noticed John Donnelly standing near the stable. It was probably he who had warned his brother. John Donnelly suddenly put down his pail, bolted into the stable, and in a few seconds reappeared leading a short-eared, whitefaced sorrel horse.

John ran with the horse towards his brother, who quickly changed direction and ran to meet them. About four or five rods from the stable door they met. Tom jumped astride the horse and started off down the farm lane towards the road. Although the horse had no saddle, Donnelly easily galloped past Constable Hodgins and in a few moments he was through the gate and heading south along the Roman Line.

John Donnelly walked over to the house and waited for Carroll to come puffing up to him.

"What the hell did you do that for?" he blurted at Donnelly, who was grinning.

Donnelly wondered if the other was hot from running, and Carroll answered, "I'll make it hot for you when I get back to Lucan. You had no business to give him that horse. I was going to arrest him and now he has escaped."

"Don't worry, Carroll," laughed John Donnelly. "Why, Tom had to take that horse into Lucan to get the shoes fixed on her. If you really want him you can find him in Kenny's blacksmith shop there."

It was a good joke, and John Donnelly laughed

and laughed. Carroll went to join Hodgins by the farm laneway and the two of them returned to their buggy.

"Well, I don't care," Carroll told Hodgins; "if he stays out of my reach I'm not particular if I catch him or not. Just as long as he stays out of the county."

The two constables drove back to the village and on the way met young Johnny Ryan, son of the man whom Tom Donnelly was accused of robbing and for which robbery they were trying to arrest him.

"I saw Tom Donnelly ride by on the sorrel horse a few minutes ago," young Ryan yelled out to Carroll. "He was riding real fast."

They told young Ryan to keep an eye out for him and continued on to Quigley's threshing.

"Tom Donnelly escaped from us on a horse when we tried to arrest him," explained Hodgins. "Can we have a horse to follow him?"

The threshers at Quigleys were still idle because of the broken machine. They told the constables that "horseshoes and other things that were in the sheaves" had broken it, and that it was the Donnellys who had hidden them there in order to spite the Quigleys for joining the society. Some of the men seemed eager for an excuse to leave the threshing. A horse was taken out of the horse power of the threshing machine and handed over to Constable Hodgins, who thereupon set out in search of Tom Donnelly. Many of the threshers followed on foot, their pitchforks over their shoulders.

The countryside was scoured but no Tom Donnelly could be found. James Maher, who had gone to Granton to see Dr. Lang on business that day, could not join the party but saw them searching on his way to the village. He met them again on his way back. Towards evening, some of the search party stopped in at the Cedar Swamp Schoolhouse and there met Martin McLaughlin riding a horse home from Lucan. McLaughlin called an impromptu meeting of the Peace Society, and it was decided to catch Tom Donnelly at all costs. He thereupon set out to ride the concession lines of the township and so continued late into the night.

Big Jack Kennedy joined up with James Carroll and together the two went back to the Donnelly farmhouse. Although it was after dark, Carroll again demanded entrance in the name of the Queen and again went through the house. Once more they returned to Whalen's Corners, Kennedy and Hodgins going in while the others, about a dozen in all, remained outside in a wagon on the road.

Young Johnny Ryan had kept his ears and eyes sharp. He followed the tracks of Tom Donnelly's horse into a bush pasture belonging to Patrick Quigley and behind the farm of Timothy Toohey. Late in the afternoon he saw James Donnelly, Sr., enter the bush pasture on foot. A short time later Donnelly came out leading his short-eared, whitefaced sorrel horse, which he took back to his farm.

In company with Big Jack Kennedy, Carroll and Hodgins had gone to Granton. On Kennedy's advice Carroll went to see James Grant, J.P., who appeared sympathetic to the cause of the anti-Donnelly faction. The constables laid a charge against John Donnelly of assisting in an escape. The J.P. issued a warrant and handed it to Carroll, but as it was by that time too late for further action, the two constables went to stay overnight at Kennedy's place.

Carroll arrested John Donnelly the following day. As he was being taken in, Donnelly suggested to Carroll that he had not really wanted to arrest his brother Tom the previous day. "If you had come down early in the morning you might have got him easily, before he knew anything about it," he told Carroll. He also intimated that Carroll had gone to Lucan to get Constable Hodgins and then over to Will Donnelly's in order to give him plenty of time to take warning and escape. John said that he thought Carroll was afraid of his brother Tom. "And furthermore," said John, "I'm not afraid of this case. I will beat you on it."

Donnelly was taken before James Grant in Granton, who took bail for his appearance. Grant wrote to Crown Attorney Hutchinson for advice and at the hearing of the case, held in Granton on Tuesday at two o'clock, John Donnelly appeared without legal counsel. After the testimony of the witnesses, Grant committed him for trial at the Interim Sessions of the Peace. Donnelly was indignant at what appeared to him to be a manifest

James Grant, Justice of the Peace from Granton (G. Grant)

accused James Maher of abusing Lewis for putting up bail for John. But Maher denied it, saying of Lewis, "I always used him decent, and he always used me decent."

40

POOR MIKE

Will Donnelly had become very uneasy about the obviously organized and persistent opposition against his family and felt that Father John Connolly bore an unjust animosity towards them. In an attempt at conciliation he asked two different men to arrange a meeting with the priest, but both told him there was no use in it and that the priest would not listen to them. Donnelly then decided to communicate the matter to Bishop John Walsh by letter. It read:

October 11th, 1879
Biddulph

Bishop Walsh
St. Peter's Cathedral
London

Most Reverend Sir:

If you will allow this humble servant to communicate with your Lordship on a matter of great importance I will be ever grateful to your Reverence. I wish to bring it to your Lordship's attention that there has been formed in the parish of St. Patrick's in Biddulph a society which I understand is a sworn association, each member taking an oath of secrecy. Now I am not aware that the Catholic Church allowed such a sworn party to exist in its midst. I believe that Father Connolly, the priest here, is the founder and head of this party and there are members of it who are in direct opposition to our family. Our name is continually referred to in church in connection with crimes supposed to have been committed by us but the names of

injustice. He immediately went to see Edmund Meredith for legal advice. Meredith advised him that before he could be found guilty of aiding an escape of a prisoner, it would have to be shown that there was in fact a prisoner. In other words, the arrest of Tom Donelly would have to be established first, and Tom had not on that occasion been arrested. Meredith told John Donnelly that if he were convicted he would have an action for damages.

In the meantime, Michael Blake had carefully considered the matter of laying a charge against John Donnelly for perjury and, having consulted his brother about it, on October 22 swore out an information. John Donnelly was again arrested, this time while in London. Standing bail for him on the charge were Thomas Keefe and John Lewis, a tavernkeeper of London. Later, the Donnellys

Bishop John Walsh

others who are known to have committed crimes are never even hinted at. For an example I put forward the case of young Jim Maher and Jack Darcey, as everyone knows, who stole the bells off a respectable Protestant man's cutter at the gate of St. Patrick's church while Father Connolly was reciting prayers at the funeral of Mrs. Andy Keefe. The priest never reprimanded the young men in church. Also, young Hugh Toohey broke his father's ribs in anger but these things were never spoken of to the people from the altar.

I believe the priest here is prejudiced against our family and I wish your reverence to bring us face to face before you, and decide who is wrong, and if I am wrong in this matter I will lower myself lower than the worm that crawls.

As for my character and reputation and that of our family I am pleased to refer your Lordship to some of the most respectable men in Biddulph, that is to say, Mr Patrick Nangle, Mr. Stephen McCormick, Mr. Dennis Darcey, Mr. John McIlhargey, Mr. Michael

Crunnican, J.P., Mr. James Keefe and Mr. Robert Keefe, as to whether we are guilty of all the crimes laid to us. They did not become members of the society.

Father Connolly was present at two or three law suits in which our family was involved and I do not think that is a fit place for a clergyman to be. Without meaning to show disrespect to your Lordship in any way I beg of you, for God and in Justice, to do something about the disbanding of this society formed against us for if something is not done I am sure it will end in bloodshed.

Your humble and obedient servant, &c.
WM. J. DONNELLY. [1]

Upon receipt of the letter, the bishop noted merely that Donnelly was ignorant of the correct form of address of a bishop as "Your Excellency", and he simply turned it over to Father John Connolly. Donnelly never received a reply to the letter. Tom Donnelly remained in hiding until Monday, October 20. He then went into London in company with his father and an old friend of the latter, Mitchell Haskett, and surrendered to Sheriff William Glass. Glass took the prisoner to John Peters, J.P., before whom the father and Haskett stood bail to the sum of four hundred dollars for his appearance at the next assizes on the Ned Ryan robbery charge.

On the following Sunday, Father Connolly told his congregation that William Donnelly had been impudent enough to send a letter to the bishop. He intimated that its tone was disrespectful, in that it was not addressed to the bishop in a language which the dignity of the position demanded. The priest went on to name the residents of Biddulph whom Donnelly had set out in the letter as character references and rebuked them for having allowed their names to be used. "What kind of men are you?" he demanded. "Do you want to put me out of the country?"

After church service, some of the men protested to the priest that they had not given Donnelly permission to use their names. They added, however, that if the bishop wrote to them concerning the family, they could say nothing but what was favourable if it was of their personal knowledge and not hearsay.

William Donnelly felt increasingly frustrated at

William Glass, sheriff of the county of Middlesex and brother of lawyer David Glass

Edmund Meredith, a London lawyer who became the favourite counsel of the Donnellys after David Glass left the city

the impasse with the parish priest. He wrote to Father Flannery in St. Thomas, relating the family's troubles and telling how the priest in Biddulph was opposed to them because of, as he considered, the influence of their enemies. He concluded:

> I am tired of Biddulph, and would be very thankful if you would use your influence in getting me a position elsewhere, no matter how humble it might be.[2]

According to Donnelly, Father Flannery was very kind in his reply, and although he regretted that he knew of no vacancy at the time, he promised to give a recommendation whenever he required one. He said he was sorry that his enemies had caused such ill-feeling between him and Father Connolly.

John Donnelly had his lawyer, Edmund Meredith, apply to the County Judge. At the Interim Sessions of October 24, the charge against him

of assisting his brother's escape was put over to the Spring Assizes, to await the result of the Ned Ryan robbery case against Thomas. On Thursday, October 30, the charge of perjury laid against John by Michael Blake came on for trial before William Stanley, J.P., in Lucan. Blake, the lawyer-brother of the complainant, conducted the case for the prosecution, while Meredith again appeared for the defendant.

When the first prosecution witness, James Carrigan, attempted to state what he had heard John Donnelly testify to in the Thompson cow trespass case, defence counsel objected. The information was alleged to be defective.

> Mr. J. J. Blake, counsel for the plaintiff, applied to have the information amended, which was done under protest by Mr. Meredith, counsel for the defendant, he (Meredith) submitting that the amendment

was not an amendment but a new charge in full.[3]

Stanley allowed the amendment and the rest of the witnesses were heard. Among them were James Carroll, Michael Blake, William Thompson, Pat Breen, John Kennedy, Patrick J. Dewan, and James Maher. During their testimony Meredith stood up. "I object to this," he argued. "As the written evidence of John Donnelly at the previous trial is in existence it should be produced as the proper evidence against him on this occasion."[4]

The magistrate reserved his decision for a week and immediately wrote to Crown Attorney Hutchinson in London for advice. Hutchinson was not able to answer the letter until November 6, and as his reply was not at hand when court reconvened, the case was put over to November 11 at 4 o'clock in the afternoon. By then Hutchinson's reply had come, and it read:

November 6th, 1879.

re John Donnelly – Perjury

I have been from home or would have answered you sooner. I have read the evidence in this case. I don't think you can properly convict the defendant on the evidence. The examination taken before Mr. Peters should have been the ground work for the prosecution. The information should have set out the examination before Mr Peters which was sworn to and signed by the defendant, and the written examination itself should have been produced at the examination before you. I think you had better dismiss the case.[5]

The magistrate followed the advice and John Donnelly was discharged.

The following Sunday, Father John Connolly displayed his anger in the pulpit at the result of this case. He referred again to the callousness and indifference of the magistrates of Lucan and stated that if they failed to convict in a case of perjury when the evidence was clear, then they also became a party to the perjury. James Carroll, listening to the words of the priest, decided to champion the contention and was nothing if not determined. Persuaded that Donnelly had beaten the charge on a mere technicality, the following Saturday, November 15, Carroll wrote the Crown Attorney requesting blank forms of informations and warrants and enclosing eighteen cents in payment.

Then, on the following Thursday, Carroll went back to James Grant, the Granton J.P., and laid a fresh charge of perjury against John Donnelly.

Constable Carroll re-arrested John Donnelly on the new charge and took him before Grant. Donnelly protested that he had already been discharged upon the exact same complaint and demanded that he be released. He even produced a Certificate of the Dismissal of the charge. But the magistrate adjourned the case and wrote to the Crown Attorney for advice. Donnelly consulted his lawyer, Edmund Meredith, who advised him to let the magistrate have his way if he persisted. "If he sends you for trial," Meredith told Donnelly, "he will be liable for damages for an unwarrantable proceeding."

Crown Attorney Hutchinson again suggested that the charge against Donnelly be dismissed, but when the case came up again at two o'clock in the afternoon of Tuesday, November 25, James Carroll was present to argue the case for the prosecution. He stated that the previous charge against John Donnelly had been brought by Mr. Michael Blake, that it had been dismissed "through the objections of a lawyer on some technical point", that the case had not really been tried on its merits, and that the present charge was laid by Carroll himself and was therefore different from the previous one. John Kennedy was at court with Carroll. James Grant decided to ignore the advice of the Crown Attorney and committed Donnelly for trial. He allowed him, however, to be released on bail.

It was a rainy day in Waterford, Ontario, on Tuesday, December 9, 1879, and the crews of the Canada Southern Railway had quit early. One of them, William Lewis, left his boarding house at Mrs. Best's at six o'clock and went over to Slaght's Hotel, where he knew other men from the railway crews would be gathered and where some of them boarded, among them Michael Donnelly.[6] In the bar-room Lewis had a drink with a fellow employee, James Marrs, and then left the room In a few minutes Michael Donnelly walked into the hotel and met Marrs in the reading room next to the bar-room.

"Let's have a bowl, neighbour," Donnelly said, indicating with a gesture and nod of his head that

Michael Donnelly

he wanted him to come into the bar-room for a drink. But Marrs had to go to the washroom instead, and Donnelly thereupon went into the bar-room alone. Charlie Slaght, the young son of the hotel proprietor, got him a drink.

Donnelly began a conversation about fighting dogs with an elderly gentleman named McCrimmon. "I've got a dog that can lick any dog," McCrimmon said.

"Sez who?" retorted Donnelly. "Why, I've got a bulldog at home that can lick anything of its weight in Ontario."

"Well, in that case," the old man replied in a jocose manner, "I haven't got a dog at all. But I can lick any dog myself."

"How's that?" Donnelly asked, just a trifle irked.

"Well," replied McCrimmon, "I can whip any dog with my clothes off. A dog won't fight me with my clothes off."

"You may whip the dog," Donnelly said, "but you cannot whip its master." Taking off his coat Donnelly pulled out his watch and held it in his hand, adding, "I have no money but I'll put my watch on it."

William Lewis came back into the bar-room just then and saw Donnelly and McCrimmon in animated conversation.

"You don't want to hop on that man now, do you, Mike?" Lewis called out.

Donnelly whirled and glared at Lewis. "No one is touching him," he said, "and it is none of your business if there was." Donnelly then put his watch on the bar counter and said, "Why, I could take your heart out and lay it alongside this watch in ten minutes if I had a mind to."

"Oh, you are always shooting off your mouth," Lewis answered.

Mike Donnelly jumped at Lewis and shoved him. "Do you want anything of me?" he demanded in a loud voice.

Marrs ran from the washroom and darted between the two men, taking hold of Donnelly and turning him away from Lewis. "Let's not have any trouble, boys," he said.

When the men seemed to have settled down, Marrs returned to the washroom, and Michael Donnelly turned his back on Lewis, leaned his elbow on the bar counter, and began talking to one Francis Perry, who stood near by.

William Lewis suddenly came up behind Donnelly and slapped him on the back of the head near the neck. Donnelly immediately whirled around and made for Lewis.

"Damn you!" he cried out at him.

Someone yelled "Fight!" and suddenly there was a great commotion of people running into the bar-room from the reading room, the washroom, and outside. Donnelly lunged at Lewis, grabbing hold of him with one arm and striking him with the other. Being taller and heavier than the other, Donnelly handled him easily. He shoved him behind the bar counter, but Lewis snatched at Donnelly and caught hold of his vest with one hand. As they were about to stumble, Donnelly released his grip in order to steady himself and just as he did so, Lewis put his hand into the pocket of his pants and pulled out a knife. He had concealed it there earlier, with the blade already open and pointed downwards.

Lewis slashed at Donnelly with an upward motion, the blade penetrating his right groin. It cut into the femoral vein by one inch and went on into the abdomen. The blood poured out. Donnelly reeled back in a daze. He threw up his hands and cried out at Marrs who had come running, "My God, neighbour, I'm stabbed."

Donnelly began quickly to unbutton his pants, staggered, and would have fallen but for Marrs, who grabbed hold of him. Jim Muir caught him on the other side and they carried him, bleeding profusely, into the washroom.

Muir was almost in tears as he tried to reassure

Donnelly. "We'll get a fresh boarding place, Mike," he said. "I'll not board in a hotel again."

Dr. Alexander Duncombe's house was next door to the hotel and someone ran to get him. The doctor hurried in, but there was nothing he could do to stop the loss of blood. Michael Donnelly died in about fifteen minutes. Lying in his own blood, a fine specimen of a man, he was twenty-nine years and one month old.

William Lewis remained in Slaght's Hotel until he heard that Donnelly was dead. Then he walked out, the bloodied knife still in his hand. Returning to Mrs. Best's boarding house, he sat down for supper with his fellow boarders, putting the knife down beside his plate. During the meal he spoke to

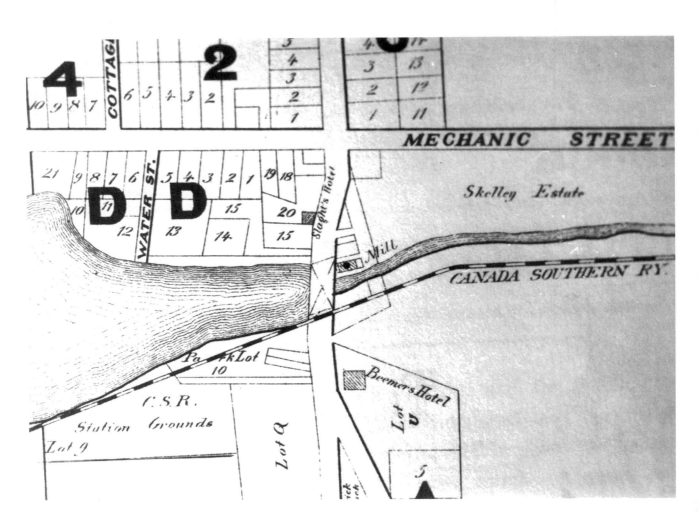

Map of Waterford showing the location of Slaght's Hotel and the Canada Southern Railway and grounds (*Historical Atlas* of Haldimand-Norfolk)

Robert Brooks. "I had a row with Donnelly," he said, "and Bob, I've fixed him. And that's the knife that did the business."

The news of Michael Donnelly's death was sent to his family back in St. Thomas. The two children, Kitty and young Jimmy, were both too young to comprehend what had happened, but they knew something was wrong when their mother became hysterical with grief and remained so for days on end. The corpse was fetched from Waterford by his brothers, and a wake was held for Michael Donnelly at the old homestead on the Roman Line. The coffin was laid out in the parents' bedroom on the huge bedstead with its high posts reaching almost to the ceiling. One of the bed ticks was taken off by Mrs. Michael O'Connor, and the white valance curtain was removed from the bottom of the bed. Many old friends of the family attended the wake, and one of them, Robert Keefe, Sr., remembered that he helped to lift up the body. The weird and mournful cry of the keening was heard into the late hours of the night, and there was great lamentation and sorrow in the Donnelly house.

The mourning at the farm became a double wake when old William Maloney, who had farmed for years on the other side of the road, died the day after Michael Donnelly. To the enemies of the family it was a kind of supernatural sign, for it was on Maloney's farm twenty-two years before that Jim Donnelly had killed Pat Farrell. As Mrs. Maloney was ill, Maloney's corpse was also brought to the Donnelly house. Following the first wake, Michael Donnelly's coffin was taken out of the front bedroom and placed in the other little chamber, to be replaced on the big bed by Maloney's corpse, which was then waked in turn.

The entire Donnelly family came home to the funeral of Michael Donnelly, except for Robert, who was still in Kingston. Will Donnelly and Norah, Jenny Currie from her home in Glencoe, Patrick from Thorold, where he left his partner Becker in charge of their wagon-manufacturing firm, all came. Michael's grief-stricken widow from St. Thomas and some of her family were there also. Michael O'Connor and his wife, Mary, came from Lucan along with their children, in-

cluding young Johnny and his sister Bridget. James Feeheley was there, but Patrick Donnelly noticed that Feeheley's brother, William, did not come.

Many Protestant friends of the Donnellys came to pay their respects. The morning of the day of the funeral was cold, and when William Kent and his daughter arrived at the farm, the house was already crowded. Many of the visitors stood around outside in small groups. Tom Donnelly came out of the house and asked Kent's daughter to go inside and warm herself. She went in and Kent followed. It was the first time he had ever been in the house. Soon the sad procession with the two coffins started off and wended its way down to St. Patrick's Church, some five miles away.

James Carroll did not attend the Donnelly funeral, but he intently watched everyone who came and went at the Donnelly farm that day. Carroll boarded at William Thompson's during the three weeks before Christmas that year, in the course of building a new pig-pen for the Thompsons. He slept in the attic portion of the house, the bare logs of which were stuffed with rags and newspapers to keep out the cold. It was one big room, floored, and containing two beds. Lying in his bed, Carroll could look out through the only window in the attic, which was about 12 feet from ground level. It was an old and shaky window, also stuffed with rags, and consisted of nine lights each 7 by 9 inches. But it looked right over the Donnelly farmhouse 480 yards away.

Michael Donnelly was buried at half past eleven o'clock on Friday, December 12. He was laid to rest beside his brother James near the back of the cemetery beside St. Patrick's Church. Father John Connolly conducted the ceremony. On grounds of compassion to allow him to attend his brother's funeral, Robert Donnelly was released from Kingston Penitentiary after serving twenty-one months, but it appears he did not get back to Biddulph in time for the funeral.[7]

The widowing of Nellie Donnelly with her two small children was a great shock. Michael Donnelly had in many ways been a champion of the family, for he had combined physical prowess with great energy and initiative. For him to be struck down was a sobering event for his brothers, and as

St. Patrick's Church and Cemetery

they entered St. Patrick's Church for the funeral service, they must also have been reflecting upon their past lives and the ephemeral nature of human life, and struck, too, with the fact that none of them had been in the church for many a long month.

After the funeral mass and burial, Tom Donnelly asked to speak privately to the priest. He and Father Connolly had a talk about the troubles in the township over the past several months. Donnelly showed contriteness and acknowledged to the priest that he had been the cause of at least some of that trouble. He told the priest that much of his problem arose from liquor and gave his pledge to the priest to forswear the future use of the evil liquid in all its forms.

The Peace Society of the Catholic Settlement of Biddulph rejoiced at the news of the death of Michael Donnelly, but did not remain idle. Two days before Christmas Day that year, William Casey took his oath in London that he was the owner of two hundred acres of freehold land in Biddulph Township and was therefore qualified to become one of Her Majesty's Justices of the Peace in and for the County of Middlesex. The names of Michael Blake and Patrick Breen had been among the names first put forward, but it turned out that because of "pollytickle feeling" there were others who would have a better chance. Casey was known as a Clear Grit, and his name and Martin Darcey's were substituted. Casey thus became a Justice of the Peace sworn to uphold the law of the land.

William Casey was nobody's fool. About ten

222   *The Donnelly Album*

years before, he had moved from Usborne Township to a farm on the Roman Line a mile and a half south of the Donnellys. He had purchased the land, Lot 23 in the sixth concession, from the cousins of his wife, the Ryder brothers. Patrick (Grouchy) Ryder was in fact named after Rachel Casey's father, who some twenty years earlier had been accused of the murder of the Englishman Brimmacombe, along with William Casey and his brother Thomas. Casey had eleven children, and was fifty-two years of age when he was appointed

a J.P. along with Martin Darcey, Martin McLaughlin, and Philip Mowbray. Only Mowbray was not a member of the Biddulph Peace Society.

On Christmas Eve, 1879, James and Johannah Donnelly went to see Father John Connolly. Both old people had become reconciled with the priest at the funeral of their son and since then had felt more comfortable in his presence. They went to confession and afterwards had a long talk with the priest. For two hours Johannah Donnelly gave

(UWO)

Father Connolly a detailed history of the family from the time of their leaving Ireland and eventual settlement on the Roman Line of Biddulph. James Donnelly himself did not say much.

"The old man," Father Connolly said later, "although a good old man, whom I liked, was not the sensible sort of man that I could talk to like I could to the old woman."

During their conversation Mrs. Donnelly acknowledged that her boys had been in a lot of trouble, but she said she was using her influence to get them to reform. "I'm gittin' me bhoys to go to confession, Father," she said, "and although they don't come here, they go in London."

"Is it possible!" exclaimed the priest.

"Yes," she said on leaving, "and Father Connolly, I am goin' to git not only me own bhoys but all the Biddulph bhoys to reform."

These were the last words she spoke to the priest and Father Connolly mused on them after she left. The old woman must, he thought, have a considerable influence on her boys and he wondered if John, in particular, would come to him for confession.

Christmas was a quiet time in the Donnelly household that year. Mrs. Patrick Whalen from across the road dropped in for a social visit. Mrs. Whalen had always kept a certain distance between herself and her notorious neighbours, calling Johannah "Mrs. Donnelly" rather than the more familiar "Judy" which a more intimate friend like Mrs. Michael O'Connor might use. Christmas time was about the only occasion she ever crossed the Donnelly threshold any more.

41

GROUCHY

The day after Christmas, Crown Attorney Charles Hutchinson was paid a visit by John Donnelly. He complained that the Granton magistrate, James Grant, had committed him for trial at the assizes on the charge of perjury on which he had already once been acquitted. Hutchinson wrote to Grant for an explanation. Grant replied on December 29, saying he felt justified in the course that had been taken.

Just after the New Year began, death again visited the Donnelly house. This time old Mrs. Maloney followed her husband to the grave and she was also waked at Donnelly's. It was becoming a regular house of death.

Many rumours circulated in the township at the beginning of the year 1880. One of them was that from the recent actions of the Peace Society the Donnellys had come to realize that their supposed criminal activities would be seriously curtailed in the future, and that unless they did something to break up the society, "they would be cleaned out themselves." They thereupon resolved on a plan of action. It was to burn down the barns of twelve of the leading members of the society, one by one, in order to intimidate them. "It is said," went the rumour, "that the names of these men were hinted at in public by the Donnellys themselves." At first, no one paid much attention to the rumours.

On Wednesday, January 14, 1880, Michael Quigley married Martha, a daughter of Robert Keefe, Sr., of the Roman Line. Father John Connolly did not perform the ceremony. He was disappointed when the Donnelly brothers did not come to confession and had warned the Keefes about their friendship with them, but they said they would not forsake their old friends. The priest had left in a huff to visit his former parishioners in Quebec and was not available when the time for the wedding ceremony arrived. This did not stop the determined couple, who procured another priest from Mount Carmel Church in Stephen Township. He performed the wedding mass at the Donnelly Schoolhouse. The party then retired to celebrate at the home of the bride's father, about a mile north of the Donnelly farm.

Robert Keefe, despite the disapproval of the priest and showing the stubbornness of his native Kilkenny, invited the Donnelly boys to the wedding celebration. Included in the invitation was Robert, home from Kingston and spending part of the holiday season with his parents. But because of the recent death in the family, the boys were at first reluctant to go until Mrs. Donnelly persuaded them they should not miss it. She also urged Bridget to accompany the brothers and had specially engaged Bridget O'Connor of Lucan, an accomplished seamstress, to make a petticoat for her for the occasion. The O'Connor girl had brought the garment out from the village that very day for its final fittings and finishings. But Bridget Donnelly's diffidence could not be overcome. She was a stranger, she said, had not been specifically invited, and would not go.

It was just before dark, therefore, that John, Bob, and Tom set out for Keefe's. Will Donnelly came down from Whalen's Corners to join his brothers. Many of the younger set of the neighbourhood also attended the wedding, including those from both pro-Donnelly and anti-Donnelly factions. Martha, a daughter of James Keefe and first cousin of the bride, had some time before married into the Ryder family, and among the guests were young Jim Ryder, his brother Pat, and his sister Mary, who at the time was on very friendly terms with William Feeheley. The Feeheley boys themselves lived just next door to the Keefes, where the wedding reception was being held, the Feeheley farm being diagonally opposite the Ryder place at the first intersection north of the Donnelly farm.

Left at home in the Donnelly house were the two old parents and the two young Bridgets. The girls sat themselves down by the stove, Bridget Donnelly busying herself with knitting a stocking and the O'Connor girl working on some sewing for Mrs. Donnelly. Mr. and Mrs. Donnelly pulled up chairs and sat with them, Johannah Donnelly peering through her spectacles at an old newspaper, reading slowly and painfully the printed lines in the dim light of the lamp. Jim Donnelly had a bad cold and coughed a lot.

After a time Bridget O'Connor said musingly, "They must be having a good time."

"Yes, they are having a good time," Bridget Donnelly replied.

At ten o'clock Bridget Donnelly rose and prepared tea and cakes, which they all sat down and ate in silence, and about eleven o'clock they retired to bed. Bridget O'Connor spent a restless night. The three females slept three in one bed, Mrs. Donnelly's huge frame in the middle. The old man in the next bedroom, separated only by a one-inch board partition, coughed frequently and kept the O'Connor girl awake much of the night. At a late hour as she heard a wagon pass by on the road, Jim Donnelly's little dog, which Detective Harry Phair of London had given him, barked. Dozing off then, she was next awakened about fifteen minutes after four in the morning by the clanking of the stove lid in the kitchen. On opening her eyes she noticed the reflection of the fire in the stove on the window in the partition between the kitchen and the front room.

Mr. Donnelly was up, lighting a fire. He came to the door of the women's bedroom and said, "The schoolhouse is on fire."

The two young girls jumped out of bed and went to the front door of the house.

"It's the schoolhouse," said Bridget Donnelly.

"No," replied the other girl, "it's not the schoolhouse. It's something else."

The two girls came back into the house.

"The fire is at Ryder's," Jim Donnelly said to them as he poked at the fire in the stove. "His fine buildings are gone."

Jim Donnelly was right. Over at the Ryder farm, Grouchy Ryder was awakened from his bed by the noise of flames crackling in the winter sky. Looking out he saw the west side of his barn ablaze. It was the building which stood farthest south and only about 125 feet from the roadway.

"The barn's on fire! The barn's on fire!" he

yelled out. "Quick. Get up. Get the things out."

Ryder quickly pulled on his clothes and ran out to the barn. He threw open the door and, groping through the smoke-filled stables, managed to reach the frightened horses, which he led out through the stalls.

Even though daylight would soon break in the east, at the house of Robert Keefe the dancing at the wedding was in full swing. Someone suddenly noticed the flames in the southeast sky and the dancing and gaiety quickly subsided. Everyone crowded to the windows and many of the wedding guests went outside for a better look.

"It looks like Ryder's place," someone said, the farm being only about half a mile away.

"Where's the Ryders?" another asked.

Young Paddy Ryder had left the dance earlier in the evening, but Jim and Mary were still there. They quickly set off for home. Curiously, many of the other guests did not follow them. Young Patrick Keefe said he was afraid to go over, and Thomas Keefe, although he said he was not at all on bad terms with the Ryders, thought "it was just as safe to stay away." None of the Donnelly brothers went over, but one of them was heard to say, "Oh, this will be the end of us now."

Grouchy Ryder's barn and nearby outbuildings were soon but a pile of ashes. The embers of the fire were still smouldering, however, when Ryder swore that it was the Donnellys who had done the deed. Early the next morning young James Keefe was passing Ryder's place when Grouchy Ryder came out to the road.

"Don't that look hard," Ryder said to Keefe, pointing to the burned buildings. Keefe said it did, and Ryder continued, "I know the fire-bug that did it, but by God I'll fix him and put him in a way he will never burn another barn again."

Ryder took a cow over to Bill Thompson's later that day for safe-keeping until a new barn was built. He told Thompson he would "law anyone he suspected of setting his barns on fire".

"Even the Donnellys?" Thompson asked.

Ryder nodded grimly. That same day he sent out all his boys and his brothers into the Catholic Settlement to summon a meeting of the Peace Society of Biddulph for that night. About twenty-five

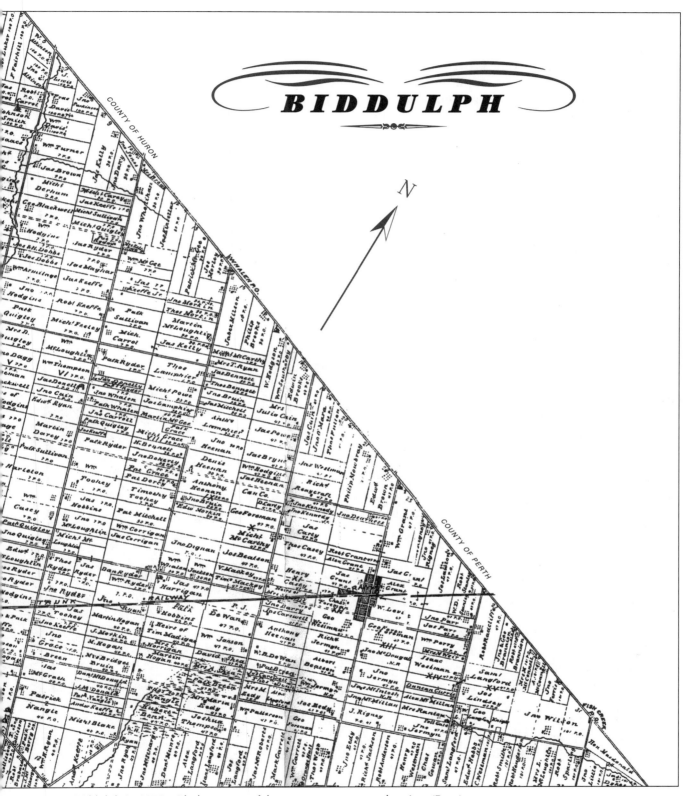

Biddulph in 1878 with the names of the property owners at that time (Page)

or thirty members came, and James Harrigan acted as chairman. They talked about the fire, how it was started, and in what manner the case against the Donnellys could be proved.

James McGrath had been summoned to the meeting by Grouchy Ryder's brother, Tom. The McGraths were among the most respectable of the Catholic Settlement families. A brother of James was a priest, Father Michael McGrath, who for the two years prior had been in charge of the Catholic Church at Bothwell in the southwestern part of Middlesex County. Another brother, John, was a medical doctor, while a sister, Annie, was an accomplished musician. The parents, old Matthew and Bridget McGrath, lived with their son James

in Biddulph. The entire family had come to the township as relative newcomers in 1870 and in the same year they built their large log house on Lot 31, concession seven, just half a mile from St. Patrick's Church on the Roman Line.[1]

James McGrath, aged thirty-six, had married Rebecca Fogarty and they had four small children, the oldest six years of age. The Fogartys came from McGillivray Township and were neighbours of, and related to, the Thompsons, whose daughter Maggie had once been courted by William Donnelly. It was the house of Rebecca's mother, Ellen Fogarty, that Will and his cohorts had invaded in search of the Thompson girl back in 1874, and that had been again invaded by a couple of masked

Grouchy Ryder's barn. Note the date (1880) on the gable of the barn built to replace the one alleged to have been fired by the Donnellys.

228 *The Donnelly Album*

men a couple of years later. Mrs. Fogarty had driven off the marauders but they were, she suspected, part of the Donnelly gang. Referring to the reason for his coming to the meetings of the Biddulph Peace Society, James McGrath said, "I thought some of my neighbours would think I was lenient to those who were keeping the place as it was, so I joined the Society."

John Purtell had been working for James McGrath for about six weeks at the time of the Ryder fire. Purtell did not go to the Cedar Swamp Schoolhouse with his boss but went instead to Dan Keefe's. He had always been on friendly terms with the Keefes and the Donnellys and in the previous year had been employed by both the pro-

Patrick "Grouchy" Ryder

Donnelly and the anti-Donnelly factions. Before McGrath's, he had worked for Patrick Dewan and Martin Hogan. Purtell was a popular hired man and recommended by the farmers as not afraid of a good day's work, even though he had acquired a criminal record when convicted a few years before of stabbing a German man in the Ellice huckleberry marsh during a Sunday outing. For this misdemeanour he had served three months in jail.

Purtell was said by some to be a great coward, while others thought him a dim-witted sort of fellow. He had been raised by the Ryders, particularly by Sideroad Jim Ryder and Tom Ryder, for he had lost his mother in childhood and his poor, drunken father was not much of a parental guide.

Sideroad Jim Ryder, with whom Purtell lived during much of his youth, was forty-five years old in 1880. Like most of the Ryders he was of small stature, with dark eyes and long, bushy dark-brown hair, and he sported a full, grizzled beard of great length. He had grown up on the Roman Line, and although he had served as a "volunteer" in the Fenian Raid scare of the 1860s, he was not the brightest person in the world. He could not read or write, and although he was able to play the card game "Forty-fives", he had to quit when it came to more sophisticated games, such as euchre.

Sideroad Jim's brother Grouchy was also short and wore grey whiskers. Pat Ryder, aged fifty-three, had reached prosperity comparatively early, having acquired among other property the old Pat Farrell farm (but not without a squabble with old Mick Feeheley). He had a large family of boys, the eldest being named James, the "young Grouch" referred to by Mrs. Donnelly.

Grouchy Ryder's youngest brother was Tom, thirty years of age, who had inherited the old Ryder place upon the death of the patriarch of the family. Tom Ryder had "the appearance of a morally weak man rather than that of a bold and desperate one". Although his forehead was high, it was "somewhat narrow and sunken", and his face was also "narrow and sharp", with a very prominent Roman nose and a wide mouth. His hair, including his moustache and chin whiskers, was light blond, "verging on white". It was, all in all, a hard face to forget.

Tom Ryder was married to Katherine Mackey, whose brother, Valentine, attended the meeting of the Biddulph Peace Society to discuss the Ryder barn fire. "The fire was a great loss," Mackey told his brother-in-law.

"It would have been a greater loss," Tom Ryder replied, "if his horses had been burned." And Ryder told Mackey that his brother had lost twelve hundred bushels of oats, four hundred bushels of

A letter from Will Donnelly about Grouchy Ryder's reaction to the burning of his barn (UWO)

wheat, and four hundred bushels of barley, as well as fifteen tons of hay, in the fire.

Following the meeting, Grouchy Ryder decided to lay a charge of arson. It was between ten and eleven o'clock that night when he reached the home of William Casey, the newly appointed Justice of the Peace, and made out the charge against William, John, Robert, and Thomas Donnelly. But Casey was a shrewd man. He talked the matter over with Ryder and pointed out that, as sure as Ryder was that it was the Donnellys who had committed the crime, there would still have to be the formality of evidence in its traditionally acceptable form before a conviction could be made. Had not Ryder's own sons and daughter been at the Keefe wedding celebration and seen the Donnelly brothers there with the other guests? Why, Ryder's own witnesses might very well supply the alibi evidence! Even though Thomas and Robert Donnelly's whereabouts the whole evening were not entirely satisfactorily accounted for, Ryder was persuaded to hold up the matter of the arrests for the time being, until some evidence could be obtained to support the charge.

The next day Grouchy Ryder, in company with his two sons, James and Patrick, drove his wagon past the Donnelly farm to pick up John and Michael Carroll, who were to assist in cutting timber for the barn which Ryder intended to rebuild immediately. On the road they met a couple of the young Keefes. Tom Donnelly was with them .

"You burned my barns," said Ryder to Donnelly. Tom made no reply. Ryder set his mouth grimly and drove off, convinced in his own mind that he had found the guilty person.

The next day was Saturday and Will and Norah Donnelly paid a visit to the farm of his parents, where they found Mrs. Donnelly making preparations to leave home. She was accompanying Robert back to Glencoe, planning to visit not only Bob's wife but her daughter Jane, who was staying with Mike's widow in St. Thomas. Jenny Currie had rented a house just down the street from Nellie Donnelly and was helping her out during the first difficult weeks of widowhood.

No sooner had Bob Donnelly and his mother left than word of their departure reached the ears of Grouchy Ryder. Ryder was sure they were fleeing from arrest. He made inquiries concerning the probable destination of the mother and son, questioning among others Zackariah McIlhargey, at whose home Bob Donnelly would often be found, since it was the abode of several attractive and unattached young ladies.

"Have you seen Bob Donnelly?" asked Ryder.

"He's gone to the woods in Michigan," McIlhargey replied. He had no reason to make such answer, he later explained, and never knew why he said it, as he had no idea where Donnelly was at the time.

Grouchy Ryder collected the stories of threats made by Mrs. Donnelly from Mrs. William McLaughlin, Mrs. Patrick Quigley, and Mrs. Patrick Whalen. Insinuations were made along the Roman Line that Mrs. Patrick Whalen in particular knew much more than she would admit. A story made the rounds that during the Ryder barn fire Mrs. Donnelly had come over and, sidling up to Mrs. Whalen, had whispered, "Don't be afraid. The fire will not spread over here, for we noted the direction of the wind before it was set!"

On Saturday, January 17, 1880. Pat Ryder was grouchier than usual when he returned to William Casey to lay a new information against Mrs. Donnelly, charging her with aiding and abetting arson. For good measure, James Donnelly, Sr., was also charged. Casey issued the warrant and handed it to Ryder, who immediately took it to James Carroll to be executed. Carroll quickly repaired to the Donnelly farm, taking old Jim Donnelly into custody and hustling him down the road to William Casey's, where he was bound over to appear at his trial. Then he set out after Mrs. Donnelly.

Arriving in St. Thomas that evening, Carroll went first to see James Fewings, the Chief of Police. He showed the Chief his warrant. Yes, the Chief knew of the Donnellys and he knew where Michael Donnelly's widow lived. To oblige Carroll, he went around and saw old Mrs. Donnelly in the house that very afternoon and came back to report to Carroll. The two of them went to make the arrests.

Jim Currie answered the knock on the door of Nellie Donnelly's house. They asked for Robert Donnelly and he answered. "He's not here. He's gone to the woods."

When they asked for old Mrs. Donnelly, Nellie Donnelly told them she was over at her daughter's house down the street. The constable and the Chief went down the street to Jenny Currie's and arrested Johannah Donnelly. Although it was between six and seven o'clock in the evening, Carroll insisted that the prisoner must accompany him back to Biddulph that very night.

"I will go with you, Mother," Jenny said. "I do not trust him. If you go alone with him he will try to get you to make a statement. I must go with you."

Carroll balked. He said that if Mrs. Currie insisted on going along he would ask Chief Fewings to provide another officer to assist him, as he did no wish to handle two women alone. Who would pay the expenses of the extra officer, asked the Chief? After some argument Jenny Currie agreed to pay the cost, and Chief Fewings ordered Constable George Speers to accompany them.

By the time the party of four set off from St. Thomas in a sleigh wagon it was ten o'clock at night. Before departing, Carroll promised to inform the Chief about the outcome of the case. Constable Speers accompanied the others as far as London, which was reached early in the morning, and it was then agreed that Speers could return while the remaining three continued on.

They reached Biddulph on Monday morning. Carroll got hold of William Casey and he bailed Mrs. Donnelly over for her trial on January 22 in Lucan. The bondsmen for Johannah Donnelly were George Hodgins and James Keefe, in the amount of $500 each. Hodgins was a Protestant and an Orangeman.

Jenny Currie accompanied her parents back home to the Donnelly homestead and stayed overnight. When she saw the high-posted bed in her parents' bedroom she sighed, "There's where poor Mike spent his last night." She returned next morning to St. Thomas.

Bail Bond for James and Johannah Donnelly in the arson case (UWO)

42

LAW

Pat Ryder told James Carroll that the witnesses against Jim and Johannah Donnelly were reluctant to go to court.

"We will serve them with subpoenas if necessary," Carroll declared.

Someone then informed Carroll that Constable Wild Bill Hodgins had an outstanding warrant for the arrest of James Feeheley who had returned to Biddulph a few months previously. It arose out of the Ned Ryan robbery case. Hodgins was working at winter threshing at a farmer's near Granton, but he took the time to return to his home in Lucan and hand over to Carroll the outstanding warrant, along with a pair of handcuffs and a revolver. Carroll made no explanation for the request and Hodgins asked for none.

On the day that the arson case against the elder Donnellys came up in Lucan, James Carroll met James Feeheley on the road to Lucan.

"I hear you have a warrant for me," Feeheley said warily. "What's it about?"

"That's my business," replied Carroll.

"I don't know how you've got a warrant against me," Feeheley went on, trying to draw the other out, "or what it's for."

They walked along side by side for a while, until after a few moments in silence Carroll looked sharply at Feeheley and asked, "Do you associate with the Donnellys?"

Feeheley was a little surprised, but was not afraid of Carroll and told him so. Carroll ignored the hostility. "The Peace Society has been got up in Biddulph to put down all bad works," he told Feeheley. "Tom Donnelly and that whole gang must be stopped, and they will be stopped one way or another. I tell you, the Donnellys are bad company. You ought to shun them."

Carroll went on to intimate that if Feeheley did not associate with the Donnellys in future, he would not pursue the matter of the warrant which was out against him. There may also have been some talk, perhaps far more persuasive in the mind of Feeheley, that in his absence the Donnellys had attempted to push the blame for both the Ned Ryan robbery and the shooting at Sam Everett upon Feeheley.

When James Carroll reached Lucan, he went to the Lucan Council Chamber above the lock-up on William Street, where William Casey was already on hand. At two o'clock Mr. and Mrs. Donnelly appeared for their trial. Grouchy Ryder, the complainant, stood up and said that the prosecution had not sufficient time to gather evidence and asked that the case be adjourned. It was put over for trial to Granton on January 27. Casey, having become a trifle uneasy at being on the other side of the bench for a change, had already spoken to James Grant and Philip Mowbray, who agreed to sit on the case provided it were held in Granton.

After court, James and Johannah Donnelly stopped in to visit their old friends Michael and Mary O'Connor, who lived in a small log house set on posts on Princess Street in the village, near the tracks. Mrs. Donnelly wanted to pick up some sewing from Bridget O'Connor, and Mr. Donnelly wanted to arrange for Bridget's younger brother, John Jeremiah O'Connor, to come to the farm and look after the livestock when the family went to court on January 27. Young Johnny O'Connor said he would go. The young lad was a bright boy about fifteen years old, although he went by a younger age.[1] He liked to go over to the Donnelly farm whenever the opportunity arose, for he looked up to the Donnelly brothers and their father, and they, in turn, liked him and treated him well.

On his return from Lucan that day, James Feeheley did not stop in at the Donnelly place as he would normally have done. "I was afraid to be seen coming out of their house," he explained later, "because they were said to be bad company."

James Carroll was on the road a great deal in those weeks. Between Granton and Lucan he met Sam Hodgins, a county constable who lived in the eastern part of Biddulph Carroll borrowed Sam Hodgins' handcuffs, explaining that Wild Bill Hodgins had asked for the return of the other pair. Sam readily agreed and said he would leave them with Thomas Culbert, one of the Granton hotel proprietors. When Carroll picked up the cuffs from Culbert in the last week of January, he had two pairs, for he had not returned the first pair to the other constable.

Father Connolly, on his return home from Quebec in the latter part of January, was angry when told of the wedding of Martha Keefe to Michael Quigley at the Donnelly Schoolhouse and the burning of Ryder's barn that night. William Toohey, a trustee of St. Patrick's School and one of the few members of that family who were still on good terms with the Donnellys, told Will Donnelly that the priest had a long meeting with Grouchy Ryder at the priest's house. Ryder told the priest all about the burning of his barn and his reasons for suspecting the Donnellys. Mrs. Donnelly had been going up and down the line making threats against his son for having taken part in the search for Thompson's cow. Tom Donnelly had smirked at Ryder the day after the fire. Bob Donnelly had been away from the dancing at Keefe's for a long time. And the rest of the brothers were over at Keefe's wedding laughing, drinking, and dancing while the barn burned. Was Tom Donnelly there? the priest asked. Oh, yes, he was laughing and drinking with the rest of them. The priest mused darkly to himself, "Tom Donnelly took the pledge from me and now he has broken it."

Out loud the priest murmured, "Damn the schoolhouse, and damn the wedding. It was the cause of the fire, and the simple, gaudy little bride."

On the following Sunday, January 25, Father Connolly mentioned the Ryder fire in his sermon and said he hoped that the parties responsible would be brought to justice. He offered a reward of $500 for private information leading to the detection of the person or persons responsible for the crime.

"The priest cursed the family from the altar," Timothy Toohey later claimed. Toohey had been a Biddulph Township councillor for many years and his word carried weight. "As Catholics we are bound to believe," Toohey went on, "that the curse of a priest would prove true. Father Connolly cursed them again and again, and once said to the old woman that she would be made an example of in the ditch." Others denied that the priest had cursed the Donnellys by name. The priest himself denied it. But all were in agreement that he did say he hoped that a ball of fire would fall from heaven on the house of those who burned Ryder's buildings. There was no doubt in anyone's mind at whom the words were directed.

The next day Father Connolly had occasion to speak to a cousin of the "simple, gaudy little bride", daughter of James Keefe and wife of the schoolteacher, Stephen J. Patton. The subject of the arrest of Mr. and Mrs. Donnelly and their imminent trial came up in conversation and the priest expressed a hope that the diabolical crime of incendiarism would be brought home to them.

"Why, Father Connolly," protested Mrs. Patton, "Mr. Donnelly is a very old man. He would not, at his time of life, have any hand in such a crime as that."

The priest's reply was sharp. "He is a wicked old man," he said, "and is capable of doing anything."

When the Donnelly arson case came up in Granton on January 27, it was again postponed, at the request of Ryder and Carroll, to January 29. Following the adjournment, Carroll made another visit to the Donnelly farmhouse, this time to serve a subpoena upon Bridget Donnelly. Carroll was not sure what testimony the young niece of James Donnelly might give, but he was bound to leave no stone unturned in attempting to obtain a conviction. He also served a subpoena upon Bridget O'Connor at her home in Lucan.

From house to house Carroll went, particularly in the vicinity of the Donnelly farm, trying to elicit any kind of incriminating evidence, his presence creating a turmoil in many households along the Roman Line. Martin Darcey accompanied Carroll to the home of John Doherty and asked the latter to come over to John Cain's house. Cain lived immediately south of the Donnellys, and Carroll's younger brother, Michael, worked for him. They began to talk about Doherty's joining the Biddulph Peace Society. Doherty was inclined to be friendly with the Donnellys. He had no quarrel with them, he said; besides, he was a brother-in-law of Dan Keefe, who had been intimate with the family for many years. He wondered exactly what the peace society was all about. The others did their best to explain its purpose of putting down all depredations in the township, but the subject always seemed to revolve around the Donnellys. Martin Darcey worked himself up into a frenzy in denouncing them, his high cheekbones flushing with anger, his great head of bushy hair and his blond goatee shaking in near-apoplexy. At one point in the animated discussion John Cain reached up and took a stick out of the hole in the chimney support, brandishing it in the air.

"By God," he exclaimed, "before a week is out I will bury this stick in Tom Donnelly's skull."

Doherty was taken aback at Cain's passion. "But this is a sworn party," he protested.

"Yes," came the reply, "but nobody can prove anything against us."

"Well," replied Doherty, suddenly making up his mind, "I will have nothing to do with a sworn party. And I will have nothing to do with putting a stick in a man's head."

John Doherty left Cain's house and returned to his own farm, which was on the first sideroad south of the Donnelly place and directly behind Patrick Farrell's old farm. The latter now belonged to Grouchy Ryder, who let William Casey keep some hogs on it that winter. Doherty would often see either Casey or the Ryders at the farm tending their livestock, sometimes the two of them together. Casey was married to Ryder's cousin and both were members of the Peace Society, Doherty knew.

When the arson case came up for trial on January 29, the Donnellys fetched the little O'Connor boy from Lucan, along with his sister, Bridget, who had been subpoenaed. Then they all piled into a wagon and drove down to Granton for the trial, leaving Johnny to tend the livestock.

Court was held in Middleton's Hotel on the Main Street of Granton in a little anteroom which was thirteen feet square. The three Justices of the Peace all crowded into the little room, along with the lawyers (the Donnellys had retained William McDiarmid of Lucan, and Ryder had hired John J. Blake of London), defendants, witnesses, and

spectators, to permit the majesty of the law to take its course.

Patrick Ryder was the first sworn and related how his barn burned down the night of the Keefe wedding. The two Bridgets then gave their testimony of sleeping on either side of Mrs. Donnelly, being awakened in the night, and looking out to see the fire. The evidence left no doubt that the barn had been burned, but there was not a tittle of testimony to show what connection the defendants had with it. When the weakness of the prosecutor's case became embarrassingly apparent, Jim Carroll got up and protested that the prosecution was having difficulties in getting witnesses to come to court. Even when served with subpoenas, the ladies of the Roman Line wanted nothing to do with courts and law. Worse still, said Carroll, when he went to serve a subpoena upon Mrs. Patrick Whalen, her husband had taken an axe to him, threatening "by the mother of God" to brain him with it. Warrants would have to be issued for the witnesses, and even at that, he said, they might refuse to testify by reason of fear. The case for the prosecution might indeed fail, he concluded, and he was getting so disgusted with the entire affair that he was almost ready to throw up the whole case.

But William McDiarmid then rose to his feet and informed the court that his clients did not intend to let the matter rest if the prosecution failed to prove its case, as seemed likely. He intimated that in his clients' opinion the charges were in the nature of vexatious proceedings, and had been laid without any real foundation; in such cases, he had advised them, the defendants had a good cause of action against the complainant for malicious prosecution and intended to pursue a claim for damages.

James Carroll then asked for an adjournment to enable him to make one last effort to round up the witnesses. At least one of the magistrates, Philip Mowbray, perceived that the case for the prosecution was a shaky one at best and wanted to dismiss the charge then and there, but William Casey was loath to let the defendants off so easily. The other J.P., James Grant, influenced by his friendship with Carroll and Kennedy, sided with Casey. A compromise was finally reached. One more ad-

Bridget Donnelly   Sworn   live in Biddulph   Live with Mr. Donnelly Senr   have been there over a year steady – Was present when Miss Conners visited with us – I don't think Miss Conners visited us more than three times in four or five month – Miss Conners was present at the Wake   staid all night and the day of the Funeral – Can't say if Miss Conners ever staid at Donnellys only the night of the Wake and the night of the Wedding – Miss Conner and I remained at home after the Funeral, thought it was a large funeral – Can't say where Miss Conners slept on the night after the funeral – I don't think Miss Conners was at our house at any time only when she came with some sewing on the day of the Wedding – I did not go to the Wedding the boys went   Mr and Mrs Donnelly myself and Miss Conners remained at home boys went to wedding before dark family went to bed at Eleven o'clock   had tea just before going to bed Can't remember whether the boys had supper or not before going out to wedding – I made some biscuits for the last Tea – A conversation was going on as I but I can't say what it was – We all went to bed together   I went with Mrs. Donnelly and Miss Conners – Have no idea of what time I got up, Mr. Donnelly came in and told us the School house was on fire – A waggon passed and Mrs. Donnelly called Mr. Donnelly to get up – I don't remember of Miss Conner sleeping with me at any time but the night of the Wedding   When Mrs. Donnelly called Mr. Donnelly to get up it was just four o'clock – After getting up Mr. Donnelly lighted the Kitchen fire   Shortly he called there was a fire We got up and went to the front Door   Uncle and I said it was the Schoolhouse   Miss Conner said it was not the School house   she saw the smoke coming over the School house – did not stay looking at the fire we went back to the Kitchen   and went to bed again till the fire lighted up – did not know it was Ryders till the next day after daylight – Bridget Conner left some time next day but I cannot say when – none of the family made any remark about the fire on the day after it took

place – was subpoenaed on Saturday 24th Jany – I saw Miss Conner since the fire, I asked her if she was subpoenaed   had no conversation with any one about the evidence I was to give – I cannot think about if Bridget Conner came there only one night Cannot say what that night was   Have no recollection of having any conversation about the fire but can't say – I might have told Miss Conner of the dog barking and a Waggon passing but I can't say – don't remember of speaking to Bridget Conners of the fire was at Mr. Donnelly's when a party of men came looking for a Cow – The family sometimes speak of being persecuted never   heard them saying they would make there tormenters suffer – did not hear Mr. Donnelly say that Mr. Ryder's fine buildings were gone – I was very much disturbed by Mr. Donnelly coughing two weeks but on this particular night I was awake all night – I spoke with no one as to what evidence I was to give

Crossexamined   Mr. Donnelly slept in the next room   heard no person up that night   can't say if the Bedroom door was shut or not   was sitting in the Kitchen on the night after the boys went to the Wedding – no person came into our house as far as I recollect on the morning after the fire the Donnelly boys were not anxious to go to the Wedding on account of the Death of a Brother – don't recollect if Mr. Donnelly say to the boys go to the Wedding   the reason I did not go was because I was a stranger   no one advised me to go   Mrs. Donnelly slept in the middle between me and Miss Conners and was not out of the bed all night

Bridget Donnelly

Wm. Casey J.P.

James Grant J.P.

Philip Mowbray J.P.

(UWO)

journment only would be allowed, but on the strict understanding that the case would be disposed of the next time it came up. If no better evidence were forthcoming, the charges would be dismissed. On this basis the case was adjourned to Wednesday, February 4, 1880.

When the crowd extracted itself from the little anteroom of Middleton's Hotel and poured out into the fresh winter air, it was between seven and eight o'clock in the evening. Tom Donnelly had asked Jim Feeheley to come to Granton that day. Tom had brought with him his loaded seven-shooter revolver and told Feeheley about it during the hearing. As friend and foe alike squeezed out of the doorway, Jim Feeheley, as if to demonstrate his continuing loyalty to the Donnelly family, suddenly confronted the Ryders and began to abuse them, calling them cowards and fools for hauling such old people about in the courts.

"Stop that talk," Carroll warned him, "or you'll be arrested."

Feeheley thereupon turned on Carroll and began to curse and swear at him, challenging him to a fight right then and there. The confrontation took place right in front of the window of the little anteroom where court had been held, and the three magistrates peered out the window at the scene. Carroll stalked back into the hotel to ask the magistrates for a warrant to arrest Feeheley, but the magistrates refused, and Carroll then grew very angry and said he would arrest him without a warrant. He began to flip furiously through the pages of his constable's handbook but in a moment regained his composure, put the book away, and left.

Shortly after, Carroll laid a charge against old Patrick Whalen for taking the axe to him and the following day he went out and arrested Whalen.

Mr. and Mrs James Grant of Granton. Grant was a Justice of the Peace who sat on the trial of James and Johannah Donnelly in the arson case. (G. Grant)

Jim Donnelly saw them drive off in the constable's buggy. Carroll took his prisoner to Granton and had him bound over for his trial to Wednesday, February 4, 1880, the same day that the Donnelly arson case was finally to be disposed of.

PLANS

A meeting of the Peace Society was called for immediately. It was a time for decisive action. Everybody from the inner circle came. It was confirmed that unless Father Connolly specifically enjoined such action, the society should again visit the Donnelly homestead on the night of Tuesday, February 3, the day before the Ryder arson case. Each of the Donnelly men would be handcuffed and taken out. They would be hanged to a tree by the neck or the heels and tortured until they made a full confession of all their crimes and promised not to prosecute any of the members of the society. Then, upon their own confession, they would be sent to the penitentiary for long terms. The precise working out of the plan was a little vague, but the intent was clear. It was not exactly intended to kill them, it was understood, but the burden of the proceedings would be "to bring them as near the dissolution point as possible".

To ensure that the unexpected presence of strangers did not interfere with the plan, accomplices would be required. The Feeheley boys,

Father John Connolly

especially James, were the logical choices. The plan was explained to them and Jim Feeheley agreed to visit the Donnelly farmhouse on the night appointed, to ensure that all was normal in the household. He would also visit the William Donnelly house, where, he was told, Big Jim Keefe was in on the plans and would also be there in the capacity of spy.

In the meantime, the intervening days would be used to summon home those who might assist in the action, to approach the priest, to influence waverers, and to establish alibis.

Father Connolly was furious when he heard of the probable outcome of the Ryder arson case. The following Sunday, February 1, James Carroll sat in the congregation of St. Patrick's Church and listened intently to the sermon. The priest mentioned again the evils that had befallen the parish and denounced witnesses who would not come for-

ward to give evidence against guilty parties. He alluded to the reward of five hundred dollars which he himself offered for the detection of the wicked persons and vowed that the guilty would eventually be punished, if not by the laws of man, then by the laws of God. He said again that a ball of fire would fall from heaven upon the house of those who burned the barns of Patrick Ryder. Some of his listeners were sure that divine retribution had been called upon the heads of the Donnellys by name, although the priest denied it. There were others who related that the priest met with the leaders of the Peace Society after church and told them that he had done his best. He could do nothing more to handle the Donnellys, he was alleged to have said, and they were to go ahead and do what they thought best.[1]

The old enemy of the Donnellys, James Maher, Sr., was also at church on Sunday, February 1. Following mass he had dinner at Andrew Keefe's, after which the two men went to the home of Jerry McDonald, who was married to Maher's sister. All that day they discussed the priest's Peace Society. Maher and Keefe also arranged to go to Stratford the following day on business. Young Pat Keefe had skipped the country, leaving behind a note which both men had endorsed, and they had now to compromise the matter.

The next day Maher and Keefe took the train from Lucan and did their business in Stratford. But as there were no passenger trains going beyond St. Marys that night, they hopped a freight train back, and as it was late by the time they reached Lucan on Monday evening, they took a room at Walker's Hotel near the Lucan railway station. Before they went to sleep, Maher drank a bit too much. He began to complain about the Donnelly family. "It was they who shaved my horses' tails," Maher blubbered, "and whoever did that, there is nothing bad enough to be done with them."

Meanwhile, early in the morning of Monday, February 2, Will Donnelly went to the home of his parents to pick up the light buggy. He was slightly startled when he walked into the kitchen of the house and saw his mother sitting in front of the stove, clad only in long, red flannel underwear, toasting her rheumatic joints. She made such a ludicrous sight that Will burst out laughing. In such a get-up, he joked, she would scare the devil himself. Johannah Donnelly broke into tears.

"Oh, William," she sobbed, "if ye had the sare trouble on ye whot I have, ye wud not joke so readily." She shook with grief, and her son, now sobered, asked what was the matter. "Oh, Will," she sobbed, "me heart is broken. They are draggin' meself and the owld man all over the counthry thryin' to fasten that burnin' on us."

The son stood silent at the old woman's bitter tears. Just then his father came in. Will Donnelly felt uncomfortable and made to depart.

"Well," he said, "I am in a hurry this morning. I must get the buggy and be off."

"Hold, hold, Will," said James Donnelly to his son, "I will not hear uv id. Stay a while. Must ye go so soon? Put the horse up and have a bid uv sup wid us. Perhaps ye will not have the chance to ate many more meals wid me."

William Donnelly was touched by the earnest entreaty of his father's voice and manner. He hesitated, and the old man continued. "Shure, I'm goin' to Granton on Wednesday for thrial, an' it may be they'd hang me," he said, "an' thin we'd niver meet agin."

The son agreed to stay a while. "But Mother," he said to the old lady as he doffed his coat, "if you are being ill-used, you had better go up to Father Connolly and ask him to use his influence. Ask him to have the Ryders stop the prosecution."

This only caused a fresh flood of tears from the old woman. "Shure, he knows the way they are usin' us, widout me goin' to tell 'im," cried Mrs. Donnelly. And the old woman wept some more and went on, "If Father Connolly had only acted like Father Girrard before, and heard no stories, it wud save us a great dale of throuble wid the neighbours."

The old man then said he thought the priest's talk in the church had the effect of keeping good, honest neighbours from visiting their house or being friendly to them, even though they still wished the family well. In one sense, said the old man sadly, Father Connolly could not be blamed because they, the Committee faction, were with the priest night and day filling his ears with lies

about them. And he related to his son that he had heard shortly before that two of his neighbours had gone through the parish collecting oats for the priest and had called in at every house on the Roman Line except the Donnelly place. The old man shook his head. First-class neighbours would no longer neighbour with the family as they had for many years before.

"The people are afraid uv the priest," Mrs. Donnelly piped in, "an' for that reason stay away from me and the rest uv us."

The three of them continued talking about the Peace Society, and about James Carroll always coming around to serve warrants and other legal process. In the large front room of the house in one of the corners opposite the bedrooms, old Mr. Donnelly pointed to some guns. The son went over to inspect the arsenal. There was a rifle that his father had owned before going to Kingston Penitentiary, the very gun he had taken a shot at Pat Farrell with twenty-five years before. It was always kept loaded. Beside it was an old musket and alongside it a recently acquired firearm, a shotgun borrowed from one of the Feeheley boys shortly after the search for Thompson's cow. The old man vowed he would defend his home against further intrusion. Picking up Feeheley's gun, he loaded it and handed it to his son.

"Guns we have plinty," said the old man and pointed out that Will's own five-shooter lay in a drawer of the bureau in the front room, along with a breech-loading single-shot pistol. In addition, there was Tom's seven-shooter in the little bedroom off the kitchen, where Tom usually slept.

But the talk of violence and the society faction depressed Will Donnelly. He left shortly after, in low spirits and with a sense of foreboding.

The morning of February 3 began like any other day in the Donnelly household. Joseph Whalen, one of the boys from across the road, met Tom Donnelly on the road about nine o'clock in the morning and exchanged a few words with him. Later that day old Jim Donnelly sat down at the kitchen table, donned the spectacles he was wont to use despite the fact that he could neither read nor write, and asked one of his sons to pen a letter to Alderman Edmund Meredith, the London lawyer. The letter was probably written by Tom, and read:

February 3rd, 1880.

Mr. Meredith:

SIR – On the fifteenth of last month Pat Ryder's barns were burned. All the vigilance committee at once pointed to my family as the ones that did it. Ryder found out that all my boys were at a wedding that night. He at once arrested me on suspicion, and also sent a constable after my wife to St. Thomas. The trial has been postponed four different times, although we are ready for our trial at any time. They examined a lot of witnesses but can't find anything against us. Ryder swore that we lived neighbours to each other for thirty years and never had any deferences, and had no reason for arresting us only we are blamed for everything.... The presiding Magistrates are old Grant and a newly made one, Casey. They are using us worse than mad dogs. Mr. McDermid is attending on our behalf.... They had the first trial in Lucan,

John Robinson Armitage and his store where Jim Donnelly made his last purchase (Stanley)

and then adjourned to Granton simply to advertise us. We have to appear tomorrow again, and I am informed they are going to send us for trial without a tittle of evidence. If so I will telegraph you when we start for London to meet us at the City Hotel, and get us bailed to take our trial before the judge, and I want you to handle the case in our behalf. There is not the slightest cause for our arrest, and it seems hard to see a man and woman over sixty years of age dragged around as laughing stocks.

YOURS TRULY,
JAMES DONNELLY, SEN. [2]

Later that day Tom Donnelly hitched a pair of horses to the wagon, for there had been so little snow that winter that there had been no sleighing as yet, and the roads were very rough. The father and son drove in to Lucan to post the letter. Patrick Whalen saw them ride off from across the road.

After calling in at the Post Office they dropped in at Armitage's store. Picking up a few small articles, James Donnelly turned to the clerk as he went to leave and said, "Charge them to the Queen, boy, I may niver return to pay you agin."

The two men then went to call at the home of the O'Connors. James Donnelly said they wanted to pick up the cutter, for as the whole family would be going to the trial in Granton the next day, an extra vehicle was required to fetch the lawyer from the village. O'Connor told them that William Donnelly had taken the cutter. Donnelly, Sr., then asked if young Johnny O'Connor could come again to look after the livestock. The young lad was over at William Hutchins' place sawing wood and one of his sisters was sent to fetch him. The Donnellys liked the boy, "as dacint a lad as iver sat fut in Biddulph", according to his mother's opinion of him. And it was an opinion that was generally accepted.

"Father wants you home," said Johnny's sister, and he came.

"Put on yer overcoat, Johnny," Mrs. O'Connor told her son. "Yer to go down wid Mr. Donnelly an' Tom here, fer they want ye to feed the things while they go to Granton tomorrow."

It was about four o'clock when the three of them drove east out of the village and then north along the Roman Line towards the Donnelly farm. It was an hour and a half before sunset and the cold winter sun gleamed bleakly across the frozen but almost bare fields. The horses galloped along smartly and the wagon wheels bumped in and out of the frozen ruts. They were going rather too fast and recklessly, thought William Casey, the Biddulph J.P., who stopped whatever chore he had been doing and watched them pass by his farm.

On reaching the farmhouse the old man and the young boy got off the wagon and went into the house to get warm, while John came out to help his brother unhitch the horses. Before putting them away they watered them at the pump near the front door. The two young men then trooped into the house and sat down by the stove with the young boy to munch apples which Johannah Donnelly had told Bridget to fetch from the little fruit cellar under the front room. In a little while a meal had been prepared and they all ate.

After supper John Donnelly said he would go over with the pony to Keefe's, and then to his brother Will's, and bring home the cutter for court the next day. He also wanted to take the money in the house for safekeeping. Throwing an overcoat over his rough working shirt he went out, his brother Tom and young Johnny O'Connor following. John threw the harness over the pony's neck and rode off. It was still only about five o'clock. Tom Donnelly then gave the boy a blanket and asked him to cover his horse while he went to get feed for the pigs, coming back in a few minutes with the feed and a whip which he handed to the boy. He told the youngster to keep the pigs away from the trough while he emptied the feed into it. When this task was done, Donnelly went up to the loft and threw some hay down for the horses. They then returned to the house.

William Carroll, younger brother of Constable James Carroll, was boarding at William

The Roman Line in winter

Thompson's at the time. He had gone over to Cain's to visit his still-younger brother, Michael. On his way back, William Carroll saw Tom Donnelly and Johnny O'Connor returning from the barn to the house.

Inside, Tom Donnelly told Bridget to get some more apples, and they again munched on them beside the stove. The winter sun disappeared over the horizon.

For an ordinary week-night during the winter, there seemed to be an unusual amount of activity among the farmers of Biddulph. Long James Toohey later denied that he had been over at Pat Breen's that evening but, yes, he had gone over to Jeremiah McDonald's. To get some seed barley, he said. And, oh, yes, he had been at Breen's that day, although not in the evening, mind you. He and James Harrigan were fence viewers, and they had gone to Breen's "to settle a dispute about a watercourse between Breen's and Thomas Nangle's". Martin McLaughlin was seen near the Widow Harrigan's and was also at Pat Breen's that afternoon. He said:

> I went over to see him on business; some lots had been taken from our school, and Mr. Breen was appointed arbitrator on the case.[3]

Long James Toohey arrived at Breen's about ten minutes after McLaughlin. Young Pat Ryder was seen at Breen's too, around nightfall. Ryder had gone first to Maher's, and then "part of the way to Quigley's to get Purtell," he said. Patrick O'Shea was at Breen's that night also.

Tom Ryder claimed that his brother, Sideroad Jim, his brother-in-law, Valentine Mackey, and Long James Toohey had all come over again that evening to his house. Mackey lived on a small six-acre parcel of land with no timber and had come over to see about cutting some stove bolts off the Ryder farm. Toohey said he had gone over to Ryder's to borrow a logging chain and had left at ten o'clock. Before he left, however, they had played some cards, "Forty-fives" first and then euchre, at ten cents a game. Mackey stayed on after Toohey left in order to win back some of the money he had lost earlier.

John and Robert Cutt, who lived on Ned McLaughlin's farm just a quarter of a mile up the road from Tom Ryder's, had been asked to come over on Monday night, also to cut stove bolts. The Cutts did not go on Monday, they claimed, but went on Tuesday night instead. They said that Tom Ryder was not at home, and although they sat and waited with Mrs. Ryder until long after she put the children to bed, Tom Ryder had still not got home when they left at half past ten.

Some of the persons out on the roads had not been in Biddulph for some time but appeared unexpectedly in the township. Michael Heenan had been 150 miles away from home at Colpoy's Bay, the jumping-off point for the Michigan lumbering district, but quickly came back to Biddulph. All that Monday he had helped his father thresh with Martin Hogan's machine, which had been hired for the occasion. William Donnelly saw him on the

Michael Heenan, a sketch by Robert Harris

road that day and recognized him from his size. Martin McLaughlin went to Heenan's earlier in the day, and Hogan saw him in conversation with Big Anthony Heenan in the haymow. Dennis Heenan, too, was a long way from home in January, in company with Ted Toohey, but both suddenly appeared back in Biddulph at the end of the month.

And Joseph Caswell, who had moved from the township in 1878 and settled in Bothwell, made a trip to Biddulph in the first week of February. Caswell considered himself a failure. The sole cause of that failure, in his opinion, was the Donnelly family, who drove him out of Biddulph. "The Donnellys burned us out up home," the Caswell boys would say. On this occasion Caswell had come back to bring down some hay. On Monday, February 2, a telegram was delivered to the Caswell place near Bothwell instructing the boys to go "up home" at once. The boys hurriedly left to catch the 10 p.m. train for London but were angry that the message had not come sooner, for it had been sent in time for its receipt the previous Saturday.

Big Jack Kennedy went over to Dennis Carty's that evening, along with Wild Bill Hodgins and James Bryan. All but Kennedy were Protestants, or, more accurately, non-Roman Catholics, for the Cartys went to no church. Most of them had but lately been befriended by Kennedy. Kennedy left with Bryan and Hodgins and got home at 9:30 that evening, but James Bryan afterwards said he had gone over to Kennedy's to get some medicine for his children later that night and saw Kennedy there while the clock struck two. He was sure it had not been the previous night.

Young Jim Ryder went outside about 8 o'clock in the evening to see "the things", as the Biddulphers called the livestock. He chased a strange dog out to the road and there happened to meet James Carroll, with whom he then walked over to Thompson's. Ryder asked Carroll if the witnesses were ready for the next day's resumption of the arson case, and after chatting for ten or fifteen minutes, during which William Feeheley and the McLaughlin girls passed, he went home to bed. Jim Carroll said he then went in to Thompson's, talked to him about building a

drive-shed, and went to bed with his brother William in the upstairs bedroom.

Earlier that day James Carroll had chatted with one of the Toohey girls at Thompson's gate. Pat Quigley had gone over to Thompson's that evening "to borrow a saw". Jim Ryder's brother, Morris, had also limped over to William Thompson's earlier in the day to notify William Carroll that he would be required by the Ryders in the bush the next day. The Ryders were busy cutting timber for the rebuilding of their barn, and Morris had cut his foot with an axe during that job.

That evening young Tom Keefe had received a letter and had taken it over to his uncle Robert Keefe's on the next farm, where his cousin, young Bob Keefe, would read it for him. Upon his return, Tom Keefe was accompanied back to the gate of

William Feeheley, in later years

his own farm by his cousin, and on the way they saw someone approaching on horseback from the north. As he came closer, they saw it was young Pat Ryder. He was carrying what appeared to be a gun.

"He's gathering the factions," said young Tom Keefe. "They're going to shoot up the country at the trial tomorrow."

Meanwhile, Mr. and Mrs. Donnelly, Tom, Bridget, and Johnny O'Connor sat around for a time munching on apples. Although there were two coal-oil lamps in the house, only a candle was lit that night. The old man got up and said he was turning in, announcing that the boy would be sleeping with him. Tom said Johnny could sleep with him in his bed off the kitchen if he wanted, but the old man insisted the boy sleep in the big bed with him. James Donnelly thereupon said his prayers in the kitchen, went to his room and took off his clothes, and went to bed.

Johnny O'Connor had slept a few nights previously in the old man's bed, between old Mr. Donnelly and John Donnelly, and he knew it was a nice big bed. The boy slipped off his outer pair of pants, tucked them under the stove in the kitchen, and followed the old man into the bedroom. He took off his other pair of pants, laid them down in the bedroom with his coat, and crawled over the old man to the inside of the bed, where he settled down to sleep. He noticed that the old man was using his greatcoat as a pillow.

As Johnny O'Connor was dozing off to sleep he heard a new voice in the kitchen. It was James Feeheley, who had dropped in to see his friends just before the two women and Tom were about to have their tea. He said he had been working at their own farm that day with his brother William and William Whalen and had returned home with Whalen to play cards. The McLaughlin girls had also come over to Whalen's, but when they left, Feeheley decided to go home to bed and had just dropped by to say hello. He declined to take any tea.

They talked for a few minutes about the impending court case. Tom Donnelly again asked his friend to accompany them to Granton in the morning, and he agreed. As they talked, Feeheley

detected the voice of old Jim Donnelly in the bedroom addressing someone whom he took to be his son John, who usually slept with him, after the old man and Bridget had exchanged a brief word identifying the visitor. When Feeheley left, Tom accompanied him out to the corner of the kitchen, where they bid each other good night. Tom returned and retired to his little bedroom off the kitchen.

CLUBS

The house of John Doherty on the Swamp Line stood four rods from the road on the first sideroad south of the Donnelly place. Shortly after twelve o'clock midnight Doherty heard a voice outside, and going to the door he saw about fourteen or fifteen men skulking down the sideroad towards the outlying farm of Grouchy Ryder on the Roman Line. When they heard Doherty open the door, they scampered off the roadway and behind a stable which stood close to it. Doherty, thinking they were after his horses, ran out of the building. The gang of men made off towards the Roman Line, but not without Doherty's recognizing several of them, including Big Jack Kennedy, Pat Dewan, John, Dennis and Michael Heenan, John Lanphier, and James Harrigan.

This group met others who had congregated at the unoccupied farm of Ryder. The ghost of murdered Patrick Farrell must have been hovering in their midst, for it was this very farm which Farrell had owned when felled by the hand of James Donnelly a generation before. Among the crowd which gathered were the Ryders. In addition to Grouchy himself there were his sons, young Jim and Patrick, Jr., and his brothers, Sideroad Jim, Thomas, and Daniel. Martin McLaughlin was there, along with his brother John. Others were Long Jim and Ted

Toohey, John Cain, the James Mahers, father and son, John and Patrick Quigley, Patrick Breen, James McGrath and his hired man, John Purtell, Anthony Heenan, Michael Heenan, Dennis Heenan, Michael Blake, John Ryan, William Thompson, Ned Ryan and his son, young Johnny Ryan, John Darsey, John Bruin, Michael Madigan, and James Kenny. Altogether there were about thirty-five men, including James Carroll.

Some of the men wore disguises. Long Jim Toohey was dressed in women's clothes, one or two had their faces blackened with stove soot, while others were heavily muffled with scarves. Big Michael Heenan, a burly farmer of twenty-four years of age, with a broad, open face and an imperial beard and moustache, was draped in a long, dark cloak "which came right down over him". Many of the men, however, wore no disguises at all. John Kennedy had on a black fur cap, and James Carroll wore a soft, black felt hat, a black coat, and a pair of grey trousers.[1]

At about one hour past midnight after several quarts of *usquebaugh*, the water of life, had been gulped down, the gang of men set off to cover the half-mile distance to the Donnelly farmhouse. Two or three of the men carried guns, Tom Ryder had a pitchfork, Purtell an axe, and Pat Quigley and Jim Toohey each had a shovel. Most of them simply carried a club or short wooden stake of ordinary cordwood, chopped at one end to form a handle. Some were eighteen inches long and some three feet. At least one was two inches square with

The Donnelly farm, a sketch made by Robert Harris in 1880. The appearance of the house was copied from the Thompson farmhouse next door, which was said to be identical. (PEI)

a whittled grip. It began to snow lightly. William Feeheley and John Whalen, crouching behind Whalen's fence, saw the crowd of men approach the Donnelly farmhouse as the dogs at the Whalen farms began barking. That was not unusual, for they always barked when anyone passed by.

The men surrounded the house, and James Carroll stepped up to the kitchen door and slowly pushed it open. Doors were not locked in Biddulph or anywhere else in Ontario in those days. All was quiet inside, only the sound of heavy breathing breaking the silence. Carroll tiptoed into the house. He was quite familiar with its interior, for in the previous few weeks he had gone through it on searches more than once. Carroll made out the form of Tom Donnelly lying in his bed in the little room off the kitchen. He was sleeping heavily. Carroll pulled out the handcuffs he had borrowed from Constable Hodgins, and walking quietly over to the bed, he deftly slipped them on the wrists of his unsuspecting victim and snapped them closed. Tom Donnelly roused himself.

"What the hell?" he murmured, trying to shake the sleep from his brain and confounded at finding himself handcuffed.

"You're under arrest," said Carroll. "Now get up and light a candle, will you?"

Tom Donnelly sat up. As soon as his mother had heard Carroll's voice, she got up and came bustling into the kitchen. She picked up a candle from the kitchen table and lit it. "Bridget, Bridget," she called out. "Get up and light a fire."

Bridget Donnelly jumped out of bed and began to dress. Carroll picked up the candle from the table, went into the front room, and looked into the bedroom where old Mr. Donnelly and young Johnny O'Connor slept. Jim Donnelly stirred himself.

"Where's Jack?" Carroll asked.

"He's not home," the old man muttered sitting up, and in doing so throwing the bedcovers over on the young boy.

Bridget Donnelly had donned her clothes and gone out into the kitchen, where Mrs. Donnelly handed her a knife to make shavings for a fire.

"Where's Jack?' Carroll asked again;

"I told you before, Jack's not home," Jim Don-

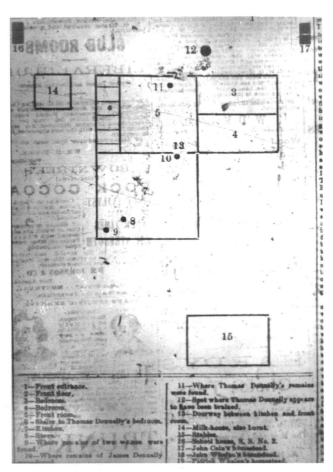

Plan of the Donnelly farmhouse (*London Daily Advertiser*)

nelly answered gruffly, and then added, "What have you got against us now?"

"I've got another charge against you," Carroll said.

The old man began to pull on his pants. Carroll had stepped back from the door of the bedroom and waited in the front room, holding the candle. He whistled as he waited while the old man ducked into his pant braces and ambled out into the kitchen carrying his boots. When he saw his son in shackles he stopped, surprised.

"What? Tom, are you handcuffed?" he exclaimed.

"Yes," Tom answered. "He thinks he's smart."

The old man slipped on his boots in the kitchen and clumped back into the bedroom.

"Where's me coat?" he said in a raised voice. "Does anyone know where me coat is?"

Mrs. Donnelly answered that she did not. Jim

Donnelly groped around the bedroom in the halflight.

"Here," he called out to Carroll, "hold the light here while I dress, will ye?"

Carroll came over to the door of the bedroom again, still holding the candle in his hand. Johnny O'Connor, now fully awake at the commotion, picked up the greatcoat from the bed where he lay and held it out for the old man, as if to say, "Here it is." Jim Carroll looked right at the boy and saw him hand the coat to old Donnelly, who took it and went out to the kitchen again, this time followed closely by Carroll. Tom Donnelly had by this time put on his pants, having got his mother to undo and refasten his brace buckles, which he could not slip over his shoulders because of the handcuffs .

"All right," said Tom Donnelly, raising his voice. "Read the warrant."

"There's lots of time for that," Carroll said in a loud, excited voice.

The next instant Carroll let out a whoop. The door to the kitchen burst open and the crowd of men rushed in. They started whooping and howling. With their clubs they began at once to beat the old man and the old woman and Tom Donnelly. Stricken with terror, the girl Bridget flew out of the kitchen and into the front room, heading for the narrow stairway to the loft. Johnny O'Connor jumped out of the bed and ran after her but was brought up short when Bridget slammed the door shut behind her at the bottom of the stairway. Without even trying to open the door, he quickly whirled around and ran back into the old man's bedroom. As he passed the doorway to the kitchen he caught a fleeting glimpse of a wild and bloody melee in which the three Donnellys were being battered. Several of the men, including Jack Quigley, wielded their clubs so effectively that they were ever after referred to as "Clubby", while Long Jim Toohey was said to have suffered a black eye in the melee, a bad omen for him, for a black eye was said by the old Irish to be the devil's mark. Johnny O'Connor scrambled under the bed, cowering behind a large clothes basket that was tucked under it.

In the kitchen old Jim Donnelly fell in a few moments, his skull broken in by repeated blows at the hands of his old nemesis, James Maher. Mrs. Donnelly was a large and strong woman and her long, sturdy arms fended off the initial blows.[2]

As for Tom, as soon as the men rushed in he began to whoop and thresh about wildly, flailing away with his feet as well as his manacled hands. He ducked and kicked and swung, and, bursting through his attackers, he ran through the centre doorway of the house into the front room and through it to the front door. With barely a pause, he put his shoulder to the door and it almost came off its hinges as it burst open. He ran out, the whole time whooping at the top of his voice. But waiting outside the front door was, among others, Tom Ryder with pitchfork at the ready. Tom Donnelly did not get more than ten feet from the door when he was struck down. He raised himself up on his knees, but the pitchfork was thrust into him again and again. "Oh! Oh! Oh!" he cried out and fell crumpled to the ground. The blood spurted out in great gobs from the multiple wounds left by the steel tines, and in a moment a great spreading patch of red stained the freshly fallen snow under him.

Inside, Johannah Donnelly shrieked at the top of her voice above the howls of her attackers. She fought courageously but was beaten to her knees. "A minute to pray," she gasped.

"Pray, you bitch," Carroll replied, "you have prayed too long already."

He struck at her. On her knees she crawled, trying to follow her son through the doorway, but made it only inside the front room and fell there.

Outside, young James Maher, James Toohey, and Patrick Quigley picked up Tom Donnelly and carried him back, face down and feet first, into the house. Johnny O'Connor heard the handcuffs rattle in the front room as they struck the floor, and peeking out from under the bed, he saw Tom Donnelly's stockinged feet. The men stood around the prostrate form almost as if in disbelief at what they had finally done. Donnelly let out a moan.

Someone cried out, "Hit this fellow on the head with that shovel and break his head open."

One of the men – it was either Jim Toohey or Pat Quigley – stepped up and struck the fallen man three or four heavy blows on the head.

"Fetch the candle here." said James Carroll.

He reached down, fumbled for the keyhole, and unlocked the handcuffs, taking them off the unconscious man's wrists and putting them in his pocket.

"Where's the girl?" someone asked.

"Look upstairs," another answered.

Several of the men tramped upstairs. There was a short scuffle, a muffled scream of terror by the girl, and the men returned in a few moments, one of them carrying her limp body across his shoulders. "It's all right," he said.

Bridget Donnelly was carried into the kitchen and dumped over the body of James Donnelly, lying senseless at the northwest angle of the kitchen near the stove.

During the wild melee no one had paid any attention to Jim Donnelly's little dog, which had begun to yelp in terror when the men burst into the house. Now, one of the men went over to the dog, which was still barking, and cracked its head with one swipe of his club. John Purtell ran over with his axe and chopped off the dog's head, kicking it almost under the stove. Old Jim Donnelly, lying a few feet away, groaned.

The men then dumped the coal oil from the lamps, splashing it around the room and on the beds, and set fire to it. "It will burn off and go out," one of them said.

More fuel was splashed around and they waited for the fire to get going. When the flames were blazing, the whole troop tramped out of the house through the kitchen door where they had come in.

Johnny O'Connor waited a few moments in terror, hardly daring to breathe and scarcely believing that they had left. What if they should change their minds and come back, he thought, terror-stricken. The flames above him leapt higher and he realized he would have to get out or be burned to death. Scrambling out from under the bed, he seized his coat and tried to beat out the flames with it. But the fire was beyond beating out or smothering. Then he thought he heard Tom Donnelly breathing in the front room. He quickly pulled on his pants and went to run out of the bedroom but hesitated for a split second, not knowing which way to turn. Tom Donnelly lay within two feet of the front door, his head pointing

Johnny O'Connor. This photograph was taken within a day or two of the Donnelly massacre and shows the boy posed in the clothes he wore when he escaped the burning house. (*Maclean's* magazine)

north. Johnny thought he heard him breathing but he wasn't sure. Then came the flashing thought – worse still, he might be dead! This frightened him even more and he bounded to the left, away from the front door. But at the doorway between the front room and kitchen he was struck again with the utmost panic when he found the door almost shut. He shoved with all his might and it opened, but in pushing the door he stepped on the body of Mrs. Donnelly. She groaned, and sheer terror seized the boy. His heart pounding, he squeezed through the doorway and raced through the kitchen and out into the open air. On his way through, he saw that the door to Tom's bedroom was open, and he caught a glimpse of the severed head of Jim Donnelly's little dog near the stove.

Johnny O'Connor hardly felt the cold ground on his bare feet. Racing to the corner of the house, he hesitated for an instant when he heard the crowd of men in the distance from the direction of the Donnelly Schoolhouse. But they were far enough away, and he raced up the laneway, over the fence, across the road, and through the gate of Mr. Patrick Whalen. Up the Whalen laneway he fled. In the darkness he ran past the house and was approaching the barn when he heard the Whalen dog barking behind him and realized he had gone too far. Turning around, he ran back to the house and pushed the door open. "Get up! Get up!" he shouted. Mrs. Whalen came out of the bedroom in her nightclothes.

"Call up the boys," he cried. "There's a fire. Call up the boys to quench it!"

"What?" stammered Mrs. Whalen. "What is it? Quench what fire?"

"Over at Donnelly's," the boy exclaimed, wondering why Mrs. Whalen hesitated so. Mrs. Whalen's face clouded darkly at the boy.

"We'd all be killed if we went over there, boy," she blurted at him. "Now simmer down and tell us what happened."

Johnny O'Connor jabbered excitedly, "A lot of people came with blackened faces and wearing women's dresses and drove the Donnellys into the woods. Tom's body is lying there in the house, and they've set it on fire."

Grizzled old Patrick Whalen came out of his room to hear what was happening.

"Did you see anyone?" Mrs. Whalen asked.

"Yes."

"Who ?"

"I saw Jim Carroll."

"Whisht, boy." Mrs. Whalen exclaimed sharply to the boy. "Shut up or you'll get into trouble."

They looked at the clock. It was a little beyond half past one.

Meanwhile, after leaving the Donnelly house, the mob held a short discussion near the Donnelly Schoolhouse about what they would do next. It was quickly decided that now the work was started it must be finished. They would have to get that devil of a cripple, Will Donnelly. Jim Keefe, too, would have to be finished off, for he was too good a friend of Donnelly's. They immediately set out for Whalen's Corners. It was a distance of one hundred and twenty feet short of three miles by sideroad and concession line. As they trudged along, they cast many a fearful glance back over their shoulders to watch the progress of the fire back at the Donnelly house. The flames soon licked up to each of the bodies lying in the house. The four, if they had not already given up the ghost, all soon died of suffocation. Before long, the blaze lit up the night sky of Biddulph.

Over in the fifth concession to the west of the Donnellys', in the Protestant section of Biddulph, John Dagg was tending a sick member of his family. He saw the light of a fire in the east over the trees but could not tell exactly where it originated. Five miles further to the west, Joe Simpson saw the fire in the early morning hours across the flat fields; from that distance it appeared as "a small, tall blaze".

Over at Will Donnelly's place at Whalen's Corners, Will and Jim Keefe had drawn firewood from the latter's woodlot in Usborne, from a maple tree about sixteen inches in diameter. As the tree had only been felled a couple of weeks earlier, it was green, but good for slow burning through the long winter nights. After drawing the last load late in the afternoon, Will's father-in-law, John Kennedy, Sr., dropped in for a short visit. He stayed for about half an hour, took tea, then left about dark. After supper John Donnelly came with the pony. He took nothing to eat, for he had had his tea at home, but he stayed in the kitchen to chat with Norah while Will and Keefe went out to the woodshed behind the kitchen to split wood for the night. They were still out there around nine o'clock when Big Martin Hogan dropped in for a visit. Hogan had been threshing at Heenan's but had finished there and had moved his machine down to Morkin's at Whalen's Corners for the next job. Keefe and Will soon entered, each with an armful of wood which they dropped into the wood box, and then they all sat and talked.

A half-hour later Norah put a chunk of wood into the stove and went to bed. The four men continued their discussion. "We stayed up talking about the Vigilance Committee," Will said. Keefe finally left for home at half past eleven. The remaining three men continued in conversation for a while longer, and when Hogan got up to go Will said, "Mr. Morkin has a large family and they will all be in bed. You had better stay here."

Hogan agreed to spend the night, and he and John retired to the inside bedroom where Will spread a new buffalo robe over the bed.

"You might need this," he said, pointing to the holes in the ceiling where the plaster had fallen off.

"Well, there's plenty of fresh air in here, any-way," said John as they settled into bed, Hogan on the inside.

As he wound the clock Will noticed it was half past midnight. Putting another heavy stick of wood into the stove, he went to bed. His wife, then between four and five months pregnant, had taken the outside position in the four-foot-wide bed, and Will tried playfully to nudge her over. "Push in," he said, but when Norah did not move, he climbed over and settled down on the inside.

It was about two hours later that the Peace Society reached Whalen's Corners. Once again, as at the Donnelly homestead, the men surrounded the house. This time, however, none of them was anxious to make entry. They determined to get Donnelly into the open instead.

A few of the men went to the stable, which

Will Donnelly's house at Whalen's Corners where John Donnelly died (Montreal *Standard*)

housed Will's prize breeding stallion, Jack's Alive. They beat the horse mercilessly, in order to lure someone from the house, but to no avail. No one inside stirred. Martin McLaughlin and young Jim Ryder then approached the side door of the house, McLaughlin carrying a rifle and Ryder a shotgun. Creeping under the small verandah which sheltered the side door, young Jim Ryder called out, "Will! Will! Fire! Fire! Open the door!"

Will Donnelly heard it and woke. He recognized the voice as that of young Ryder, whom he had known since the young man's birth. John Donnelly also heard it and roused himself. He got up, and as he walked through his brother's bedroom toward the door he mumbled, "Will, someone is calling for you. I'll let them in."

A voice outside shouted, "Is that you, Will?"

John replied, "Yes."

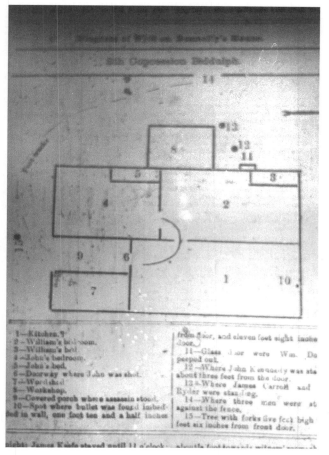

Floor plan or Will Donnelly's house (*London Daily Advertiser*)

As he opened the door a blaze of lead from each gun blasted into his chest and groin The shot from Ryder's shotgun blew over thirty holes in John's chest, piercing his lungs and breaking his collarbone as well as several ribs both front and back. The bullet from McLaughlin's rifle passed clean through his groin and dug itself into the frame of the little window at the rear of the kitchen. The wadding from Ryder's shotgun, a piece of newspaper about the size of a human hand, glanced off John's forehead and fell into the room.

Mortally wounded, John Donnelly fell back into the kitchen. "Oh! Oh! Will, I am shot!" he moaned.

McLaughlin and Ryder ran immediately toward the front of the house, on the way firing seven more shots into the air in quick succession.

Inside the house Big Martin Hogan and William and Norah Donnelly all sat up in their beds. "Call Hogan," William Donnelly whispered to his wife.

Hogan, sitting motionless, hissed, "Keep quiet. It's you they want." He continued to sit unmoving on the edge of the bed for two long minutes.

"Oh, Will," Norah cried out, "I can hear the blood in Johnny's throat. I'm going to get up and go to him if I am shot for it."

As she got out of bed she caught a glimpse of her husband reaching over to lift up a corner of the blind. Will peered through the window and saw John Kennedy and Jim Carroll standing near the corner of the house, Carroll being only about nine feet from the bed in which he sat. Beyond the front fence he saw three men, whom he took to be Big Mike Heenan, William Carroll, and Young Pat Ryder.

"Brother-in-law rests easy at last," said Kennedy with a note of finality in his voice.

Carroll said, "What next?"

William Donnelly lowered the blind. Norah had lit a lamp which was resting on the floor of the bedroom. She screamed when she saw John Donnelly bleeding to death in the kitchen. "Oh, Will," she cried, "He's dying."

"Draw him in," he whispered to her.

She tried to pull John into the bedroom but could hardly move him.

Will addressed his next whisper to Hogan.

"John's shot," he said. "Pull him in here."

Hogan got down on all fours, crept out to John Donnelly, and dragged him into the bedroom, his body leaving a bloody trail on the floor. John Donnelly managed to mumble a few words. "My God, Will, I am murdered," he said. "May the Lord have mercy on my soul."

Norah looked at Hogan. "Is he dying?" she asked.

"Yes," he answered.

She went back into the kitchen and got a piece of blessed candle and gave it to Hogan, who cupped it into John's hand and held it there. Norah went back to the kitchen for some holy water. John Donnelly died in about five minutes.

Hogan stayed crouched on the floor, then pulled back under the bed in which William Donnelly and his wife had been sleeping. He shook so much that the whole bed trembled.

"Will, get up," Norah said.

Hogan hissed at her, "Hold your tongue! Hold your tongue! Let him be where he is. What good can it do?"

Will merely said, almost to himself, "Good God, I always thought they would do this."

The three of them stood huddled in the house without moving for almost three hours.

The Peace Society of Biddulph trudged onward in the snow, past William Donnelly's and towards the farm of Big Jim Keefe, which lay just inside Usborne Township. They were halfway there when Jim Feeheley confronted them.

"I helped to put one son of a bitch out of the way," he later said about his participation in the butchery. "And I know others who put four more away." But he now said simply, "There's been enough bloodshed tonight, boys. Let's go home."

And they did. Jim Feeheley agreed that "The Donnellys were a hard lot." But he added, "There is not many of them left, God damn them."

Thus ended the days of the Donnellys in the Township of Biddulph.

AFTERMATH

After the better part of an hour had elapsed, old Pat Whalen went over to his son John's house 184 yards distant. John Whalen was "shaking like a leaf", but they finally screwed up enough courage to go over to the Donnelly house. Mrs. Whalen got Johnny O'Connor some shoes and stockings, and he accompanied them, along with young Joe Whalen. They could not get close to the front door because of the heat and smoke but could plainly see near it a great pool of blood.

Peering through the windows of the house, they saw that little could be done, to save the bodies, glimpses of which they caught through the flames. One of the windows almost bowled old Whalen over as it popped out of the blazing building from the heat which had built up inside. The four of them could do nothing more than move away from the building a light buggy that had been left near the house. They then returned to Pat Whalen's, and Johnny O'Connor went to bed with the Whalen boy to await the dawn.

At the Donnellys' the entire house was soon enveloped in flames. When the floor boards burned away, Tom Donnelly's charred body settled down upon the steaming apples and potatoes in the little cellar below him, the head eventually separating from the body. The same thing happened to the other bodies.[1] All that remained of the Donnelly house after several hours were the two logs that formed the front steps.

The Vigilance Committee had not doubted for a moment that they had killed Will Donnelly. But Will was alive and cursing his enemies. "Yes, the skulking bastards," he swore, "they thought they had put me out of the way when they fired the shots, but I will live to see this whole thing through."

Will waited in his house until almost dawn before dressing and going next door to his neighbour, William Walker. At his request, Walker checked the tracks in the snow with him for future testimony in court. Donnelly dug out of the window frame the bullet which had passed through his brother John, and picked up for preservation as evidence the wadding from the buckshot, which consisted of pieces of the newspaper the *Catholic Record*. Then he checked the stallion in the stable, found it relatively unharmed, and rode it over to Jim Keefe's to tell him of John's death. On his return, he asked Walker to drive the cutter over to the old homestead to inform his parents. Walker went and found the Donnelly house burned to the ground, then stopped in at Whalen's just long enough to tell them of the other death at Whalen's Corners.

Early in the morning, just as it was getting light, old Pat Sullivan came south along the Roman Line to investigate the fire he had seen in the night. He got as far as Thompson's, where William Thompson was getting ready to take some grain for milling to Exeter that day.

"Where's the fire?" Sullivan asked Thompson.

Thompson seemed unconcerned. "Over at Donnelly's," he replied simply.

"Bedad, I'll go home thin," said old man Sullivan and returned quickly to his own home.

William Thompson later claimed that he was not aware that his next-door neighbours had been murdered until he had travelled thirty miles to Exeter, where he was informed of it by John Farmer, a storekeeper there.

James Carroll had court business in Granton that day. The Donnelly arson case was coming up, as well as his own case against old Pat Whalen for having taken an axe to him. According to Mrs. Thompson, when the Carroll brothers woke up next morning and saw only smoking ashes where the Donnelly house had stood, the sole comment they made was, "It's a cold morning to be without a house!" James Carroll rode his pony to Granton early in the morning past the smoking ruins. On the way he passed William Casey, the magistrate,

also on his way to Granton to sit on the cases in question. Pat Whalen, too, went to Granton to tidy up the Carroll axe case, although he had previously arranged through an intermediary, Martin Curtin, to settle the matter.

Johnny O'Connor had breakfast at Whalen's. Some of John Carroll's family, some of the Tooheys, and other neighbours had come over and, with the arrival of the news of John's death brought by Walker, there was great excitement in the household. In the confusion, Johnny O'Connor decided to get home as fast as he could and, slipping on a hat of Theresa Whalen's, he went back over to the Donnelly farm, got a horse out of the stable, and rode it home to Lucan.

On seeing him enter the house wearing the girl's hat, his mother burst out laughing and asked him where his overcoat was. Young Johnny O'Connor thereupon broke into tears. He told his mother through his sobs that his coat had been burned in the Donnelly house and that the Donnellys themselves had been burned up with it, and the house destroyed over their heads.

Michael O'Connor took his son down to Porte's post office and sent telegrams to Patrick Donnelly in Thorold and to Robert and Jenny, to inform them of the awful news. The police authorities in London were notified. The word of the multiple murders spread like wildfire, and the entire village began to buzz with excitement.

Soon after arriving in Granton that morning, James Carroll and William Casey experienced a double shock. First, they learned that young Johnny O'Connor had already related events of the massacre. Then they learned that Will Donnelly was still alive! Astounded by this news, Carroll became frightened. He immediately hired a horse and buggy from one of the Granton hotel proprietors, Thomas Culbert, and drove to Whalen's Corners to verify the latter fact with his own eyes. Others of the Vigilance Committee were equally astounded. Martin Darcey and his friends, being afraid to check for themselves, sent a little boy to Whalen's Corners to bring back a report.

John's body and the bodies of the other four, scraped up out of the ashes, were taken to the home of Michael O'Connor. Undertaker John

Murdy was called in to prepare them for burial, his bill for burying John Donnelly coming to thirtyfive dollars and for the other four bodies four dollars.

Pat Donnelly arrived from Thorold and a wake was held on two successive nights, February 4 and 5, one for the four resting in one coffin and the other for John Donnelly alone.

Jenny Currie arrived by stage from London at six o'clock on Thursday evening. When she entered the small log house and saw the coffins of her dead parents and brothers, she went into hysterics, continuing in this state for nearly the whole of that night. "The unfortunate girl being the observed of all observers, scream after scream is wafted out on the night air, the reverberanon of which strikes terror in the hearts of the listeners," wrote one eye-witness.

A couple of hours after midnight on Friday, Robert Donnelly arrived from St. Thomas. "He wept like a child," it was reported, "and finally fell fainting at the coffin of his brother John." After a while he regained his composure and went over to the other coffin.

> After gazing intently at them for some time, he picked up the burnt heart of his father and kissed it tenderly. He then performed the same act on the liver of his brother, Thomas.[2]

But his brother William said, "Don't be a fool," and directed him to be taken to the house next door, which also belonged to the O'Connor family.

The funeral, on Friday, February 6, was a large one. Five hundred people had assembled at the O'Connor house and the procession which set off for the church was over half a mile in length and contained about sixty or seventy teams of horses and sleighs. Wild rumours circulated in the village. One was that Father John Connolly not only had refused to allow the family to be buried in St. Patrick's Cemetery but had ordered the disinterment of the remains of young James Donnelly and Michael Donnelly, and that the old corpses and the recent ones would all then be buried in the Anglican Church Cemetery. All of the rumours proved to be false.

Father Connolly met the two caskets at the

John Murdy, the Lucan undertaker who prepared the bodies of the Donnellys for burial (E Murdy)

church door and preceded them up the aisle followed by the members of the family and the rest of the mourners. The mass for the dead having been concluded, the church fell silent. The priest turned to the congregation at the foot of the altar. He began to speak in a voice low and choked with emotion. "My beloved brethren," he began haltingly, "you are in the presence of the most solemn scene that has ever been brought before the gaze of humanity." Then he stopped, overcome by emotion. "My heart is broken," he cried out in a flood of tears, and turning his back on the people he leaned on the altar and wept like a child for several minutes .

> At the same time sobs broke forth from Mrs. Curry and the woman sitting next to her, while Patrick and Robert Donnelly, who sat in the seat before them, although they managed to suppress their tears, were

observed to shake like branches in a gale. William Donnelly's features were tightly set, showing the iron will that he is possessed of, but still he was not unmoved.[3]

Father Connolly finally recovered his composure and turned again to address the assembly. He again began haltingly, but as he spoke he gradually regained more and more control. He talked of the laws of God and man, the spilling of innocent blood, and the day of Judgment. He mentioned the victims by name, and said:

It might be thought that I was not in friendship with the family. But I can say truly that I have no enmity against them. With the old people I always agreed, particularly with the old woman. She came frequently to confession, and it was only on last Christmas Eve that she told me of all the sorrows and troubles of her life.[4]

Father Connolly again almost broke down with emotion at this point, but continued:

On that night the old woman told me she was trying to get her boys to come to confession. But they did not come and here is the consequence. O, God of Heaven, forgive them.

At this point he was again overcome and once more leaned on the altar and wept. The entire church was again filled with the weeping and sobbing of the women.

Patrick Donnelly then rose from his seat in the congregation and said in a loud and clear voice, "Father Connolly, I want you to give a detailed account." The priest turned and appeared quite astonished at the sound of Patrick Donnelly's voice speaking out in church in that way. He hesitated and seemed confused. Then he said, "Perhaps it would be just as well that I should tell something of my trouble with the boys."

Father Connolly then went on to relate the incident of the taking out of Kelly's horse, the letter which William Donnelly wrote to him, his conversation with the boys at Whalen's threshing and how he felt deceived by them. "As to the formation of the Vigilance Committee," he went on,

I had not much to do. I was not present at any of its meetings, but I had unbounded confidence in the men

that belonged to it, and believe that they are incapable of committing such a terrible murder as this one. It was outside of them, and my suspicions rest on others. I can't understand how it took place.

The priest concluded by pointing out the terrible disgrace that had been brought upon the parish by the murders and wondered if the people of the district could ever live it down. The ceremony was concluded by his blessing the coffins. They were taken out and consigned to earth in the family plot at the rear of the cemetery beside the church. After the funeral the Donnelly family members were invited to tea with the priest and they all accepted the invitation. In private, the priest expressed to them his personal sorrow at the turn of events in Biddulph .

William Thomas Trounce Williams had assumed the position of Chief of Police in the city of London in October 1878, having been recommended for the position by Chief Justice Harrison as a result of his commendable part in the suppression of the Catholic riots in Toronto. He took charge of the investigation of the massacre of the Donnellys. Arrests were soon made. Taken into custody were James Carroll, John Kennedy, Jr., Martin McLaughlin, Thomas Ryder, James Maher, Sr., James Maher, Jr., John Darcey, Grouchy Ryder, Pat Ryder, Jr., Michael Heenan, William Carroll, John Purtell, Mrs. James Maher, and the Mahers' hired man, James Shea.

James Carroll was asked, on the pretext of requiring his presence as a constable, to accompany the policemen to Lucan from his Uncle Maher's house. As they drove by the blackened remains of the Donnelly house, one of the police said to him, "There's the remains of Old Decency." Carroll said nothing and refused even to look at the ruins. He was formally arrested in Lucan.

When Detective Murphy brought Michael Heenan in, the latter told the police officer that he believed in lynch law — that it worked well in the western United States and should work in Biddulph, too.

Several of the prisoners were lodged for a time in the tiny cells of the Lucan lock-up, and three or four officers were posted in the little building to guard them. A few anxious moments occurred

Chief W. T. T. Williams

James Shea, sketch by Robert Harris (PEI)

when a special constable of the village went home for supper, taking with him the only key to the little lock-up and leaving prisoners and guards all cooped up inside.

When young Paddy Ryder was arrested and was being taken to London by Detective Enoch Murphy, the latter said to him, "This is a sad affair."

"I believe in Texas law," Ryder replied.

The Mahers' hired man, James Shea, was an old pensioner, a British Army veteran. By the time he was taken into custody the cells of the London Gaol were so full that he was placed in the corridor of the male cells for a few days. He turned out to be a garrulous and good-natured old man, who whiled away the time by telling war stories. In a few days he was released, along with the senior James Maher, Mrs. James Maher, and Pat "Grouchy" Ryder. The others were also released except for James Carroll, Martin McLaughlin, John Kennedy, Thomas Ryder, James Ryder, and John Purtell.

The day after the murders John Cutt was working in Thomas Ryder's bush. A tree fell on him, and he lay pinned under it for four hours before he was finally found and carried out of the bush by his brother Tom and Mike McLaughlin. He died the next night. On the night of the Donnelly massacre, it was John Cutt and his brother Robert who had waited in vain for Thomas Ryder to return home, and it was the Cutts who stated that when Long Jim Toohey shortly after the murders returned a saddle he had borrowed from the family, he had a black eye. The Cutts left Biddulph that summer.

The Caswell boys returned home four or five days after the murders. The tavernkeeper at Sutherland Corners, near the place where they lived, remembered seeing them come back in a borrowed buggy and by a strange route, the buggy being returned by Mrs. Caswell about two weeks later. The Caswells were reported to have told some strange stories about the Donnelly murders, but the boys clammed up after a few days and ever after refused to talk about it. A coat and a shirt with blood on the front and the sleeves were found hidden in the woods on the route the boys were supposed to have taken.

When the Biddulph Township Council held a meeting on February 10, the week following the Donnelly massacre, Patrick J. Dewan of the Catholic Settlement did not put in an appearance. There were rumours he had suffered an injury about a week before and was recuperating.

A belief was held by many that a photograph of the eyes of a murder victim, when enlarged, would reveal the reflection of the murderer, and one of the Lucan photographers, John S. Thom, did in fact photograph John Donnelly in his coffin. It was said, however, that the murderers felt quite safe on this account because of the darkness in which the deed had been committed.

Reporters from all over the country flocked to Lucan. The villagers soon became wary of them. The following dialogue was taken down by one reporter:

"Bez yees a reporter?"
"I am."
"Then I tell yees all o' yees ought to be kicked into *hell*. Yees be all as bad as one another!"[5]

About ten days after the murder of his parents and his brothers, William Donnelly received the following letter which had been posted at Sarnia. It read:

Port Huron, Michigan
February 11th, 1880

William Donnelly — You and your relatives have been a disgrace and a curse to our country. Your chances are favourable to leave now. If you delay our friends will assist you so take warning. If your brother Patrick remains at Lucan he will take his chances with our friends for assistance when we think proper.
Yours truly,
ONE WHO SAW YOUR MOTHER AND FATHER FALL.[6]

Will suspected that the letter had been posted by a man named Lewis, who had been working with Patrick Breen up to the time of the murders but had disappeared from Biddulph right after and had apparently gone to Port Huron.

Another letter was sent to William Donnelly from near Barrie, Ontario. Will suspected, from its style and format, that it had come from "the retired sailor", John J. Blake, the London lawyer whose brother was a leading member of the Biddulph Vigilance Committee. This letter read:

Mulmur, Feb. 8, 1880
Wm. Donnelly, Lucan
Sir —...You know well enough whom the slugs were intended for that took effect in your brother John. It was a slight miscarriage but it was as well to get Jack out of the way. There may be a slug or two left for you if you don't be careful...I am not a man that does anything by halves. My motto is "root and branch" when a family had to be exterminated by reason of their depredatory and incendiary acts, and I believe you are a member of such a family....
Yours warningly,
ONE WHO KNOWS WHAT HE KNOWS.[7]

Still another letter, written in a disguised hand on a piece of paper torn from a commercial ledger, read:

TO ROBERT AND WILLIAM DONNELLY:
This is to notify you that the Honest and Law-abiding People of Lucan wishes you to remove from this villeg at once, or you May be Moved some knight & your colegs will be remembered. Your Brother Jim was shot here by our polece man in 1877 in the act of incendrey cans, your rowdey ism in our streets waylaying & robbery, burnings, cutting our horses throats, Murdering. Dan Clark's murder is not forgotten, Deluding our femails, robbing them of their character & other bad acts.
A FRIEND TO LUCAN AN SITIZEN.[8]

Some of the people said of these letters, "Bill Donnelly wrote them himself to stir up public feeling in his favour."

One letter-writer to the *Globe* stated in apparent seriousness:

...Nine out of ten thinking people that I have conversed with in Oxford and Middlesex Counties believe William Donnelly to be the murderer....[9]

The St. Mary's *Argus* said:

No one regrets that the community is rid of most of a family who have made themselves a terror....[10]

The *Exeter Times* was a little more charitable.

We knew, personally, several members of the family, and had their lives been cast in different places, had they but pursued a different course in life, and possessed more charitable feelings towards their neighbours, they would not have come to such an ignominious end...but their excellent talents were distorted by unbridled passion.[11]

HEARINGS

Coroner Thomas Hossack of Lucan immediately began the inquest and rounded up fifteen of the villagers to form the jury. They were William Henry, shoemaker; John Bawden, constable, builder, and village councillor; James Mayo, labourer; William Benn, druggist; J. W. Orme, merchant; William Pratt, pop manufacturer; John Judge, blacksmith; Thomas Cubbins, miller; George Kernick, engineer; Thomas Robinson, carpenter; William Quigley, shoemaker; Jacob Palmer, carpenter; John Maguire, carriage builder; Henry Wilson, clerk; and E. R. Hodgins, bricklayer. The inquest opened in the Lucan Public School, in a large upstairs room known as the Town Hall, at 7 o'clock in the evening of Thursday, February 5. Only the evidence of the three Whalens — Patrick, John, and Joseph — was taken at that first session, and on the advice of the Crown Attorney the hearing was then adjourned to the following Wednesday.

Public opinion in "the troubled district" was typified by the following comments heard in the streets. Said one woman, "It's no more than they deserved," while another old lady was heard to say, "Shure, we're agin the law and we'll not lave it a leg to shtand on." And a Justice of the Peace of the neighbourhood said, "I wonder what they are making all the fuss about? Why don't they leave the two sides to themselves? Things will settle down by and by."

When the inquest was resumed on February 11, the funerals had taken place and most of the suspects had been arrested and lodged in London Gaol. The aggressive and pugnacious Hugh Macmahon of London was retained by lawyer John J. Blake as the leading defence counsel. The two lawyers travelled to Lucan for the resumption of the inquest. This session was held in the Council Room above the lock-up, because the school trustees refused a second entry to the Town Hall room. It was again crowded from wall to wall with jurors, lawyers, witnesses, reporters, and spectators.

The crowd became visibly excited when the diminutive Johnny O'Connor pushed his way through the throng and picked up the Bible to be sworn as a witness. Wearing an old brown overcoat and with his hair shorn since the day of the massacre, he told his story:

Thomas Donnelly came down to father's on Tuesday morning about 3:30 or 4 to get our cutter to go to Cranton; Mr. Donnelly came down to father's to get some things he had left there; then old Mr. Donnelly asked to let me go down and stay till next day.... Tom and John Donnelly put in the horses; Tom and John then came in and sat down for a while, and Bridget Donnelly went for some apples, and then went and got supper; then John went out and got the pony, threw the harness over his neck and went for the cutter...after taking apples old Mr. Donnelly told me to get off my shoes and go to bed with him; then Tom said I was to go to bed with him; but the old gentleman made me go to bed with him; I then went and while in bed I heard someone talking in the kitchen; the old man and Bridget thought it was James Feeheley; then went to sleep; between twelve and two o'clock a man came into the house to arrest the old man and Jack; the old man said Jack was not in...the old man dressed himself....[1]

"Do you know the man who came in?" asked Crown Attorney Hutchinson.
"Yes," replied the witness.
"Who was it?"
"It was James Carroll, the constable."

A charge of electric excitement ran through the room. Hugh Macmahon immediately jumped up and objected to the continuation of the hearing unless the person named were present. The Crown Attorney disagreed and instructed the Coroner to proceed. After some legal wrangling the examination continued:

Carroll stood at the door holding the candle...the old man got his coat and went out into the kitchen.... Tom then said, "Yes, he thinks he's smart," and asked Carroll to read the warrant, when Carroll answered, "There's lots of time for that"; then a whole crowd jumped in and began to hammer them with sticks...then Tom ran through the front room.... Bridget ran upstairs; I went to run after but she shut the door and I went back and got under the bed and hid behind a clothes basket; they started to hammer Tom outside...then carried Tom into the house again.... then heard someone say, "Hit that fellow with a spade and break his skull open"; Tom was then hit three or four times with a spade.... I saw the man Ryder and Purtell standing near the bedroom door.[2]

Once again, when Johnny O'Connor named Ryder and Purtell, a wave of excitement swept through the room. The youthful witness concluded his testimony by telling of the setting on fire of the bedclothes, the departure of the men, and his flight over to Whalen's house. The inquest was then adjourned for one week.

Reporters from everywhere continued flocking to Lucan. Gordon Brown of the Toronto *Globe* called a young artist named Robert Harris into his office and instructed him to go to London for on-the-spot sketches of the prisoners. Harris was at that time in his early twenties but later became Canada's most famous portrait artist. He reported

Hugh Macmahon

Johnny O'Connor, sketch by Robert Harris. The boy had had his hair short-cropped since the night of terror at the Donnelly farmhouse. (PEI)

his experiences in a letter to his mother a few days later:

>...I got into the prison after some trouble and saw the first batch, four in a cell, three in another. I got my book out and jotted one fellow down. They saw it and knew what I wanted so there was a general covering up. However I got the ones I wanted in spite of their efforts. In the next cell I found two old villains lying on their stomachs with their heads covered over. Their mouths gave me a store of good stout language and bade me begone. I resorted to all kinds of tricks but could not get a look at them.[3]

But Harris persisted, following the prisoners to Lucan by train on the day the adjourned inquest was to resume. The prisoners themselves had been dispatched by a double rig by way of the Proof Line, and upon Harris's arrival at the Clandeboye train station he found the Hawkshaw Omnibus Line to Lucan temporarily out of operation, necessitating a two-and-a-half-mile walk through mud to reach the village. On his arrival he learned that Coroner Hossack was ill and the inquest had again been adjourned. Harris rented a rig to follow the prisoners back to London and induced the constables in charge to stop for a drink at one of the taverns.

>The prisoners tried to keep their faces covered but I nailed them and returned to Lucan triumphant. Next morning the *Globe* reporter and I went out to the scene where four of the people were killed and burnt and I got a sketch of the place.

When more of the prisoners were picked up, Harris was telegraphed and went back to the jail in London. Again,

>I was received with vollies of oaths.... However, I hung on till feeding time and got a look at the men I wanted just as they were getting their bread and soup...I got one old villain just as he was running from the wicket holding a cake in one hand and a mug in the other. Like Lot's wife he could not help giving one glance over his shoulder as he fled.

The "old villain" caught by Harris was James Maher, Sr. The jailer glanced at the portrait frozen in pencil on Harris's pad and burst out laughing. "Damn it," he exclaimed, "he's took 'im."

The inquest was finally resumed again on Tuesday, March 2. Chief W. T. T. Williams of London was in charge of the little courtroom, which was so crowded that when proper track could not be kept of prisoners, witnesses, and jurors, the Chief got upset.

>...Whilst waiting for Hogan to turn up, momentary confusion was caused by one of the jury leaving the room and the prisoners conversed freely with their friends. Upon resuming, one of the jury was not to be found and the Chief of Police stepped up to the Coroner's table and said, "I want to go home." "What!" said Mr. Hutchinson and the Coroner in one breath, "Are you sick?" The chief, "I am not well...it is utterly impossible to look after both jurymen and prisoners with the staff I have here..."[4]

But the absent juror arrived, order was restored, and the Chief agreed to stay. The inquest evidence was finally completed and the jury retired to consider its verdict.

While the deliberating jurors were nominally locked up for the night, they treated the occasion in a festive spirit, assisted by one of the local merchants who sent up a pailful of beer. Their voices could be heard into the wee hours bawling out the ditty "We won't go home till morning". A verdict was rendered the next day with two jurors dissenting. It stated that the Donnellys were killed "by some party or parties unknown".

In the meantime, the preliminary examination into the criminal charges of murder and arson laid against the prisoners commenced and proceeded at the same time as the drawn-out inquest. The testimony in these proceedings was heard in London before Justices of the Peace John Peters and James Fisher. This hearing, too, went on for several days, sometimes at the City Hall whenever the larger courtroom in the Court House was pre-empted. One day, before court opened, the spectators mistook an inoffensive man named McCabe, who was up on a charge of petty fraud, for one of the Biddulph defendants, and declared, "He looked every inch a murderer."

When the real Biddulph defendants were brought into court, they were so numerous that they occupied not the prisoner's dock but the jury seats. The preliminary hearing began on Saturday, February 21. Crown Attorney Charles Hutchinson appeared along with Edmund Meredith, who had been retained by the Donnelly family. On the defence side were Hugh Macmahon and John J. Blake.

Johnny O'Connor repeated his story and was cross-examined by counsel for the defence. The following occurred in that cross-examination:

Mr. Macmahon — Where is Thomas Ryder?
Witness — There he is. (Pointing to Thomas Ryder.) (Sensation).
Mr. Macmahon — If we were to prove that he was not there you would be very much mistaken, I presume?
Witness — I saw him there, and knew him.[5]

During the cross-examination a dog fight broke out "which enlivened the proceedings and increased the excitement". At other times during the proceedings a little colour was added in other ways:

The friends of the prisoners have been in the habit of supplying them with apples, oranges, etc., in the court. An enthusiastic relative, panting to introduce a novelty in the diet waltzed in with a long walking stick of striped candy in each hand for the prisoners.[6]

Crown Attorney Hutchinson had great difficulty in obtaining information from some of the witnesses, particularly if it involved the machinations of the Biddulph Peace Society, now almost always referred to as the Vigilance Committee. He questioned old Patrick Whalen about it:

Mr. Hutchinson — Did you ever attend any meeting of the Vigilance Committee?
Witness — Yes; I went once to a meeting at the Cedar Swamp School House... did not go to the meeting alone; they were talking funny there; there was nothing done; don't know who summoned me to attend.
Mr. Hutchinson — Try and recollect who you went with.
Witness — I needn't try.
Mr. Hutchinson — But you must try and recollect. Will you swear you don't recollect who it was went to the Committee with you?
Witness — I can not swear, and can't remember.
Mr. Hutchinson — Who were at the meeting?
Witness — I can't tell.
Mr. Hutchinson — Have some regard for the truth, sir, as an honest and respectable man. Remember

you are sworn before God and this audience to tell the truth.
Witness — Sure and would I not be an honest and respectable man?
Mr. Hutchinson — Who were there?
Witness — I passed no remarks upon anyone.
Mr. Hutchinson — Who were there, sir?
Witness, with a fierce look, said — I passed no remarks upon it. (And turned his back to Mr. Hutchinson.)

The Crown Attorney threatened to commit the old man for contempt, and he finally admitted seeing at the meeting James Carroll, John Kennedy, Martin McLaughlin, and Michael Feeheley. But he refused to admit he knew anything of what business was transacted. The questioning continued:

Mr. Hutchinson — Did you sit there like Quakers?
Witness — I don't know how Quakers sit.
Mr. Hutchinson — Quakers sit around without speaking until the spirit moves them. Did you do that?
Witness — Begorra, I did not see any spirits there.[7]

A great many other witnesses were heard. The evidence of William Donnelly was anticipated with great excitement, and he finally gave his testimony on Saturday, February 28, being allowed to sit while testifying, for he had been ill for several days. He stated, in part:

Martin Hogan and his brother John Donnelly stayed in the house that night... wife went to bed before twelve; the three men sat up talking about the Vigilance Committee; about half past two witness was awakened, was disturbed by John coming out of his room... heard someone hallooing, "Fire! Fire! Open the door, Will"; witness heard the door open, and immediately heard two shots fired in rapid succession; John fell back... as he fell he said, "Will! Will! I am shot! May the Lord have mercy on my soul!" ...the next thing witness did was to turn the corner of the blind and look out; saw John Kennedy, James Carroll and James Ryder there... witness saw three men standing near the gate; witness thought it was William Carroll, Michael Heenan and Patrick Ryder, Jr.; would not swear to them... witness swore positively to Kennedy, James Carroll and James Ryder... the voices were those of Martin McLaughlin and James Ryder....[8]

Will Donnelly gave a great deal of other evidence relating to his familiarity with the men he identified, and the background of his enmity with them. He was vigorously cross-examined by Hugh Macmahon. Referring to the day that Donnelly routed the crew with his fiddle, William Donnelly said: "McLaughlin had a blackthorn."

"Oh, well," replied the lawyer, "I carry a blackthorn every day."

"Yes," said Donnelly, "but you don't act like a Zulu, do you?"

Macmahon was content to leave the exchange with the remark, "It seems like Zululand out there in Biddulph sometimes."

The investigative efforts of Police Chief Williams seemed sometimes to be amateurish, and he became almost an object of derision during the proceedings. Said Mary Thompson in the witness-box on one occasion, "He took an old cloak of my grandmother's and wanted to know which of the men had that on." The comment provoked great laughter among the spectators in court. Again, when the Chief in his evidence told of putting a mark opposite the chamber in which he found a certain cartridge of a certain gun, he could not tell which chamber it was because the mark was between the two chambers. "It was one of the two," he said lamely.

Charles Hutchinson, the Crown Attorney, took a strong personal dislike to Hugh Macmahon during the preliminary hearing sessions. The feeling was reciprocated. "I am very angry indeed to see the manner in which the learned counsel for the Crown has conducted this case," Macmahon once proclaimed to the Bench. Some of the spectators applauded the remark, soon followed by hisses from the pro-Donnelly faction. High Constable Groves in charge of courtroom decorum was scandalized:

After Captain Groves had shouted himself hoarse in shouting "Silence in the Court!" order was restored....[9]

On another occasion the Crown Attorney confided to a friend: "I fear I lost my balance yesterday with Macmahon, as he did also. Fools both probably — but the man offends me in every way...."

The preliminary examination was finally concluded and the evidence was held sufficient to put the prisoners on trial. Of the thirteen persons who had been held on suspicion, only eight were committed for trial: James Carroll, John Kennedy, Martin McLaughlin, Thomas Ryder, James Ryder, John Purtell, William Carroll, and Patrick Ryder, Jr. The last two were allowed out on bail. The rest of them settled down to await the assizes. Johnny O'Connor was considered so valuable a witness for the prosecution that he was taken from the charge of his parents and given over to the care of Constable Charles Pope, a black policeman of kindly disposition. The young boy grew quite attached to Pope, but the boy's parents drove both the constable and the Crown Attorney to distraction by attempting to extract privileges and favours, including special living accommodations and cash expense allowances. Johnny O'Connor once told the constable, "As we are not getting our money and Mr. Hutchinson is going back on us, I hope the prisoners get off, and they will get off, too!" Pope finally quit the assignment in exasperation; he thought that the parents drank too much, although he liked Johnny and considered him a decent young lad.

On several occasions Father John Connolly visited his jailed parishioners. And Charles Hutchinson wrote:

E. Meredith attended the Catholic Church in Biddulph last Sunday in company with Blake, the Biddulph counsel for the prisoners — and afterwards dined at Father Connolly's. There may have been no harm in it, of course, but it doesn't look well, considering the state of the feeling, and that he has pocketed a $250 retainer on behalf of the Donnelly family, for which he has done next to nothing.[10]

47

TRIALS

The next step in the proceedings was the opening of the Spring Assizes for the County of Middlesex, set for Monday, April 12, 1880. Excitement buzzed in and around the old Court House on the banks of the Thames at the corner of Dundas and Ridout streets when Mr. Justice Adam Wilson, the same judge who had sentenced Bob Donnelly to prison two years before, took his seat on the bench. The courtroom was jammed, while many who were turned away at the doors milled around outside. In addition to Blake and Macmahon, the distinguished lawyer William Ralph Meredith

appeared for the defence. The prosecution was headed by Hamilton's Aemilius Irving, an advocate fierce of visage and thunderous of voice, who in his day was one of the most dreaded of prosecutors. He was assisted by James Magee of London, who had been retained by the Province of Ontario to represent the public interest. It was an imposing array of legal talent. Macmahon, Magee, and William Ralph Meredith later became Justices of the Supreme Court of Ontario, and Meredith, in particular, was one of the finest jurists ever to grace the bench in the province.

The Crown first applied to the court to change the venue of the trial to a different county town, on the grounds that Middlesex County was in a state of excitement in which a fair trial could not be held. The Judge took the motion under consideration overnight and the next day denied the application. But he decreed that the trial should not proceed, in view of the excitement alleged to be prevailing and in order to allow his decision to be

William R. Meredith

Aemilius Irving

James Magee

appealed. The case was put over to the Fall Assizes. The reaction of the defendants was noted:

A smile of satisfaction passed over the faces of the prisoners when they heard they would not be taken elsewhere for the trial.[1]

They were returned to their cells in the old jail behind the Court House to await the appeal of Wilson's decision. In March, the mother of John Kennedy died and he applied to be released to attend the funeral but was refused. Bob Donnelly went to the Kennedy house to pay his respects, driving a horse and buggy belonging to his brother William, which he had to leave some distance from the house because of the many other vehicles in the laneway. He returned to find the buggy broken to bits.

Later in the spring the trial of William Lewis, charged with the murder of Michael Donnelly, came up at the Simcoe Spring Assizes on Friday, May 7, and was presided over by Mr. Justice Matthew Cameron. Defence counsel for Lewis was a Simcoe lawyer named Charles S. Fuller, the case for the Crown being prosecuted by John Crerar, of Hamilton. The trial was short, lasting

only a day. Friends of the deceased, such as James Muir, fireman on the gravel train, and James Marrs, neighbour of the dead man, gave evidence of the events of the day, along with Freeman Slaght, the hotel proprietor, and several other witnesses. The background of the dispute between Lewis and Donnelly, which appeared to have nothing to do with Biddulph affairs, was only lightly skimmed over. The defence attempted to make capital out of the fact that Pat Donnelly had assisted the Crown in serving subpoenas on one or two of the witnesses. The jury retired and soon brought back a verdict of Not Guilty on the charge of murder but Guilty of manslaughter. Mr. Justice Cameron sentenced Lewis to five years in the Kingston Penitentiary. The local newspaper, the Norfolk Reformer, was very critical of the verdict. It felt that Lewis should have been convicted of murder in view of the premeditation implied in his vow to "fix" Michael Donnelly.

Back in London, jail was so boring for the Biddulph defendants that Carroll, Purtell, McLaughlin, and Tom Ryder asked to break stones in the jailyard. The other two, John Kennedy and Jim Ryder, preferred to stay in their cells, and the latter got quite fat. The newspapers reported on them occasionally:

Purtell, Carroll and Jim Ryder were in one cell; the married men, Kennedy, McLaughlin and Tom Ryder in another... There were 46 prisoners in London Gaol in the fall of 1880, 30 males and 16 females. Among the males was a 105-year old man, charged with vagrancy.[2]

When the Crown appealed the decision of the Assize Court judge denying the change of place of trial, the appeal was heard by the full court of three judges at Osgoode Hall, and it was deemed necessary to transport the prisoners to that city. They went by train to Toronto and then by cab from the station to the venerable law courts, and through the famous cow-gates. During the lunch break they were presented with a huge fruit-cake baked on the Roman Line. Affidavits supporting the change of venue were filed with the court, along with affidavits opposing it by the prisoners and their friends. Chief Justice Hagerty and Justices Cameron and Armour dismissed the appeal, again

James Carroll. At the time of the Donnelly murders he was about twenty-seven years of age, although in this photograph and the Harris sketches he looks older. (*Maclean's* magazine)

Martin McLaughlin

John Purtell, sketched by Robert Harris (PEI)

denying a change in the place of trial.

The prisoners returned to London to await the Fall Assizes. and during the rest of the summer were said to be "all in good spirits, but suffer somewhat from the heat and want of home liberties and comforts". It was reported that

> Every morning they all take an hour's exercise during which they indulge in short races, jumping and other athletic contests.[3]

And it seems they were not totally deprived of home liberties and comforts, for Jailer Joseph Lamb proved very friendly, allowing them special privileges such as tobacco, food treats, and nocturnal visits by the spouses of Martin McLaughlin and Big Jack Kennedy. When these irregularities came to light, however, Lamb was dismissed from his post. But there came to his rescue a couple of Biddulph Vigilantes who had not long before been under his care, Grouchy Ryder and James Maher. They helped to remove the former jailer's effects to Lucan, where Lamb opened a grocery store.

The Government of Ontario offered a reward of four thousand dollars for information leading to

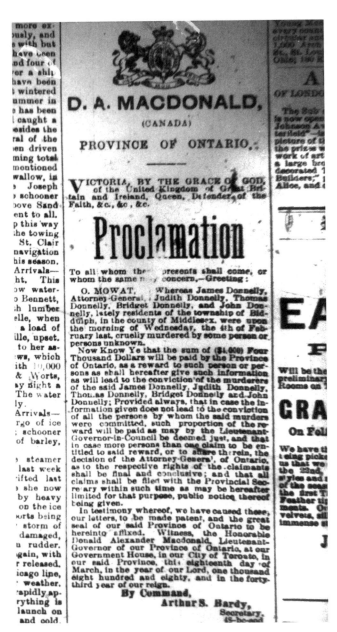

(*London Daily Advertiser*)

the discovery of the murderers of the Donnellys. The reward caused great controversy and was deeply resented by the accused men and their families. As a result of it, the O'Connors in particular came to be looked upon with hatred and scorn, as indicated by a letter that Johnny O'Connor's father wrote about this time to one of the London papers.

To the Editor of the *Advertiser*.

SIR,

On Saturday evening last in the Market Square an auctioneer was vending a good many articles, and among the many things set up for sale was a buggy. A large crowd surrounded the auctioneer, and your correspondent and some of the notorious Biddulphites were in the crowd. The Biddulpher that I have reference to is Patrick Ryder, alias Grouchy, the father and brother of two of the prisoners accused of the Donnelly massacre. Mr. Grouchy addressed me and said, "Mick, buy the buggy, the county will pay for it." I could then and there have told Mr. Grouchy Ryder that I ever lived by my own honesty and industry, and never asked the Crown or county to provide any comfort for me without coming by it legitimately. It is a well known fact that I never before troubled Crown or county, and would not be thus insulted were it not for my own civility in allowing my son Johnny O'Connor to oblige the late Donnellys by going to their place on the night of the tragedy, and had Mr. Grouchy's friends remained at home that night, said their prayers and gone to bed as I did, I would not be in a position to be thus insulted...

Yours, etc.,

London, May 18th.

MICHAEL O'CONNOR.[4]

The Fall Assizes finally opened in late September, presided over by Mr. Justice John Douglas Armour, a strong-willed judge who would brook no interference in the running of his court. The Grand Jury returned True Bills against all six of the prisoners, and the trial was fixed for Thursday, October 4. The defendants were given the right, however, for separate trials and the Crown chose to proceed first against James Carroll, charged with the murder of Judith Donnelly. On the first day of trial the courtroom was filled to overflowing. Aemilius Irving, president of the Hamilton Law Association and later Treasurer of the Law Society of Upper Canada, again appeared for the Crown, assisted by James Magee who appeared on behalf of the province. Defence counsel, as before, were Hugh Macmahon and William R. Meredith, assisted by John J. Blake.

James Carroll had shaved off his chin whiskers for the trial and was wearing an imperial.

Justice John Douglas Armour

His moustache had been given a fierce twist, and this assisted him in getting up a bold look upon his entrance into Court, but the glare of his eyes and stern expression of countenance speedily gave way to an anxious look....[5]

The climax of the trial was once more the testimony of young Johnny O'Connor. Again he told his straightforward story. In substance it was the same as previously related at the inquest and again at the preliminary hearing, differing only in sufficient detail to show that it was genuine. The cross-examination by Hugh Macmahon of the young boy was long and searching, but it did not break down anything of importance. William Donnelly was cross-examined by Meredith and he, too, came through it unscathed. Upon completion of the Crown's case, the defence made no motion to dismiss for lack of sufficient evidence but went straight into the defence testimony.

The defence was alibi. William and Mary Thompson swore that the Carroll brothers had spent the entire night at the Thompson farmhouse and could not possibly have been out that night. Mrs. Thompson said she distinctly remembered the brothers depositing their boots near the stove, and the boots were still there when the clock struck twelve midnight, for she had had to get up in the night for medicine. Many other witnesses were called to prove alibis for the others. John Kennedy swore that James Bryan had come over in the night to get some medicine for his children and that although he stayed but a few minutes, the clock struck two during that short time. Mr. Magee asked Kennedy in cross-examination, "Is it not remarkable how many occurrences happened at two o'clock that night?" and Kennedy had to agree it was.

John Purtell testified that he had spent the night in the McGrath house where he worked, and several of the McGraths confirmed that he could not possibly have left the house without their knowledge. Temperance McLaughlin, the 21-year-old daughter of the defendant Martin McLaughlin, swore that she came downstairs in the night from her second-floor bedroom and saw her mother and father in bed just as the clock struck two. She got a drink and went back to bed.

Another defence witness was Valentine Mackey. When he took the witness box the following exchange occurred:

Mr. Magee — Did you kiss the book?
Witness — Yes, sir.
Mr. Meredith — It is not fair to speak in that way to the witness.
Mr. Magee — It struck me that he didn't, that's all.
His Lordship — No, he didn't kiss the book. Have him sworn.
Mackey then kissed the book with a resounding smack and said — Is that the way?[6]

When the defence witnesses were finished, the Crown called reply witnesses and there was much swearing as to the honesty and reputation of William Donnelly. In all, a total of almost one hundred witnesses had paraded to the witness box before the testimony was concluded.

Friday and part of Saturday were spent in the addresses of counsel. Hugh Macmahon made a brilliant address to the jury on behalf of the prisoners, using all of his considerable forensic skill. He was thorough and logical, and particularly adept at seizing upon every shred of testimony which could in any way be favourable to the defendants and which he skilfully wove into a persuasive pattern of logic. One of the most telling points he made was this: If the murderers did not hesitate to shed the blood of an innocent girl in order to hide their crime, then why did they let Johnny O'Connor survive, if the boy was right in swearing that it was James Carroll who was there and that he looked right at him while holding the candle at the doorway? Mr. Justice Armour followed the lawyers with his charge to the jury, which was definitely weighted against the prisoner. It was reported:

> The evidence against the prisoner was clearer than is customary in most murder trials, while his faint alibi was founded only on the testimony of those who were plainly interested in shielding him from punishment.[7]

When the jury retired, a verdict of Guilty was generally expected.

Late on Saturday, October 9, the jury straggled back into the courtroom, and the foreman wearily announced that they were unable to agree and that there was no prospect of agreement. They stood seven for acquittal, four for conviction, and one undecided. The Judge discharged the jury and remanded the prisoners in custody for their trial at the next court.

A member of the jury named Rodgers was interviewed and reported to have said, "I wouldn't go for conviction if I had seen them do the deed!"

Very little of event occurred between the end of Carroll's first trial and the beginning of the next, except that the Crown Attorney had great difficulty with the O'Connors. One day Mick O'Connor took his son Johnny to Lucan but got drunk on the way back and could have seriously jeopardized the Crown's case if something had happened to the young boy. A fragment of a letter was found in Berlin (later renamed Kitchener), which indicated

the writer may have known something of the murders in Biddulph, but the clue could not be followed up. William Donnelly did his best to hunt up fresh evidence, along with Sam Everett. Although witnesses such as Luke Nangle, Pat Bennett, and John Doherty were found who could have implicated some of the accused persons, they could not be persuaded to repeat their statements in court. An attempt was made to obtain a confession from John Purtell, considered a weakling, but nothing came of it, and Purtell proved to be remarkably cool and self-possessed in the witness box.

The second trial was unusual in that the government took the precaution of setting up a special commission of two Justices to try the case: Mr. Justice Featherston Osler and Mr. Justice Matthew Cameron. The trial opened on Monday, January 24,1881, a bitterly cold day in the middle of winter. Special tickets of admission had been printed up for the occasion:

> The blue ones are season tickets while the red ones are only for one day's admission.[8]

One of the London newspapers quoted the Toronto *Mail*'s "excited report":

> When the Court opened all the Biddulphers were on hand — men who had their noses bitten out by the roots, men who had left some of their ears in the mouths of their antagonists, men who bore the scars and scratches of many a faction fight, clustered in the corridors and damned the constables because they were not admitted.[9]

Those who were disappointed "stormed and swore, and at one time in a rush for the doors nearly overcame the constables...."

The same counsel appeared at the second trial and the evidence was much the same, except that the death of John Donnelly was barely mentioned. The Crown had apparently decided that Will Donnelly's evidence merely gave the defence an opportunity to attack the character of the murdered victims. Johnny O'Connor once again repeated his story. When the young boy came to the part where he thought the gang of men had killed Bridget Donnelly, the prisoner Carroll became violently ill. He was removed from the courtroom clutching his stomach. After Carroll's recovery, the testimony continued, and when the young boy

Justice Matthew C. Cameron

Justice Featherston Osler

related how he thought Mrs. Donnelly was still breathing when he stepped over her body, Carroll again took sick. Below, in the cells, when the name of Johnny O'Connor was dropped by one of the jail attendants, Buckshot Jim Ryder muttered bitterly, "That son of a bitch will swear anything."

This time it was Meredith who cross-examined the boy. His questioning

> was conducted with a great deal of tartness... the questions were put in a strong, though perhaps not loud, tone of voice but were poured in with such rapidity that the boy hardly had time to sandwich his answers between them, allowing not a second for hesitancy or deliberation.[10]

It seemed, however, to make little difference to Johnny O'Connor's story, and the witness "appeared to keep remarkably cool".

Aemilius Irving, for the Crown, questioned young Dennis McGee as to the purposes of the meetings of the Biddulph Peace Society.

> Mr. Irving — How often were you there?
> Witness — Three or four times.
> Q. — What business was done the first time?
> A. — I don't remember anything being done.
> Q. — What was done the second time you were there?
> A. — I don't remember.
> Q. — What was done the third time?
> A. — I don't remember.[11]

There was some question about the efficacy of the Protestant Bible — it had a cross on it — on which the witnesses were sworn. "Some of the friends of the prisoner," it was reported, "were recently heard to remark that an oath taken on that book would not be morally binding." The officials seemed to have taken the rumour seriously, or perhaps it was a stratagem of the defence, but in any event a Catholic Bible was produced in court just before the witness Mary Hastings O'Connor was called to the stand.

Mary O'Connor, the mother of young Johnny, had gone to the Attorney General's office in Toronto to try to collect the provincial government's reward. The defence had discovered that she had made the trip and was determined to exploit the point. Informers, after all, were anathema to the Irish. The fact that Mrs. O'Connor had a fist-fight with Mrs. Patrick Whalen and her daughter Teresa in the witnesses' anteroom just prior to her being called into the witness-box did not help her composure during her cross-examination by Hugh Macmahon. Part of it, interspersed with laughter from the spectators, went as follows:

Q. — Did you hear of a reward being offered?
A. — I din't hear it, sir.
Q. — What?
A. — Somebody has been talking to me about the reward.

...

Q. — You were in Toronto a short time ago?
A. — I was, sir, an' what of it?
Q. — Did you see the Attorney-General?
A. — To see who?
Q. — The Attorney-General?
A. — No, sir, I did not see the Attorney-General.

...

Q. — Now, tell me where you went in Toronto?
A. — I went to the office.
Q. — What office?
A. — The Attorney-General's office.
Q. — What did you want there?
A. — I wanted to see what kind of a place it was.

...

Q. — So you only went to see what kind of an office the Attorney-General had?
A. — Maybe I did and maybe I didn't, and I don't want to be questioned any longer.
His Lordship — People in your position don't usually travel a great distance at considerable expense merely to see an office in a city.
A. — Poor people, I suppose, can't go and see things as well as rich folks?[12]

Mr. Justice Cameron finally dismissed her from the witness-stand with the remark that not a word she said could be believed.

By Tuesday, February 2, ninety witnesses had been heard. The trial had proceeded with good dispatch, however, for proceedings commenced in the morning "at 9 o'clock or half past and [went] on with only a half hour lunch break until six in the evening." The trial had even continued through Saturday afternoon, a time when court usually adjourned. With the conclusion of the evidence on Tuesday, the counsel made their addresses to the jury. Mr. Macmahon argued from half past one o'clock until four and Mr. Irving

then addressed the jury for two hours, following which the court adjourned.

The winter was a cold one but that night was especially frigid, with the thermometer sinking to 24 degrees below zero, Fahrenheit. By eight o'clock next morning it was still 20 below, but this notwithstanding, "the living stream began to set steadily in towards the Court House" for the last day of the trial.

The notebook of Mr. Justice Featherston Osler recorded the events of the day succinctly:

9:30   Cameron J. charges the jury.
11:15   Jury retires.[13]

Mr. Justice Cameron's charge to the jury was a contrast to that at the first trial. He was careful to point out to the jurors that simply because Carroll was proved to be a member of the Vigilance Committee, that did not make him guilty of the murder. It was definitely more favourable to the defence than the previous jury instruction.

While the jurors were deliberating in the jury room, the Crown proceeded to arraign two of the other prisoners. John Purtell and Thomas Ryder were brought up from the cells and placed in the prisoner's dock. The selecting of the second jury was begun and, after nearly forty challenges and directions to stand aside, several jurors were sworn.

At 2:57 p.m. the jury in the Carroll case returned to the courtroom. The clerk asked the foreman if they had reached a verdict. They had. The foreman then announced: "My Lords, we find the prisoner not guilty of murder."

The ensuing eruption of excitement was quickly suppressed. William Donnelly was not in the courtroom. The lawyers then continued as if nothing of moment had occurred, but when eleven jurors in the second case had been sworn and a twelfth had been selected, Aemilius Irving rose.

"My Lords," he said, "I ask that this juror be not sworn. The Crown under the circumstances is not prepared to proceed with the trial of these prisoners. Carroll has just been acquitted. The evidence against these men is the same as that which was presented against the last prisoner. I do not foresee any different verdict in their case from that which has just been rendered. I therefore ask that their cases of arson, the killing of the unfortunates, and the burning of the building, go over to the next assizes. The Crown is ready to consider the question of bail for all of the accused."

The last statement was greeted with happy astonishment by the prisoners and their friends. The Crown had virtually given up the prosecution. Bail was quickly arranged in amounts surprisingly small: $500 for each prisoner, with two sureties of $200 each.

James Carroll was then returned to the dock, and Mr. Justice Cameron addressed him:

James Carroll... you are now acquitted of the charge of the murder of Judith Donnelly, but not from the charge of which you may yet be placed on trial, for the murder of James Donnelly, Thomas Donnelly and Bridget Donnelly. The jury in your case have

taken a most favourable view, and I hope a correct view has been taken by them, and I sincerely hope you have not been guilty of the atrocious crime laid to your charge. There is one point, however, I must dwell on. You, James Carroll, are a member of the constabulary of your county and you have in the discharge of your duties as a constable exhibited the utmost disparity. It has been plainly shown you were particularly anxious to prosecute the Donnellys, and if you have suffered a year's imprisonment you have yourself to blame for it. This, together with the continual dread and uncertainty hanging over you... may be regarded by you in some measure as a punishment for your dereliction of duty in the discharge of your duties as a constable. I trust you will leave the dock a better and wiser man. You are discharged.[14]

When the words "You are discharged" were

The jury at the second trial of James Carroll

uttered, James Carroll and the other defendants were almost carried out of the courtroom by their friends. When they reached the foot of the stairs and the few possessions kept for them by the jail officials were handed over, cheer after cheer was raised as they were carried along by the boisterous crowd.

The jury was so proud of itself that it marched down in a body to the photographic studio of Frank Cooper and had its picture taken. They were all Protestants, and consisted of John Carrothers, William Hooper, Horace Hyatt, John Lambert, George M. Francis, James F. Elliott, Dugal Graham, James A. Watterworth, James Dores, Hopper Ward, Asa Luce, and Benjamin Kilburn.[15]

"Some of the jurors," it was reported, "said that they would have found Carroll guilty had it not been that they thought such a verdict would have ultimately resulted in the hanging of half a township ."

Meanwhile, the crowd accompanying the released prisoners, grown to almost a thousand people, continued along King Street until it reached the City Arms Hotel. They pushed into the hotel.

Soon every room on the ground floor was packed. Then followed a scene of great confusion, everybody shaking hands with the released men and then with everybody else. The wives of the lately accused persons embraced their husbands; tears of joy were shed, and one or two of the friends could not refrain from dancing an Irish jig in honour of the occasion.[16]

Back in Lucan the verdict was posted up in front of the Post Office. As soon as the notice went up

crowds of people began to collect upon the streets and it was a study to notice the effect of the verdict. Even the school children, when they spelled out the three words "Verdict Not Guilty," were seen rejoicing in a manner that could not be mistaken... [17]

Later that evening some of the crowd were drinking in the bar-room of the Western Hotel in London and discussing the case when Bob Donnelly suddenly appeared. He walked up to the bar, turned around to the crowd, and cried, "I want all of you murderers to come and have something."

No one accepted the invitation and Robert Donnelly left. The same thing occurred shortly after at the City Hotel in London.

The newspaper editorial writers waxed eloquent on the verdict. Said the *Exeter Times*:

The experience of the Crown in the Biddulph murder trial ought to be enough to convince people that the offering of large rewards for the apprehension and conviction of murderers is an evil practice.... The only result of such an offer would be to cast doubt and suspicion upon the most direct evidence.... Take the case of Mrs. O'Connor.... Having a suspicion of the mother, there was naturally a suspicion that the son had been coached and instructed to look to the $5,000.... The offering of the reward was the kindest act the Government could have done the prisoner.[18]

The Toronto *Globe* editorialized:

Stronger evidence, both direct and circumstantial, has rarely been brought against any man who in the face of it escaped the gallows.[19]

The *Detroit Free Press* commented:

The two ends of Canada differ somewhat. At New Westminster, British Columbia, four men were hung last week for the murder of one man, while at the border of Old Westminster, in Ontario, one man was acquitted who was shown to have murdered four persons.[20]

48

SEQUEL

John Purtell remained in London but the rest of the released men returned to Lucan almost immediately. While the married men hurried to their homes, Carroll and Buckshot Jim Ryder stayed several hours in the village celebrating. All of them spent the ensuing weeks "having a happy time in Biddulph as they [went] from house to house enjoying the hospitality of their friends."

A fund was established to defray the $4,000 it cost to defend Carroll. Only two men in Lucan — it was doubtless said with some exaggeration — refused to subscribe to it. For the same purpose, an open meeting of the Biddulph Peace Society was held at the Cedar Swamp Schoolhouse and attended by news reporters, as well as Catholics and Protestants from all parts of the district. Speeches were made just as at political meetings of the day.

Most of the participants in "the Biddulph Tragedy", as the local people referred to the massacre, continued to haunt the scene of the crime. The surviving Donnelly brothers, James Carroll and the other Vigilantes, Father Connolly, and many lesser actors in the drama occasionally caused ripples of excitement in the aftermath. Father Connolly admitted that he had been to some extent misled as to the character of the Donnellys and that certain elements of the Peace Society had taken advantage of him. He had fully expected to be arrested as an accomplice, but Will Donnelly was adamant on the subject.

"I won't hear of it," Will declared. "It's a thing I never dreamt of and never will countenance for a minute. I believe that Father Connolly acted wrongly in his treatment of our family, but his motives in organizing the society at the church were for the best. They departed from his simple foundation, but unknowingly to him. I don't suspect for a second that he knew or had anything to do with the murder."

Robert Donnelly was less charitable. On Sunday, April 14, 1880, he walked into the Donnelly Schoolhouse where Father Connolly was holding church service and nailed a poster on the wall.

"Mr. Donnelly," the astonished priest said, "what are you putting on the wall?"

"It's the reward poster for the murderers," Bob grimly replied.

"I do not think this is the proper place for that," said the priest, "and I ask you to take it down."

"I will not take it down," Donnelly answered. "I think this is the right place. You've got the rest of the murderers around you."

Of the surviving brothers, Bob Donnelly seemed most obsessed with a passion for immediate vengeance. One Saturday when he met James Carroll on the sidewalk opposite Barney Stanley's store in Lucan, he ran into him with his shoulder. Carroll laughed it off. A few minutes later, as Carroll passed in front of the Queen's Hotel, Bob's voice came booming out from the doorway of the tavern loud enough for everyone in the street to hear: "You can tell by that man's shoulders he is a murderer!" Carroll walked on, ignoring the taunt. But Donnelly followed him, and as he came up jostled Carroll off balance. Still the latter refused to retaliate. He went instead to the office of William Stanley to lay a charge. The J.P. said he had no blank forms and asked Carroll to come back on Monday. Carroll then went to see his old Peace Society friend and magistrate, William Casey, but the latter persuaded him to drop the matter.

"Donnelly only wants to keep the name of the place in disrepute," said Casey, "to furnish items for second-class news mongers."

The brothers vowed that the Donnelly homestead property would not be sold. "None of the Vigilants will ever get it," Will Donnelly declared, "either by purchase or in any other way while we live." The land was leased to old Michael Feeheley, one of the two men who had given evidence on behalf of James Donnelly on his trial for murder many years before.[1]

Mick Feeheley, however, died shortly after,

leaving a bankrupt estate and the mortgage on his own farm in default. One of his largest creditors turned out to be James Maher. It seems that Maher and Feeheley had endorsed another note for young Pat Keefe, who had skipped the country without paying. Maher had paid up and claimed Feeheley's portion of it. But the Feeheley farm was sold under the mortgage to old Michael Carroll, who happened to live across the road from the property.

The remaining members of the Feeheley family were sorely disappointed at the turn of events. Some of the Cains, to whom they were related, had emigrated to Saginaw, Michigan, years before and the Feeheleys now planned to join them. But they were loath to leave Biddulph dead broke. James and William Feeheley let it be known that Old Carroll, "respactable" or not, would not be allowed to take possession of their farm without an additional payment of $500, made direct to them, "for the goodwill of the place". But when Old Carroll decided to pay the extra money, this in turn aroused the ire of James Maher, who

> forbade Carroll paying the $500, he (Maher) claiming that sum as a part of the Feeheley general estate to which all creditors might resort.[2]

Maher's nephew, James Carroll, also forbade payment of the goodwill money. Thus thwarted, the Feeheley brothers threatened to tell all they knew about the Donnelly murders. They openly accused James Carroll of being a murderer. When Father Connolly discovered that the entire murder investigation was in danger of being revived, he went to see the widow of Mick Feeheley and handed over a portion of the sum her sons had demanded.

Patrick Donnelly had in the meantime gained the confidence of the Feeheley boys, who had been, after all, his boyhood chums. Jim Feeheley confessed to Pat that Johnny O'Connor had sworn the truth. He had everything right, said Feeheley, except that John Purtell was not at the murders. According to Feeheley, young O'Connor had mistaken either William Carroll or young Pat Ryder for Purtell. (Sam Everett, on the other hand, at about the same time claimed to have received authentic information that Purtell had indeed been among the mob, along with Purtell's employer, James

Patrick Donnelly

McGrath.) Feeheley also admitted that while on the witness-stand at the first trial of Carroll, he had almost broken down and confessed his part in the whole affair. Before he could act, however, the court was adjourned for the day.

The Feeheleys left for Saginaw shortly after. But before their departure, James Feeheley came to blows with John Bawden in Lucan and was badly beaten. After the fight, Feeheley was taken to the hotel room of one Francis M. West to lick his wounds. West was an erstwhile amateur investigator who had arrived in Lucan in December, attracted from the United States by the notoriety of the Donnelly murder case. He related that Feeheley

> sat down on the bed and began to cry and said he got no show in the fight, that he knew he would die a hard death but he would not give in to Old Christ himself...[3]

Feeheley also lamented: "Both parties are against

me, the Donnellys and the Vigilants. My backbone is gone now. My old man knew too much for the whole of us while he was alive."

By the time the police authorities had pieced together all the new evidence in the case, the Feeheleys had settled in Saginaw and both brothers had obtained jobs at an iron foundry there. They refused to return to Canada voluntarily to give evidence. "In Canada," they said, "witnesses are treated the same as prisoners."

Nevertheless, charges of aiding and abetting the murder of Thomas Donnelly were laid against the Feeheley brothers in Canada, and proceedings to extradite them from Michigan were taken. Brought back to London for preliminary hearing, true bills against them were found by the Grand Jury at the Fall Assizes in 1881, but their trial was delayed until the following spring. However, after due deliberation the Deputy Attorney General of the Province of Ontario informed the Crown Attorney of Middlesex that the government had spent enough on the Donnelly prosecutions, and in view of the state of the evidence and considering the probabilities of acquittal, he refused to allow the case to go further. The Feeheleys were thereupon released on bail, and the case against the rest of the suspects was allowed to die. No one ever paid a legal penalty for the murders of James, Johannah, John, Thomas, and Bridget Donnelly.

One by one the surviving Donnellys abandoned the district. With the release of the Feeheleys, Pat Donnelly returned to his blacksmith and carriage-making trade in Thorold. He eventually acquired the Mansion House Hotel in that town, and for the remainder of his life kept tavern either in Thorold or in nearby St. Catharines, where he raised a family of two sons and three daughters. Pat died in 1914, and the last of his children, Mame, died in Detroit in 1970. Of his sons, John Donnelly never married and Matthew Donnelly lived with his wife for only a few months and had no children. Two of Patrick's grandsons through the female line, however, live in the St. Catharines area today, one of them boasting a family of seven sons and two daughters.

Will Donnelly's older daughter, named Jo-Anna after her grandmother, was born while Will and Norah continued to live in Lucan for the year or two following the Carroll trials. In the fall of 1881 Will and Bob Donnelly, with others, were arrested on a charge of attempting to burn down the huge grist mill of Stanley & Dight, which stood near the Lucan lock-up. The principal prosecution witness was the erstwhile private detective Francis M. West, who, under the guise of a music teacher, had attempted to work up a case against first the Vigilantes and then the Donnellys. West related, "Bob Donnelly said that if he thought the mill would go on Saturday he would not leave until Sunday." Three prominent and smirking spectators at the trial were ex-constable James Carroll, Buckshot Jim Ryder, and Big Mike Heenan. The Donnellys were acquitted.

Will Donnelly left the district following the trial. For a short time he operated a hotel in Bothwell, where his only son, John William Donnelly, was born in 1883. A little later he settled down in the hotel in Appin, sometimes called the St. Nicholas. Here was born his only other child, Nora. While his health remained, it was said that Will Donnelly would walk around the village of Appin with a couple of guns sticking from his belt and decorated with red tassels, the latter to denote police permission to carry weapons for self-protection. He also continued playing his fiddle until his last long illness, making up ditties deriding his enemies to go along with the music.

William Donnelly died at Appin on Sunday, March 7, 1897. He was fifty-two years old and for the last couple of years of his life had been confined to his bed. His only son was thirteen years old at his death and remembered him well. All three children of William Donnelly married, but only the daughters bore children. Thus it was that John William Donnelly, when he died in 1973 in Detroit, carried the family name to the grave, for notwithstanding a long and happy marriage of over fifty years to a girl from Pittsburgh, he remained childless.

Jenny Currie returned to her family in the Glencoe area and raised a family of five sons and six daughters. She died in 1916. At least two of her sons survive at the time of this writing, but the Curries remain sensitive on the subject of the Donnelly family.

Robert Donnelly followed his sister to the Glen-

The Stanley and Dight grist mill in Lucan. If finally burned down in 1899. (Stanley)

coe area, where he unsuccessfully applied for the job of constable. He returned to his native district in the spring of 1893. The house on the Donnelly farm was rebuilt, and many of the residents helped in the work. But when one of those who were assisting drove into a neighbour's farm to water his horse, the farmer's wife told him, "You're welcome to water, but not the man you're working for."

On another occasion Pat Grace of the Swamp Line held a bee to haul manure. It was a hot day, and as the well on Grace's farm was not a very good one, some of the men went over to the excellent well of a neighbour for a drink. The neighbour was Pat Darcey. The second time the men went over, they found a crude notice posted on the pump. It read:

No water for blackfeets here. Go to old Donnelly's homestead and you will get all you want.

(When William Donnelly was queried as to the meaning of the term "blackfeets", he answered, "I don't know, unless it is to distinguish those who belong to the Vigilance Committee from those who don't, and whose sympathies and feelings are with us and on the side of law and order....")[4]

In 1901 Bob Donnelly also went into the hotel business when he, along with his nephew James Michael Donnelly, purchased the old Western Hotel on William Street in Lucan. James Michael was the only son of Mike Donnelly. After the sale of the hotel, Bob Donnelly continued to live in Lucan with his wife and nephew in a neat frame house on south Main Street. He died in 1911,

276 *The Donnelly Album*

without children, and is buried in St. Peter's Cemetery in London. "His mind got weak," it was said, "and he spent the last year or two in the Ontario Hospital for the Insane." His widow, Annie, remained in Lucan until her death.

James Michael Donnelly died in 1938, a bachelor. His sister, Catherine, thereupon sold the family homestead, which had been restored by Bob Donnelly to its original full size of one hundred acres with the purchase of the old Cain farm.[5] Catherine also died childless. Michael Donnelly's widow remarried, following her first husband's tragic death, and lived a happy new life in Cleveland. There were several issue of her second marriage, but they knew little of Nellie Hines' first husband, believing only that he had been killed in a railroad accident.

Part of the Donnelly legend consists of an Irish curse which it is said fell upon the heads of each of the Vigilantes who participated in the butchery of the family. The legend has been nurtured over the years. In 1910 a newspaper reported, "It is a peculiar fact that of all the persons said to have been connected with the tragedy, though many of them were comparatively young, scarcely any are living today, and many of them died a violent death." And upon Patrick Donnelly's death in 1914, the *Thorold Post* referred to the murders and stated:

The mystery was never fully solved by the courts, and no one convicted, but one uncanny echo was a prophecy by Patrick that none of the alleged murderers would die in bed, which prophecy, strange to relate, was realized to its awful fulness, each one coming to a violent end.[6]

The story of the curse or prophecy originated, at least in part, in the office of the Crown Attorney within a few minutes after the conclusion of the trial of James Carroll which resulted in his acquittal. Aemilius Irving, the Crown prosecutor, was commiserating at the outcome of the trial in private with the three remaining Donnelly brothers and their sister Jenny. As the latter sobbed tears of anguish and frustration, Irving consoled her with the words: "Do not cry, my dear woman, there is a just God

Norah Donnelly shortly before her death in 1937 (John W. Donnelly)

who sees all. He will try the case without lawyers or jury, and He will give you ample satisfaction in the way of retribution before ten years pass."

The Vigilantes laughed at the alleged curse on their heads until the following holiday season. Then, on Christmas Day, 1880, at Grundy's Crossing just north of Lucan, a terrible accident on the train tracks took the lives of James McGrath, his wife Rebecca McGrath, brother Matthew McGrath, and his cousin Ellen Blake. James McGrath was a prominent member of the Vigilance Committee. Ellen Blake was his niece, and sister of Michael Moony Blake and John J. Blake, secretary and lawyer for the Biddulph Peace Society respectively. Mrs. McGrath was a Fogarty. Her mother was related to the Thompsons, who had been involved with the Donnellys in the affairs of Maggie, the charivari, and the cow. The deaths were attributed to supernatural events: "The ghosts of the murdered Donnellys came up from the ditch and held the horses until the train struck."[7]

During the remainder of his life William Donnelly encouraged the stories of the curse. He kept one of his mother's arm bones out of her casket and vowed he would not allow it to be buried until the family had obtained vengeance. He kept a diary which purported to show that the divine hand of retribution fell heavily upon the Peace Society members and their families. In 1893 he wrote:

… In the 13 years, 34 persons who were either directly or indirectly concerned in that slaughter have met their just deserts, and as none of them have been murdered, a direct visitation from Almighty God must have been the cause I will not be personal but I will say several were killed by the London, Huron &

Bruce train. More were found dead in bed without any apparent cause. More fell into a well. More dropped dead. More died suffering the agonies of a mad dog, and a few are in the asylum, while the majority of those living are homeless and not worth a dollar, though well off 13 years ago.[8]

Supporters of the Vigilance Committee of Biddulph disputed the claims of William Donnelly, but it is true that every misfortune or sudden or unnatural death of anyone in any way connected with the society was ever after attributed to the curse.

James Carroll remained in the district for a time. He brought legal proceedings against his two uncles for mismanaging his father's estate and for failing to abide by the last will. Then he left and was seen in Kimberley, British Columbia, in the

The hotel at Appin where Will Donnelly died in 1897 (H. F. Bardwell)

winter and summer of 1907-8. He was then living with his widowed sister, Mrs. Maguire, who owned and operated the Falls View Hotel in the nearby settlement of Marysville. "He appeared to have very few friends or acquaintances and spoke only to the few he seemed to know. He spent the rest of his life in the rugged East Kootenays and died in 1915 in St. Mary's Hospital, New Westminster, B.C.

Of the other six defendants in the Donnelly murder trials, John Purtell soon disappeared from the district but McLaughlin, Kennedy, and the two Ryders stayed for years after. Martin McLaughlin was reported alive in 1929, in his ninety-third year. Big Jack Kennedy's wife died prematurely in 1888, and Kennedy himself had a close call with death six years later when he was just barely rescued in time from a room in the London hotel of

James Michael Donnelly, son of Mike Donnelly (John W. Donnelly)

John Donnelly, son of Patrick; John William Donnelly, son of Will; and Matthew Donnelly, son of Patrick

Catherine Donnelly Crosman, the daughter of Mike Donnelly (C. Andrewes)

A new house was built on the Donnelly farm some years later on the site of the original house.

his friend, Jerry McDonald. The gas cock had been left on and the door of the room was locked. Kennedy survived until 1902. Pitchfork Tom Ryder appears to have quit Biddulph ten years after the Donnelly murders, but his nephew, Buckshot Jim Ryder, stayed on. One day in 1893 the latter quarrelled over a horse trade with Alfred Dignan, who then occupied the Donnelly place. Ryder called Dignan out to the gate and there, Dignan claimed, pulled a knife. But Dignan wrestled it away from him and stuck the blade into Ryder some twenty times before the fight ended.

The fate of some of the other Peace Society members is known. Patrick J. Dewan died in his bed in 1891 at age 50 from congestion of the lungs, after a week's illness. Will Donnelly attributed his death to the curse. Pat Breen died unexpectedly. James Heenan died in June 1900 at age 41; James Kelly in June 1882 at the same age; Thomas Lanphier in 1886 at age 37; Michael

Sullivan in 1883 at age 25; Patrick Sullivan in June 1883 at age 33. John Darsey died in February 1883 at age 55 and Martin Darcey died at age 40. The latter was married to Bridget Cain whose mother was a Toohey. Timothy Darcey fell through the slide-hole of a Winnipeg fire hall on a harvest excursion in 1910 and was killed. William Feeheley died of apoplexy in Saginaw, Michigan, in 1926. James Maher, Sr., survived until 1901, but his wife, Ellen Cain, died five years after the massacre at age 46, while their young son Willy, who as a lad of 15 stayed all day following the murders watching the Donnelly house smoulder, died two years after his mother at age 23. A daughter died a few years later at age 17. James Maher, Jr., was reputed to have died suddenly, too, in 1917, while in the granary of his barn. He could not be moved, and the priest had to climb a ladder to give him the last rites. Sideroad Jim Ryder's wife, Katherine, died in 1882 at age 45, while young Patrick Ryder died in 1903 at age 41, leaving his widow, Lizzie Heenan, daughter of a Vigilante and sister to two others. Peg-leg Brown, a notorious criminal, shot to death in London Michael Toohey, a policeman and brother of Spadey Jim Toohey. The latter's wife died in 1884 a few weeks after the death of their young son shortly after Christmas. Toohey himself was fatally injured by a falling rack. Michael O'Mara died in 1884, also at the age of 26. He was related by marriage to Toohey through Toohey's second wife. James Quigley died in August 1880 at the age of 31 .

Others connected with the Biddulph Vigilante Committee suffered misfortune. John Joseph Blake went to British Columbia and prospered for a time when he became the first city solicitor of Vancouver. But he later fell on hard times and was eventually disbarred in 1896 for improperly withholding money from a client, and died a pauper in a rooming house three years later. Of another Vigilante family it was reported in 1887:

John Bruin, Sr., age 83, of the Cedar Swamp Line, near Granton, attempted suicide the other day by cutting his throat with a razor.[9]

The old stagecoach rival of the Donnellys, John Flanagan, had not only kept a tavern and a store but also served as clerk of the Division Court and treasurer of the Township of Biddulph. In the early part of 1890, in financial straits, he absconded with two or three thousand dollars of cash which rightly belonged to others. His creditors forced a sale of his properties. Although Flanagan was later located in Texas and agreed to sign bankruptcy papers, he refused to return to Canada. His brother, Patrick, died in Winnipeg at age 45 from a paralytic stroke. In 1889 John Quigley's house on the Roman Line burned to the ground during a raging winter storm, and Quigley was forced to flee with his family of nine children and carrying his aged father from the flaming house in his arms.

The fate of others connected with the Donnelly massacre is unknown. In 1910 when reports came out of Blind River in Northern Ontario that a William Carroll had escaped from an insane asylum after having been arrested on a charge of murder in a lumber camp, it was assumed by many

that he was the brother of James Carroll of the Biddulph Vigilance Committee. But this William Carroll turned out to be a different man. He was of the Protestant Carrolls in the Saintsbury district of Biddulph, and the St. Patrick's Church he had attended in the township was the Protestant St. Patrick's![10]

Again, the fate of Johnny O'Connor remains a mystery. He was reported alive in 1946, living near Detroit, and would then have been about 80 years of age. But he was also reported as living in Toronto in his nineties, while still other reports had him dying in California — and in Saskatchewan, and in Ohio, and in Winnipeg, as well as several other places. Fred Dobbs, of Exeter, related:

Johnny O'Connor visited my father and mother one fall evening. I should think about 1934 or 1935. He stayed talking till 2 a.m., and even though his bed was made up for him he would not stay. He said he came to Lucan just to visit them. He came in the dark and must leave in the dark. At that time he was living in Winnipeg and did not wish to enlarge on his home or past any more than he had been fairly prosperous with a happy family life.

Father John Connolly remained pastor at St. Patrick's Parish for fourteen long years after the murders. When the old frame church — then being used as a school — burned down, he was instrumental in building a new brick schoolhouse, in 1885, which stands near the road today. No one will ever know how much of the Donnelly story came out in Father Connolly's confessional, but it is entirely likely the priest heard more than one death-bed repentance, despite the stories which still circulate of the tardiness of the friends and families of dying Vigilantes in fetching the priest. Father Connolly himself experienced a close brush with death in 1893 when a passing train almost hit him on the tracks at Tavistock Station. He finally left St. Patrick's on January 24, 1895, after completing fifteen years of service in Biddulph almost to the day. He went to the church at Ingersoll where he remained until 1907, and in that year, in poor health, he left for a trip to Ireland. He died in 1909.

For decades after the Donnelly massacre, ghost stories abounded in Biddulph. Zackariah

McIlhargey's daughter Kate told the following tale:

The priest of St. Patrick's once asked my father many, many years after the murders what old Jim Donnelly looked like. My father described him. The priest then said, "Well, I saw his ghost in here just now, kneeling and praying there in the church. I first thought he was just someone who wanted to go to confession but when I went over to the box to open the door and looked back, he was gone."

Over the years, as in many parts of rural Ontario, the population of the farm community of Biddulph gradually declined. Many families drifted to the cities of Detroit, London, and Windsor. By 1946 the population of Lucan had dwindled to six hundred.

TODAY

It is ironic that while those of the anti-Donnelly faction were in the end successful in ridding the township and the village of the family, they left a different legacy to their descendants. The massacre has forever linked the name Donnelly with Biddulph and Lucan. Instead of being endured as just another family of hooligans and forgotten with their passing, the Donnellys have become folk-heroes whose story seizes the imaginations of many a schoolboy, preacher, tradesman, secretary, or businessman. It has a wide and fascinating appeal to people in all walks of life.

In the 1920s an Easterner goes on a harvest excursion to the Saskatchewan prairies, and when he applies for a job, the farmer asks him where he is from. "London, eh?" says the farmer to the man's reply. "A city fellow. Why, I'll bet you don't know the front end of a horse from its back end." The Easterner is a little irked and tells the farmer he said London only to identify the general district of his origin — that he really comes from a little country village near London. The farmer seems a

little interested and asks, "What place?"

"It's a place called Lucan," says the Easterner, who is thereupon surprised to be hired on the spot, and all that summer after working hours is regaled, by the farmer with tales of the Donnellys. The young Easterner admits later that the Saskatchewan farmer knew more about the story and about Lucan at the time of the Donnellys than he.

Another man, born and raised near Goderich, Ontario, travels to the United States in the 1960s and lands up working in a hotel in Las Vegas, Nevada, in the midst of country that was once the American Wild West. Someone at the hotel happens to have heard of the Donnelly family of Lucan, and the man tells the others he was born near the place where the events occurred. Ever after, the man is regarded with a little awe, and his acquaintances call him by the nickname "Donnelly.[1]

In the 1970s a young secretary is on a month's holiday from her home in Glasgow, Scotland, and is being given a ride to London, Ontario. Does she have friends in London? Oh, yes, but the real reason she is going there is to see the famous Donnelly tombstone in St. Patrick's churchyard, which she understands is near the city, and she will ask her friends to take her there.

In Biddulph and Lucan itself, understandably enough, the subject of the Donnellys was for a long time suppressed. Several inhabitants of seventy or eighty years of age, who were born, raised, and lived almost their entire lives in Lucan, admitted that they were grown men or women before they ever heard of the story![2] It is no wonder, therefore that curious strangers who come to gawk in the little village are sometimes met with cold stares, indifference, or sometimes plain rudeness when they ask about the Donnellys. It is not, as the strangers more often than not think, that the local people are keeping to themselves their secrets. It is usually because they know little about the subject themselves! However, it should be stated that there are a few enterprising and relatively recent arrivals in the village who will sell the unsuspecting tourist "genuine artifacts, guaranteed" to have belonged to the Donnelly family. Tom Donnelly must have had dozens and dozens of hats survive him!

Although suppressed for a couple of generations or more in many local circles, the Donnelly story was kept alive outside the district in many of the farming communities of Canada, and particularly, but not exclusively, in Ontario. The family is talked about by the people of these communities as if they had been alive yesterday, and almost everyone knows someone who was related to someone who was involved in the story. Even more curious, many others claim to be blood relatives of the Donnellys, without the slightest foundation in fact, while many more know someone who claims to be so related. The name itself is fairly common: within fifteen or twenty miles of the Donnelly homestead itself lived several other families of the same name, both Catholic and Protestant, but totally unrelated to the Donnellys of the Roman Line.

According to many visitors to Biddulph, the story arouses great emotions still in parts of the Catholic Settlement. A Biddulph farmer, Kelly, wrote not long ago, "I firmly believe that these people deserve a lot more respect in their deaths than you are allotting them," and did not wish to be further contacted on the subject. Another woman in Etobicoke thought a presentation of the Donnelly story "unsavoury", and it upset her terribly.

Even when the story is heard for the first time it often arouses the strongest emotions. Many seem to experience greater outrage at cruelties inflicted upon horses than upon human beings. Otherwise sound and rational citizens become obsessed with the tale and cannot wait for a free day to journey to Lucan to savour the atmosphere and perhaps attempt to conjure the phantoms of the famous Roman Line.

There are a few genuine sites left in Biddulph and Lucan which go back to the days of the Donnellys. One of the oldest buildings is the McIlhargey tavern, built around 1850, which sits on the London highway near the southern edge of Lucan. On the main street of the village stands the white frame house where Robert Donnelly lived for a few years, and further along are the Crunnican-McIlhargey block and the Central Hotel. The Western Hotel, or Donnelly House as it was called when Bob Donnelly operated it, stood on William

Street near the railway station until it was razed for street-widening in Canada's Centennial Year in 1967, the very time when all other communities in the land were trying to preserve their historic old buildings.[3] And, still in the village, there is one old log house in the southwest part, and now extensively renovated, which was supposed to have been built in the pioneering days of Biddulph Township.

Outside Lucan, at the corner of the London highway and the Roman Line, stands St. Patrick's Church. Beside it is the cemetery where, until 1964, stood the famous tombstone with the words "MURDERED" cut after the names of the five victims who died on the night of February 3 and 4, 1880. Erected in 1889, it stood for exactly seventy-five years, attracting thousands of visitors. With the publication of books on the story in 1954 and again in 1962, the stone became a magnet for many thousands more, until the parish priest became vexed with the publicity and, it was alleged, the damage to church property caused by the visitors. In 1964 the stone was removed. This action, in turn, stirred up the ire of a few of the descendants of the family, who disputed the action of the diocese, but an agreement was finally made whereby a new stone was erected omitting the offending word.[4]

The Cedar Swamp Schoolhouse still stands, but along the Roman Line itself few, if any, of the farmhouses exist which were there at the time of the Donnellys. Some of the barns go back to that day, including that on the Grouchy Ryder farm, which was rebuilt in 1880. And until 1972, on the northeast corner of the Donnelly farm itself stood the Donnelly Schoolhouse, forlorn, abandoned, and weathering the onslaughts of nature and the acquisitive instincts of the souvenir hunters, who one by one hauled away many of the yellow bricks which were later added to its original frame construction.[5]

Near the site of the schoolhouse, a farmhouse stands on the Donnelly farm beside the spot where the original hewed-log house stood. For a few years in the early 1970s, a recently arrived American, Walter Fults, lived across the road from this house on the old John Whalen farm. He had never heard of the Donnelly story until his arrival in

Biddulph, but was amazed at the interest of visitors. "Some of them come poking around here," he said, "almost expecting to find the embers from the fire in 1880 still smouldering."

And there are the letters, some telling some weird and wonderful versions of the story, as in the following:[6]

The original tombstone that marked the family grave for seventy-five years from 1889 to 1964

Bill Donley was very much in love with his cousin Bridget but his affections were not returned as she had given her promise to a younger brother, so Bill was very much upset.... No one ever knew how many were in the group who helped commit that terrible crime as Bill Donley disappeared that night and was never seen or heard of for many years.... The lad who escaped hid in some neighbour's barn and was not found for at least two days after....

Wrote another correspondent:

I think that these people had as much a part in the history of Canada as Billy the Kid had in the U.S.A.

Another young person wrote:

I cannot bring myself to put down the words to explain my sympathy towards the Donnellys.... I myself did an in-depth thesis on the Donnellys and found my sources going from one extreme to the other. It was either they were the meanest, thieving people or the dearest, kindest people.

Another student chose to make as a school project an exact replica of the Donnelly farmhouse both inside and outside. Another young girl of thirteen wrote from Toronto:

...I became fascinated by the Donnelly story. I even did a project on them in school.... I Loved the Donnellys so much; I worshipped Tom. My friend and I would carve crosses with the initials T. D. out of soap and give them to each other.... I wanted this summer to visit their grave and I might take some moss from the tombstone. With this moss I would put it in plastic and put it under my pillow.... Instead of praying to the God most people pray to I pray to Tom....

Thus it appears that while the Donnellys may have been removed from Biddulph, in the folk history of Canada at least, they are alive and thriving.

The new tombstone without the offending word "murdered"

NOTES

Chapter 1 Handspikes

[1] The circumstances of Patrick Farrell's death are derived from the depositions of the eye-witnesses at the inquest held a few days after the event and, as in almost every case throughout this book, the words attributed to a character appear from the source to have been actually spoken. The inquest notes are preserved at the Public Archives of Canada, Ottawa, hereafter cited as PAC.

[2] Mitchell Rawson, "The Steps of Dan Donnelly", *Sports Illustrated,* April 17, 1961, E-18. Dan Donnelly was supposed to have been mockingly knighted by the Prince Regent (later George IV) after the bout.

[3] William Carleton, Introduction to "Traits and Stories of the Irish Peasantry", *The Works of William Carle*ton, 2 vols. (1881; reprint ed., Freeport, N.Y.: Books for Libraries Press, 1970), vol. 1, p. 662.

[4] *Goderich Signal,* Sept. 16, 1862.

[5] Carleton, "The Tithe Proctor", *The Works of William Carleton,* vol. 2, p. 361.

[6] Carleton, "Wildgoose Lodge", *The Works of William Carleton,* vol. 1, p. 944.

[7] *London Daily Advertiser,* April 20, 1874; *London Free Press,* Aug. 19, 1960.

Chapter 2 Biddulph

[1] Patrick Woulfe, *Irish Names and Surnames* (1923; reprint ed., Baltimore: Genealogical Publishing Co., 1967), p. 505.

[2] Source of this story is E. J. McAuliffe, genealogical researcher, Dublin, Ireland.

[3] Toronto *Globe,* Feb. 12, 1880. Donnelly's likeness was drawn posthumously by Robert Harris, based on descriptions by his surviving children and others who knew him.

[4] Descriptions of Donnelly's appearance and character are compiled from the Goderich Gaol Register (1858) and the various newspapers in 1880.

[5] The courtship and early marned life of James and Johannah Donnelly are narrated in "The Donnelly Murders", a paper by Alice McFarlane, read in 1946 to the London and Middlesex Historical Society, much of the source of which was, in turn, Zackariah McIlhargey, an intimate friend of the Donnelly family from early days. McIlhargey's daughter, Kate Ryan, of Dublin, supplied additional details to the author, as did John W. Donnelly, son of William; Tom Newman, grandson of Patrick; and Spencer Armitage-Stanley, local historian and genealogist of Lucan and Biddulph.

[6] William Henry Smith, *Canada: Past, Present and Future,* 2 vols. (Toronto: T. McLear, 1851), vol. 2, p. 196.

[7] The Ryders, Mahers, Tooheys, Cains, Carrolls, and Farrells were all connected by marriage. Part of the connection was, curiously enough, through the Orange Shoebottoms: London Township pioneer John Shoebottom married Mary Maher; her daughter Hanorah married James Ryder, who came out with James Donnelly.

[8] B. Drew, *The Narrative of Fugitive Slaves in Canada* (1856; reprint ed., Toronto: Coles, 1972), p244.

[9] *Ibid., p.* 245.

[10] Accounts of Wilberforce are derived, in addition, from Land Registry Office records and newspaper accounts, such as *London Free Press,* May 15,1937; Aug. 9,1943; Aug. 27,1966; July 29,194-; Jan. 2, 1960; *Exeter Times,* March 30, 1876; and census records.

[11] The evidence in the trials may be found in A. Brewster's *A Report of SevenTrials at the Clonmel Assizes of 1829* (Dublin: Milliken, 1830).

[12] Big Jim's career was chronicled in *History of the County of Middlesex* (Toronto: Goodspeed, 1889). Other sources are *London Free Press,* May 1, 1948, and Feb. 1, 1964.

[13] Surveyor McDonald's notes are preserved at Public Archives of Ontario, Toronto, Marcb 16, 1836

[14] Heber Davis to author, April 2, 1972.

Chapter 3 Factions

[1] Accounts of these early engagements which resulted in petty law cases are preserved in the Regional History Collection of the University of Western Ontario, London. The abbreviabon UWO in these notes indicates references to this collection, from which the following papers were consulted: Huron County, Clerk of the Peace, Coroner's Inquests, 1841-1904; Huron County Clerk of the Peace, Schedules of Convictions, 1841-1903; Huron County, Clerk of the

Peace, Returns of Convictions, 1841-1912; Huron County, Clerk of the Peace, Criminal Cases, 1841 – 1933; Huron County, Sheriff's Records, 1842 – 1916; Huron County, Court of Queen's Bench proceedings, 1851 – 55; Huron County, Clerk of the Peace, Correspondence, 1841 – 1918; Middlesex County, Clerk of the Peace, Criminal Records, 1844 – 1919; Middlesex County, Clerk of the Peace, Coroner's Inquests, 1832 – 1904; Middlesex County, Clerk of the Peace, Court of Quarter Sessions, Returns of Convictions, 1869 – 1908; Charles Hutchinson, Middlesex County Crown Attorney and Clerk of the Peace, Papers (1826 – 93), letter-books (1835 – 1910), personal letter-books (1871 – 80); Middlesex County Assessment Rolls, 1862 – 95; Goderich Gaol Register, 1841 – 77; Chancery dockets; manuscripts; Donnelly family papers.

2 Despite the locating of the Keefe tavern by previous writers at Elginfield, there seems little doubt that it was really at the Church Corners beside St. Patrick's. This is borne out by contemporary records, such as the Brimmacombe inquest evidence and the depositions in the case of the Orange riot at Keefe's tavern on election day, 1857, and is confirmed by Fred McIlhargey, Lucan, whose relatives ran the tavern in later years.

3 The books of the Canada Company are preserved at the Public Archives of Ontario, Toronto. Other sources of the land dispute are the Biddulph Assessment Rolls and Land Registry Office Records.

4 1851 Census.

5 Exeter Times, July S, 1888.

6 Huron Court Records (UWO), 1854.

7 History of the County of Middlesex, p. 461. Other sources of the trouble between blacks and whites in Biddulph are the Goderich Gaol Register; Huron Court Records (UWO); London Free Press, Feb. 22, 1936, and March 7, 1942.

8 In their book In the Days of the Canada Company (1896; reprint ed., Toronto: Coles, 1972), p. 238, Robina and Kathleen Macfarlane Lizars referred to "the Hodgins (in which tribe were Big Jim, Little Jim, Jerry Jim, Big Billy and Little Billy, and Little Billy's Lenny, Longworth George, Dublin Tom, Peeler Tom and Naygur Tom)" and said, doubtless referring to Big Jim himself, "one of these celebrities was a magistrate who could neither read nor write; but an axehandle was much more effective than a quill at election time."

9 The papers relating to the Brimmacombe inquest and preliminary hearing are preserved in the Public Archives of Canada, Ottawa, 1857-65 (PAC).

10 St. Marys Argus, July 29, 1858; Huron Court Records (UWO), 1857-58; Goderich Gaol Register; Toronto Globe, Sept. 10, 1880; census records (1851, 1861, 1871) are the sources of the account of the Tooheys.

11 Letter to the Provincial Secretary, Aug. 29, 1859 (PAC), with similar sentiments expressed in the depositions of some witnesses, e.g. Sarah McGee and Alice McGee.

Chapter 4   Kingston

1 Inquest notes (PAC).

2 John Holmes to Governor General, Oct. 15, 1857 (PAC) .

3 PAC.

4 Huron Court Records, 1857 (UWO).

5 Comments on John Wilson are from History of the County of Middlesex, p. 135, while details of the arrest and trial of James Donnelly are mainly from Huron Court Records (UWO), 1857-58.

6 On one occasion, as Mayor of London, he also served as magistrate and, hauling himself up in his own court on a charge of "drunk and disorderly", dutifully found himself guilty and imposed a fine of four dollars. This he promptly paid by transferring the sum from his left-hand to his right-hand pocket, as he was allowed to collect all fines in his magisterial capacity. He then returned half the amount to the original pocket on grounds of remission for previous good conduct. While the grounds of remission were questionable, Cornish in later years left for the Great Northwest and became the first mayor of Winnipeg.

7 The other jurymen werc Joseph Wilson, Patrick Gibson, Thomas Hunter, Alexander McNaughton, Andrew Kidd, Richard Tindett, Peter Campbell, John Davidson, and Thomas Farquhar.

8 History of the County of Middlesex, p. 135.

9 The existence of the petitions are known from sources preserved at the Public Archives of Canada, but the petitions themselves, like the actual depositions of witnesses at the trial of Donnelly, have not yet turned up.

10 William Carleton, perhaps facetiously, described the dish in "The Three Tasks", The Works of William Carleton, vol . 2, p. 668: "An Irish family, of the cabin class, hangs up in the chimney a herring, or 'small taste' of bacon, and as the national imagination is said to be strong, each individual points the potato he is going to eat at it...the act communicat[ing] the flavour of the herring or bacon, as the case may be, to the potato..."

11 The relationship is a deduction only, based on the

assertion of Will Donnelly's daughter Nora that her grandfather Donnelly came to Canada with a brother, on John Donnelly's undoubted presence in Biddulph at this time, and on his friendship with John Kennedy and Michael Ryan. His eventual fate was related by John W. Donnelly, of Detroit. On the other hand, the Goderich Gaol Register lists John's arrival in Canada as 1852, although the Register was not particularly reliable.

[12] McFarlane, "The Donnelly Murders", p. 4.

[13] Michael Helm, *Civil Disorders in Biddulph Township, 1850-1880* (Thesis equivalent, Montreal: Sir George Williams University, 1970).

[14] Toronto *Globe*, Sept. 10, 1880.

[15] *Ibid.*

[16] *Huron Signal,* Nov. 14, 1882.

Chapter 5 Scholars

[1] Huron Court Records (UWO), December 19, 1861.

[2] The altar is now in the possession of the author.

[3] Information concerning Jenny, as well as others of the family, is derived from newspaper accounts, census records, death certificates where available, and personal contact by the author with descendants.

[4] A photograph of him is in private hands and, although viewed by the author, was not available for publication.

[5] The statements appeared in newspapers in 1880, chiefly in the Toronto *Globe*.

[6] Aside from the usual sources already noted, details of Will Donnelly were obtained in conversation with his only son.

[7] McFarlane, "The Donnelly Murders", p. 21.

[8] *Montreal Standard*, Dec. 21,1946. An interview with Dearness, who lived to a remarkable age, was also reported in the *London Free Press*, May 23, 1946.

[9] *London Daily Advertiser,* May 23, 1881.

[10] Undated notes of Hugh McKinnon (UWO).

[11] *Huron Expositor,* Feb. 20, 1880.

Chapter 6 Lucan

[1] The history of Lucan Village given here is, of course, very sketchy and touched upon only as it relates to the Donnelly story. Main sources of information are newspaper accounts, census records, court records, assessment rolls, land registry records, and other sources already mentioned in other connections.

[2] *London Free Press*, Feb. 8, 1964.

[3] Toronto *Globe*, Feb. 6, 1880.

[4] *Ibid.*, March 17, 1880.

[5] The account of that day is from the *Huron Expositor,* Aug. 29, 1879.

[6] *London Daily Advertiser,* Aug. 14, 1872.

[7] As told by Patrick McGee, the grandson.

[8] *London Daily Advertiser,* Sept. 29, 1879.

[9] *Ibid.,* May 2, 1872.

[10] *Ibid.,* April 5, 1877.

Chapter 7 Return

[1] Some of the details of the Donnelly house are obtained from Robert Harris's sketches of the Thompson house made in February 1880, copies of which were obtained from Harris's papers preserved in Prince Edward Island at Confederation Centre, Charlottetown, through the courtesy by Moncrieff Williamson.

[2] Much of the information relating to the inside of the house was gleaned from the evidence of the witnesses in the trial of James Carroll for murder, notably the witnesses John O'Connor and William Donnelly.

Chapter 8 Caswell

[1] *London Daily Advertiser,* March 14, 1872.

[2] *Exeter Times,* March 13, 1876.

[3] London *Daily Advertiser,* June 17, 1874.

[4] Story related by Gerald Lanphier to the author.

[5] *London Daily Advertiser,* Sept. 1, 1871.

[6] The account of Caswell is derived in the main from the *London* Daily *Advertiser,* Feb. 11, 1880.

Chapter 9 "Femails"

[1] Sources of these family traditions were Elizabeth Quigley of London, Spencer Stanley of Toronto, Mrs. C. J. Scott of Hamilton, all of whom were born and raised in Biddulph or Lucan, as well as Frank Ryan of St. Thomas, whose aunt met her husband on the Donnelly stagecoach; Rev. Robert E. McGrath of Ottawa, a grandson of Biddulph Vigilante James McGrath; and William Yonkers of Florida, grandson of Michael Donnelly's widow.

[2] John's wife remained in Lucan a short while after their separation but finally went to St. Thomas, where, it was said, she contracted a bigamous marriage with a man named Hind, but about which John never troubled her: *London Daily Advertiser,* Dec. 29, 1871; Feb. 9,1880; May 23, 1881; Toronto *Globe*, Feb. 13, 1880; March 3, 1880; Biddulph Assessment Rolls.

[3] William, Patrick, Michael, and Robert were eventually married – Pat to a girl from Niagara Falls, New York, named Mary Donnelly (no relation). Part of the family genealogy is set out in the affidavits of Alex McFalls and James Sutton, M.D., of Lucan, dated July 26, 1901, and filed with me Probate Court of Huron County, Michigan. Robert married Annie Currie, sometimes spelled Curry, a sister of his brother-in-law,

James Currie. (Death Certificates, Office of the Registrar General of Ontario)
4 Notes of the evidence by Mr. Justice Featherston Osler, in *R. v. Carroll* (2nd trial), 1881, preserved at Osgoode Hall, Toronto.
5 The attempted abduction of Maggie Thompson is derived mostly from accounts in the *London Free Press,* Feb. 10 and April 10,1874, and the *Exeter Times,* Jan. 22 and Feb. 5, 1874.
6 *Exeter Times,* Jan. 22, 1874.
7 As related by members of the Currie family.

Chapter 10   Hawkshaw

1 There are, of course, many descendants of James and Johannah Donnelly, but none through the male line.
2 Stagecoaching and hotelkeeping were closely related, and all three of the surviving boys, Will, Pat, and Bob, at one time or another owned hotels in later life. William Donnelly may have become first associated with Hugh McPhee of the Revere House, Lucan, as his bartender about 1865, according to McPhee's character evidence in *R. v. Carroll,* 1880.
3 *London Daily Advertiser,* Sept. 16, 1869.
4 *Ilbid,* April 18, 1872.
5 *Ibid.,* June 20, 1872.
6 Keefe's background is derived from an account in the *Exeter Times,* June 14, 1888, some of it seeming a little far-fetched.
7 *London Daily Advertiser,* Nov. 29, 1872.
8 Correspondence by the author with the Post Office, Ottawa.
9 Related by Mel Westman, Biddulph.
10 *London Daily Advertiser,* Oct. 18, 1877.

Chapter 11   Barnum

1 Much of the material of this chapter, as in the case of several subsequent chapters, was derived from newspaper sources of the year or years in question, in this case most notably rhe *London Daily Advertiser, London Pree Press,* and *Exeter Times* of 1873 and 1874.
2 *London Daily Advertiser,* Sept. 2, 1873.
3 *Ibid.,* Sept. 10, 1873.
4 *Ibid.*
5 *London Daily Advertiser,* Oct. 4, 1873.
6 *Ibid.,* Aug. 1, 1873.
7 Notes made by Spencer Stanley, Toronto, among his personal papers.
8 *Exeter Times,* April 15, 1874.
9 *Ibid.,* July 2,1874,
10 *Ibid.,* April 30, 1874.
11 The passenger incidents were derived from Jenny R.

Lewis's *Birr and Beyond* (Birr Women's Institute, 1958); and the *Huron Expositor,* Feb. 20, 1880.
12 Hawkshaw apparently disputed the result of the fight, as appears from a conversation with the Reverend Donaldson in 1879, in which he referred to his opponent as the second-youngest of the boys, althongh he named him (apparently in error) as Mike.
13 London *Daily Aduertiser,* May 27, 1874.
14 *Exeter Times,* July 15, 1874.
15 *London Free Press,* Feb. 21, 1874.
16 *Exeter Times,* Dec. 10, 1874.

Chapter 12   Flanagan

1 The place was also called Irishtown, the Village of Ireland, and McGillivray Post Office, but was renamed Clandeboye when the London, Huron and Bruce Railway came through in 1875. Early records indicate that Pat Flanagan's original log tavern was on the McGillivray side of the road, later moved to the opposite side and named the Victoria House.
2 Jenny R. Lewis, *Sure An' This Is Biddulph* (Biddulph, 1964). Although there appears to have been some controversy about the date, it seems quite clear from newspaper accounts, particularly one in the *London Free* Press, Jan. 1, 1874, that the new St. James was completed at the end of 1873.
3 *Exeter Times,* Jan. 13, 1875.
4 *London Daily Advertiser,* June 2, 1875.
5 McFarlane, "The Donnelly Murders", p. 5.
6 Land Registry Office, Bad Axe, Michigan, August 20, 1874.
7 *London Daily Advertiser,* March 17, 1875.

Chapter 13   Dan Clark

1 The circumstances of Dan Clark's demise are derived from the depositions of the inquest (UWO).
2 James Donnelly, Jr., gave evidence at the inquest and, curiously, made an X to his deposition, although he was capable of signing his name. The circumstance smacks strongly of the old Irish subterfuge of thumb-kissing, described by William Carleton in "The Geography of an Irish Oath", *The* Works of *William Carleton,* vol. 2, p. 920, in the belief that such a trick thereby avoided the binding of the deponent's conscience and was not a sin.
3 The Suttons themselves had been accused of arson in the early days of the district, and Dr. Sutton was a close friend of the Donnellys for many years, from the time when the physician set up shop in Irishtown where Dennis Sutton once kept store. A Catherine Donnelly was his long-time housekeeper.

4 Facts of the Gibbs case are derived from the papers and docket (UWO).

5 The London Gaol Register entry for April 6, 1875, described James Donnelly, Jr., as "intemperate in habits", p.77.

6 Facts of the Easdale case are derived from the depositions (UWO) and newspapers accounts.

7 Toronto *Globe*, March 4, 1880.

8 The success of the fire company was erratic. Three years after the first one was formed, there were still complaints that it was "the ambition of each Lucanite to act either as chief engineer or 'branch man'", leaving few hands to "run the machine": *London Free Press*, March 22, 1877.

9 Hines was a Catholic who had married a Presbyterian girl named Mary McGowan from around Brucefield, Ontario.

10 According to Catherine Andrewes, of London, a descendant of her sister, Ellen Hines turned Catholic when she married Mike Donnelly.

Chapter 14   Berryhill

1 Which of the Donnelly brothers was involved in this incident is not revealed by the inquest papers (UWO), although in all probability it was Michael.

2 *Exeter Times*, Aug. 19, 1875.

3 *London Daily Advertiser*, Sept. 8, 1875.

4 The events leading up to the Berryhill fight are partially reconstructed from the undated notes of the Crown Attorney, Charles Hutchinson, who later prosecuted the charges arising out of it (UWO).

5 Berryhill, in fact, was partially blinded in the injured eye as a result of the fight: per his deposition, March 10, 1876(UWO).

Chapter 15   Falling Out

1 The charge was never proceeded with for lack of evidence. That he was charged is derived from McFarlane, "The Donnelly Murders", p. 6, and the William Porte Diary, in private hands (based on Spencer Stanley's notes among his personal papers).

2 St. Patrick's Cemetery, Biddulph.

3 John Kennedy, Jr., marned Johanna Kenny, daughter of a Lucan blacksmith.

4 Mrs. Kennedy once went so far as to accuse her son John openly of having committed murder (Hamilton *Spectator*, Feb. 10, 1880) shortly before her death in 1880. And John Kennedy, Sr., died of a heart seizure in a Granton hotel in 1883 during a heated argument, which in all probability concerned his relations with the Donnellys (*Exeter Times*, March 30, 1893).

5 William Flanagan stood John Kennedy's bail in 1881.

6 *Exeter Times*, Feb. 3, 1876.

7 *Ibid.*

8 *London Free Press*, Jan. 3, 1876.

Chapter 16   McKinnon

1 Reid had Lucan connections in that a sister married William E. Stanley, who worked in Barney Stanley's store, while a brother served as county constable in the village for a time. Furthermore, the Reids may have been related to Alex Calder, of London, with whom the Donnellys once ran stage but had a falling-out (Spencer Stanley, interview).

2 From the date on his tombstone in Dawson City, Yukon.

3 Hamilton newspaper clipping about the nme of his death in scrapbook, Hamilton Public Library.

4 McKinnon returned to Hamilton in later life and became Chief of Police there but again lost the job after several years when his actions as chief were called into question. Details of his career are derived also from the Hamilton *Spectator*, Oct. 29, 1886; G. M. Adam (ed.), *Prominent Men of Canada* (Montreal: National Publication Co. of Canada, 1931 – 32), p. 126; G. V. Torrance, *The Hamilton Police Department (Hamil*ton, 1971).

5 Hamilton newspaper clipping in scrapbook, Hamilton Public Library.

6 *London Free Press*, Feb. 26, 1876.

7 Flanagan's hiring of McKinnon is confirmed from the correspondence of Charles Hutchinson, the Middlesex County Crown Attorney, including letters written byMcKinnon, particularly Feb.26, 1876, and by Hutchinson to the office of the provincial Attorney General.

8 Much of McKinnon's version of events is paraphrased from his interviews recorded in the Toronto *Globe*, March 4, 1880, and the Hamilton *Spectator*, Feb. 9, 1880.

9 Paraphrased from the Torooto *Globe*,   March 4, 1880.

10 *London Free Press*, Dec. 7, 1875.

11 *Exeter Times*, Dec. 30, 1875.

12 Records of St. Patrick's Roman Catholic Church, Biddulph.

Chapter 17   Rhody

1 Even Jenny was implicated in the case of The Queen, by complainant Robert Orme, versus Gray and William Donnelly, in that she was prepared to give evidence against the complainant, although the case never got to trial.

2 Glass's two brothers served as Sheriff and Deputy-Sheriff for the County of Middlesex, so that all of them knew the Donnelly boys.

3 Per William Donnelly in the preliminary hearing of *The Queen v. Carroll* (1880), printed evidence from the papers of Aemilius Irving, Q.C., preserved by the Provincial Archives of Ontario in Toronto.

4 Henry Ferguson once wrote the Crown Attorney that "there was three constables sent from London city to the Donnellys they spent nearly two days and a night and did not make the arrests, and my [son] Charles arrested on the arson case one of them and gave him up to Squire O'Neil to appear before me on the next Saturday," in all likelihood referring to the case of James Donnelly, Jr., charged with the arson of Flanagan's stable. Robert Hill O'Neil, J.P., the first reeve of Lucan, "was a great friend of the family and assisted them in many ways".

5 Correspondence of Charles Hutchinson, County Crown Attorney (UWO).

6 *Ibid.*

7 *Ibid.*

8 Deposition in the case (UWO).

9 Correspondence of Charles Hutchinson, County Crown Attorney (UWO).

10 *Ibid.*

Chapter 18   Fitzhenry's

1 *Exeter Times,* Jan. 20, 1876.

2 *London Daily Advertiser,* Feb. 1, 1880, per Valentine Mackey; 1871 Census. Almost the entire account of the incidents at the Revere House and Fitzhenry's are taken from the depositions of Reid, Bawden, and Coursey (UWO).

3 Benedict Kiely, *Poor Scholar* (London: Sheed & Ward, 1947), p 13.

4 Toronto *Globe,* March 4, 1880.

5 *London Free Press,* March 3, 1880.

6 McKinnon designated Michael Donnelly, but I believe Thomas was the correct brother on the grounds that 1) it was Bawden who arrested Michael; 2) there was no other account of the arrest of Tom at this time, yet there is no doubt he was taken into custody; 3) it was Tom who was generally conceded to be the most dangerous of the brothers; and 4) McKinnon admitted having trouble distinguishing the names of the brothers.

7 *Donnelly v. Bawden* (1876-77), 40 Upper Canada Queen's Bench Law Reports, 611.

8 James Atkinson was appointed a county constable not long afterward.

Chapter 19   Assizes

1 The list is compiled from informations actually laid, such as the arson of Flanagan's stable in Lucan, depositions (UWO), newspaper accounts, and reports of court cases such as *Donnelly v. Bawden* (1876 – 77), 40 U.C.Q.B. 611.

2 For example, the charge preferred by John Bawden, according to the information actually laid, was "that he hath been informed and hath just cause to believe that James Donnelly, John Donnelly, Thomas Donnelly, Robert Donnelly, William Donnelly and William Farrell of Lucan and Biddulph did on or about the 4th day of October 1875 at the village of Lucan aforesaid feloniously set fire to and burn the stable of Patrick Flanagan." It was never proceeded with.

3 Donnelly, Sr., used the trips to London to transact other business, such as his St. Patrick's Day trip to his lawyer's office to sign the deed to a further slice of land for the Donnelly Schoolhouse plot (Land Registry Office, London, Ontario).

4 "A groggery with imposing interior has just made its appearance on one of our principal streets," a newspaper reported in August 1874, and "an alluring shingle, invitingly extended, holds out inducements to heated pedestrians to draw nigh and partake of the fluids…" Respectable churchgoers of the village were outraged at the unlicensed establishment, especially when "men in a state of intoxication frequent at the place," wrote W. W. Lee, licence inspector to the County Crown Attorney. Lee called on the shebeen and found a regular bar "with bottles, glasses, whiskey, wine and pop", and when he pointed out to the O'Connors that they were liable to prosecution, Mrs. O'Connor answered defiantly, "We will keep liquor for our boarders!" O'Connor was arrested by Rhody Kennedy, then acting as constable, but the latter claimed to have been drugged by Mick while being taken to the J.P.'s office and O'Connor had to be retaken.

5 Toronto *Globe,* March 4, 1880.

6 *London Free Press,* April 1, 1876

7 Records of the Central Prison, Toronto.

Chapter 20   Damages

1 St. Patrick's Roman Catholic Church records.

2 *London Daily Advertiser,* March 2, 1876.

3 Much of the material from this chapter is gleaned from the letter copybooks and correspondence of the County Crown Attorney (UWO).

4 *London Daily Advertiser,* June 13, 1876.

5 *Quoted in London Daily Advertiser,* Nov. 10, 1876.

[6] The Crown Attorney's letter copybooks under date Dec. 27, 1876 (UWO).

[7] *London Daily Advertiser,* Dec. 27, 1876.

[8] *Ibid.,* Dec. 14, 1876.

[9] The Crown Attorney's letter copybooks under date Jan. 26, 1877 (UWO).

[10] *Donnelly v. Bawden* (1876 – 77), 40 U.C.Q.B. 611.

Chapter 21   Terror

[1] *London Daily Advertiser,* Feb. 1, 1877.

[2] *Ibid., March* 8,1877.

[3] *London Free Press,* March 22, 1877.

[4] *Ibid,* April 16, 1877.

[5] *Ibid.,* May 5, 1877.

[6] *Exeter Times,* June 7, 1877.

[7] In fact, he ascribed death in his certificate to "inflammation of the lungs", according to the office of the Registrar General of Ontario.

[8] The reconstruction of events is not without difficulties in that, at this particular time, newspaper reporting of events in Lucan seemed to be running at times two or three weeks after the actual occurrence. For example, the attack on Joe Watson on April 28 was reported in the *Advertiser* on May 2, in the *Free Press* on May 5, and in the *Exeter Times* only on May 10. In the shooting behind the Queen's Hotel the Tuesday referred to seems to have been May 15, the day of young James Donnelly's death. "The previous (Sunday) night"indicates that the account was written May15, since no "outrages" took place on any of the Sunday nights between May 13 and June 5, and that it was Monday, May 14, when the suspicious persons behind the Queen's were fired at. This is probably when young Jim Donnelly was shot, if he was shot at all.

[9] Timothy Carey happened to be a brother-in-law of Martin McLaughlin, who was raised on the farm next but one to the Donnellys.

[10] *London Daily Advertiser,* May 31, 1877.

[11] *Ibid.,* June 14, 1877.

Chapter 22   Politics

[1] In 1863 when Thomas Scatcherd was elected over William Watson, Biddulph formed part of West Middlesex Riding: William Horton, *Memoir of the Late Thomas Scatcherd* (London, Ont., 1878).

[2] The Conservative *Exeter Times,* on the other hand, in its issue of February 18, 1875, had no intention of letting this equivocation go by. "Electors of North Middlesex should remember that Mr. Scatcherd, their representative," it stated, "voted for the pardon of the murderer Riel, notwithstanding his denunciation of the late Government for not bringing him to justice."

[3] *London Daily Advertiser,* Aug. 12, 1878.

[4] *Ibid.,* Sept. 3, 1878.

[5] *Exeter Times,* Feb. 5, 1874. Glass served as Mayor of London, later as City Solicitor of Winnipeg and as Speaker of the Manitoba Legislature. He also claimed to be one of the last persons to interview President Abraham Lincoln.

[6] *Exeter Times,* Jan. 25, 1875.

[7] *London Daily Advertiser,* Sept. 15, 1875.

[8] *Ibid.,* Oct.6, 1875.

[9] *Ibid.,* July 12, 1877.

[10] The modern name for this place is Denfield.

[11] *London Daily Advertiser,* Oct. 9, 1877.

[12] *Ibid.,* Dec. 20, 1879.

Chapter 23   Lambs

[1] While Thomas Edison's incandescent light had been reported in the newspaper, the invention was not yet a practical reality.

[2] Depositions in *John Harrigan v. James Hogan,* 1854 (UWO).

[3] Michael Feeheley had been one of the two defence witnesses in the murder trial of James Donnelly. As with the case of another early crony of Donnelly, John Kennedy, Sr., they were no longer on speaking terms.

[4] Maggie's brother, William, was married to Mary Carroll, daughter of "the respectable" Michael Carroll, whose sister, in turn, was marned to Robert Keefe, Sr. The connection with the Carrolls never at any time interfered with the Keefes' close friendship with the Donnellys.

[5] *London Daily Advertiser,* Aug. 13, 1877.

[6] The Chief of Police of nearby London earned $1,000 a year, while a constable made $1.25 a day.

[7] *London Daily Advertiser,* Dec. 13, 1877.

[8] *Ibid,* Aug. 6, 1878.

[9] Crown Attorney Hutchinson's correspondence, letter from J. Gnnn, Sept. 8, 1877 (UWO).

[10] *London Daily Advertiser,* Sept. 19, 1877.

[12] *Ibid,* Dec. 6, 1877.

[13] *Ibid,* June 7, 1877.

[14] Hogan skipped out on his bondsmen and failed to appear at the 1878 Fall Assizes when his mother was acquitted, but later gave himself up and was similarly acquitted.

[15] *London Daily Advertiser,* Jan. 10, 1878.

[16] *Exeter Times,* Jan. 10, 1878.

[17] *London Daily Advertiser,* March 20, 1878.

[18] *Ibid,* Jan. 24, 1878.

[19] *Exeter Times.* Jan. 10. 1878.

Chapter 24   Ned Ryan
1 *London Daily Advertiser,* Feb. 21, 1878.
2 Much of the account of the Ryan robbery is gleaned from Ryan's own depositions made first in 1878 and then a year later when the case was revived (UWO).
3 His brother, Michael, drank himself to death in Martin Fogarty's house (Inquest, Oct. 7, 1869) (UWO).
4 It was the heyday of the American Wild West where, only a short time before, Custer and his troops were massacred at the Little Big Horn by Sitting Bull and his braves and where, just about this time, James "Wild Bill" Hickok was shot to death in a poker game in the Black Hills District.

Chapter 25   Two Years
1 Everett's deposition, 1878 (UWO).
2 *London Daily Advertiser,* March 20, 1878.
3 Based on Hines's testimony in the Thompson cow trespass case in 1879. Francis M. West also reported that William Feeheley confirmed it was Robert Donnelly who shot at Everett (UWO).
4 Main sources for the account of the fight are McFarlane, "The Donnelly Murders", p. 7, the William Porte Diary (notes made by Spencer Stanley among his personal papers), and the London *Daily Advertiser,* April 1, 1878, the last-mentioned putting the location of it at Kenny's blacksmith shop.
5 *London Daily Advertiser,* April 1, 1878.
6 *Ibid.*
7 At the same time James Donnelly, Sr., arranged a mortgage on the Donnelly homestead to pay David Glass's fee of $100 to defend the case (Land Registry Office, London, Ontario).
8 *London Daily Advertiser,* April 1, 1878.
9 *Ibid*
10 *London Daily Advertiser,* April 2, 1878.
11 *Ibid.,* June 13, 1878.

Chapter 26   Coughlin
1 *London Daily Advertiser,* Jan. 22, 1878.
2 *Exeter Times,* July 31, 1879.
3 Barney Stanley had just come back from a summer excursion to the "Auld Sod".
4 *London Daily Advertiser,* April 8, 1879.
5 *Exeter Times,* May 30, 1878.
6 *London Daily Advertiser,* Sept. 1, 1875.
7 Toronto *Globe,* Feb. 7, 1880.
8 *London Daily Advertiser* Aug. 10, 1878.
9 *Exeter Times,* Aug. 29, 1878.
10 *Ibid,* July 23, 1874.
11 *London Daily Advertiser,* Aug. 19, 1878.

Chapter 27   Carroll
1 Hamilton *Spectator,* Feb. 16, 1880.
2 The O'Carroll lands were forfeited following Cromwell's subjugation, but with the restoration of the Stuarts ten years later Charles Carroll petitioned Charles II for their return. He was given instead 60,000 acres in Maryland, which formed the base of the family's fortune in the New World, making them the greatest landowning family in America at the time of the American War of Independence. The third Charles Carroll signed the Declaration of Indepedence; a relative, John Carroll, became the first bishop in the United States in 1879.
3 *London Daily Advertiser,* Aug. 10, 1878.

Chapter 28   October
1 Jerry McDonald was not, strictly speaking, James Carroll's uncle but was married to Carroll's Aunt Eleanor. Jim Carroll called her Aunt Ellen and one of his sisters was named after her.
2 McFarlane, "The Donnelly Murders", p. 7.
3 *Ibid.*

Chapter 29   Wolfskin
1 H. B. Pollard, *The Secret Societies of Ireland* (Dublin: P.Allen, 1922),sums it up on page 8: "...in 1745 the Catholics were again granted the right of public worship, so the need for the Defenders as secret protectors of the faith vanished. Despite this, the organisation endured as a primitive secret society enforcing its own laws and disregarding all others...remaining inherently Catholic, and exacting a mythical sense of comfort from this peculiar perversion of the faith..."
2 Charles J. Kikham, the most famous of Tipperary authors, wrote in 1870 in *Knocknagow, or, The Homes of Tipperary* (Dublin: Gill, 1962) of the black cloud over Clonmel from the day of Father Sheehy's execution and the attitude of the common pcople to his memory .
3 Two months after the priest's execution his cousin, Edward Sheehy, and two farmers, one of them named Farrell, were also executed on similar testimony.
4 The secret agrarian societies often set about their deadly business wearing straw masks or blackened faces and with women's clothes or with their shirts pulled out at the waist to cover their other garments, hence the name Whiteboys. Other names included Levellers, Straw Boys, Rakers, Right Boys, and, of course, Defenders.
5 Thomas D'ArcyMcGee,*A Popular History of Ireland,* 2 vols. (New York: Sadlier & Co., 1863), p. 642.

[6] According to Donaldson, Hawkshaw named the Donnelly brother he was supposed to have thrashed as Mike, but referred to him as second from the youngest, which would make him, as is more likely, Robert.

[7] Norah Donnelly was badly enough frightened by the episode to persuade her husband to move into the hamlet of Whalen's Corners on the following March 27, 1879.

Chapter 30   Arrest

[1] William Hutchins, otherwise known as Short Bill or Dark Bill, defeated for reeve of the village William Stanley, known as Long Bill or White Bill, and was popular with many of the villagers despite his support of the Reform party in federal and provincial politics, which did not sit well with the ruling clique of Stanleys. The village elections of 1878 were said to be a repetition of "the Pacific Scandal on a small scale but more interesting to Lucanites". (London Daily Advertiser, Dec. 22, 1878).

[2] London Daily Advertiser, Feb. 12, 1879.

[3] Ibid., Feb. 1, 1879.

[4] Ibid., April 17, 1879.

[5] Ibid., April 24, 1879.

[6] Exeter Times, March 13, 1879.

[7] William Kerby Atkinson was an Ailsa Craig storekeeper, vice-president of the Huron & Middlesex Fire Insurance Company, perennial promoter of the Northern Middlesex Agricultural Fair, and correspondent for the London Daily Advertiser, under the byline Northern Sparks. Like William Porte, he also kept a pet crow.

Chapter 31   Combat

[1] London Daily Advertiser, April 15, 1879.

[2] James M. Donnelly grew up to be a lonely, brooding man who often wondered what his dead father and uncles and their parents were really like. In later life he helped his uncle, Robert Donnelly, operate the Western Hotel in Lucan in the early 1900s.

[3] The account of this incident is derived from the notes of Mr. Justice Cameron, the presiding judge in the case of William Lewis for the murder of Michael Donnelly in May 1881. The judge's notebook is preserved at Osgoode Hall and was perused by the kind permission of Chief Justice Gale of the Supreme Court of Ontario.

Chapter 32   Kelly's Horse

[1] London Daily Advertiser, May 2, 1879.

[2] Ibid., May 7, 1879.

[3] Most of the account of the taking out of Kelly's horse and its repercussions is taken from William Donnelly's

narrative in the Toronto Globe, March 2, 1880, although Father Connolly mentioned it in his funeral sermon in 1880.

[4] The letter is not a verbatim reproduction but a reconstruction based on a careful perusal of Donnelly's account of it in the Toronto Globe, March 2, 1880.

[5] Exeter Times, April 17, 1879.

[6] Ibid., Sept. 4, 1879.

Chapter 33   Society

[1] From a photograph of the book itself, a copy of which was kindly provided by Orlo Miller.

[2] There is some confusion as to the actual time of Tom Donnelly's visit to Ryder's farm to forbid the threshing of Ryan's grain. John Cain was reported in the Toronto Globe, Oct. 7, 1880, as having stated it was "the fall", whereas in the London Daily Advertiser, Feb. 1, 1881, it was reported as "June".

[3] This information was obtained from Peter Bench's daughter, Marie, of St. Catharines, as well as from letters in her possession written by the school trustee, James Harrigan, and the parish priest, Father John Connolly.

Chapter 34   Martin

[1] Some information about the McLauglins was obtained from Patti McLaughlin, then living in Burlington, Ontario, whose husband was a direct descendant of William McLaughlin who lived on the next farm but one to the Donnellys.

[2] This information was obtained from Patrick McGee, of Thorndale, Ontario, whose mother, prior to her marriage, was housekeeper to Father John Connolly, and also from Nora Lord, of Levack, Ontario, daughter of William Donnelly.

[3] Exeter Times, May 15, 1879.

Chapter 35   Heifer

[1] Much of the information concerning the lost cow, the search, and the repercussions was obtained from the many depositions in the several resulting court cases, including the depositions of James Donnelly, Sr., John Donnelly, Tommy Hines, and many of the members of the society (UWO).

[2] See William Carleton's "Traits and Stories of the Irish Peasantry", The Works of William Carleton, vol. 2, for countless examples of the correct rendering into English of the pre-Famine Irish peasant's dialect.

Chapter 36   Fiddle

[1] The author has so far been unsuccessful in identifying the tune of this march.

[2] London Daily Advertiser, Sept. 29, 1879.

Chapter 37 Petitions
[1] The entire petition was reproduced in the *London Daily Advertiser*, Feb. 7, 1880.

Chapter 38 Trespass
[1] The Donnellys had always, for example, neighboured at harvest time with the Daggs, whose farm backed on the rear of the Donnelly farm.

Chapter 39 Escape
[1] M. C. Cameron, of Goderich, to Charles Hutchinson, Oct. 29, 1879 (UWO).

Chapter 40 Poor Mike
[1] Again, this is not a verbatim reproduction but a reconstruction based on a careful perusal of William Donnelly's account of it, as reported in the Toronto *Globe*, March 3, 1880.
[2] Again, a reconstruction based on the report in the Toronto *Globe*, March 3, 1880.
[3] Depositions (UWO).
[4] The source of this statement is a note in the deposition of James Carrigan. As in several of the cases of depositions preserved in the Regional History Collection (UWO), it is unclear, from its face or its place in the files, to which case the document belongs, but this information can usually be deduced from its contents.
[5] Charles Hutchinson to W. Stanley, Nov. 6, 1879 (UWO).
[6] The circumstances of the death of Michael Donnelly were obtained from the newspaper files of the *Norfolk Reformer*, May 21, 1880, preserved in Simcoe, Ontario, which reported the inquest in full and the trial. Many valuable details were obtained also from the notebook of the trial judge, Mr. Justice M. Cameron, preserved at Osgoode Hall and perused by the kind permission of Chief Justice Gale of Ontario.
[7] Robert's home at this name was in Glencoe, where he had left his wife Annie, but he found it difficult to settle down with her both before and after his term of imprisonment. He returned to Glencoe following his release but after the holiday season went back to the home of his parents. William Porte saw him in Lucan on Sunday, January 11, 1880, as noted in his diary.

Chapter 41 Grouchy
[1] Information about the McGrath family was obtained from the *Rodney Mercury*, June 14, 1967, and from Rev. Father Robert E. McGrath, of Ottawa, a grandson of James McGrath.

Chapter 42 Law
[1] Reported testimony of his godmother, Temperance McLaughlin, in the *London Daily Advertiser*, Feb. 1, 1881, and the Toronto *Globe*, Feb. 1, 1881, and census records would appear to indicate that Johnny O'Connor's age was closer to fifteen years than twelve, as generally reported.

Chapter 43 Plans
[1] This version was related by Elizabeth Quigley, of London, daughter of Caleb Quigley, of Lucan, and granddaughter of William Quigley, Lucan shoemaker.
[2] Hamilton *Spectator*, Feb. 5, 1880.
[3] Toronto *Globe*, Oct. 9, 1880.

Chapter 44 Clubs
[1] Details of the massacre were obtained from many sources, including the testimony at the inquest, the preliminary hearing, and the two trials of James Carroll, which testimony was gleaned from the depositions, the newspaper reports, and the notebooks of the trial judges. Additional information, much of which did not become public knowledge at the time of the trials, was obtained from the correspondence of Charles Hutchinson, the County Crown Attorney.
[2] Additional details of the murders were published in the *Exeter Times*, May 26, 1881, alleged to be the confession of the Feeheley brothers. While the account was ridiculed at the time, it sounds fairly authentic in that it fits well with the other evidence.

Chapter 45 Aftermath
[1] As the bodies burned, the heads separated from the trunks, and it was because of this, and the fact that one or two of the skulls were stolen (or, at least, attempts at stealing them were made for they merely crumbled on contact), that the rumour spread that the victims had been beheaded.
[2] Toronto *Globe*, Feb. 9, 1880.
[3] *Ibid.*, Feb. 7, 1880.
[4] *Ibid* .
[5] *London Daily Advertiser*, Feb. 12, 1880.
[6] Hamilton *Spectator*, Feb. 20, 1880.
[7] *Ibid.*, March 3, 1880.
[8] *Ibid.*, March 2, 1880.
[9] Toronto *Globe*, March 16, 1880.
[10] Quoted in *London Daily Advertiser*, Feb. 7, 1880.
[11] *Ibid.*, Feb. 13, 1880.

Chapter 46 Hearings
[1] *London Daily Advertiser*, Feb. 11, 1880.
[2] *Ibid.*

[3] The date of Harris's letter is February 23, 1880, and it is preserved in Confederation Centre, the Fathers of Confederation Memorial Building Trust, Charlotte-town, Prince Edward Island. A copy was supplied through the courtesy of Mr. Moncrieff Williamson, Director, Confederation Art Gallery and Museum.

[4] London *Daily Advertiser,* March 3, 1880.

[5] *Ibid.,* Feb. 23, 1880.

[6] *Ibid.,* March 13, 1880.

[7] *Ibid.*

[8] *Ibid.,* Feb. 28, 1880.

[9] *Ibid,* Feb. 27, 1880.

[10] Charles Hutchinson to Aemilius lrving, June 29, 1880 (UWO).

Chapter 47   Trials

[1] Toronto *Globe,* April 14, 1880.

[2] *London Daily Advertiser,* Oct. 5, 1880.

[3] *Ibid., July* 26, 1880.

[4] *Ibid.,* May 19, 1880.

[5] *Ibid.,* April 13, 1880.

[6] Toronto *Globe,* Oct. 9, 1880.

[7] Albert R. Hassard, *Famous Canadian Trials* (Toronto: Carswell, 1924), Chapter V.

[8] *London Daily Advertiser,* Jan. 25, 1880.

[9] *Ibid.,* Feb. 4, 1881.

[10] Toronto *Globe,* Jan. 27, 1881.

[11] *London Daily Advertiser,* Jan. 29, 1881.

[12] Toronto *Globe,* Jan. 27, 1881.

[13] Notebook of Justice Osler, Osgoode Hall.

[14] *London Daily Advertiser,* Feb. 3, 1881.

[15] The jurors came from the following municipalities of Middlesex: John Carrothers, Adelaide; William Hooper, Biddulph; Horace Hyatt, Caradoc; John Lambert, Caradoc; George M. Francis, Strathroy; James F. Elliott, Westminster; Dugal Graham, Strathroy; James A. Watterworth, Mosa; James Dores, Westminster; Hopper Ward, Metcalfe; Asa Luce, Caradoc; Benjamin Kilburn, Delaware.

[16] *London Daily Advertiser,* Feb. 3, 1881.

[17] *Exeter Times,* Feb. 4, 1881.

[18] *Ibid.*

[19] Quoted in *London Daily Advertiser,* Feb. 4, 1881.

[20] *Ibid.,* Feb. 7, 1881.

Chapter 48   Sequel

[1] Old Feeheley thought himself in command of the situation, according to a note by William Donnelly found among the correspondence of Charles Hutch-inson (UWO): "About the time of the row about the $500 I was speaking to Jas. Feeheley. He said he was going to tell all – He said he would have told immediately after the murder only for his father-He said there was a mortgage on his farm, and the father's plan was to keep the murderers in his power, and the farm could never be sold for the mortgage, as no one would dare come in and buy it."

[2] *London Daily Advertiser,* May 23, 1881.

[3] Notes of Francis M. West, Correspondence of Charles Hutchinson (UWO).

[4] *London Free Press,* June 24, 1880.

[5] The purchaser was Patrick Leo Michael Harrigan, a son of James Harrigan of the Swamp Line. Pat Harrigan died in a fire in the old Harrigan home on June 2, 1966.

[6] *Thorold Post,* May 22, 1914.

[7] Two persons in the sleigh survived the accident, Annie McGrath, a younger sister of James and Matthew, who jumped out of the vehicle in time, and the McGraths' little girl, Nellie, a babe in arms all bundled up. Ellen Blake was to have taught school at the Cedar Swamp School the following year.

[8] *Exeter Times,* Feb. 9, 1893.

[9] *Exeter Advocate,* Aug. 4, 1887.

[10] Material for this chapter was obtained from later newspaper reports and particularly the *Exeter Times* and the *Exeter Advocate,* from St. Patrick's Cemetery records, and from correspondence and interviews by the author.

Chapter 49   Today

[1] The stories were related by Clarence Lewis, Lucan, and Harry Ryan, Toronto.

[2] For example, Elizabeth Quigley, Clarence Lewis, Spencer Stanley.

[3] The author has saved a few bits and pieces from the hotel, such as parts of the front door and the stairs, which he purchased within a day or two of its demolition.

[4] Nora Lord, daughter of William Donnelly, led the negotiations with the parish in replacement of the marker with a new stone, and her actions were concurred in by her brother.

[5] The author has in his possession a few mementoes of the schoolhouse, including desks, the altar, and the old cast-iron stove.

[6] All the letters are taken from the author's correspondence.

INDEX